W9-DIW-730

ENGLISH AS A SECOND LANGUAGE CURRICULUM RESOURCE HANDBOOK

A Practical Guide for K-12 ESL Programs

KRAUS INTERNATIONAL PUBLICATIONS
A Division of The Kraus Organization Limited
Millwood, New York

Consulting editor:

Sarah Hudelson
Professor, College of Education
Arizona State University, Tempe, Arizona

Contributing editors:

Graciela Italiano
Educational Consultant
Los Angeles, California

Patricia Rounds
Professor, American English Institute
University of Oregon, Eugene, Oregon

First Printing 1993
Printed in the United States of America

Library of Congress Cataloging-in-Publication Data

English as a second language curriculum resource handbook:
    a practical guide for K–12 ESL programs.
        p.   cm.
    Includes bibliographical references and index.
    1. English language—Study and teaching—Foreign
speakers—Handbooks, manuals, etc. I. Kraus International Publications.
PE 1128.A2E472   1993   92-46196
428'.0071'2—dc20

Printed on recycled paper

CONTENTS

PART III: TEXTBOOKS, CLASSROOM MATERIALS, AND OTHER RESOURCES

PUBLISHER'S FOREWORD

T HE *English as a Second Language Curriculum Resource Handbook* is one of a new series of practical references for classroom teachers, curriculum developers, education faculty, and student teachers. The handbook is designed to provide basic information on the background of ESL programs, as well as current information on publications, standards, and special materials for K-12 ESL. Think of this handbook as the first place to look when you are revising or developing your ESL program—or if you need basic resource information on ESL any time of the year.

This handbook does not seek to prescribe any particular form of curriculum, nor does it follow any set of standards or guidelines. Instead, the book provides a general grounding in ESL teaching, so that you can use this information and then proceed in the direction best suited for your budget, your school, and your district. What this handbook gives you is a sense of the numerous *options* that are available—it is up to you to use the information to develop the appropriate curriculum or program for your situation.

How To Use This Handbook

There are various ways to use this resource handbook. If you are revising or creating an ESL program, you should read the Series Introduction (for an overall sense of the different philosophies of curriculum and how this will affect the program you develop), chapter 1 (for basic background on the trends and research in K-12 ESL), and chapter 2 (for practical advice on needs assessment for Limited English Proficiency students). With this background, you can go through the other

chapters for the specific information you need— ranging from topics and skills to be covered at various grade and ability levels (chapter 4) to state requirements (chapter 5) to publishers and producers (chapter 11).

If you know what type of information you need, check the Table of Contents for the most appropriate chapter.

What's in the Handbook

The *Introduction* provides an overview of the ideologies and philosophies that have affected American curriculum through the years. This section will acquaint you with the various ideologies, so that you can determine whether your school is following one such philosophy (or a combination), and how this might influence the development of your curriculum. The Series Introduction is generic by design, since these ideologies pertain to all subject areas.

Chapter 1 provides an overview of *Trends and Issues* in ESL programs. This chapter discusses the development of present-day curriculum and looks at the directions ESL teaching is taking. The major research works are cited so that you can get more detailed information on particular topics.

Chapter 2 provides practical steps on *Assessing Student Needs* in your school or district and on customizing an ESL program to meet their needs.

Chapter 3, *Funding Curriculum Projects*, lists funding for programs that are studying or developing curriculum. Along with addresses and phone numbers, the names of contact persons are provided (wherever possible) to expedite your gathering of information.

Chapter 4 outlines *Topics and Skills* in teaching ESL from kindergarten to grade 12. This is not meant to be a pattern to follow, but instead is a reflection of the way in which many specialists structure their ESL programs and what current research recommends.

Chapter 5, *State-Level Curriculum Guidelines: An Analysis,* describes the statewide frameworks and discusses the various emphases, philosophies, and coverage among the state materials.

Chapter 6, *State-Level Curriculum Guidelines: A Listing,* supplements the previous chapter by listing addresses of state departments of education and their publication titles.

Chapter 7 discusses *Testing as an Assessment Tool.* Covered are such topics as evaluating appropriate tests for ESL assessment, the characteristics of tests, testing procedures, a review of commercial ESL tests, and alternative assessment methods.

Chapter 8 is an annotated list of *Recommended Curricular Materials* for ESL; these publications can help guide you in developing lessons and programs.

Chapter 9 discusses *Ideas for Special Projects.* The chapter describes a number of books that can provide ideas for special projects to enhance ESL instruction as well as help develop lessons around what students are learning in their regular classes. The books cover language teaching through pictures, drama, songs, games, holidays, and so on.

Chapter 10 gives information on *Children's Trade Books* that can be used in ESL classes. This chapter discusses resources to use in finding these trade books; it also provides selected listings of picture books, poetry books, folk tales, and other appropriate works.

Chapter 11 is an annotated list of *Curriculum Material Producers* of textbooks, videos, software, and other materials for use in K-12 ESL instruction.

Chapter 12, *Statewide Text Adoption,* lists the ESL textbooks adopted by each state.

Chapter 13 is an *Index to Reviews* of ESL textbooks and supplementary materials. Since these items are reviewed in a wide variety of publications, we have assembled the citations of appropriate reviews in index form (cited by title, author, publisher/distributor, subject, and grade level).

Chapter 14 provides a list of *Kraus Curriculum Development Library* (KCDL) subscribers; KCDL is a good source for models of curriculum guides in all K-12 subject areas.

In an appendix we reprint a state-generated ESL guide, to provide one example for creating your own curriculum materials.

Acknowledgements

The content of this handbook is based on numerous meetings and discussions with educators and curriculum specialists across the country. Our thanks go to the curriculum supervisors in schools across the United States; the faculty at education departments in the colleges and universities we visited; and curriculum librarians. Special thanks go to the members of the Curriculum Materials Committee (CMC) and the Problems of Access and Control of Education Materials (PACEM) committee of the Association of College and Research Libraries' Education and Behavioral Sciences Section (ACRL/EBSS). Our meetings with the committees during American Library Association Conferences continue to provide Kraus with valuable ideas for the handbooks and for future curriculum projects.

We also acknowledge with thanks the assistance of Marjorie Miller Kaplan, Ruth Eisenhower, Alan Aycock, and the indexers at AEIOU, Inc.

Your Feedback

We have a final request of our readers. At the back of this handbook is a user survey that asks your opinions about the book, its coverage, and its contents. Once you have used this book, please fill out the questionnaire—it should only take a minute or so—and mail it back to us. If the form has already been removed, please just send us a letter with your opinions. We want to keep improving this new series of handbooks, and we can do this only with your help! Please send questionnaires or other responses to:

Kraus International Publications
358 Saw Mill River Road
Millwood, NY 10546-1035
(914) 762-2200 / (800) 223-8323
Fax: (914) 762-1195

SERIES INTRODUCTION

P. Bruce Uhrmacher

Assistant Professor of Education

School of Education, University of Denver, Denver, Colorado

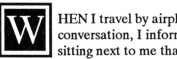HEN I travel by airplane and desire conversation, I inform the person sitting next to me that I'm in education. Everyone has an opinion about education. I hear stories about teachers (both good and bad), subject matter ("The problem with the new math is . . ."), and tests ("I should have gotten an A on that exam in seventh grade"). Many people want to tell me about the problems with education today ("Schools aren't what they used to be"). Few people are apathetic about schooling. When I do not wish to be disturbed in flight, however, I avoid admitting I'm in education. "So, what do you do?" someone trying to draw me out asks. I reply matter-of-factly, "I'm a curriculum theorist." Unless they persist, my retort usually signals the end of the dialogue. Unlike the job titles *farmer, stockbroker,* or even *computer analyst,* for many people *curriculum theorist* conjures few images.

What do curriculum theorists do? The answer to this question depends in part on the way curriculum theorists conceive of curriculum and theory. The term *curriculum* has over 150 definitions. With so many different ways of thinking about it, no wonder many curriculum theorists see their task differently. In this introduction, I point out that curriculum theorists have a useful function to serve, despite the fact that we can't agree on what to do. In short, like economists who analyze trends and make recommendations about the economy (and, incidentally, who also

agree on very little), curriculum theorists generate a constructive dialogue about curriculum decisions and practices. Although curricularists originally fought over the word *curriculum,* trying to achieve conceptual clarity in order to eliminate the various differences, in time educators recognized that the fight over the term was unproductive (Zais 1976, 93). However, the problem was not simply an academic disagreement. Instead, curricularists focused on different aspects of the educational enterprise. At stake in the definition of curriculum was a conceptual framework that included the nature of the role of the curricularist and the relationships among students, teachers, subject matter, and educational environments. Today, most curricularists place adjectives before the term to specify what type of curriculum they're discussing. Thus, one often reads about the intended, the operational, the hidden, the explicit, the implicit, the enacted, the delivered, the experienced, the received, and the null curriculum (see glossary at the end of this chapter). Distinctions also can be made with regard to curricularist, curriculum planner, curriculum worker, and curriculum specialist. I use the terms *curricularist* and *curriculum theorist* to refer to individuals, usually at the college level, who worry about issues regarding curriculum theory. I use the other terms to refer to people who actually take part in the planning or the implementation of curriculum in schools.

In order to trace the development that has

brought the field of curriculum to its present state, I will begin with a brief overview of the progression of curriculum development in the United States. First, I examine issues facing the Committee of Ten, a group of educators who convened in 1892 to draft a major document regarding what schools should teach. Next, I focus on the perennial question of who should decide what schools teach. Curriculum was not a field of study until the 1920s. How were curriculum decisions made before there were curriculum specialists? How did curriculum become a field of study? We learn that the profession began, in part, as a scientific endeavor; whether the field should still be seen as a scientific one is a question of debate. Finally, I provide a conceptual framework that examines six curriculum "ideologies" (Eisner 1992). By understanding these ideologies, educators will discern the assumptions underlying various conceptions of curriculum. Then they should be able to decide which ideology they wish to pursue and to recognize its educational implications.

What Should Schools Teach?

In the nineteenth century, curriculum usually meant "the course of study," and what many educators worried about was what schools should teach. Under the theoretical influence of "mental discipline" (derived from the ideas of faculty psychologists), many educators believed that certain subjects strengthened the brain, much like certain exercises strengthened body muscles. Greek, Latin, and mathematics were important because they were difficult subjects and thus, presumably, exercised the brain. By the 1890s, however, with the great influx of Italian, Irish, Jewish, and Russian immigrants, and with the steady increase of students attending secondary schools, a concern grew over the relevance and value of such subjects as Greek and Latin. Why should German or French be any less worthy than Greek or Latin? In addition, students and parents raised further questions regarding the merits of vocational education. They wanted curricula that met their more practical needs.

While parents pressed for their concerns, secondary school principals worried about preparing students for college, since colleges had different entrance requirements. In 1892 the National Education Association (NEA) appointed

the Committee of Ten to remedy this problem. Headed by Charles W. Eliot, president of Harvard University, the committee debated and evaluated the extent to which a single curriculum could work for a large number of students who came from many different backgrounds with many different needs. In its final report, the committee suggested that colleges consider of equal value and accept students who attended not only the classical curriculum program, but also the Latin scientific, the modern language, and the English programs.

By eliminating the requirement of Greek for two of the programs and by reducing the number of required Latin courses, the committee broke with the traditional nineteenth-century curriculum to some degree. Yet, they were alert to the possibility that different kinds of curriculum programs taught in different ways could lead to a stratified society. Eliot had argued that the European system of classifying children into "future peasants, mechanics, trades-people, merchants, and professional people" was unacceptable in a democratic society (Tanner and Tanner 1975, 186). The committee believed all should have the opportunity for further studies under a "rational humanist" orientation to curriculum, a viewpoint that prizes the power of reason and the relevance and importance of learning about the best that Western culture has to offer.

The committee's report met with mixed reviews when it came out. One of its foremost opponents was G. Stanley Hall, a "developmentalist," who argued that the "natural order of development in the child was the most significant and scientifically defensible basis for determining what should be taught" (Kliebard 1986, 13). According to Hall, who had scientifically observed children's behavior at various stages of development, the committee did not take into account children's wide-ranging capabilities, and it promulgated a college-bound curriculum for everyone, even though many high school students would not go to college. Rather than approaching curriculum as the pursuit of a standard academic experience for all students, Hall and other developmentalists believed that knowledge of human development could contribute to creating a curriculum in harmony with the child's stage of interest and needs.

Thus far I have indicated two orientations to curriculum: the rational humanist and the developmentalist. We should understand, however, that at any given time a number of interest groups struggle for power over the curriculum. Historian Herbert Kliebard observes:

> We do not find a monolithic supremacy exercised by one interest group; rather we find different interest groups competing for dominance over the curriculum and, at different times, achieving some measure of control depending on local as well as general social conditions. Each of these interest groups, then, represents a force for a different selection of knowledge and values from the culture and hence a kind of lobby for a different curriculum. (Kliebard 1986, 8)

Who Should Decide What Schools Teach?

Thinking about curriculum dates back in Western culture to at least the ancient Greeks. Plato and Aristotle, as well as Cicero, Plutarch, and Rousseau, all thought about curriculum matters in that they debated the questions of what should be taught to whom, in what way, and for what purposes. But it wasn't until 1918 that curriculum work was placed in the professional domain with the publication of *The Curriculum* by Franklin Bobbitt, a professor at the University of Chicago. Although supervisors and administrators had written courses of study on a piecemeal basis, "Professor Bobbitt took the major step of dealing with the curriculum in all subjects and grades on a unified and comprehensive basis" (Gress 1978, 27). The term *curriculum theory* came into use in the 1920s, and the first department of curriculum was founded at Teachers College, Columbia University, in 1937. Of course, the question arises: If curricularists (a.k.a. curriculum specialists, curriculum theorists, and curriculum workers) were not making decisions about what should be taught in schools prior to the 1920s, then who was?

As we have seen, national commissions made some of the curricular decisions. The NEA appointed the Committee of Ten to address college–high school articulation in 1892 and the Committee of Fifteen to address elementary school curriculum in 1895. In the early 1900s the NEA appointed another committee to develop fundamental principles for the reorganization of secondary education. Thus, university professors, school superintendents, and teachers made some curricular decisions as they acted in the role of acknowledged authorities on national commissions.

Along with commissions, forces such as tradition have shaped the curriculum. One long-time student of curriculum, Philip Jackson, observes:

> One reason why certain subjects remain in the curriculum is simply that they have been there for such a long time. Indeed, some portions of the curriculum have been in place for so long that the question of how they got there or who decided to put them there in the first place has no answer, or at least not one that anyone except a historian would be able to give. As far as most people are concerned, they have just "always" been there, or so it seems. (Jackson 1992, 22)

Jackson also notes here that subjects such as the three R's are so "obviously useful that they need no further justification"—or, at least, so it seems.

Texts and published materials have also been factors in shaping the curriculum. Whether it was the old *McGuffey Readers* or the modern textbooks found in almost any classroom in the United States, these books have influenced the curriculum by virtue of their content and their widespread use. According to some estimates, text materials dominate 75 percent of the time elementary and secondary students are in classrooms and 90 percent of their time on homework (Apple 1986, 85). Textbook writers are de facto curriculum specialists.

National Commission committees, tradition, textbooks, instructional materials, and the influence from numerous philosophers (e.g., Herbart and Dewey) were focal in deciding what schools should teach. Of course, parents, state boards of education, and teachers had their own convictions as to what should be in the curriculum. However, as the United States moved toward urbanization (30 percent of 63 million lived in cities in 1890; over 50 percent of 106 million lived in cities in 1920 [Cremin 1977, 93]), new factors influenced schooling. In particular, the industrial and scientific revolutions commingled in the minds of some to produce new ways of thinking about work. Franklin Bobbitt applied these new ideas to education. Influenced by Frederick Winslow Taylor, the father of the scientific management movement, Bobbitt assumed that the kinds of accomplishments that had been made in business and industry could be made in education. What was needed was the application of scientific principles to curriculum.

Briefly, Bobbitt believed that "educational engineers" or "curriculum-discoverers," as he called them, could make curriculum by surveying the array of life's endeavors and by grouping this broad range of human experience into major fields. Bobbitt wrote:

> The curriculum-discoverer will first be an analyst of human nature and of human affairs. . . . His first task . . . is to discover the total range of habits, skills, abilities, forms of thought . . . etc., that its members need for the effective performance of their vocational labors; likewise the total range needed for their civic activities; their health activities; their recreations, their language; their parental, religious, and general social activities. The program of analysis will be no narrow one. It will be as wide as life itself. (Bobbitt 1918, 43)

Thus, according to Bobbitt, curriculum workers would articulate educational goals by examining the array of life's activities. Next, in the same way one can analyze the tasks involved in making a tangible object and eliminate waste in producing it, Bobbitt believed one could streamline education by task analysis, by forming objectives for each task, and by teaching skills as discrete units.

Bobbitt's push for the professionalization of curriculum did not replace other factors so much as it added a new dimension. By arguing that schools needed stated objectives and that curricularists should be chosen for the task since they were trained in the science of curriculum, Bobbitt opened up a new line of work. He and his students would be of direct help to practitioners because they would know how to proceed scientifically (analyze the range of human experience, divide it into activities, create objectives) in the making of curriculum, and this knowledge gave curricularists authority and power. The world was rapidly changing in communications, in agriculture, in industry, and most of all in medicine. Who could argue with the benefits of science?

If Franklin Bobbitt created the field of professional curriculum activities, Ralph Tyler defined it. In his short monograph, *Basic Principles of Curriculum and Instruction* (1949), Tyler offered a way of viewing educational institutions. He began his book by asking four fundamental questions that he believed must be answered in developing curriculum:

1. What educational purposes should the school seek to attain?
2. What educational experiences can be provided that are likely to attain those purposes?
3. How can these educational experiences be

effectively organized?
4. How can we determine whether these purposes are being attained? (Tyler 1949, 1)

Tyler devoted one chapter to each question. Unlike some curricularists, Tyler did not say what purposes a school should seek to attain. He recognized that a school in rural Idaho has different needs from an urban one in Boston. Rather, Tyler suggested that schools themselves determine their own purposes from three sources: studies of the learners themselves, studies of contemporary life, and studies from subject matter specialists.

Tyler, like Bobbitt before him, wished to bring order to the complex field of education. Although there are differences between the two men, both believed there was work to be done by professional curricularists. Both men trained students in the field of curriculum, and both believed in the liberal ideals of rationality and progress. Curricularist Decker Walker summarizes the tradition that Bobbitt and Tyler started as follows:

> Since Bobbitt's day, planning by objectives (PBO) had developed into a family of widely used approaches to curriculum improvement. As a method of curriculum materials design, PBO focuses early attention on developing precise statements of the objectives to be sought. If the process is to be fully scientific, the selection of objectives must be rationally justifiable and not arbitrary. (Walker 1990, 469)

While Bobbitt and Tyler taught students how to become professional curricularists and encouraged them to conduct research, to write, and to attain university positions, differences of opinion on what curricularists should be doing soon mounted. At issue was not only the utility of scientific curriculum making, but also the specific endeavors many curricularists pursued.

A Framework for Thinking about Curriculum

Tyler produced a seminal work that provided curriculum workers with a way of thinking about curriculum. While some elaborated on his ideas (Taba 1962), others wondered whether indeed Tyler provided the best questions for curricularists to think about. During the 1970s, numerous educators began to seek other ways of thinking about curriculum work. William Pinar, for example, asked, "Are Tyler's questions . . . no longer pertinent or possible? Are they simply cul-de-sacs?" (Pinar 1975, 397). Reconceptualizing the term *curriculum* (race course) from the verb of the Latin root, *currere* (to run a race), Pinar goes on to argue:

> The questions of *currere* are not Tyler's; they are ones like these: Why do I identify with Mrs. Dalloway and not with Mrs. Brown? What psychic dark spots does the one light, and what is the nature of "dark spots," and "light spots"? Why do I read Lessing and not Murdoch? Why do I read such works at all? Why not biology or ecology? Why are some drawn to the study of literature, some to physics, and some to law? (402)

More will be said about Pinar's work later. My point here is that curriculum theorists do not necessarily agree on how one should approach thinking about curriculum. By trying to redefine curriculum entirely, Pinar drew attention to different aspects of the educational process.

Out of this continuing discussion among curricularists, various ideologies—beliefs about what schools should teach, for what ends, and for what reasons—have developed (Eisner 1992). In this section, I present six prominent curriculum ideologies that should prove useful in thinking about developing, adapting, or implementing curriculum. While these ideologies are important, they are not the only ones. Elliot Eisner writes of religious orthodoxy and progressivism and excludes multiculturalism and developmentalism. Some authors may include constructivism rather than developmentalism.

I remind the reader that few people actually wear the labels I describe. These conceptualizations are useful in helping one better articulate a set of assumptions and core values. They help us see the implications of a particular viewpoint. They also help us understand issues and concerns that may otherwise be neglected. Sometimes ideologies are specified in mission statements or some other kind of manifesto; at other times, ideologies are embedded in educational practice but are not made explicit. Rarely does a school adhere to one curriculum ideology—though some do. More often, because public schools are made up of people who have different ideas about what schools should teach, a given school is more likely to embrace an array of curricular ideas. While some readers may resonate strongly with a particular ideology because it expresses their inclinations, some readers may appreciate particular ideas from various ideolo-

gies. In either case, it may be a good idea to examine the strengths and weaknesses of each one. Later in this chapter I argue that one does not need to be ideologically pure in order to do good curriculum work.

Rational Humanism

We have already seen, in the historical example of Charles Eliot and the Committee of Ten, an early exemplar of rational humanism. During Eliot's day, rational humanists embraced the theory of mental discipline, which provided a handy rationale for traditional studies. Why study Greek and Latin? Because these subjects exercised the mind in ways that other subjects did not. While mental discipline fell by the wayside, rational humanism did not. From the 1930s through the 1950s, Robert Maynard Hutchins and Mortimer Adler championed the rational human-istic tradition, in part by editing *The Great Books of the Western World*. Hutchins argued that the "great books" offer the best that human beings have thought and written. Thus, rather than reading textbooks on democracy, science, and math, one ought to read Jefferson, Newton, and Euclid.

Today, one may find the rational humanist ideology in some private schools and in those public schools that have adopted Adler's ideas as represented in the *Paideia Proposal* (Eisner 1992, 310). In short, the Paideia plan provides a common curriculum for all students. Except for the choosing of a foreign language, there are no electives. All students learn language, literature, fine arts, mathematics, natural science, history, geography, and social studies.

While Adler endorses lecturing and coaching as two important teaching methods, the aspect of teaching Adler found most engaging was maieutic or Socratic questioning and active participation. In essence, maieutic teaching consists of a seminar situation in which learners converse in a group. The teacher serves as a facilitator who moves the conversation along, asks leading questions, and helps students develop, examine, or refine their thinking as they espouse particular viewpoints. This process, according to Adler, "teaches participants how to analyze their own minds as well as the thought of others, which is to say it engages students in disciplined conversation about ideas and values" (Adler 1982, 30).

Another important educational feature of these seminars is that one discusses books and art

In a follow-up book to *The*
Adler (1984) provides a K–12
ding list in which he recom-
;arten to fourth grade Aesop,
el Silverstein, Alice Walker,
ez-Silva, Langston Hughes, and
Dr. Seuss, among other authors. I indicate these
authors in particular because the charge that
Adler's program embraces only the Western
European heritage is not entirely accurate. While
Adler would argue that some books are better
than others, and that, in school, students should
be reading the better ones, one can see that Adler
includes authors who are not elitist and who are
from culturally diverse backgrounds.

Developmentalism

Another approach to curriculum theory, which
was discussed briefly in the historical section of
this chapter, is developmentalism. Although a
range of scholars falls under this heading, the
basic point is that, rather than fitting the child to
the curriculum, students would be better served if
the curriculum were fitted to the child's stage of
development. Why? One argument is that doing
otherwise is inefficient or even detrimental to the
child's development. It would be ridiculous to try
to teach the Pythagorean theorem to a first
grader, and it could be harmful (to use a fairly
noncontroversial example) to teach a fourth
grader to master throwing a curve ball. By
understanding the range of abilities children have
at various ages, one can provide a curriculum that
meets the needs and interests of students. Of
course, while the stage concept cannot pinpoint
the development of a particular child at a given
age, it serves as a general guide.

One might also pay attention to the idea of
development when creating or adapting curriculum because of the issue of "readiness for learning." There are two ways of thinking about
readiness. Some educators, in their interest to
hurry development, believe that encouraging
learners to perform approximations of desired
behaviors can hasten academic skills. In this case,
one tries to intervene in apparently natural
development by manipulating the child's readiness at younger and younger ages. The research
findings on whether one can greatly enhance
one's learning processes are somewhat mixed,
but, in my opinion, they favor the side that says
"speed learning" is inefficient (Duckworth 1987,
Good and Brophy 1986, Tietze 1987). I also think

the more important question, as Piaget noted, is
"not how fast we can help intelligence grow, but
how far we can help it grow" (Duckworth 1987,
38).

A different way of thinking about readiness
for learning concerns not how to speed it up, but
how to work with it effectively. Eleanor
Duckworth, who studied with Piaget, believes the
idea of readiness means placing children in
developmentally appropriate problem situations
where students are allowed to have their own
"wonderful ideas." She believes that asking "the
right question at the right time can move children
to peaks in their thinking that result in significant
steps forward and real intellectual excitement"
(Duckworth 1987, 5). The challenges for teachers
are to provide environmentally rich classrooms
where students have the opportunity to "mess
about" with things, and to try to understand
children's thought processes. Students should
have the opportunity to experiment with materials likely to afford intellectual growth, and
teachers should learn how their students think. In
this approach to curriculum, mistakes are not
problems; they are opportunities for growth.

The developmental approach to curriculum
teaches us to pay attention to the ways humans
grow and learn. One basic idea underlying the
various theories of human development in regard
to curriculum is that the curriculum planner
ought to understand children's abilities and
capabilities because such knowledge enables one
to provide worthwhile educational activities for
students.

Reconceptualism

As noted earlier with Pinar's use of the term
currere, during the 1970s numerous individuals
criticized the technical aspects and linear progression of steps of the Tyler rationale. Loosely
labelled as reconceptualists, some educators felt
the following:

> What is missing from American schools . . . is
> a deep respect for personal purpose, lived
> experience, the life of imagination, and those
> forms of understanding that resist dissection
> and measurement. What is wrong with
> schools, among other things, is their industri-
> alized format, their mechanistic attitudes
> toward students, their indifference to
> personal experience, and their emphasis on
> the instrumental and the out of reach. (Pinar
> 1975, 316)

Reconceptualists have focused on Dewey's

observation that one learns through experience. Given this assertion, some important questions arise. For example, how can teachers, teacher educators, or educational researchers better understand the kinds of experiences individual students are having? To answer this question, reconceptualists employ ideas, concepts, and theories from psychoanalysis, philosophy, and literature.

Another question that arises when one reflects on understanding experience is, How can teachers provide worthwhile conditions for students to undergo educational experiences? Maxine Greene divides educational experiences into two types: "an education for having" and "an education for being." Education for having is utilitarian—for example, one may learn to read in order to get a job. Some students need this kind of experience. Education for being is soulful—one may learn to read for the sensual qualities it can provide. All students, she says, need the latter kind of experience. One problem is that the latter has often been neglected or, if not, often provided for the talented or gifted at the expense of others (Green, 1988a).

In their effort to reperceive education, reconceptualists such as Maxine Greene, Madeleine Grumet, and William Pinar do not usually offer specific educational ideas that are easily implemented. In part, this is because the kind of education with which they are concerned is not easy to quantify or measure. In general, reconceptualists do not believe their theories and ideas need quick utilization in schools in order to validate their worth. If in reading their writings you think more deeply about educational issues, then I think they would be satisfied.

Nevertheless, I can think of two practical challenges for education that stem from their writing. First, how could you write a rigorous and tough-minded lesson plan without using objectives? What would such a lesson plan look like? Second, if you wanted to teach students a concept such as citizenship, how would you do it? Rational humanists would have students read Thomas Jefferson or Martin Luther King, Jr. Reconceptualists, however, would wonder how teachers can place students in problematic situations (i.e., in the classroom or on the playground) where students would grapple with real issues concerning citizenship.

Critical Theory

The idea of critical theory originated at the Institute for Social Research in Frankfurt ("the Frankfurt school") in the 1920s. Today, scholars who continue to recognize the value and importance of Marxist critiques of society and culture draw from and build on ideas from critical theory. In education they reveal, among other things, that schooling comprises a value-laden enterprise where issues of power are always at play.

For instance, while many people perceive schools as neutral institutions, places that will help any hard-working student to get ahead in life, critical theorists suggest that, on the contrary, schools do not operate that way. Michael Apple points out, "Just as our dominant economic institutions are structured so that those who inherit or already have economic capital do better, so too does cultural capital act in the same way" (Apple 1986, 33). According to Apple, schools reflect the general inequities in the larger society. Rather than changing society through cultural transformation (teaching students to question or to be independent thinkers), schools actually maintain the status quo through cultural reproduction.

Unlike some curricularists who try to appear neutral in exercising judgments about curriculum matters, Apple's values are well known. He believes in John Rawls's insight that "for a society to be truly just, it must maximize the advantage of the least advantaged" (Apple 1979, 32). Apple encourages curricularists to take advocacy positions within and outside of education. While critical theory makes for a powerful theoretical tool, one question frequently asked of critical theorists is how this information can be used in the classroom. Teachers point out that they may not be able to change the school structure, the kinds of material they must cover, or the kinds of tests that must be given. Although admittedly application is difficult, one high school English educator in Boston who employs the ideas of critical theory is Ira Shor.

In an activity called "prereading," for example, Shor tells students the theme of a book they are about to read and has them generate hypothetical questions the book may answer. At first students are reluctant to respond, but after a while they do. Shor believes this kind of exercise has numerous functions. First, it provides a bridge for students to decelerate from the "rush of mass culture" into the slow medium of the printed word. Habituated to rock music and MTV, students need a slow-down time. Also, after creating a list of questions, students are curious how many will actually be addressed. Students may still reject the text, says Shor, but now it won't be a result of alienation. Perhaps most importantly, prereading demystifies the power of the written word. Rather than approaching the text as some kind of untouchable authority, "students' own thoughts and words on the reading topic are the starting points for the coordinated material. The text will be absorbed into the field of their language rather than they being ruled by it" (Shor 1987, 117).

Critical theory offers a radical way of thinking about schooling. Particularly concerned with students who are disenfranchised and who, without the critical theorists, would have no voice to speak for them, critical theory provides incisive analyses of educational problems.

Multiculturalism

In some ways, multiculturalists have an affinity with the critical theorists. Though critical theory traditionally is more concerned with class, most critical theorists have included race and gender in their analyses and discussions. Multiculturalism, however, deserves its own category as a curriculum ideology because it is rooted in the ethnic revival movements of the 1960s. Whether the purpose is to correct racist and bigoted views of the larger community, to raise children's self-esteem, to help children see themselves from other viewpoints, or to reach the child's psychological world, the multicultural ideology reminds educators that ethnicity must be dealt with by educators.

One major approach to multicultural education has been termed "multiethnic ideology" by James Banks (1988). According to Banks, Americans participate in several cultures—the mainstream along with various ethnic subcultures. Therefore, students ought to have cross-cultural competency. In addition to being able to participate in various cultures, Banks also suggests that when one learns about various cultures, one begins to see oneself from other viewpoints. The multiethnic ideology provides greater self-understanding.

When teaching from a multiethnic perspective, Banks advises that an issue not be taught from a dominant mainstream perspective with other points of view added on. This kind of teaching still suggests that one perspective is the "right one," though others also have their own points of view. Rather, one should approach the concept or theme from various viewpoints. In this case, the mainstream perspective becomes one of several ways of approaching the topic; it is not superior or inferior to other ethnic perspectives. In addition to what takes place in the classroom, Banks also argues that a successful multiethnic school must have system-wide reform. School staff, school policy, the counseling program, assessment, and testing are all affected by the multiethnic ideology.

Cognitive Pluralism

According to Eisner, the idea of cognitive pluralism goes back at least to Aristotle; however, only in the last several decades has a conception of the plurality of knowledge and intelligence been advanced in the field of curriculum (Eisner 1992, 317). In short, cognitive pluralists expand our traditional notions of knowledge and intelligence. Whereas some scientists and educators believe that people possess a single intelligence (often called a "g factor") or that all knowledge can ultimately be written in propositional language, cognitive pluralists believe that people possess numerous intelligences and that knowledge exists in many forms of representation.

As a conception of knowledge, cognitive pluralists argue that symbol systems provide a way to encode visual, auditory, kinesthetic, olfactory, gustatory, and tactile experiences. If, for example, one wants to teach students about the Civil War, cognitive pluralists would want students not only to have knowledge about factual material (names, dates, and battles), but also to have knowledge about how people felt during the war. To know that slavery means by definition the owning of another person appears quite shallow to knowing how it feels to be powerless. Cognitive pluralists suggest students should be able to learn through a variety of forms of representation (e.g., narratives, poetry, film, pictures) and be able to express themselves through a variety of forms as well. The latter point about expression means that most tests, which rely on propositional language, are too limiting. Some students may better express themselves through painting or poetry.

One may also think about cognitive pluralism from the point of view of intelligence. As I mentioned, some scholars suggest that intelligence may be better thought of as multiple rather than singular. Howard Gardner, a leading advocate of this position (1983), argues that, according to his own research and to reviews of a wide array of studies, a theory of multiple intelligences is more viable than a theory about a "g factor." He defines intelligence as follows:

> To my mind, a human intellectual competence must entail a set of skills of problem-solving—enabling the individual to resolve genuine problems or difficulties that he or she encounters and, when appropriate, to create an effective product—and must also entail the potential for finding or creating problems—thereby laying the groundwork for the acquisition of new knowledge. (Gardner 1983, 60–61)

Gardner argues that there are at least seven distinct kinds of human intelligence: linguistic, musical, logical–mathematical, spatial, bodily–kinesthetic, interpersonal, and intrapersonal. If schools aim to enhance cognitive development, then they ought to teach students to be knowledgeable of, and to practice being fluent in, numerous kinds of intelligences. To limit the kinds of knowledge or intelligences students experience indicates an institutional deficiency.

Applying Curriculum Ideologies

While some teachers or schools draw heavily on one particular curriculum ideology (e.g., Ira Shor's use of critical theory in his classroom or Mortimer Adler's ideas in Paideia schools), more often than not, a mixture of various ideologies pervade educational settings. I don't believe this is a problem. What Joseph Schwab said in the late 1960s about theory also applies to ideologies. He argued that theories are partial and incomplete, and that, as something rooted in one's mind rather than in the state of affairs, theories cannot provide a complete guide for classroom practice (1970). In other words, a theory about child development may tell you something about ten-year-olds in general, but not about a particular ten-year-old standing in front of you. Child developmentalists cannot tell you, for example, whether or how to reprimand a given child for failing to do his homework. Schwab suggested one become eclectic and deliberative when working in the practical world. In simpler terms, one should know about various theories and use them when applicable. One does not need to be ideologically pure. One should also reflect upon

one's decisions and talk about them with other people. Through deliberation one makes new decisions which lead to new actions which then cycle around again to reflection, decision, and action.

To understand this eclectic approach to using curriculum ideologies, let's take as an example the use of computers in the classroom. Imagine you are about to be given several computers for your class. How could knowledge of the various curriculum ideologies inform your use of them?

Given this particular challenge, some ideologies will prove to be more useful than others. For example, the rational humanists would probably have little to contribute to this discussion because, with their interests in the cultivation of reason and the seminar process of teaching, computers are not central (though one of my students noted, that, perhaps in time, rational humanists will want to create a "great software" program).

Some developmentalists would consider the issue of when it would be most appropriate to introduce computers to students. Waldorf educators, who base their developmental ideas on the writings of philosopher Rudolf Steiner (1861–1925), do not believe one should teach students about computers at an early age. They would not only take into account students' cognitive development (at what age could students understand computers?), but they would also consider students' social, physical, and emotional development. At what age are students really excited about computers? When are their fingers large enough to work the keyboard? What skills and habits might children lose if they learned computers at too early an age? Is there an optimum age at which one ought to learn computers? Waldorf educators would ask these kinds of developmental questions.

Developmentalists following the ideas of Eleanor Duckworth may also ask the above questions, but whatever the age of the student they are working with, these educators would try to teach the computer to children through engaging interactive activities. Rather than telling students about the computer, teachers would set up activities where students can interact with them. In this orientation, teachers would continue to set up challenges for students to push their thinking. Sustaining students' sense of wonder and curiosity is equally important. In addition to setting new challenges for students, teachers would also monitor student growth by trying to understand student thought processes. In short, rather than fitting the child to the curriculum, the curriculum is fitted to the child.

Reconceptualists' first impulse would be to consider the educational, social, or cultural meaning of computers before worrying about their utility. Of course, one should remember that there isn't one party line for any given ideological perspective. Some reconceptualists may be optimistic about computers and some may not. Although I don't know William Pinar's or Madeleine Grumet's thoughts on computers, I imagine they would reflect on the way computers bring information to people. Pinar observes that place plays a role in the way one sees the world (Pinar 1991). The same machine with the same software can be placed in every school room, but even if students learn the same information, their relationship to this new knowledge will vary. Thus, to understand the impact of computers one needs to know a great deal about the people who will learn from and use them. Having students write autobiographies provides one way to attain this understanding. Students could write about or dramatize their encounters with technology. After such an understanding, teachers can tailor lessons to meet student needs.

Critical theorist Michael Apple has examined the issue of computers in schools. Though he points out that many teachers are delighted with the new technology, he worries about an uncritical acceptance of it. Many teachers, he notes, do not receive substantial information about computers before they are implemented. Consequently, they must rely on a few experts or pre-packaged sets of material. The effects of this situation are serious. With their reliance on purchased material combined with the lack of time to properly review and evaluate it, teachers lose control over the curriculum development process. They become implementers of someone else's plans and procedures and become deskilled and disempowered because of that (Apple 1986, 163).

Apple also worries about the kind of thinking students learn from computers. While students concentrate on manipulating machines, they are concerned with issues of "how" more than "why." Consequently, Apple argues, computers enhance technical but not substantive thinking. Crucial political and ethical understanding atrophies while students are engaged in computer proficiency. Apple does not suggest one avoid computers because of these problems. Rather, he wants

teachers and students to engage in social, political, and ethical discussions while they use the new technology.

Multiculturalists would be concerned that all students have equal access to computers. Early research on computer implementation revealed that many minority students did not have the opportunity to use computers, and when they did, their interaction with computers often consisted of computer-assisted instruction programs that exercised low-level skills (Anderson, Welch, Harris 1984). In addition to raising the issue that all students should have equal access to computers, multiculturalists would also investigate whether software programs were sending biased or racist viewpoints.

Finally, cognitive pluralists, such as Elliot Eisner, would probably focus on the kinds of knowledge made available by computers. If computers were used too narrowly so that students had the opportunity to interact only with words and numbers, Eisner would be concerned. He would point out, I believe, that students could be learning that "real" knowledge exists in two forms. If, however, computers enhance cognitive understanding by providing multiple forms of representation, then I think Eisner would approve of the use of this new technology in the classroom. For example, in the latest videodisc technology, when students look up the definition of a word, they find a written statement as well as a picture. How much more meaningful a picture of a castle is to a young child than the comment, "a fortified residence as of a noble in feudal times" (*Random House Dictionary* 1980, 142).

In addition to learning through a variety of sensory forms, Eisner would also want students to have the opportunity to express themselves in a variety of ways. Computers could be useful in allowing students to reveal their knowledge in visual and musical as well as narrative forms. Students should not be limited in the ways they can express what they know.

Each curriculum ideology offers a unique perspective by virtue of the kinds of values and theories embedded within it. By reflecting on some of the ideas from the various curriculum ideologies and applying them to an educational issue, I believe educators can have a more informed, constructive, and creative dialogue. Moreover, as I said earlier, I do not think one needs to remain ideologically pure. Teachers and curricularists would do well to borrow ideas from the various perspectives as long as they make sure

CURRICULUM IDEOLOGIES

Ideology	Major Proponent	Major Writings	Educational Priorities	Philosophical Beliefs	Teachers, Curriculum, or Schools Expressing Curriculum Ideology	Suggestions for Curriculum Development
Rational Humanism	R. M. Hutchins M. Adler	The Paideia Proposal (Adler 1982) Paideia Problems and Possibilities (Adler 1983) The Paideia Program (Adler 1984)	Teaching through Socratic method. The use of primary texts. No electives.	The best education for the best is the best education for all. Since time in school is short, expose students to the best of Western culture.	Paideia Schools. See Adler (1983) for a list of schools.	Teach students how to facilitate good seminars. Use secondary texts sparingly.
Developmentalism	E. Duckworth R. Steiner	Young Children Reinvent Arithmetic (Kamii 1985) "The Having of Wonderful Ideas" and Other Essays (Duckworth 1987) Rudolf Steiner Education and the Developing Child (Aeppli 1986)	Fit curriculum to child's needs and interests. Inquiry-oriented teaching.	Cognitive structures develop as naturally as walking. If the setting is right, students will raise questions to push their own thinking.	Pat Carini's Prospect School in Burlington, VT.	Allow teachers the opportunity to be surprised. Rather than writing a curriculum manual, prepare a curriculum guide.
Reconceptualism	W. Pinar M. Grumet	Bitter Milk (Grumet 1988) Curriculum Theorizing (Pinar 1975) Curriculum and Instruction (Giroux, Penna, Pinar 1981)	Use philosophy, psychology, and literature to understand the human experience. Provide an "education for having" and an "education for being."	One learns through experience. We can learn to understand experience through phenomenology, psychoanalysis, and literature.	See Oliver (1990) for a curriculum in accordance with reconceptualist thinking.	Write lesson plans without the use of objectives. Curriculum writers ought to reveal their individual subjectivities.
Critical Theory	M. Apple I. Shor P. Freire	Ideology and Curriculum (Apple 1979) Teachers and Texts (Apple 1986) Pedagogy of the Oppressed (Freire 1970) Freire for the Classroom (Shor 1987)	Equal opportunities for all students. Teaching should entail critical reflection.	A just society maximizes the advantage for the least advantages. Schools are part of the larger community and must be analyzed as such.	See Shor's edited text (1987) for a number of ideas on implementing critical theory.	Curriculum writers ought to examine their own working assumptions critically and ought to respect the integrity of teachers and students.
Multiculturalism	J. Banks E. King	Multiethnic Education (Banks 1988) Multicultural Education (Banks and Banks 1989)	Students should learn to participate in various cultures. Approach concept or theme from various viewpoints.	Students need to feel good about their ethnic identities. All people participate in various cultures and subcultures.	See King (1990) for a workbook of activities teaching ethnic and gender awareness.	Make sure that text and pictures represent a variety of cultures.
Cognitive Pluralism	E. Eisner H. Gardner	"Curriculum Ideologies" (Eisner 1992) The Educational Imagination (Eisner 1985) Frames of Mind (Gardner 1983)	Teach, and allow students to express themselves, through a variety of forms of representation. Allow students to develop numerous intelligences.	Our senses cue into and pick up different aspects of the world. Combined with our individual history and general schemata, our senses allow us to construct meaning.	The Key School in Indianapolis.	Curriculum lesson plans and units ought to be aestetically pleasing in appearance. Curriculum ought to represent a variety of ways of knowing

they are not proposing contradictory ideas.

The chart on page 11 summarizes the major proponents, major writings, educational priorities, and philosophical beliefs of each curriculum ideology covered in this chapter. (Of course, this chart is not comprehensive. I encourage the reader to examine the recommended reading list for further works in each of these areas.) In the fifth column, "Teachers, Curriculum, or Schools Expressing Curriculum Ideology," I indicate places or texts where readers may learn more. One could visit a Paideia school, Carini's Prospect School, or the Key School in Indianapolis. One may read about reconceptualism, critical theory, and multiculturalism in the listed texts. Finally, in the sixth column, "Suggestions for Curriculum Development," I also include interesting points found in the literature but not necessarily contained in this chapter.

Recommended Reading

The following is a concise list of recommended reading in many of the areas discussed in this chapter. Full bibliographic citations are provided under *References*.

Some general **curriculum textbooks** that are invaluable are John D. McNeil's *Curriculum: A Comprehensive Introduction* (1990); William H. Schubert's *Curriculum: Perspective, Paradigm, and Possibility* (1986); Decker Walker's *Fundamentals of Curriculum* (1990); and Robert S. Zais's *Curriculum: Principles and Foundations* (1976). These books provide wonderful introductions to the field.

The recently published *Handbook of Research on Curriculum* (Jackson 1992) includes thirty-four articles by leading curricularists. This book is a must for anyone interested in research in curriculum.

For a discussion of **objectives** in education, Tyler (1949) is seminal. Also see Kapfer (1972) and Mager (1962). Bloom refines educational objectives into a taxonomy (1956). Eisner's (1985) critique of educational objectives and his notion of expressive outcomes will be welcomed by those who are skeptical of the objectives movement.

Good books on the **history of curriculum** include Kliebard (1986), Schubert (1980), and Tanner and Tanner (1975). Seguel (1966), who discusses the McMurry brothers, Dewey, Bobbitt, and Rugg, among others, is also very good.

Some excellent books on the **history of**

education include the following: Lawrence Cremin's definitive book on progressive education, *The Transformation of the School: Progressivism in American Education, 1876–1957* (1961). David Tyack's *The One Best System* (1974) portrays the evolution of schools into their modern formation; and Larry Cuban's *How Teachers Taught: Constancy and Change in American Classrooms, 1890–1980* (1984) examines what actually happened in classrooms during a century of reform efforts. Philip Jackson's "Conceptions of Curriculum and Curriculum Specialists" (1992) provides an excellent summary of the evolution of curriculum thought from Bobbitt and Tyler to Schwab.

For works in each of the ideologies I recommend the following:

To help one understand the **rational humanist** approach, there are Mortimer Adler's three books on the **Paideia school**: *The Paideia Proposal: An Educational Manifesto* (1982), *Paideia Problems and Possibilities* (1983), and *The Paideia Program: An Educational Syllabus* (1984). Seven critical reviews of the Paideia proposal comprise "The Paideia Proposal: A Symposium" (1983).

For works in **developmentalism** based on Piaget's ideas see Duckworth (1987, 1991) and Kamii (1985). Among Piaget's many works you may want to read *The Origins of Intelligence* (1966). If you are interested in Waldorf education see Robert McDermott's *The Essential Steiner* (1984) and P. Bruce Uhrmacher's "Waldorf Schools Marching Quietly Unheard" (1991). Willi Aeppli's *Rudolf Steiner Education and the Developing Child* (1986), Francis Edmunds's *Rudolf Steiner Education* (1982), and Marjorie Spock's *Teaching as a Lively Art* (1985) are also quite good.

A general overview of the developmental approach to curriculum can be found on pages 49–52 of Linda Darling-Hammond and Jon Snyder's "Curriculum Studies and the Traditions of Inquiry: The Scientific Tradition" (1922).

Two books are essential for examining **reconceptualist** writings: William Pinar's *Curriculum Theorizing: The Reconceptualists* (1975) and Henry Giroux, Anthony N. Penna, and William F. Pinar's *Curriculum and Instruction* (1981). Recent books in reconceptualism include William Pinar and William Reynolds's *Understanding Curriculum as Phenomenological and Deconstructed Text* (1992), and William Pinar and Joe L. Kincheloe's *Curriculum as Social Psychoanalysis: The Significance of Place* (1991).

Some excellent works in **critical theory** include Paulo Freire's *Pedagogy of the Oppressed* (1970) and *The Politics of Education* (1985). Apple's works are also excellent; see *Ideology and Curriculum* (1979) and *Teachers and Texts* (1986). For an overview of the Frankfurt School and the application of Jürgen Habermas's ideas, see Robert Young's *A Critical Theory of Education: Habermas and Our Children's Future* (1990).

For an application of critical theory to classrooms see the Ira Shor–edited book, *Freire for the Classroom* (1987) with an afterword by Paulo Freire.

In **multicultural education** I recommend James Banks's *Multiethnic Education: Theory and Practice* (1988) and Banks and Banks's *Multicultural Education: Issues and Perspectives* (1989). Also see Gibson (1984) for an account of five different approaches to multicultural education. Nicholas Appleton (1983), Saracho and Spodek (1983), and Simonson and Walker (1988) are also important. Edith King's *Teaching Ethnic and Gender Awareness: Methods and Materials for the Elementary School* (1990) provides useful ideas about multicultural education that could be used in the classroom. John Ogbu's work (1987) on comparing immigrant populations to involuntary minorities is also an important work with serious educational implications.

Important works in the field of **cognitive pluralism** include Elliot Eisner (1982, 1985, 1992) and Howard Gardner (1983, 1991). Some philosophical texts that influenced both of these men include Dewey (1934), Goodman (1978), and Langer (1976).

For $20.00, the Key School Option Program will send you an interdisciplinary theme-based curriculum report. For more information write Indianapolis Public Schools, 1401 East Tenth Street, Indianapolis, Indiana 46201.

Glossary of Some Common Usages of Curriculum

delivered curriculum: what teachers deliver in the classroom. This is opposed to Intended curriculum. Same as operational curriculum.

enacted curriculum: actual class offerings by a school, as opposed to courses listed in books or guides. *See* official curriculum.

experienced curriculum: what students actually learn. Same as received curriculum.

explicit curriculum: stated aims and goals of a classroom or school.

hidden curriculum: unintended, unwritten, tacit, or latent aspects of messages given to students by teachers, school structures, textbooks, and other school resources. For example, while students learn writing or math, they may also learn about punctuality, neatness, competition, and conformity. Concealed messages may be intended or unintended by the school or teacher.

implicit curriculum: similar to the hidden curriculum in the sense that something is implied rather than expressly stated. Whereas the hidden curriculum usually refers to something unfavorable, negative, or sinister, the implicit curriculum also takes into account unstated qualities that are positive.

intended curriculum: that which is planned by the teacher or school.

null curriculum: that which does not take place in the school or classroom. What is not offered cannot be learned. Curricular exclusion tells a great deal about a school's values.

official curriculum: courses listed in the school catalogue or course bulletin. Although these classes are listed, they may not be taught. *See* enacted curriculum.

operational curriculum: events that take place in the classroom. Same as delivered curriculum.

received curriculum: what students acquire as a result of classroom activity. Same as experienced curriculum.

References

Adler, Mortimer J. 1982. *The Paideia Proposal: An Educational Manifesto*. New York: Collier Books.

———. 1983. *Paideia Problems and Possibilities*. New York: Collier Books.

———. 1984. *The Paideia Program: An Educational Syllabus*. New York: Collier Books.

Aeppli, Willi. 1986. *Rudolf Steiner Education and the Developing Child.* Hudson, NY: Anthroposophic Press.

Anderson, Ronald E., Wayne W. Welch, and Linda J. Harris. 1984. "Inequities in Opportunities for Computer Literacy." *The Computing Teacher: The Journal of the International Council for Computers in Education* 11(8):10–12.

Apple, Michael W. 1979. *Ideology and Curriculum.* Boston: Routledge and Kegan Paul.

———. 1986. *Teachers and Texts: A Political Economy of Class and Gender Relations in Education.* New York: Routledge and Kegan Paul.

Appleton, Nicholas. 1983. *Cultural Pluralism in Education.* White Plains, NY: Longman.

Banks, James A. 1988. *Multiethnic Education: Theory and Practice.* 2d ed. Boston: Allyn and Bacon.

Banks, James A., and Cherry A. McGee Banks, eds. 1989. *Multicultural Education: Issues and Perspectives.* Boston: Allyn and Bacon.

Bloom, Benjamin S., ed. 1956. *Taxonomy of Educational Objectives: The Classification of Educational Goals, Handbook 1: Cognitive Domain.* New York: McKay.

Bobbitt, Franklin. 1918. *The Curriculum.* Boston: Houghton Mifflin.

Cremin, Lawrence A. 1961. *The Transformation of the School: Progressivism in American Education, 1876–1957.* New York: Vintage Books.

———. 1977. *Traditions of American Education.* New York: Basic Books.

Cuban, Larry. 1984. *How Teachers Taught: Constancy and Change in American Classrooms 1890–1980.* White Plains, NY: Longman.

Darling-Hammond, Linda, and Jon Snyder. 1992. "Curriculum Studies and the Traditions of Inquiry: The Scientific Tradition." In *Handbook of Research on Curriculum: A Project of the American Educational Research Association,* ed. Philip W. Jackson, 41–78. New York: Macmillan.

Dewey, John. 1934. *Art as Experience.* New York: Minton, Balch.

Duckworth, Eleanor. 1987. *"The Having of Wonderful Ideas" and Other Essays on Teaching and Learning.* New York: Teachers College Press.

———. 1991. "Twenty-four, Forty-two, and I Love You: Keeping It Complex. *Harvard Educational Review* 61(1):1–24.

Edmunds, L. Francis. 1982. *Rudolf Steiner Education.* 2d ed. London: Rudolf Steiner Press.

Eisner, Elliot W. 1982. *Cognition and Curriculum: A Basis for Deciding What to Teach.* White Plains, NY: Longman.

———. 1985. *The Educational Imagination.* 2d ed. New York: Macmillan.

———. 1992. "Curriculum Ideologies." In *Handbook of Research on Curriculum: A Project of the American Educational Research Association,* ed. Philip W. Jackson, 302–26. New York: Macmillan.

Freire, Paulo. 1970. *Pedagogy of the Oppressed.* Trans. Myra Bergman Ramos. New York: Seabury Press.

———. 1985. *The Politics of Education.* Trans. Donaldo Macedo. South Hadley, MA: Bergin and Garvey.

Gardner, Howard. 1983. *Frames of Mind.* New York: Basic Books.

———. 1991. *The Unschooled Mind: How Children Think and How Schools Should Teach.* New York: Basic Books.

Gibson, Margaret Alison. 1984. "Approaches to Multicultural Education in the United States: Some Concepts and Assumptions." *Anthropology and Education Quarterly* 15:94–119.

Giroux, Henry, Anthony N. Penna, and William F. Pinar. 1981. *Curriculum and Instruction: Alternatives in Education.* Berkeley: McCutchan.

Good, Thomas S., and Jere E. Brophy. 1986. *Educational Psychology.* 3d ed. White Plains, NY: Longman.

Goodman, Nelson. 1978. *Ways of Worldmaking.* Indianapolis: Hackett.

Greene, Maxine. 1988a. "Vocation and Care: Obsessions about Teacher Education." Panel discussion at the Annual Meeting of the American Educational Research Association, 5–9 April, New Orleans.

———. 1988b. *The Dialectic of Freedom.* New York: Teachers College Press.

Gress, James R. 1978. *Curriculum: An Introduction to the Field.* Berkeley: McCutchan.

Grumet, Madeleine R. 1988. *Bitter Milk: Women and Teaching.* Amherst: Univ. of Massachusetts Press.

Jackson, Philip W. 1992. "Conceptions of Curriculum and Curriculum Specialists." In *Handbook of Research on Curriculum: A Project of the American Educational Research Association,* ed. Philip W. Jackson, 3–40. New York: Macmillan.

Kamii, Constance Kazuko, with Georgia DeClark. 1985. *Young Children Reinvent*

Arithmetic: Implications of Piaget's Theory. New York: Teachers College Press.

Kapfer, Miriam B. 1972. *Behavioral Objectives in Curriculum Development: Selected Readings and Bibliography.* Englewood Cliffs, NJ: Educational Technology.

King, Edith W. 1990. *Teaching Ethnic and Gender Awareness: Methods and Materials for the Elementary School.* Dubuque, IA: Kendall/Hunt.

Kliebard, Herbert M. 1986. *The Struggle for the American Curriculum, 1893–1958.* Boston: Routledge and Kegan Paul.

Langer, Susanne. 1976. *Problems of Art.* New York: Scribners.

McDermott, Robert A., ed. 1984. *The Essential Steiner.* San Francisco: Harper & Row.

McLaren, Peter. 1986. *Schooling as a Ritual Performance: Towards a Political Economy of Educational Symbols and Gestures.* London: Routledge and Kegan Paul.

McNeil, John D. 1990. *Curriculum: A Comprehensive Introduction.* 4th ed. Glenview, IL: Scott, Foresman/Little, Brown Higher Education.

Mager, Robert. 1962. *Preparing Instructional Objectives.* Palo Alto, CA: Fearon.

Ogbu, John. 1987. "Variability in Minority School Performance: A Problem in Search of an Explanation." *Anthropology and Education Quarterly* 18(4): 312–34.

Oliver, Donald W. 1990. "Grounded Knowing: A Postmodern Perspective on Teaching and Learning." *Educational Leadership* 48(1): 64-69.

"The Paideia Proposal: A Symposium." 1983. *Harvard Educational Review* 53 (4): 377–411.

Piaget, Jean. 1962. *Play, Dreams and Imitation in Childhood.* New York: Norton.

———. 1966. *Origins of Intelligence.* New York: Norton.

Pinar, William F., ed. 1975. *Curriculum Theorizing: The Reconceptualists.* Berkeley: McCutchan.

Pinar, William F., and Joe L. Kincheloe, eds. 1991. *Curriculum as Social Psychoanalysis: The Significance of Place.* Albany: State Univ. of New York Press.

Pinar, William F., and William M. Reynolds, eds. 1992. *Understanding Curriculum as Phenomenological and Deconstructed Text.* New York: Teachers College Press.

The Random House Dictionary. 1980. New York: Ballantine.

Saracho, Olivia N., and Bernard Spodek. 1983. *Understanding the Multicultural Experience in Early Childhood Education.* Washington, DC: National Association for the Education of Young Children.

Schubert, William H. 1980. *Curriculum Books: The First Eight Years.* Lanham, MD: Univ. Press of America.

———. 1986. *Curriculum: Perspective, Paradigm, and Possibility.* New York: Macmillan.

Schwab, Joseph J. 1970. *The Practical: A Language for Curriculum.* Washington, DC: National Education Association.

Seguel, M. L. 1966. *The Curriculum Field: Its Formative Years.* New York: Teachers College Press.

Shor, Ira, ed. 1987. *Freire for the Classroom: A Sourcebook for Liberatory Teaching.* Portsmouth, NH: Heinemann.

Simonson, Rick, and Scott Walker, eds. 1988. *The Graywolf Annual Five: Multi-Cultural Literacy.* St. Paul, MN: Graywolf Press.

Spock, Marjorie. 1985. *Teaching as a Lively Art.* Hudson, NY: Anthroposophic Press.

Taba, Hilda. 1962. *Curriculum Development: Theory and Practice.* New York: Harcourt Brace Jovanovich.

Tanner, Daniel, and Laurel N. Tanner. 1975. *Curriculum Development: Theory into Practice.* New York: Macmillan.

Tietze, Wolfgang. 1987. "A Structural Model for the Evaluation of Preschool Effects." *Early Childhood Research Quarterly* 2(2): 133–59.

Tyack, David B. 1974. *The One Best System: A History of American Urban Education.* Cambridge: Harvard Univ. Press.

Tyler, Ralph W. 1949. *Basic Principles of Curriculum and Instruction.* Chicago: Univ. of Chicago Press.

Uhrmacher, P. Bruce. 1991. "Waldorf Schools Marching Quietly Unheard." Ph.D. diss., Stanford University.

Walker, Decker. 1990. *Fundamentals of Curriculum.* New York: Harcourt Brace Jovanovich.

Young, Robert. 1990. *A Critical Theory of Education: Habermas and Our Children's Future.* New York: Teachers College Press.

Zais, Robert S. 1976. *Curriculum: Principles and Foundations.* New York: Thomas Y. Crowell.

CURRENT TRENDS IN ESL CURRICULUM

by Else V. Hamayan
Director of Training and Services
Illinois Resource Center, Des Plaines, Illinois

OVER the last ten years, views regarding English as a second language (ESL) instruction have changed significantly. Several previously held assumptions have changed, and new methods have emerged for helping students develop proficiency in English as a second language. Traditional ESL methods and approaches, which tended to focus on the form and structure of English, have been found to contradict the way in which language naturally develops, making the second language learning process more tedious and cumbersome for the learner than it needs to be. Beliefs that we learn a second language by forming habits and that pattern drills and repetitive grammar exercises reinforce good habits in the second language are not well founded. Instructional methods that stem from these beliefs do not allow a second language to emerge in natural developmental stages, making it difficult for most second language learners (Corey, Pfleger, and Hamayan 1987).

We have moved from teaching isolated units within a language to teaching language as a whole, interrelated system. We have moved from approaches that focus explicitly on the form of language to those that give much more importance to the content or the message. We have also seen a broadening of approaches and instructional strategies used in ESL classrooms. Consequently, the changes in the way that ESL is taught have led to a change in the organization of ESL classrooms from a teacher-centered environment to one that is more learner- and activity-centered, where teachers and students are partners in the learning experience.

These instructional changes have stemmed from our views about language, about second language learning, and about the role that teachers and students play in the learning process. Language is currently seen as a complex, vital, and constantly changing system of communication whose sum is larger than its parts. We no longer conceptualize language simply on the basis of the units that constitute it, such as the sounds, letters, syntactic rules, or words that are part of language. Rather, meaning is now seen to be inherent in and conveyed by the interaction of those units within a social or functional context (Chaika 1982; Lindfors 1987).

Views regarding language learning have also changed: language learning is now seen as an active endeavor in which the learner plays a significant role, generating the language he or she is learning and altering the learning process in individualized and culturally determined ways. Reading, for example, is not seen as a matter of turning letters into sounds or a process of decoding words; rather, reading is now seen as a process of communication between a writer and a reader (Goodman 1984; Goodman and Goodman 1978; Smith 1982). The reader is seen primarily as a *meaning maker* (Rigg 1986), and, as such, is viewed as bringing to the language learning process a whole array of individual characteristics that play a vital role in making sense out of a written linguistic environment.

Thus, the role of the learner has changed from that of a passive recipient of knowledge about the language he or she is learning, and from an automatic applier of rigid language rules, to an active decision-maker in the language learning process and a creative generator of newly acquired language. This notion applies to very young learners as well as to older students. The characteristics that any learner brings with him or her to the classroom affect the way and the rate at which the second language is learned. Attitudes and motivation (Gardner and Lambert 1972), personality characteristics and learning style preferences (Tucker, Hamayan, and Genesee 1976), and native language proficiency (Cummins 1984) are a few of the individual learner characteristics that have been found to play important roles in the second language learning process.

The learner's cultural background is also seen as an important factor in the language learning process, and it shapes the way that information in the new language is internalized and comprehended (Heath 1986). Second language learning is a culturally embedded process (Heath 1983), and the mismatch between the ESL classroom culture (and perhaps the school culture in general) and the student's home culture can sometimes lead to difficulties in the second language learning process. Thus, using—or including the use of—the learners' culture as a basis for ESL instruction is becoming a common feature of many ESL classrooms (for example, see Au and Jordan 1981).

Because of the active role that the learner plays in the second language learning process, the role of the ESL teacher has changed from knowledge giver to facilitator of the learning process. The teacher gives the student the opportunity to engage in the process of using and developing language (Altwerger, Edelsky, and Flores 1987; Weaver 1990). The ESL teacher helps to mediate the English-speaking world to the student by framing, selecting, focusing, and feeding back experiences in the second language in such a way that learning takes place. For example, if a student is struggling over the words of a text, the teacher may direct the student's attention to the illustrations accompanying the text, and may get the student to guess and predict

the general sense of the passage before focusing on the text itself. (This is similar to the notion that Feuerstein (1982) introduced to describe the best environment for children with special needs. He suggested that difficulty in academic settings often occurs because children have not been taught to focus their attention on significant events and ideas in their environment. A teacher can help the student to learn.) In many ways, the teacher becomes the student's partner in learning (Calkins 1983; Graves 1983), and many instructional decisions may be made jointly by a teacher and his or her students.

These changes have given rise to three general and significant trends in the field of teaching ESL. The first comes from the awareness that proficiency in a second language needs to emerge holistically and naturally through the use of functional language used for authentic purposes. The second is based on the idea that a second language is best learned when the content of instruction forms an important component of language instruction. The third major trend comes from the realization that there is no single method of teaching that is ideal for all ESL learners.

This chapter describes these trends and discusses the implications for curriculum design, choice of materials, and use of instructional strategies. Implications of these trends for assessment procedures are also discussed briefly as they emerge, since assessment and instruction are closely interrelated.

The Natural and Holistic Development of ESL

One of the major shifts over the last ten years in the way ESL is taught is reflected in the awareness that a second language needs to emerge holistically and naturally through functional language that is used for authentic purposes. Although the natural emergence of a second language is only one of three processes through which a second language develops, it deserves special attention, since it has only recently begun to be incorporated into second language teaching. The developmental processes characteristic of second language learning are: (1) automatic habit formation, (2) conscious rule learning, and (3) the natural emergence process noted above. The first two processes are reviewed briefly and the third is discussed in more detail.

Second Language Learning Processes

Through the first process, memorization of chunks, second language learners pick up "chunks" of language, which are usually phrases used frequently in everyday conversation, or language that is the focus of a particular ESL lesson (Hatch, Peck, and Wagner-Gough 1979). These chunks eventually become part of the student's verbal repertoire, even though the student may initially not understand the exact meaning of the chunk of language and may use it inappropriately.

Automatic language learning, which usually results from repeated exposure to a word, phrase, or sentence, gives the learner access to automatic responses and is particularly useful to (and typical of) the beginning level ESL student (Hanania and Gradman 1977). Because this process often bypasses meaning, however, it contributes neither to understanding the internalized rules of the language nor to the authentic use of the second language (Krashen and Scarcella 1978). A belief by many ESL educators and researchers in the importance of this second language acquisition process is likely to have led to audiolingual teaching methods (Lado 1964) that stressed the use of repetition and pattern drills and emphasized memorization as an integral learning tool.

The second process reflects a more conscious knowledge of the rules of the language and is the product of formal *learning* (Krashen 1981). Through this process, the learner develops knowledge about the second language and is able to manipulate the rules of grammar, phonology, and semantics. This type of knowledge may well underlie metalinguistic proficiency and more cognitively demanding language processing. And yet, the surface skills that develop through this process may not transfer very far beyond the ESL classroom or even a language exercise.

There is some indication that conscious knowledge about language comes into play only when the task at hand is focused on the form of language itself, as in a language test, for example (Houck, Robertson, and Krashen 1978; Krashen, Butler, Birnbaum, and Robertson, 1978). The type of language proficiency that results from this process develops primarily through formal instruction where the focus of lessons is on language per se. This approach is typically seen in structured ESL method textbooks and basal readers where the focus is explicitly on language. It is, in fact, useful in contexts where the target

language is studied for academic purposes alone, and not for interaction or functional conversation. But, significantly, this situation usually does not apply in the typical ESL classroom.

Habit formation and mastery of the rules of language typify the more traditional approaches to teaching ESL, based on structural approaches to learning, referred to here as formal structural approaches.

The third process is based on research that suggests that second language students learn ESL much the same way as English-speaking children learn their first language (Dulay, Burt, and Krashen 1982). This process, which Krashen refers to as *acquisition* (1981), reflects an implicit knowledge of a language and the ability to use it in authentic contexts. The type of language proficiency that results from this process develops primarily through structured and unstructured exposure to and use of the second language in a meaningful context. Through this process, language emerges through natural developmental stages whereby students begin with a silent stage that precedes production. When production occurs, it emerges in stages: in the earlier stages, for example, students might produce only single-word utterances, which eventually turn into longer phrases and sentences (Hakuta 1976; Ervin-Tripp 1974). Errors occur as a natural and inevitable part of the development of a second language. Rather than trying to avoid errors, teachers who base their instructional approaches on this process use information obtained from observing second language errors to determine the strategies that a learner may be using.

Typically, this process underlies holistic approaches to ESL instruction where the focus rarely is explicitly on language; rather, lessons are arranged around topical themes that are chosen primarily on the basis of their importance to the learners. Thus, holistic ESL instruction for K–12 students usually centers around academic content area topics that the students encounter in the mainstream classroom, or around social topics with relevance to the students' daily lives.

The next section describes the characteristics of formal structural approaches to second language development and points out some of the shortcomings of the exclusive use of these approaches. Some tenets of the holistic approach to ESL instruction will also be discussed.

Characteristics of Formal Structural Approaches to Second LanguageDevelopment

The fact that language is a complex system led some ESL educators in the past to believe that language is learned more easily when it is broken down to its smallest units and when it is taught in a piecemeal fashion. It is this misconception that has led to ESL teaching approaches in which the sounds of English, individual syntactic rules, groups of words, or the separate structures of language are taught in isolation. Krashen and Seliger provide a definition of formal language instruction that is useful for this discussion. According to them, the special features of formal language instruction are "(1) the isolation of rules and lexical items of the target language and (2) the possibility of error detection and correction" (Krashen and Seliger 1975, 173). Formal structural approaches vary in the extent to which they incorporate different teaching methodologies, but they share some common characteristics.

1. The focus of ESL lessons in formal structural approaches is usually on the form of language itself rather than the message or the content. Curricula are organized around language units rather than topics, and language objectives are primary in lessons rather than secondary to other cognitive, school, or academic content area objectives. Learner utterances and written products are controlled so as to minimize errors, and much attention is paid to how students say and write things rather than what they are saying or writing.

2. In formal structural approaches, isolated units of language are generally taught separately, as are the four skills of language—listening, speaking, reading, and writing. Thus, the past tense is taught as a distinct unit, and it is typical to have time set aside for oral language practice, separately from written language or reading. Often, skills are taught sequentially—first listening and speaking, then reading and writing.

3. In formal structural approaches, the materials that are used are very different from the learners' oral language in both form and content. Thus, the students may encounter ESL lessons that focus on the irregular past tense at a time when that form is not part of their usable knowledge of English. Similarly, students may read about characters and events that have very little in common with their lives. The instructional materials may not be based at all on the students' own current or past cultures and may be irrelevant to their daily activities or circumstances.

For example, lessons may feature young adolescents in a typical suburban nuclear family, whereas the ESL student may live in an urban apartment that houses extended family.

4. In a classroom where formal structural approaches are typically used, the student has very little decision-making power as to the content of instruction and little choice as to the particular tasks that make up a lesson. Those decisions are either taken by the teacher independently or are usually predetermined by the materials and the curriculum being used.

Shortcomings of the Exclusive Use of Formal Structural Approaches

Because of these and other characteristics, formal structural approaches have not been found to be very efficient and effective in developing proficiency in either a first language (Cambourne 1987) or in ESL (Hudelson 1986). First, they do not satisfy most ESL learners' need for functional language. Second, because of this lack of focus on function, the second language is forced to establish itself in an unnatural way and takes on an artificiality that is difficult to offset. Third, because of the significant attention paid to the form of language without a functional context, learning becomes unreal or abstract, and therefore meaningless and difficult. And fourth, language learning is reduced to a series of often boring and failure-prone chores.

The Lack of Functional Language. In formal structural approaches to ESL instruction, most learners' basic need for functional language is not satisfied, nor is their need to learn the social rules that govern the use of everyday language. ESL students, even if they are young children, have pressing needs to function in the second language in social situations—for example, to negotiate with peers on the playground—just as they have needs to function meaningfully in academic content areas. Since language use is fundamentally a social act that occurs in a social context, it is important for students to learn language that is functional and that fits their specific social and academic needs. An exclusively structural ESL approach may force language on the student which lacks communicative functions or which diverges widely from the student's immediate social needs.

Moreover, since most ESL students come from cultural backgrounds that are quite different from those represented in many ESL textbooks, the students end up being exposed to language that is very different from their own language, both in style and in content. When ESL students are given instructional materials that are neither directly related to their current daily lives nor to their past experiences, language learning becomes irrelevant and the motivation to become a fluent user of the second language is diminished significantly (Edelsky 1986).

The Artificial and Forced Use of Language. The second reason that exclusively formal structural ESL approaches fail is that the second language is not allowed to emerge in the natural developmental stages equivalent to those occurring in first language learning. In structural ESL classrooms, students' utterances and written products are controlled to a great extent so as to reduce the likelihood of errors. Perfection is often required long before the student is ready to be close to perfect. This requirement prevents the gradual and natural emergence of the second language and is likely to lead to an artificial type of *interlanguage* (Selinker 1972) that may not be very functional for the learner. The artificiality of some typically structural ESL tasks is exemplified by fill-in-the-blank types of worksheets, repetition drills, and controlled written exercises.

The Lack of Meaningful Input. A third aspect of exclusively formal structural approaches that makes them inappropriate for ESL learners is their tendency to focus on sounds and words in isolation. Because isolated sounds and words do not carry much meaning, activities that focus the learner's attention on these isolated units of language are relatively meaningless, and the learner is less likely to understand them or to make them part of his or her language system. These activities are less useful, or capable of being internalized, than those derived from connected prose (Goodman 1986; Krashen and Terrell 1983). By burdening the learner with relatively meaningless tidbits of language, his or her search for meaning is made more difficult.

Focusing on the form of language without explicit and direct reference to its meaning or functional relevance also forces the learner to take an abstract view of language, which may be a difficult task for many ESL learners. It may be particularly difficult for young ESL learners or those coming from atypical educational backgrounds, such as refugees or migrant students, to

treat language as something one talks about rather than something one simply does. Yet, at other times, it is this very lack of an abstract view of language that makes it essential for the ESL teacher to focus on the structures and rules of English in order to build higherorder cognitive skills. For these students, the awareness of language may not emerge naturally by itself, but it is important in developing a base for comprehending academic content materials. Because students with atypical educational backgrounds are not likely to pull out the rules governing the use of particular aspects of language, the teacher may have to direct the students' attention explicitly to the form of language in as meaningful a way as possible.

The Lack of Motivation to Learn. The final reason that exclusively formal structural approaches fail to meet the needs of ESL students, and perhaps the most important one, is that they reduce language learning to something tedious, frustrating, and too often unsuccessful. As a consequence, many students lose their motivation to engage in second language learning tasks. As the research on the role of motivation in second language learning indicates, general interest in language learning is a strong predictor of success in second language acquisition (Gardner 1985; Spolsky 1988). Analyzing language, practicing its rules—often without understanding them—and manipulating its minute units (which is typical of formal structural approaches to ESL) will turn far too many learners away from the second language learning task because such activities lack an inherently attractive incentive for most learners. Such structurally oriented activities are not only devoid of the joy of language but they also make the learner failure-prone.

In most structurally based ESL approaches, the materials that are used may also make the task of reading, in particular, and the task of second language learning, in general, extremely boring. Many ESL texts and basals, driven and buoyed by the mastery of skills and phonics, control language to such an extent that they deprive the reader of the joy of language (Routman 1988). Children, especially, do not get a feel for the rich array of sensations and emotions portrayed in the literature they read and do not get to enjoy reading in the way in which children's authors intended them (Ohanian 1987). Subsequently, they are likely to lose their motivation to read and perhaps even to use the second language at all.

The Need for Holistic ESL Instruction

The notion underlying the formal structural approaches to ESL, that is, breaking language down to its smallest parts to make it manageable for ESL learners, contradicts the most pressing need that most ESL learners have: to deal with meaning. In many ways, ESL learners learn in ways that are quite similar to children learning their first language. As Goodman (1986) has pointed out, the idea that children begin their language learning experience with isolated words (parts) and put them together to make a whole is an illusion. Children convey whole meanings even when they utter single words: thus, "up" may mean "I want to go upstairs," "pick me up," or even "put me down," depending on the context in which it is used. Meaning is also key in the second language learning process, in that the second language learner is primarily a meaning maker. Language, for most ESL students, exists for the formulation, comprehension, and transmission of meaning (Norris and Damico 1990).

Despite the complexity of language and the difficulty of the task facing the ESL learner, language is easier to learn when it is whole (Goodman 1986). Rather than working with small units of language, students learning ESL need to be introduced to English in a meaningful way, they need to make the link between meaning and language as naturally as possible, and they need to be given the opportunity to use the new language in meaningful and real contexts. Consequently, new language may be learned more easily by listening to and reading a well-illustrated story than by practicing a pattern such as the formation of the regular past tense.

One of the reasons that language is easier to learn holistically rather than in small units is that whole language carries more meaning than do isolated units that make up language, and meaning is a key element in learning. Meaningful chunks of language are easier to learn than bits and pieces of language that may not carry much meaning by themselves. Thus, despite the fact that an illustrated story is likely to contain even more unfamiliar language than a pattern exercise, students probably glean much more meaning—and consequently are more likely to internalize new language—from the story than from the grammar exercise.

The holistic view of language is also appropriate in that with real language use, all components of language are simultaneously present and interacting with one another. The ability to communicate exhibits itself through the adequate production of the sounds of English, in the case of oral language, or through the use of the alphabet, in the case of written language, as well as through the appropriate use of grammar and vocabulary. Phonology, grammar and vocabulary skills all support each other in any instance of language use.

Separating the components of language from one another and teaching them individually and out of context make the language learning task much more difficult than it needs to be. Language is almost always used in a context or a situation that allows for the creation of meaning (Norris and Damico 1990). To teach language with little or no context makes it even harder for the student. Nevertheless, there is a place for the isolated units of language (Adams 1990) that help to build a strong foundation, especially concerning literacy in the second language. The key is to place the instruction of the isolated units of language within a meaningful context, rather than teaching them in isolation as has typically been done in traditionally structural ESL approaches. This issue is addressed in more detail in a later section of this chapter.

Another issue that makes the holistic approach to ESL instruction extremely valuable is that in everyday situations the different processes of language rarely occur separately from one another. In most conversations, the participants speak and listen simultaneously; we read what we write, and sometimes we talk about what we have read. To separate the instruction of these various processes leads to language use that is rather artificial and contrived.

Teaching the Form and Structures of Language

Although the exclusive use of formal structural approaches is not appropriate for most ESL learners, attention to the rules and structures that govern language explicitly can help ESL learners gain control over their second language and develop higher-order thinking skills and learning strategies. This may be particularly important for ESL students who are coming from atypical educational backgrounds, who have had interrupted schooling, and who may not have the kind of informal training in school behavior and strategies as other students. Because of a lack of experience with school and with school-type activities, students with limited educational experience may need to be taught not just the formal aspects of language, but also strategies they can use to complete classroom tasks (Hamayan in press).

One of the reasons for teaching the formal aspects of language is that students can and do make use of such knowledge for decoding and comprehending written text (Adams 1990). The explicit teaching of reading and learning strategies has been shown to be helpful to literate adult ESL learners (Carrell, Pharis, and Liberto 1989) as well as to younger nonliterate adolescents learning ESL (Hamayan in press). Research has shown not only that effective language learners use a greater number of learning strategies but also that strategies can be taught successfully to ESL students who have not yet acquired them on their own (Chamot, O'Malley, Kupper, and Impink-Hernandez 1987; Oxford 1990).

Rather than focusing on the discrete points of language in isolation and as the goal of learning, the most effective way to teach these points of language is to integrate their structural and functional aspects. Once a meaningful context has been established, students' attention can be directed to focus on specific structures and forms of language. Any holistic activity used to engage the learner in a language task, such as shared reading of a storybook or individual creative writing, can serve as a launching pad for follow-up activities that focus on specific formal aspects of language, such as alphabetizing or changing the tenses of verbs. Following this procedure, the same language that was generated through a hands-on or a holistic type of activity can serve as the material for a decoding or phonics exercise, instead of using words or sentences from the reading text, such as the ESL series or the basal reader, for which the students may not have a strong oral base. This type of linguistic focus has been referred to as *language exploitation* (Mohan 1979), and by itself may be regarded as insufficient use of teaching material. It will become clear, however, in the section of this chapter on integrated instruction that when language focus is integrated with content area instruction, many more objectives can be accomplished.

Implications for
Curriculum and Instruction

From the discussion of the first major trend in ESL instruction, the conclusion was made that proficiency in a second language can best be developed when it is allowed to emerge holistically and naturally through the use of functional

language used for authentic purposes. The following general implications for curriculum and instruction emerge from this first trend:

1. Any ESL curriculum or classroom activity must be guided by meaning. Lessons and activities must not only be meaningful to the learner, but they must also take into account the fact that the learner will have the making of meaning as a primary goal.

2. Any ESL curriculum or classroom activity must be primarily functional for the learner. ESL students need to learn the language for what they need to accomplish in their daily lives, both socially and academically or vocationally.

3. Any ESL classroom activity must take into account and, to some extent, be based on students' cultural background. The student needs to learn the second language (English) and the culture that it represents by building on his or her existing native language skills and culture knowledge.

4. The way that any ESL class is structured must be designed to make it more likely that the student will succeed rather than fail. Any utterance or product in the second language, even if it is laden with errors, must be seen as a step forward and not as a deviation from the accurate, acceptable form it is supposed to approximate.

The following specific implications for curriculum and instruction also emerge from the issues discussed in the first section of this chapter:

1. The second or target language must be allowed to emerge in natural developmental stages rather than be strictly patterned on an artificially established notion of accuracy. This means that, initially, the learner must be allowed the opportunity to learn functional chunks of language and to go through a silent period. When language does emerge, it will probably emerge in seemingly incomplete and erroneous forms that, given the right environment, will eventually approximate accurate and acceptable forms of English.

2. Lessons must be organized topically or according to themes, rather than according to language units. The choice of the topics or themes will be based on their usefulness for the learner. Since language objectives are secondary to topical or thematic ones in this type of curricular organization, it follows that discrete points or units of language are presented together, and that the four skills of language will also be integrated with one another.

3. While surrounding the learner with accurate and rich language, the focus of the

teacher's attention will be on the content of language used in the classroom or the message being conveyed, rather than on the form of language and the way it is used.

4. Even when attention is drawn to the discrete units of language and they become the focus of instruction, they must be presented in a context that is meaningful to the learner. Students must be thoroughly familiar with the language that they focus on and manipulate.

5. The language used in the ESL classroom must be authentic rather than contrived, in that it represents real situations to which the students can relate.

6. The materials and strategies used in the ESL classroom must have some cultural relevance to the students. This may mean the use of multicultural literature as well as classroom management techniques that are in keeping with the students' preferred styles.

7. The students, regardless of their age, must be given some ownership of their own learning. They need to generate their own materials, based on their own oral language and their own background, and they need to be free to learn in the way that they feel most comfortable learning.

8. Activities used in the ESL classroom must be inherently motivating to students, both in content and in form, so that language learning does not become a chore or a burden.

Integration of Content and Language Instruction

The second major trend in teaching ESL is the integration of content area instruction with the instruction of the second language. Integrated language and content instruction enables students to develop academic knowledge and skills in the content areas while they acquire the academic language in English needed to succeed in school (Crandall 1990). The integration of content and language also allows for the development of thinking skills, which has become a current focus of ESL instruction. Thus, three components are present in integrated instruction: language, content, and cognition.

This innovative view of language instruction suggests that the content of ESL curriculum needs to be just as important as the language to be attained. Indeed, the development of one can support or lead to development in the other.

Traditionally, the main focus of ESL teachers was the instruction of language forms to second language learners. Similarly, the main focus of content area teachers was the instruction of content, with little attention paid to related language objectives. Moreover, the instruction of ESL was kept separate from and independent of the instruction of other content areas that an ESL student would typically get during a school day. Thus, what happened in the science or social studies part of the day had little to do with the ESL support a student was receiving.

An example of integration of language and content is the use of an academic content area topic within the ESL classroom. For example, the ESL teacher may do a series of activities around the topic of *Home* and may pull out of those activities foci on particular language units. Because ESL teachers are usually not bound by content area curriculum and textbook requirements, it is easier for them to plan for activities within the ESL class that are based on supplementary resources such as hands-on tasks and tradebooks.

It is only recently that educators have stopped regarding language development and content area development in isolation, but rather as mutually supporting one another (Mohan 1990). In fact, this approach to education is not confined to discussions about ESL learners but represents a more general concern for the integration of various parts of the curriculum for the general school population (Pring 1973).

One of the earliest models of instruction based on the integration of content and language for second language learners was the *immersion* model in Canada (Lambert and Tucker 1972).

In this model, English-speaking Canadian children went to school primarily taught in French and eventually developed their skills in French as a second language by learning content through that language. Second language skills were developed naturally and systematically, not by focusing on them formally but rather by focusing on the development of other academic skills. In this model, native language instruction was eventually introduced in a formal way. Since the children came from communities with strong support for and pride in their native language (English) and since English was a language of power and status in the larger society, their native language skills did not suffer when compared to their counterparts who were not learning French through the immersion model (for an extensive review of immersion programs in Canada and elsewhere, see Genesee 1987).

Although the immersion model is not feasible for many students of various native language backgrounds in the United States (Tucker 1980), some of the principles underlying the model, such as teaching the second language in an integrated fashion with content areas, have proven to be very effective for ESL learners. As the effectiveness of formal language teaching has been questioned, and with the advent of natural approaches to ESL instruction, it has become more common for language instruction to be integrated with content area instruction. This trend has had some implications for teacher roles and responsibilities, as discussed below.

In order for the instruction of language to be wholly and systematically integrated with the instruction of content, language teachers and content teachers need to cooperate with one another and mutually support one another (Mohan 1990). In some schools, the mainstream classroom teacher is responsible for both the ESL development and the content-area teaching. In that case, it would naturally be easier to integrate the various components of instruction than would be the case with separate teachers. When there is a separate ESL teacher, that teacher needs to be involved in the process of instruction planning with the mainstream classroom teacher in a coherent way. This involvement implies a departure from the traditional role that ESL and mainstream content area teachers have played, in that content area instruction has now become part of the ESL teacher's responsibility, and the development of second language proficiency has become part of the mainstream classroom teacher's responsibility. The implications of this point for staff development will be addressed further in a later section.

First, the rationale and some of the reasons for integrating language and content instruction must be addressed.

The Rationale for Integrating Language and Content

It has become increasingly clear that separating the instruction of language from the instruction of academic content areas within a school setting is not very effective for students who are attempting to become proficient in the language of instruction while they gain knowledge in the academic content areas required by the curriculum. The central idea in integrated language and content instruction is that ESL students need to learn language and content simultaneously and systematically (Mohan 1990). This means that language objectives and content area objectives must both be integral parts of any lesson presented to ESL students.

The ineffectiveness of separating language and content instruction is based on two principles. First, when ESL instruction is separated from the instruction of content, the emphasis and focus of instruction tend to shift unnecessarily to the form of the target language. As indicated in the discussion earlier in this chapter, the effectiveness of ESL instruction that focuses heavily on the form of language, with little consideration to the message or content, has been seriously questioned. Second, it has become clear that ESL students face increasingly demanding tasks dealing with the content area curriculum in a language in which they are not very proficient. By teaching language separately from content, ESL students are deprived of much-needed bodies of knowledge and skills, specifically in the area of cognitive development. Their access to the mainstream curriculum, and hence the learning of academic language, is limited until they have mastered English. The following section elaborates on these points.

Cognitive Development. The first area that benefits from the integration of language and content is cognitive development. The integration of language and content relates language learning, content learning, and the development of thinking; as such, it brings out the systematic connections among them (Mohan 1990). By integrating the instruction of language and content, cognitive development can occur more easily and in a more systematic, planned way than had no provisions been made for non-language-specific objectives (Snow, Met, and Genesee 1989). When teachers plan both for the content and language development of their ESL students, planning for cognitive development is likely to occur (Short, Crandall, and Christian 1989).

Such planning is particularly important for ESL students, since many of them find processing new abstract concepts to be a complex task, especially when the processing is taking place in a language that is difficult for them. Integrated instruction allows for systematic planning of the three central components of classroom learning: linguistic, content area, and cognitive. When instruction, whether it is provided by the ESL teacher or the mainstream content area teacher, takes into account these three components of learning, the tasks of learning language, learning content, and developing thinking skills can become much easier for the student.

Access to the Mainstream Curriculum. The second reason for integrating the instruction of language and content is that it gives ESL students more direct access to the curriculum being used with the rest of the student population, which in most cases is the mainstream population, and, oftentimes, the majority population. ESL students in many school districts may end up with a very different type of curriculum simply because their second language needs are typically taken care of outside the mainstream classroom. When efforts are made to integrate the instruction of language and content systematically, collaboration between the ESL teacher and the mainstream content area teacher is likely to occur on a regular basis.

Another programmatic consequence of integrated language and content instruction is that the services provided to ESL students become a more integral part of the mainstream school environment. Many programs for ESL students tend to isolate students who are receiving specialized support services, both restricting the range of instruction and slowing its pace (Perlman 1990). The research on effective schools clearly shows that involvement of all students in the general school curriculum is a crucial factor in quality education for linguistically and culturally diverse students (Carter and Chatfield 1986). Thus, when the ESL teacher uses a topic from a content area—for example, the Civil War—to develop students' proficiency in ESL, it gives ESL students a more direct access to the mainstream curriculum. Insofar as the education of ESL students is an integral part of a school's general goals, and insofar as the delivery of content area instruction is one of the key components of ESL students' education, the integration of language and content instruction becomes essential (Hamayan 1990).

Learning Academic Language. Another impetus for the integration of language and content is that academic language, which may vary from one content area to another, is crucial for academic success (Snow, Met, and Genesee 1989). Becoming proficient in the language of the school and in the language of academic content areas is a difficult process both because of the nature of the second language learning process itself and because of the demands set by the curriculum.

The attainment of second language proficiency is an arduous and long task. Even in the best of circumstances, a student who has the characteristics of a good second language learner in an environment that is most conducive to second language learning may well display the apparent "incompetence" that typifies second language learners and that can last as long as five to seven years (Collier 1989; Cummins 1980). At the core of this "incompetence" is the complex nature of language proficiency. Various overlapping types of language skills that are applied in different contexts and domains of interaction characterize proficiency in any language: for example, everyday social interpersonal skills, more complex and more cognitively demanding academic language skills, formal and informal language, personal introspective language, and analytic language.

The more cognitively demanding and abstract type of language proficiency is more closely related to the language that is developmentally needed in the academic content areas. As Cummins (1981) has pointed out, school success is based to some extent on a student's ability to perform high-level thinking skills in the language of instruction—English. Skills such as analyzing, classifying, and evaluating require specialized language skills. It has been suggested that this more cognitively demanding type of language proficiency needs to be developed formally and systematically (Levine 1984). The integrated approach to instruction can achieve this goal in a way that is most efficient for the student as well as the school.

The need for this academic type of language proficiency is especially evident in the higher grade levels. A look at elementary school curricula shows that the linguistic demands on students in content area classes increase with grade levels. There seems to be an increasing emphasis on literacy in the middle and upper grade levels as a medium for transmitting academic content area knowledge (Chamot 1983). The way that literacy is approached in the upper grade levels may also make the student's tasks more challenging. This emphasis on literacy as well as the way that literacy is approached invariably necessitate a command of cognitively demanding academic language skills, particularly those required in the content areas.

Some language functions, such as following directions and asking for clarification, are characteristic of all the content areas. Others, such as obtaining information from graphs and charts, are specific to some content areas (Chamot and O'Malley 1986). These specific language functions, as well as the more generalized ability to understand and express content area concepts, are some of the concerns that can be addressed through integrated language and content instruction. How this can be accomplished is the topic of the following section.

Frameworks for Integrating Language and Content

The integration of ESL and content instruction requires careful thought and planning. It cannot happen haphazardly or be left to chance. The ESL teacher cannot assume that the students sitting in a content area class are being given the opportunity to develop the language that they need for the content area lesson, nor can the content area teacher assume that his or her ESL students are receiving the appropriate kind of support in content area conceptual development that will make it easier for them to grasp new concepts in a language in which they are not fluent (Mohan 1990).

Another indirect outcome of integration, the development of thinking skills, also cannot be taken for granted. It too has to be planned for and incorporated into the general instructional framework. To date, very few frameworks have been developed to organize integrated language and content instruction and to suggest ways for ESL and mainstream content area teachers to accomplish true integration. Mohan (1979) describes several ways in which language and content area instruction can be integrated that are based on different assumptions and that place different emphasis on language and content area objectives.

Teaching the Second Language to Aid Content Area Learning. One option in integrating language and content instruction is to teach the second language directly in order to aid the second language learner in the content area classes. The objectives for this type of integrated language and content instruction are primarily language-based, and the responsibility for "integration" lies mainly with the ESL teacher.

One of the more comprehensive models available to ESL teachers to apply this type of integration was developed at the Center for Applied Linguistics (Short, Crandall, and Christian 1989; Spanos, Rhodes, Dale, and Crandall 1988). This model is based on identifying those areas of language that pose special problems for ESL students and suggests ways to use a specific content area to bolster the areas of language need. This type of instruction is constrained in that the burden of language and content integration falls on one teacher, namely, the ESL teacher. (It is however possible that a content area teacher could work in collaboration with the ESL teacher to provide a more coordinated type of instruction. For example, the content area teacher, after consulting with the ESL teacher, might do some preteaching activities that develop the particular language that is key to understanding the concept to be taught.) Still, this model provides the ESL student with some support and preparation for the content area classes.

Teaching the Second Language by Teaching Content. A second option for integrating language and content is to teach the second language by teaching content. In this framework, the assumption is that content teaching will help second language development. This framework is most effective in a situation similar to that of French immersion programs for English-speaking Canadian children. In these programs, described briefly in an earlier section of this chapter, students are able to gain knowledge in the content areas expected at their grade level and are able to gain significant levels of proficiency in their second language. The immersion model, as it has been applied in Canada, is not suitable for most language minority populations in the United States (Tucker 1980; also, see Genesee 1987 for a review of the research). However, a framework that has risen from this type of program is the one that presents ESL students with language-supported content area instruction.

Language-Supported Content Area Instruction. Two models have stemmed from this framework: the first model is that of *sheltered content area instruction*, also known as *Sheltered English*; the second model is the *cognitive academic language learning approach.* Sheltering instruction means making content-specific language more comprehensible to ESL students by using hands-on demonstrations, visual clues, and techniques such as simplifying both oral and written language, and by teaching key vocabulary through familiar concepts. Sheltered classrooms essentially use ESL instructional techniques to teach content area lessons. The language used by teachers is characterized by linguistic modifications, such as simplified (but accurate and appropriate) syntactic structures, controlled vocabulary, and shortened sentences. In addition, the teacher attempts to use language that is mostly known to students, and to allow new language to be acquired in a meaningful context.

Another characteristic of sheltered instruction is the active participation of students in the learning process. Lessons usually center on an activity, and students work in small groups to discover, on their own, solutions to problems or information about concepts being studied. Cooperative learning (Kagan 1986; Slavin 1981), which has been shown to be an effective classroom management technique to promote learning among heterogeneous groups of students, is a method that is also typically used in sheltered classrooms. (See Hamayan and Perlman 1990 for practical suggestions for modifying and sheltering instruction.)

The task of dealing with sheltered instruction usually falls to the mainstream content area teacher because it is usually in the mainstream classroom that ESL students encounter difficulty in processing abstract, cognitively demanding information in English. When instruction is sheltered, abstract content area material is taught through context-rich comprehensible language, through active student participation, and by building on students' own experiences. When mainstream teachers make an effort to modify their instruction this way, they also become conscious of the difficulty students may have developing in the language of instruction while learning new concepts (Parker 1985). Although this model calls for some collaboration between ESL and mainstream content area teachers, it still represents a partial type of integration.

The second model that is based on language-supported content area instruction is the *cognitive academic language learning approach* (CALLA) designed by Chamot and O'Malley (Chamot and O'Malley 1987; O'Malley, Chamot, and Walker, 1987; O'Malley 1988). CALLA was designed to provide transitional instruction for ESL students at the junior high and high school levels who are being prepared for mainstream content area classrooms. The program has three components: a content area curriculum that corresponds to

that of the mainstream, academic language development, and learning strategies instruction. The provider of instruction, using the CALLA model, can vary the approach depending on the extent of collaboration that exists within a school building. It is applicable within an ESL class, or a mainstream content area class, or both.

Language, Content, and Thinking Skill Are Inseparable. When language skills, content area knowledge, and cognitive development are all seen as integral parts of the same process, integrated instruction can happen in the best and truest sense. One of the frameworks that provides a model for ESL and content area teachers to work together to provide this integrated instruction is a model called *the learning web*, developed at the Illinois Resource Center (Dailey and Tobias in press). The model is based on the structure of a circular spider web, and it consists of four dimensions.

1. The web begins with the *support frame* in which teachers' basic beliefs about learners, the role of teachers, and how learning takes place, as well as the assumptions that stem from those beliefs, are established. As teachers develop the assumptions that shape curriculum and teaching, they identify critical instructional elements that are necessary in order for learning to take place in an optimal fashion. The instructional elements include components such as: cooperative learning, strategic teaching, and critical thinking; individualization of teaching based on identified individual learner characteristics; and integration of cultural values into the instruction.

2. These elements emerge during the *collaborative planning phase,* during which different teachers involved in the education of ESL students make decisions collaboratively about what is to be learned and how that learning should occur. During this phase, general instruction as well as specific instructional activities are planned.

3. The next part of the learning web, the *learning phases section,* builds on the student's prior learning and prepares the student for new learning. This consists of five steps: (a) the *experiential phase* that provides students with a common experiential base upon which to build new learning; (b) the *concept preview phase* during which students formulate a purpose for new learning and link their knowledge from the experiential phase with the new concepts to be learned; (c) the *direct instructional phase* that provides

students with direct strategic instruction and opportunities for mediating conceptual understanding; (d) the *real world transfer phase* in which new concepts are connected to the real world in personally relevant ways to ensure long-term retention; and, finally, (e) the *learner action phase* in which students take action based on their learning.

4. The last part of the learning web is the *implementation and assessment phase,* which ensures that assessment is integrated within the structure of each lesson. As instruction takes place, the teacher is directed to attend to assessing the concepts, skills, strategies on material being taught.

Because of the comprehensive structure of this approach, which begins in the planning stage and includes assessment, and because of the framework it provides for both ESL and content area instruction, integration can occur in a complete and inclusive manner. An approach such as the learning web also makes it more likely for both ESL and content area teachers to be involved in the curricular and instructional planning together.

Integration of Language and Culture

Since language and culture are so closely tied with one another, a discussion of integrated second language instruction would be incomplete if it did not address the notion that when ESL students learn English they also learn about culture. ESL teachers need to be aware of the fact that they are teaching culture simultaneously with language. One of the most important roles that teachers play vis-à-vis ESL students is that of a representative of one of the cultures present in the school, and a mediating agent in the socialization and acculturation of the student into the mainstream school community.

In the case of students who come from a cultural background that is vastly different from that of the mainstream population, the ESL teacher can play a role in developing and maintaining the social and cultural bridges between the students' home culture and that of the school (Ovando 1989). The ESL teacher can help the ESL student who comes from a cultural background that is different from that of the school by integrating the instruction of the second culture with the instruction of the second language. Students need to learn about the new culture and will also need a long time to adopt some of its

norms. This process of second culture learning can sometimes take even more time than learning the second language itself.

It is important to state that the adoption of the mainstream culture does not need to occur at the expense of the student's native culture. Students need to feel proud of their own heritage in order to be motivated to learn the new second culture (Simich-Dudgeon, McCreedy, and Schleppegrell 1989). ESL teachers can play a valuable role in creating a truly multicultural environment in the school by making the ESL students' cultures an integral part of not only their ESL curriculum but also of the mainstream curriculum. Culture can be integrated into the curriculum by taking what Banks (1988) calls the additive approach, in which cultural content, concepts, themes, and perspectives are added to the already existing curriculum without changing its structure. For example, a unit on mexican mural painting may be added to the Fine Arts curriculum. At a higher level of commitment to multiculturalism, the transformation approach (Banks 1988) can be taken, in which the structure of the curriculum is changed to enable students to view concepts, issues, events, and themes from the perspective of diverse ethnic and cultural groups. Thus, every unit of the curriculum would address an issue relevant to a particular ethnic group or ethnically diverse populations in general. For example, a unit on *Dwellings* would address issues relevant to recent immigrants, or a unit on *The Thirties* would address issues of labor among ethnic minorities.

Implications for Curriculum and Instruction

The following general implications for instruction and school design emerge from the integration of language and content:

1. Close collaboration among all teachers who work with ESL students is needed to ensure that what happens in the ESL part of the day is coordinated with what happens in the content area part of the day. This collaboration will reduce the fragmentation of instruction that is typical for students who are receiving specialized support services for special needs. It also implies that time needs to be set aside for teachers to meet and to work together on lesson plans or on larger curriculum issues.

2. Staff development activities that aim to develop cross-specialization skills among teachers must be part of the plan to integrate the instruc-

tion of language and content. ESL teachers need to become familiar with not only the various content areas that they will start supporting but also with content area teaching strategies. Similarly, content area teachers need to become familiar with issues regarding second language acquisition and with ESL techniques.

3. The ESL program, or all specialized support services provided to ESL students, must be incorporated into the activities carried out in the general school, so that the ESL part of the school becomes an integral part of the mainstream program. It hurts the learning process when ESL students feel isolated.

In addition to the above implications for general instruction, the following specific implications for curriculum emerge:

1. The ESL curriculum needs to be designed around content area themes and needs to have content area objectives as a focus of instruction in addition to the language objectives that are typical of ESL curricula. In addition, thinking skills must also be a focus in the ESL curriculum. Both of these characteristics will move the focus away from the form and structure of the language to its content.

2. The content-specific language that poses difficulties must be identified for groups of ESL students in order to provide guidance to both ESL and content area teachers as to students' specific needs.

3. Because of the importance of the cognitive academic skills in ESL, efforts must be made to identify students' proficiency in that domain.

4. ESL teachers need to become familiar with the various cultures that are represented among their student population so they can better incorporate those cultures into the general school environment as meaningfully and appropriately as possible.

Choice of an ESL Teaching Approach

The third major trend in ESL instruction derives from the realization that there is no single method of teaching that is ideal for all ESL learners. The field of teaching ESL has been characterized by what Stern (1985) has called a "century-old obsession" with the search for the perfect method to get second language learners to become proficient in the target language. In the sixties, the audiolingual method was extremely popular (Lado 1964); since its effectiveness has been successfully challenged, however, there

seems to have been an acceptance of eclecticism in language teaching (Spolsky 1988). However, a proliferation of methods, approaches, and strategies began in the seventies: the old methods—the Berlitz methods, the Ollendorf methods, the *direct method*, and the Army methods (see Titone 1968 for a historical review of ESL methods)—were replaced by equally one-dimensional new methods—the *total physical response* (Asher 1977), the *natural approach* (Krashen and Terrell 1983), *suggestopedia* (Lozanov 1978), the *language experience approach* (Nessel and Jones 1981; see also Richards and Rogers 1986 for a review of many of these newer methods).

As Spolsky points out, there are serious problems with the theoretical bases of these various methods: "Any theory of second language learning that seems to lead to a single method is wrong" (Spolsky 1988, 378). The problem with the use of a single method, especially one that is one-dimensional in nature, is twofold: (1) second language learning is far too complex a process to be taught using a single method; and (2) second language learners vary too much from one another to warrant a uniform method of teaching. Each of the methods listed may be appropriate for developing certain aspects of a second language for a certain type of second language learner under certain conditions. When one recognizes the complexity of the concept of becoming proficient in a second language, one realizes the inability of a single method to satisfy the needs of all learners.

Complexity of the Second Language Learning Process

The complexity of second language learning is indicated by the complexity of theories that attempt to explain the process. As Spolsky (1988) points out, a theory of second language learning must take into account the following notions: (1) there is no simple and single criterion according to which a second language learner can be said to know a language; (2) different combinations of conditions will lead to all the possible language proficiency outcomes; (3) not all the various conditions for language learning are necessary for learning to take place; and (4) second language learning is a social act that takes place within a social context.

The social context provides a set of conditions that influences the second language learning process. The social context includes components such as the student's sociolinguistic circumstances, the type of interaction that learners have with other languages, the function that English and the learners' native language(s) play in the community, and general attitudes toward bilingualism and multiculturalism in the community. These social components interact with individual characteristics that the learner brings to language learning, making the learning process highly varied from person to person. The tremendous differences among learners adds to the complexity of the process, making it even more difficult to choose a single one-dimensional method for teaching ESL.

Individual Differences in Second Language Learning

A number of individual learner characteristics have been identified as playing a significant role in the process of second language learning. Attitudes toward the second language and its speakers (Schumann 1976), the motivation to learn the second language and to become proficient in it (Gardner and Lambert 1972), personality traits (Tucker, Hamayan, and Genesee 1976), capabilities (Genesee 1976), previous knowledge, native language proficiency (Cummins 1980), and age (Krashen 1974) are all factors that affect the second language learning process. The social context that the learner is in also produces some individual differences in that different contexts provide different opportunities, both formal and informal, for language learning.

The great variety among ESL student populations entering the school system adds to the complexity of the second language classroom. Over the last decade, schools have accepted students with a variety of ethnic, linguistic, educational, and experiential backgrounds. Some ESL students enter school at various grade levels with little or no literacy in their native language; others come from a migrant background. Some may enter with very extensive educational experience, while others may enter high school with very limited education. Thus, characteristics of the individual learner become even more varied when the students' experiential background is taken into account, making the choice of an appropriate instructional method even more difficult and complex.

It is up to the teacher, then, to select, on the basis of the particular group of students he or she is working with, the particular combination of methods and strategies to help those students

attain the expected levels and types of language proficiency. The proliferation of methods, approaches, and strategies that can be borrowed from—both from ESL and from mainstream education—can provide the teacher with a rich resource. This calls for another change in the ESL teacher's role, from what has traditionally been an executor of instruction to a decision-maker. It also calls for the teacher to take on the responsibility of assessment in order to identify characteristics of learners that have to be considered in the choice of an instructional design and approach.

Implications for Curriculum and Instruction

The following general implications for curriculum and instruction emerge from the realization that there is no single method of teaching that is ideal for all ESL learners:

1. Decisions regarding the particular curriculum and the particular instructional approach to be used with a particular group of students must be the teacher's responsibility. This implies that the ESL curriculum may change slightly depending on the group of ESL students receiving the instruction.

2. The materials that an ESL teacher uses must be varied and cannot relate to a single approach, series, or method. Published texts must be combined with trade materials, such as literature and newspaper and magazine articles, to fit into the structure of curriculum created for a group of ESL students.

3. ESL students' characteristics and educational backgrounds must be assessed before any major decisions can be made about the most effective types of approaches (see Cloud 1991 for suggestions on assessment of educational backgrounds).

Summary and Conclusions

The field of teaching English as a second language has undergone significant changes over the last ten years that have made the profession dynamic and challenging for teachers and administrators. Instead of structuring language instruction carefully around units of language that need to be mastered by the ESL learner, teachers are looking into ways of allowing the second language to emerge naturally and holistically. Instead of simply teaching language, teachers are now concerned with combining the teaching of academic and social content to ESL students. Instead of following a set curriculum with a narrow choice of teaching strategies and instructional materials, teachers are now faced with the responsibility of choosing the best combination of approaches for a particular group of students, based on their individual learner characteristics and the learning context.

These trends in ESL instruction can produce a dynamic and effective learning environment that will help ESL students attain proficiency in English as a second language in an efficient and enjoyable way.

References

Adams, M. 1990. *Beginning to Read: Thinking and Learning about Print.* Cambridge, MA: MIT Press.

Aetwerger, B., Edelsky, C. & Flores, B.M. 1987. "Whole Language: What's New?" *The Reading Teacher 41*: 144-154.

Asher, J. 1977. *Learning Another Language through Actions: The Complete Teacher's Guide Book.* 2d ed. Los Gatos, CA: Sky Oaks Productions.

Au, K. H., and C. Jordan. 1981. "Teaching Reading to Hawaiian Children: Finding a Culturally Appropriate Solution." In *Culture and the Bilingual Classroom: Studies in Classroom Ethnography,* ed. H. T. Trueba. Rowley, MA: Newbury House.

Banks, J. 1988. *Multi-Ethnic Education: Theory and Practice.* Boston: Allyn and Bacon.

Calkins, L. 1983. *Lessons from a Child.* Portsmouth, NH: Heinemann.

Cambourne, B. 1987. "Language, Learning, and Literacy." In *Toward a Reading-Writing Classroom,* ed. A. Butler and J. Turbill. Portsmouth, NH: Heinemann.

Carrell, P., B. Pharis, and J. Liberto. 1989. "Metacognitive Strategy Training for ESL Reading." *TESOL Quarterly* 23: 647–78.

Carter, T. P., and M. L. Chatfield. 1986. "Effective Bilingual Schools: Implications for Policy and Practice." *America Journal of Education* 95: 200–34.

Chaika, E. 1982. *Language: The Social Mirror.* Rowley, MA: Newbury House.

Chamot, A. U. 1983. "A Transfer Curriculum for Teaching Content-Based ESL in the Elementary School." In *On TESOL '83,* 125–33. Washington, DC: TESOL.

Chamot, A. U., and J. M. O'Malley. 1986. *A Cognitive Academic Language Learning Approach: An ESL Content-Based Curriculum.* Rosslyn, VA: National Clearinghouse on Bilingual Education.

———. 1987. "The Cognitive Academic Learning Approach." *TESOL Quarterly* 21: 227–49.

Chamot, A. U., J. M. O'Malley, L. Kupper, and M. V. Impink-Hernandez. 1987. *A Study of Learning Strategies in Foreign Language Instruction: First Year Report.* Washington, DC: InterAmerican Research Associates.

Cloud, N. 1991. "Educational Assessment." In *Limiting Bias in the Assessment of Bilingual Students,* ed. E. Hamayan and J. Damico, 219–46. Austin, TX: Pro Ed.

Collier, Virginia P. 1989. "How Long? A Synthesis of Research on Academic Achievement in a Second Language. "*TESOL Quarterly 23*: 509–32.

Corey, K., M. Pfleger, and E. Hamayan. 1987. "A Whole Language Program for Refugee Children." *ERIC/CLL News Bulletin* 11: 1–7.

Crandall, J. 1990. "ESL through Content Area Instruction." In *Proceedings of the First Research Symposium on Limited English Proficient Students' Issues,* 429–36. Washington, DC: U.S. Department of Education, Office of Bilingual Education and Minority Languages Affairs.

Cummins, J. 1980. "The Entry and Exit Fallacy in Bilingual Education." *NABE Journal* 4: 25–29.

———. 1981. "The Role of Primary Language Development in Promoting Educational Success for Language Minority Students." In *Schooling and Language Minority Students: A Theoretical Framework,* ed. California State Department of Education, 3–49. Los Angeles: Evaluation Dissemination and Assessment Center, California State Univ.

———. 1984. "Wanted: A Theoretical Framework for Relating Language Proficiency to Academic Achievement among Bilingual Students." In *Language Proficiency and Academic Achievement,* 2–19. Clevedon, England: Multilingual Matters 2.

Dailey, J., and B. Tobias. In press. *The Learning Web.* Des Plaines, IL: Illinois Resource Center.

Dulay, H., M. Burt, and S. Krashen. 1982. *Language Two.* New York: Oxford Univ. Press.

Edelsky, C. 1986. *Writing in a Bilingual Program: Habia Una Vez.* Norwood, NJ: Ablex.

Ervin-Tripp, S. 1974. "Is Second Language Learning Like the First?" *TESOL Quarterly* 8: 111–27.

Feuerstein, R. 1982. *The Dynamic Assessment of Retarded Performers: The Learning Potential*

Assessment Device, Theory, Instruments, and Techniques. Baltimore: Univ. Park Press.

Gardner, R. C. 1985. *Social Psychology and Second Language Learning: The Role of Attitudes and Motivation.* Baltimore: Edward Arnold.

Gardner, R. C., and W. E. Lambert. 1972. *Attitudes and Motivation in Second Language Learning.* Rowley, MA: Newbury House.

Genesee, F. 1976. "The Role of Intelligence in Second Language Learning." *Language Learning* 26: 267–80.

———. 1987. *Learning Through Two Languages.* Cambridge, MA: Newbury House.

Goodman, K. 1986. *What's Whole in Whole Language.* Portsmouth, NH: Heinemann.

Goodman, K. S. 1984. "Unity in Reading." In *Becoming Readers in a Complex Society; 83d Yearbook of the National Society for the Study of Education.* Chicago: National Society for the Study of Education.

Goodman, K. S., and Y. Goodman. 1978. *Reading of American Children Whose Language Is a Stable Rural Dialect of English or a Language Other than English.* Washington, DC: U.S. Department of Health, Education, and Welfare.

Graves, D. H. 1983. *Writing: Teachers and Children at Work.* Portsmouth, NH: Heinemann.

Hakuta, K. 1976. "Prefabricated Patterns and the Emergence of Structure in Second Language Acquisition." *Language Learning* 24: 287–98.

———. 1986. *Mirror of Language.* New York: Basic Books.

Hamayan, E. 1990. "Preparing Mainstream Classroom Teachers to Teach Potentially English Proficient (PEP) Students." In *Proceedings of the First Research Symposium on Limited English Proficient Students' Issues,* 1–22. Washington, DC: Department of Education, Office of Bilingual Education and Minority Languages Affairs.

———. In press. "ESL for Students from Low-Literacy Backgrounds." In *Educating ESL Children,* ed. F. Genesee. Cambridge: Cambridge Univ. Press.

Hamayan, E. V., and J. S. Damico. 1991. *Limited Bias in the Assessment of Bilingual Students.* Austin, TX: Pro Ed.

Hamayan, E. V., and R. Perlman. 1990. *Helping Language Minority Students after They Exit from Bilingual/ESL Programs.* Program Information Guide Series, vol. 1. Silver Spring, MD: National Clearinghouse for Bilingual Education.

Hanania, E., and H. Gradman. 1977. "Acquisition of English Structures: A Case Study of an Adult Native Speaker in an English Speaking Environment." *Language Learning* 27: 75–92.

Hatch, E., B. Peck, and J. Wagner-Gough. 1979. "A Look at Process in Child Second-Language Acquisition." In *Developmental Pragmatics,* ed. E. Ochs and B. Schieffelin, 269–78. New York: Academic.

Heath, S. B. 1983. *Ways with Words.* Cambridge: Cambridge Univ. Press.

———. 1986. "Sociocultural Contexts of Language Development." In *Social and Cultural Factors in Schooling Language Minority Students,* 143–86. Sacramento: California State Department of Education.

Houck, N., J. Robertson, and S. Krashen. 1978. "On the Domain of the Conscious Grammar." *TESOL Quarterly* 12: 335–39.

Hudelson, S. 1986. "ESL Children's Writing: What We've Learned, What We're Learning." In *Children and ESL: Integrating Perspectives,* ed. P. Rigg and D. S. Enright, 23–54. Washington, DC: Teachers of English to Speakers of Other Languages.

Kagan, S. 1986. "Cooperative Learning and Sociocultural Factors in Schooling." In *Beyond Language: Social and Cultural Factors in Schooling Language Minority Students,* ed. Bilingual Education Office, California State Department of Education, 231–98. Los Angeles: California State Univ.

Krashen, S. 1974. "The Critical Period for Language Acquisition and Its Possible Bases." *Annals of the New York Academy of Sciences* 263 (19 Sept. 1975): 211–24.

———. 1981. *Second Language Acquisition and Second Language Learning.* Oxford: Pergamon.

Krashen, S., J. Butler, R. Birnbaum, and J. Robertson. 1978. "Two Studies in Language Acquisition and Language Learning." *International Review of Applied Linguistics* 39/40: 73–92.

Krashen, S., and R. Scarcella. 1978. "On Routines and Patterns in Language Acquisition and Performance." *Language Learning* 28: 283–300.

Krashen, S., and H. Seliger. 1975. "The Essential Contributions of Formal Instruction in Adult Second Language Learning." *TESOL Quarterly* 9: 173–83.

Krashen, S. D., and T. D. Terrell. 1983. *The Natural Approach.* Hayward, CA: Alemany.

Lado, R. 1964. *Language Teaching.* New York: McGraw-Hill.

Lambert, W. E., and G. R. Tucker. 1972. *The Bilingual Education of Children: The St. Lambert Experiment.* Rowley, MA: Newbury House.

Levine, L. N. 1984. "Content Area Instruction for the Elementary School ESL Student." In *On TESOL '84: A Brave New World for TESOL,* ed. P. Larson, 233–40. Washington, DC: Teachers of English to Speakers of Other Languages.

Lindfors, J. W. 1987. *Children's Language and Learning.* 2d ed. Englewood Cliffs, NJ: Prentice-Hall.

Lozanov, G. 1978. *Suggestology and Outlines of Suggestopedy.* New York: Gordon and Breach.

Mohan, B. 1979. "Relating Language Teaching and Content Teaching." *TESOL Quarterly* 13: 171–82.

———. 1990. "LEP Students and the Integration of Language and Context: Knowledge Structures and Student Tasks." In *Proceedings of the First Research Symposium on Limited English Proficient Students' Issues,* 113–60. Washington, DC: U.S. Department of Education, Office of Bilingual Education and Minority Languages Affairs.

Nessel, D., and M. Jones. 1981. *The Language Experience Approach to Reading: A Handbook for Teachers.* New York: Columbia Univ. Press.

Norris, J. A., and J. S. Damico. 1990. "Whole Language in Theory and Practice: Implications for Language Intervention." *Language, Speech, and Hearing Services in Schools* 21: 212–20.

O'Malley, J. M. 1988. "The Cognitive Academic Language Learning Approach (CALLA)." *Journal of Multilingual and Multicultural Development* 9: 43–60.

O'Malley, J. M., A. U. Chamot, and C. Walker. 1987. "Some Applications of Cognitive Theory in Second Language Acquisition." *Studies in Second Language Acquisition* 9(3).

Ohanian, S. 1987. "Ruffles and Flourishes." *Atlantic* 9: 20–21.

Ovando, C. 1989. *Multicultural Education: Issues and Perspectives.* Boston: Allyn and Bacon.

Oxford, R. L. 1990. *Language Learning Strategies: What Every Teacher Should Know.* New York: Newbury House.

Parker, D. 1985. "Sheltered English: Theory to Practice." Unpublished manuscript, California State Department of Education.

Perlman, R. 1990. *A Time for Change: Restructuring State Board Policies on the Education of Elementary and Secondary Students of Limited English Proficiency.* Springfield, IL: Illinois State Board of Education.

Pring, R. 1973. *Curriculum Integration: The Philosophy of Education.* London: Oxford Univ. Press.

Richards, J. C., and T. S. Rodgers. 1986. *Approaches and Methods in Language Teaching.* New York: Cambridge Univ. Press.

Rigg, P. 1986. "Reading in ESL: Learning from Kids." In *Children and ESL: Integrating Perspectives,* ed. P. L. Rigg and D. S. Enright, 55–91. Washington, DC: Teachers of English to Speakers of Other Languages.

Routman, R. 1988. *Transitions from Literature to Literacy.* Portsmouth, NH: Heinemann.

Schumann, J. 1976. "Social Distance as a Factor in Second Language Acquisition." *Language Learning* 26: 135–43.

Selinker, L. 1972. "Interlanguage." *International Review of Applied Linguistics* 10: 209–31.

Short, D. J., J. Crandall, and D. Christian. 1989. *How to Integrate Language and Content Instruction: A Training Manual.* Los Angeles: Center for Language Education and Research, Univ. of California.

Simich-Dudgeon, C., L. McCreedy, and M. Schleppegrell. 1989. *Helping Limited English Proficient Children Communicate in the Classroom.* Silver Spring, MD: National Clearinghouse for Bilingual Education.

Slavin, R. E. 1981. "Synthesis of Research on Cooperative Learning." *Educational Leadership* 38: 655–60.

Smith, F. 1982. *Understanding Reading.* 3d ed. New York: Holt, Rinehart and Winston.

Snow, M., M. Met, and F. Genesee. 1989. "A Conceptual Framework for the Integration of Language and Content in Second/Foreign Language Instruction." *TESOL Quarterly* 23: 201–17.

Spanos, G., N. Rhodes, T. Dale, and J. Crandall. 1988. "Linguistic Features of Mathematical Problem-Solving: Insights and Applications." In *Linguistic and Cultural Influences on Learning Mathematics,* ed. R. Cocking and J. Mestre, 221–40. Hillsdale, NJ: Erlbaum.

Spolsky, B. 1988. "Bridging the Gap: A General Theory of Second Language Learning." *TESOL Quarterly* 22: 377–96.

Stern, H. H. 1985. "Review of Methods that Work: A Smorgasbord of Ideas for Language Teachers." *Studies in Second Language Acquisition* 7.

Titone, R. 1968. *Teaching Foreign Languages: An Historical Sketch.* Washington, DC: Georgetown Univ. Press.

Tucker, G. R. 1980. "Implications for U.S. Bilingual Education: Evidence from Canadian Research." In *Focus*, vol. 2, 1–4. Silver Spring, MD: National Clearinghouse for Bilingual Education.

Tucker, G. R., E. Hamayan, and F. Genesee. 1976. "Affective, Cognitive, and Social Factors in Second Language Acquisition." *Canadian Modern Language Review* 23:214–26.

Weaver, C. 1990. *Understanding Whole Language: From Principles to Practice.* Portsmouth, NH: Heinemann.

ASSESSING STUDENT NEEDS

by Carolyn T. Linse
Resource Specialist
New England Multifunctional Resource Center, Brown University, Providence, Rhode Island

BEFORE initiating a new language program, vital preparatory work in the form of information gathering must take place. This fact finding stage provides answers to the key questions in any program: Who are the learners? Who are the teachers? Why is the program necessary? Where will the program be implemented? How will it be implemented?"
Dubain and Olshtain 1986

The ESL students walking into our nation's classrooms in the 1990s are very different from previous groups of immigrant ESL learners in that they come from a much wider variety of linguistic, educational, cultural, and political backgrounds than their predecessors. Many of the students come from the developing world and have little or no experience with formal education, while others may have attended very comprehensive educational programs (Sossa 1992). The number of immigrants legally entering the United States is a staggering 400,000 annually, according to U.S. census records, and the number of illegal immigrants is believed to equal that amount.

ESL students should not be viewed as a temporary population. Although many school officials believe that the ESL student population will stabilize or decline, experience has proven that the opposite is often true. Educators should plan programs for their current ESL students with the realization that the number of ESL students is very likely to increase.

The background of ESL students should guide both program and curriculum design. Learning becomes irrelevant for ESL students when the curriculum does not relate to their present situations or past experiences (Edelsky 1986). In order to avoid this, educators should look at the language(s) spoken by the students; the students' educational background, including literacy skills, previous schooling, and attitudes towards formal schooling; and the cultural and political background and personal characteristics of the students.

Curriculum developers must complete a comprehensive needs assessment in order to provide students with purposeful and relevant goals and activities that relate to their daily lives. School systems must compile data that is representative of the needs of students from different language, cultural, and political groups. The data should also include educational backgrounds and skills that students have acquired in both their native language(s) and English.

Chapter 1 emphasizes the need for language instruction that is meaningful and takes into account the needs of the learner. The purpose of this chapter then is to discuss what should be examined as part of a comprehensive needs assessment and the methods used to conduct the assessment. This chapter is designed to help curriculum developers identify the needs of the individuals and groups of ESL learners, in order to select the most appropriate approaches for these students. Each section discusses the needs that should be assessed, methods used to conduct the assessment, and proposes specific guidelines for incorporating the data generated into the curriculum design and delivery. It is important to determine whether the curriculum is being designed for use by mainstream content area teachers or for teachers who teach ESL exclusively.

Needs Assessment

A holistic and pedagogically sound curriculum cannot be developed without a comprehensive needs assessment. ESL students require a curriculum that uses their personal experiences, background knowledge, cultural and political history, and personal characteristics as the foundation. Students' experiences with language and education must be examined to determine what the academic or preacademic starting point should be. The needs assessment must address the intellectual and linguistic demands made on students who fully participate in all aspects of the academic, extracurricular, social English-speaking school and community environments. This chapter provides narrative instructions and charts to help educators design a needs assessment program and use the data generated from the assessment to develop a curriculum that addresses both the school and the community needs of ESL students.

It is unrealistic for educators, facing budget and staff constraints, to compile an extensive background needs assessment on every individual student, but it is feasible for educators to look at the needs of groups of students. They can begin their assessment by obtaining a representative sample of students from different linguistic, educational, cultural, and political backgrounds found in the local ESL population. Educators should be cautioned that, although there may be a number of students from the same language group and country, frequently the cultural and political backgrounds of these students may be dramatically different. Excellent examples of this situation are found in students from Eastern European countries.

The number of students required for a needs assessment will depend upon local demographics. In order to make sure that the sample used is representative of the total ESL population, the following questions should be addressed:

· How many different language groups are represented? What are the major language groups? How many speakers of each language are there?

· What is the range of educational experiences represented by students? Are there some students with extensive formal education? Are there students who lack literacy skills in their primary language and/or English?

· How many different cultural and political groups are represented?

In addition to obtaining a representative sample of students, educators must conduct a student needs assessment that provides the information necessary to design a curriculum that reflects the students' varied backgrounds. The three areas of investigation are:

· the students' backgrounds with language(s)

· the students' educational backgrounds

· the students' cultural/political backgrounds and personal characteristics

Although there is some overlap from one area to another, there is a core of different information in each area that greatly impacts curriculum development and delivery.

First, the students' knowledge and experiences with language(s) must be examined so that the program builds upon existing language skills. In addition to looking at the students' knowledge and experiences with language, it is essential to define the linguistic demands that students must meet in their first and second language(s) that enable them to have equal access to all school and community opportunities that are available to their English-speaking peers. Language is not included in the educational background section since so much of the language acquisition process occurs outside classroom walls.

Second, ESL students' educational backgrounds and attitudes toward education must be considered. This is necessary if students and their teachers are to be actively engaged in designing and achieving goals that give students a sense of purpose, personal meaning, and progress. Many students have little or no experience with the structure of American elementary and high schools. Often, ESL students find school to be a frightening and confusing place.

Finally, cultural and political factors as well as personal characteristics must be examined so that ESL learners can have a curriculum that interests, respects, motivates, and challenges them. As we begin to see a "new world order," the faces in our classrooms continue to change dramatically, often due to cultural and political conflict in the students' countries of origin. Rather than dwelling on the conflict, the curriculum should reflect the positive contributions and attributes of all cultures, subcultures, and political groups represented in the local ESL population. Educators must also examine how these factors vary from student to student because of individual characteristics such as age and gender.

Language

The goal of every ESL program should be to give students the language skills necessary for them to participate in the most challenging, personally meaningful, and cognitively demanding experiences inside and outside of the classroom in both the native-language and English-speaking communities. It is insufficient for ESL programs merely to help students acquire the minimum knowledge of conversational language and literacy skills needed to function in remedial English classes. All ESL programs should give students the linguistic and cognitive skills necessary to achieve their academic and personal goals in English and/or their native language. Figure 1 provides information for developing a language needs assessment as well as guidelines for using the information generated from the assessment.

Students are often identified and placed in ESL programs, individually and collectively, based on the native language(s) they speak. Too often, school districts use the students' test scores on language dominance tests and ESL placement tests as the only way to determine the need for ESL and bilingual programs. Language dominance tests indicate the students' stronger or dominant language at the time of testing. ESL placement tests give a broad indication of how much oral English students have acquired. These tests do not, however, provide the detailed information that educators need regarding students' experiences with language(s).

It is important for educators to know what languages are represented, what experiences and knowledge students have with language(s), and how many speakers there are of each language and each language group. The students' levels of language acquisition in their primary language and in English should also be determined. In many cases, it is also appropriate for educators to assess what students know about the structure and form of the English language. Finally, educators should examine and describe the English skills that students need in order to participate fully in the mainstream curriculum and in the local English-speaking community.

Languages Represented

The first step in compiling a profile of students' language(s) is to determine what languages the students speak. When students enter schools in the United States and come from homes where languages other than English might be spoken, home language surveys should be administered. The results of the home language survey are used to determine whether or not students should undergo further language testing for possible placement in bilingual and ESL programs. Students are then tested to determine which is their dominant or stronger language (see figures 1 and 2).

Curriculum developers need to use the information from the home language survey and language dominance tests to compile a demographic profile of all of the languages and language groups represented by students. The following questions need to be addressed:
· How many languages or language groups are represented?
· How many students speak each language or language group?
· Is it feasible to have a bilingual program for students?

Whenever possible, students should be given content instruction in their primary language since it can take five to seven years before ESL students have developed academic language proficiency (Cummins 1984). Then, while students are acquiring the prerequisite English necessary to tackle cognitively challenging tasks in English, they can also be refining their intellectual skills in their primary language.

Levels of Language Acquisition

After students have been tested to determine whether or not they need bilingual or ESL instruction, their level of language acquisition should be assessed. This testing procedure is usually more refined than the testing for language dominance. Students should be tested for their level of language acquisition in their native language as well as English because by testing the students' level of language acquisition, educators can develop a program with both realistic and meaningful expectations and tasks. Such testing should be done by qualified bilingual personnel to determine their level of social language skills as well as their academic language skills.

Figure 1

Student Language Survey

Student's Name_____ Date_____
School _____ Grade_____
Teacher _____

Circle the best answer to each question.

1. Was the first language you learned English?   Yes   No

2. Can you speak a language other than English?   Yes   No
   If yes, what language? _____

3. Which language do you use most often when you   English   Other
   speak to your friends?   (specify: _____)

4. Which language do you use most often when you   English   Other
   speak to your parents?   (specify: _____)

5. Does anyone in your home speak a language other   Yes   No
   than English?

Source: E. Hamayan, J. Kwiat, and R. Perlman, *Assessment of Language Minority Students:
A Handbook for Educators* (Des Plaines, IL: Illinois Resource Center, 1985), 17. Reproduced with permission.

Table 1. Needs Assessment: Language

Student Background and Needs	Methods for Assessing Needs	Guidelines for Curriculum Developers
What language(s) do students speak? What language groups do students represent?	Home language surveys	Whenever possible, teaching methods and materials should encourage students to develop and expand language skills in their native language(s)
What are students' levels of English language acquisition?	Language observation, checklists, and tests	Teaching methods and materials should help students build upon their existing levels of language acquisition
What prior knowledge do students have regarding the form of the English language (i.e., grammar, syntax)? What have students "learned" about the English language?	Language observation, checklists, and tests	Teaching methods and materials should help students who have studied English and "learned" specific information about language to use that prior knowledge to enhance the language acquisition process.
What language(s) and specific language skills do students need at home, at school, and in their local community?	Home language surveys; interviews, questionnaires, etc.	Whenever possible, methods and materials should take into account which language(s) students use every day and for what purpose(s).
What English language skills do students need in order to function successfully in the mainstream curriculum and in the local English- speaking community?	ESL and language arts curriculum; interviews, questionnaires; tests	Teaching methods and materials should provide students with opportunities for students to acquire meaningful and purposeful English language skills.

Figure 2

Home Background Questionnaire

1. How many years has the family been in the United States? _____

2. What is the birthplace of the parents (guardians)? Mother: _____ Father: _____

3. In what language did each parent/guardian receive most of his/her education?

   Mother: _____ Father: _____

4. How many years of schooling did each parent (guardian) complete?

   Mother: _____ Father: _____

5. What language do the parents (guardians) speak at home most of the time?

   Mother: _____ Father: _____

6. What language does the student speak with his/her parents?

   Mother: _____ Father: _____

7. What language does the student most often speak with brothers and sisters? (List each sibling and language)

Sibling	Language
_____	_____
_____	_____
_____	_____

8. What language does the student most often speak with his/her friends or playmates? _____

9. In which language are television and radio programs most often received in the home? _____

10. In which language is most print media (book, magazines, newspapers) in the home? _____

11. Does the family receive a daily newspaper? If so, in what language? _____

12. To what magazines does the family subscribe? _____

13. Does the child receive any periodicals under his/her own name? If so, in what language? _____

14. How many hours per week is the child read to? _____ In what language(s)? _____

15. How many hours per week does the child observe the parents reading? _____

    In what language(s)? _____

16. How many hours does the child read per week? _____ For what purposes? _____

    In what languages? _____

Source: N. Cloud, "Educational Assessment," in *Limiting Bias in the Assessment of Bilingual Students,*
ed. E. V. Hamayan and J. S. Damico (Austin: Pro-Ed, 1991), 18. Reproduced with permission.

Curriculum developers should strive for bilingual program models that allow learners to continue to develop and refine their first language skills while they begin and/or continue to acquire skills in English. It is much more efficient for students to develop cognitive skills in their native language and then transfer those skills into English. For example, if students have begun to develop critical thinking and reading skills in ~~the~~ their primary language, they should continue refining those skills while they are acquiring the skills necessary to do comparable tasks in English.

Structural Knowledge about the English Language

In addition to assessing students' levels of language acquisition, it is important for schools to look at the formal knowledge that students have about language. There are some students who lack the ability to communicate in English even on the most basic level but who have a sophisticated knowledge about the English language. There are many students, especially from former Soviet Bloc Eastern European countries, for example, who have studied the English language as an exercise but have not acquired the skills to communicate. These students' needs must also be assessed and addressed.

Just as it is important to analyze and build upon students' levels of language acquisition, it is also necessary to assess what students know *about* English. Educators need to determine if students have academic and structural knowledge about English that can be used to help them as they are learning to use English as a communication tool. For example, some students may have learned the conjugations of everyday regular and irregular verbs, such as *to eat*, but do not know that the word *ate* is used after someone has eaten something. Standardized, structurally based tests of language proficiency which faces on specific aspects of language, such as grammar, may be used to obtain this information.

When appropriate, educators should assess students' formal knowledge of the English language so that the written skills which they previously acquired can easily be transferred into oral skills. Learners need to know that their formal and academic study of the English language was not an exercise in futility.

Daily Language Use

Schools must also examine how students use language on a daily basis. Educators need to know which languages learners use and for what purpose, which language students value the most, and how they use language to accomplish specific, personally meaningful tasks.

Sometimes the original language assessment may be misleading. For example, during school registration parents may complete a home language survey which indicates that they speak English with the child, and the school may assume that this is the main language spoken at home. Often, however, a grandparent is the child's primary caretaker and speaks only the native language to the child.

There are a number of questions which can help clarify the range of students' language usage:

· What languages(s) do students use when talking to different family members?
· What language(s) do students use when talking to their friends?
· Do students speak in just one language at a time or do they switch back and forth from one language to another?

Educators may learn, for example, that some students accomplish all tasks outside of the classroom in their native language, such as going shopping or to the movies, while other students may be forced to use English if they wish to rent a video or buy a hamburger. This information can help curriculum developers design a program that provides students with the language skills necessary to complete tasks that are personally meaningful and can be used easily in the local community. Specific tasks that students wish to accomplish in English should also be included in the curriculum whenever possible.

English Language Demands

It is important for educators to know what English language skills are necessary to enable students to participate in all school and community activities offered in English. Too often, educators develop programs that help students to develop only social language skills. As a result of this narrow viewpoint, ESL students frequently have only the minimum skills necessary to function in remedial courses designed for mainstream English-dominant students. There are a very few students, who in spite of this program design, are able to excel academically. Unfortunately, there has been a tendency for some educators to look at these students, who are exceptions to the rule, and conclude that since some students have excelled, all ESL students should excel without any need for improving the program design.

Educators should not focus on the few students who are able to work around the obstacles. Instead, schools should design a program that will give all students the language and cognitive skills they need to take advantage of opportunities that are available to their English-speaking peers both at school and in the community.

In order to develop a language learning program that will give students the academic language skills needed to tackle the most challenging academic courses and other intellectually challenging activities, educators must first look at the mainstream curriculum. Even at the elementary school level, linguistic tasks become cognitively more demanding with increasing grade levels. Mastery of language that is needed to process information in science, social studies, and math is essential (Chamot 1983). High school advanced placement courses also need to be reviewed to determine what linguistic and cognitive skills are needed in order for ESL students to be able to compete on an equal basis for placement. These skills should be integrated into the curriculum, and students should receive specialized, often sheltered, ESL instruction until they have mastered the necessary academic language skills. These skills should be clearly delineated in the curriculum, and mastery of them should be considered necessary for all ESL students before they are permitted to leave the ESL program.

Whenever possible, students should receive instruction in their native language that focuses on the acquisition of higher level thinking skills. They are then able to transfer these skills to English more readily than if they are trying to learn a second language *and* cognitive skills in the second language simultaneously. For example, students should be taught how to do word problems in math in their primary language while they are still acquiring basic English skills. Then they will only need to learn the English necessary to do the word problems rather than both the language *and* math problem-solving skills.

In addition to academic language skills, schools should also help ESL students develop the social language skills needed for them to take advantage of opportunities often made available only to English-dominant youth. For example, students need more cognitive and language skills to qualify for a clerical job than to work as a janitor.

The language and cognitive skills necessary for students to participate in the local English-speaking community should be clearly addressed in the bilingual/ESL curriculum. When educators include and teach the skills that ESL students need to participate in the local community, they are making it possible for students to reach their potential both inside and outside the classroom doors. By helping ESL students to compete on an equal par with their English-speaking peers, they are making it possible to dispel community prejudice that too often is directed at ESL students of color.

Methods Used To Assess Language and Language Use

There are a variety of methods that can be used to assess students' knowledge and use of language as well as the language demands made by the local community. The home language survey and language dominance or proficiency tests can be used to determine if students speak a language other than English and what their dominant language is. This also helps educators determine students' level of language acquisition. Language observation checklists (Goodman and Goodman 1978), language tests, questionnaires, interviews, and mainstream language arts curriculum guides can be used to determine the demands that the school, home, and community make upon the student to use English and their native language. The data generated by these methods can help educators select language learning tasks that are very purposeful and meaningful to students.

The first step in assessing students' language dominance and proficiency is to identify the bilingual and ESL student population through a home language survey (see figure 2). Home language surveys help determine what language students have been exposed to and, possibly, speak. The survey asks what language(s) the students speak at home with parents and peers. The home language survey is a simple questionnaire that parents complete regarding the language use of their child, and it is used to determine whether or not the student should be tested for possible placement into a bilingual and/or ESL program.

The schools should provide the home language surveys in the parent's primary language and English. In some communities, with parents who lack literacy skills in their own language, the home language survey should be administered orally. Schools should be diligent in their efforts to identify students who lack experience and exposure to the English language and require bilingual and ESL services.

All students who enter our schools should complete a home language survey. If the home language survey indicates that a language other than English is spoken, then the student should be given a language proficiency test and perhaps a language dominance test. There are different language tests (described in Chapter 7) that can be used to determine students' dominant language, their level of native language acquisition, and their level of English language acquisition. This formal testing is used to place students in bilingual and/or ESL programs. In addition to formal testing, language observation checklists and interviews can show what language(s) students have acquired and how they are using it (them).

Interviews and questionnaires conducted with a representative sample of students as well as members of the native language and English-speaking communities can also provide invaluable information about how language is used in the student's home, school, and community. Interview guides and questionnaires should be given to members of all of the major linguistic and cultural groups represented by the ESL student body. Language observation checklists are a very good way to look at which languages students use at school, both inside and outside the classroom, and for what specific purposes.

By knowing how language is used, educators can select tasks, goals, and activities that are purposeful and meaningful (See table 1).

Educational Background and Attitudes toward Schooling

The ESL students of all ages who enter our public schools represent a wide range of educational experiences and attitudes toward schooling. Some students will have had extensive formal schooling, while other students have never set foot in a classroom. Many students who have not had formal school will have participated in educational experiences and activities that take place outside of the classroom. These experiences and activities should be examined and documented as being part of the students' educational experiences. In addition, the students' and their families' attitudes towards formal schooling should also be taken into account. Table 2 provides information for developing a needs assessment that examines students' educational backgrounds and attitudes towards schooling as well as guidelines for using the information generated from the needs assessment.

Educators must first examine what contact students and their families have had with formal schooling in their country of origin, in other foreign countries, and in the United States. The attitudes that accompany these educational experiences must also be investigated. Second, literacy and academic skills that students have acquired in their native language and English need to be identified and recognized as valuable starting points.

Prior Experience with Formal Schooling

Schools must determine what prior experiences students have had with formal education. Educators are facing students with wide differences in their prior experiences with formal schooling. At one end of the continuum there are students, often ages thirteen and above, who have little or no experience inside a classroom. At the other end of the continuum there are students who have gone to school six days a week for seven hours a day since the time they were four or five years of age.

Many recently arrived ESL students have had their education interrupted. Some students have spent years in refugee camps waiting for one of the few spaces in a makeshift classroom. When these students come to the United States they are often ostracized by their peers merely because they do not understand the expectations. For example, students may come from a country where there is very little water or no plumbing and not know that members of the school community expect students to flush the toilet every time they use it. The ramifications for not understanding this expectation can include being shamed by other students, teachers, staff, and administrators.

Other learners, such as children of migrant workers, have often been unable to attend school for a continuous period of time due to family relocations and the search to obtain work. Students, especially older learners ages 13–18, with little or no exposure to schooling or the school environment, generally feel extremely frightened and uncomfortable when they suddenly find themselves in our classrooms.

There is another group of ESL students who also feel ill at ease and uncomfortable in U.S. schools. These are students who have attended schools in their native countries that seem to be more serious and more academically challenging. Students may go to school for long hours, six days a week and come home to do three or four additional hours of strenuous homework. The classes in other countries may be more formal than in the United States. For example, in many countries students are expected to stand whenever they are called on in class or whenever an adult enters the room. These students are puzzled by the seemingly casual attitudes American students have toward education.

Both groups of ESL students described above need to be oriented to the expectations that American schools have for students. The formal curriculum should allocate time for all students to learn about the routines and expectations of the school. Students should be given opportunities to discuss local school expectations and compare them to the expectations made in their native countries. They also need to know what the ramifications are for not obeying rules and meeting expectations. Students need to understand the overall expectations before they can focus on specific tasks and goals. This aspect of the curriculum is just as important, if not more so, as formal academic skills and should have a prominent place in the ESL curriculum.

Attitudes toward Education

To be responsive to the needs of students, education must determine what attitudes the students and their families have toward formal schooling and education. Students all over the globe are typically educated by their families, in local schools, and by other organizations such as churches and ethnic or cultural groups. The role of public education varies from country to country and community to community within different countries. Students may be schooled through the public, state-operated schools but actually receive the majority of their education from local religious organizations.

In some countries, formal schooling is not viewed as important for reaching one's personal and life goals. In cultures that have an oral tradition and lack a traditional orthography, the education most valued by community members takes place outside of the classroom walls where young people may learn very sophisticated information about astronomy, agriculture, or fishing. Often elders are responsible for providing this valuable education.

Unfortunately, too often parents and families view the school as another obstacle which must be dealt with before the student can begin to fulfill his or her own personal objectives. The best way to find out if this is the case is by contacting and communicating with family members and individuals whom the students and family consider to be local leaders (of the same cultural and/or ethnic background). There are a number of questions which need to be addressed:

· What do parents and their families view as the role of the school?

· Do students and their families value the public schools?

· Do students and their families see the local schools as assisting students in realizing and

Table 2. Needs Assessment: Educational Background		
Student Background and Needs	**Methods for Assessing Needs**	**Guidelines for Curriculum Developers**
What experiences have students had with formal schooling? Have students had interrupted periods of school attendance?	School records; interviews	Teaching methods and materials should help students who lack continuous prior formal schooling become comfortable with U.S. schools' structure.
What do students and their families perceive as the role of schooling in their native countries and in the U.S.? Are there other ways young people are educated in their native countries?	Interviews, questionnaires, etc.	Teaching methods and materials should reflect the educational goals and the methods of instruction used in students' native countries.
What preliteracy and literacy skills do students have in their native language?	School records; tests; interviews	Whenever possible, teaching methods and materials should help students develop and expand upon preliteracy and literacy skills in their native language.
What preliteracy and literacy skills do students have in English?	School records; tests; interviews	Teaching methods and materials should help students develop and expand their English preliteracy and literacy skills.
What cognitive/academic skills do students have in their native language (for example, advanced knowledge of math and science)?	School records; tests; interviews	Whenever possible, teaching methods and materials should help students develop and expand their cognitive and academic skills in their native language.
What cognitive/academic skills do students have in English? For example, have students learned advanced scientific concepts?	School records; tests; interviews	Teaching methods and materials should help students develop and expand cognitive/academic skills in English.

fulfilling their personal aspirations and goals?
· What goals do parents have for their children?
· How can local schools help students to achieve
these goals?
· What accomplishments are families most proud
of, academic and otherwise?
· Are parents aware of all of the opportunities
that are made available to students as a result
of education?

Preliteracy/Literacy Skills
in the Student's Native Language

It is necessary for schools to know what preliteracy
and literacy skills all of their ESL students possess;
for young learners, schools should find out what
readiness skills students possess. Often when ESL
students enter school, regardless of age, they are
tested for oral language skills and dominance and
placed in a bilingual or ESL program based solely
on their oral language skills. A more comprehensive
formal assessment of students, which includes
testing for preliteracy and literacy skills, should be
conducted for every ESL student who enters school.

Many of the children who immigrate to the
United States lack basic literacy skills in their
primary language and often have little or no
experience with the printed word. This situation is
especially problematic for older learners. Although
students may lack experience with literacy in their
primary language, they often have developed oral
language skills in their first language that will
facilitate the process of learning to read and write.
The wealth of oral language skills and cultural
knowledge that students possess in their primary
language should be used as the basis for developing
preliteracy and literacy skills in that language.
Unfortunately, the instruments used to measure
students' literacy and preliteracy skills often look
only at students' prior experience with paper-and-
pencil tasks.

Schools must take a broader view of the
preliteracy skills that students have acquired in
their primary language and/or English. For example, many adolescent learners have been the
primary caretakers of younger siblings and invent
stories to amuse their younger brothers and sisters.
These students may be able to tell complex stories
orally. Unfortunately, these reading readiness skills
are not usually part of a routine ESL student
assessment. It is important to document what
intellectual skills students possess regardless of
whether or not they have acquired literacy skills.

Skills such as these, developed in students'
native languages, should easily be transferred into

English. When students enter kindergarten in the
United States, teachers view their role as helping
them gain the *readiness* or *preliteracy* skills that are
required to learn to read. These skills are necessary
for students regardless of whether or not their primary language has an orthography or writing systems.
Schools are not prepared to work with these
students and often do not see the skills they possess;
rather they view these learners as disadvantaged.

Teachers who work with older students often
do not know how to teach preliteracy skills to
students who have very little experience with
schooling and books and they are often perplexed
and frustrated by these students. Teachers must
think about the knowledge students bring to the
classroom as well as the skills students need in
order to succeed at school. Skills such as looking
from left to right and top to bottom on a page must
be consciously taught.

Whenever possible the curriculum should
provide a scope and sequence of preliteracy and
literacy skills in students' primary language(s) and
in English. The curriculum should enable students
to acquire literacy skills in their primary language
regardless of how old they are when they enter
school. If there are students who lack literacy skills
in their primary language, then a reading specialist,
preferably one who is proficient in the students'
native language, should be included in the curriculum development process. When students are
taught preliteracy and literacy skills in their primary
languages, the students' wealth of oral language and
cultural backgrounds are fully utilized.

Preliteracy/Literacy Skills in English

Just as it is important for schools to know the
preliteracy skills that their students possess in their
primary language, it is also necessary to know what
preliteracy and literacy skills students have in
English. Students have very different levels of skill
acquisition that often do *not* correspond to their
ability to read and write in their primary language
or their level of English language acquisition.

Students who do not have an opportunity to
gain preliteracy skills in their primary language
should be taught these skills in English. Just as in
primary language instruction, emphasis should be
placed on the prerequisite skills necessary for
students to be able to read and write. In some
instances, students may have very good oral
language skills in English but lack the ability to read
or write it. Other students may lack both oral and
written language skills in English. The four language skills (listening, speaking, reading, and

writing) should be integrated and taught together for students, regardless of their level of language acquisition.

The curriculum must enable students to develop and expand both preliteracy and literacy skills in English as needed. If there are a large number of students, especially older learners, who lack literacy skills in English and/or their primary language, then a reading specialist should be included in the curriculum development process. Emphasis should not be placed only on the acquisition of oral language skills in English. Instead, all four language skills should be integrated to make sure that students acquire literacy skills that are congruent with their acquisition of oral language. The amount of emphasis on preliteracy skills in English will depend on the students' level of literacy development in their primary language.

Cognitive/Academic Skills in the Students' Native Language

Schools should ascertain the students' level of cognitive development and acquisition of academic skills in their native language(s). The students' ability to perform cognitively challenging oral and written tasks in their first language should be assessed. Many bilingual students enter school with sophisticated cognitive skills from life experiences but lack the skills to do paper-and-pencil tasks. Bilingual programs should continue until students have acquired the cognitive skills in English that will make it possible for them to take advantage of every opportunity made available to their English-speaking peers.

Students may enter school in the United States with the ability to perform cognitively challenging tasks in their first language orally and/or in writing. Schools should assess skills orally and in writing. Some students will be able to do math at a level three or four times more advanced than their peers. Other students, who may not have acquired literacy skills, may have sophisticated problem solving abilities as a result of being the primary caretaker for one or more younger siblings.

Although it is very common for school districts throughout the United States to have bilingual programs, generally they cease after students have acquired basic literacy skills in their native language. As Cummins points out, it is important for bilingual programs to continue until students have acquired the skills necessary to be successful in English, usually about five years.

Schools should develop a comprehensive program for students to gain cognitive and academic skills in their primary language while they are acquiring English. Although students may not have the formal skills, they do have the foundation of oral language from which to build cognitive and academic skills while they are acquiring a second language.

Although many students may lack literacy skills in their native language, there is also a group of students who may have acquired advanced cognitive and/or academic skills in their primary language. For example, students throughout the world regularly outperform their American peers in geography, math, and science. It is important for schools to help students to continue their intellectual growth even if it means providing materials for students that are on a higher level than the ubiquitous *on grade level.*

The curriculum should provide students with opportunities to expand upon the cognitive skills they possess in their primary language(s) when they enter school. The continuum of cognitive and academic skills will depend upon students' background and will vary, based on the types of cognitive skills that students have in their primary language.

Cognitive/Academic Skills in English

Schools must ascertain what cognitive and academic skills students have acquired in English. In most ESL programs, emphasis is placed on the development of basic interpersonal communication skills and not on cognitive academic language proficiencies. As cited above, whenever possible, students should acquire cognitive academic language proficiencies in their primary language before they learn them in English.

The ESL curriculum should provide students with opportunities to transfer cognitive academic language proficiencies from their primary language to English for a period of several years before bilingual and ESL support ceases. In other cases, where students have not had an opportunity to develop extensive cognitive and academic skills in their primary language, a longer period of time and more attention must be paid to individual skills since students will be working on acquiring both language and cognitive/academic skills simultaneously.

Methods Used To Assess Educational Backgrounds and Attitudes toward Schooling

A variety of methods may be used to assess students' educational backgrounds and attitudes toward schooling. More and more educators are using ethnographic methods to assess both attitudes and skill acquisition. A variety of observation checklists, interview guides, and formal tests can be used to ascertain what language and cognitive skills students have acquired in their native language and English. Questions such as the following should be addressed:

- What was school like in your country?
- What is the purpose of schooling in your native country?
- What do you think is the purpose of schooling in this country?
- How long should students be forced to attend school? Why do you think so?
- What do your children need to know to get a good job?
- What should schools teach students?
- What should parents and family teach students?
- How can parents and schools work together?
- Do you feel comfortable at school?

Cultural and Political Backgrounds of Students and Personal Characteristics

Students who enter our schools often come to the United States as the only way to avoid war or other hardships. Often, families are forced to flee a country because of political reasons, such as war, civil unrest, severe poverty, or lack of opportunities for upward mobility. Unfortunately, when the media reports what a country or its leaders have done, there is a tendency to extend responsibility for those actions to all members of that culture or country. For example, historically there have been anti-Iraqi and anti-Iranian actions when the governments of each country have acted in an irresponsible manner. It is common for students who come from these countries to be just as opposed to their country's government. In addition, these acts are often described without the proper context or details. It is very typical of the American media to simplify the nature of conflicts that take place in a different country.

It is the school's responsibility to take into account the cultural, political, and personal characteristics of students as the curriculum is developed in order to plan activities and objectives that are realistic and purposeful. It is not the responsibility of the school to act on political matters, but it is the school's responsibility to provide equal access to school opportunities and to validate the experiences of all of the students, regardless of their political and/or cultural backgrounds. This information will help to minimize conflicts among students from different groups. Curriculum developers and planners should use the information presented in this section as a checklist to insure that all students are honored and respected, regardless of their cultural and political backgrounds. Table 3 provides information for developing a needs assessment that examines students' cultural and political backgrounds as well as guidelines for using the information generated from the needs assessment.

Country of Origin

It is helpful for educators to know why students have moved from their countries of origin to the United States. By understanding why families leave their homelands, educators can begin to understand which values are important to a particular family or group of people. Families undergo a great deal of turmoil when they come to the United States because they believe they will have a better life in this country than in their native countries. Often, immigrants view the United States as the promised land, a place where individuals can speak freely and see dreams come true.

Students may live in several different countries for extended periods of time before their families finally reach the United States. Others may feel a lack of identity because they have spent very little or no time in their country of origin, and the only ties they have are their language and the recollections shared by parents and other relatives. Some learners may never have been in their native country and may have spent extensive periods of time in refugee camps in other foreign countries, waiting to come to the United States.

The curriculum should give students opportunities to explore their cultural heritages. Students should decide which countries they consider to be home and warrant in-depth study and analysis. It is important for students to come up with their own sense of identity, such as Croatian, American-Croatian, or American. Educators should not make the mistake of just focusing attention on the study of the students' legal country of origin. For example, it would be wrong to focus all of the attention in social studies on Cambodia when students who were indeed born there may have spent more time in Thailand and feel a stronger bond to that country.

Cultural Groups and Political Groups Represented

Schools must look at all of the cultural groups represented by their students. Often generalizations about a culture are made in order for educators to understand better the group of learners that it represents. This in itself can help to make sure that students will feel comfortable with the methods and techniques being used (Ramsey 1987). There is not any one culture for any specific city, state, or country; there are numerous different cultural groups in every geographical area and region.

Educators must not look just at the country of origin to determine the students' cultural values and characteristics. For example, Mexicans traditionally have large families and have a major celebration when girls turn fifteen; however, Mexican subcultures may be very different depending upon such factors as socioeconomic status and place of residence. Unfortunately, schools often assume that students from the same country and/or cultural background will get along and will benefit from being grouped together.

It is often difficult for students who come from the same country but who have different cultures to recognize the commonalities they share with their peers. Emphasis needs to be placed on what students have in common and what they value. Culture is a very difficult concept for anthropologists, sociologists, and educators to define. It is even more difficult for students to understand. What students and their families perceive as being of prime importance is usually a reflection of cultural values.

In order for a curriculum to be authentic and meaningful, the cultural views and information about all cultures represented should be included in the curriculum. Stereotypes should be avoided. Students need to learn how to recognize similarities and differences as cultural traits and not cultural values. Students should be taught how to respect students from other cultural groups. The curriculum should provide opportunities for students to investigate and celebrate their cultures and subcultures of origin.

Methods that are generally viewed as ethnographic should be used to assess the cultural and political backgrounds of students as well as personal characteristics. Interviews and questionnaires can be used to learn about the students' countries of origin and their cultural and political backgrounds. The news media and bilingual newspapers can help educators learn about the political factors impacting their students' lives as well as individuals who are viewed as leaders. A variety of methods should be used to learn about students' cultural and political backgrounds.

Community Leaders from the Cultures and Subcultures Represented by Students

School personnel need to know which figures members of different cultural and political groups view as their leaders. These individuals can provide a valuable link between the classroom and home and should be used as a resource when planning programs for students. Leaders know not only what holidays, traditions, and festivals are celebrated but, more importantly, what is valued and should be emphasized at school. Leaders also are in a good position to differentiate between the school's responsibilities and those of the home, as well as knowing when schools are overstepping their bounds. Leaders may be teachers from a particular cultural group or a family.

Local community leaders should provide input at every stage of curriculum development and implementation. Topics that are truly of interest to students, based on their cultural backgrounds, can be learned from community leaders and from their experiences with their children. In addition, they can identify materials that might appear to be confusing or disrespectful of the students' culture of origin. Older learners who may identify with several cultures are often in a position to review curriculum as well, to determine what is culturally appropriate.

Conclusion

The ESL students who enter schools throughout the United States are a very diverse group of learners. They represent a wide range of linguistic, educational, and cultural backgrounds. Some of these youngsters come from homes where literacy and books are considered as important and necessary as food and water. Other students come from families and cultures where literacy is not a prerequisite for success. Regardless of youngsters' backgrounds, it is the responsibility of local educational agencies to design programs which enable ESL students to have equal access to the same academic and extracurricular opportunities made available to their English-speaking peers.

Table 3. Needs Assessment:
Cultural and Political Backgrounds and Personal Characteristics

Student Background and Needs	Methods for Assessing Needs	Guidelines for Curriculum Developers
What are students' country/countries of origin? Why have they moved to the U.S.?	Interviews, questionnaires, etc.; news media	Teaching methods and materials should reflect each student's country of origin and their reasons for coming to the U.S.
What cultures and subcultures do students represent?	Interviews, questionnaires, etc.	Teaching methods and materials should help students investigate and celebrate their cultural heritage.
What political and sociopolitical groups do students represent? How does this impact schooling?	Interviews, questionnaires, etc.	Teaching methods and materials should take into account the political and sociopolitical factors which directly impact the lives of students.
Which local community leaders represent students' cultural and sociopolitical backgrounds?	Bilingual newspapers; interviews, questionnaires, etc.	Teaching methods and materials should be reviewed by local community leaders.
What are the ages of students? What are the cultural expectations for students at different ages?	Interviews, questionnaires, etc.	Teaching methods and materials should be age-appropriate and take into account cultural expectations for students of different ages.
What are the cultural expectations for girls and boys?	Interviews, questionnaires, etc.	Teaching methods and materials should take into account the expectations that different cultures have for boys and girls.

References

Chamot, A. U. 1983. "A Transfer Curriculum for Teaching Content-Based ESL in the Elementary School." In *On TESOL '83*, 125–33. Washington, DC: TESOL.

Cummins, J. 1984. "Wanted, A Theoretical Framework for Relating Language Proficiency to Academic Achievement among Bilingual Students." In *Language Proficiency and Academic Achievement*, 2–19. Clevedon, England: Multilingual Matters 2.

Dubain, F., and E. Olshtain, 1986. *Course Design: Developing Programs and Materials for Language Learning.* New York: Cambridge Univ. Press.

Edelsky, C. 1986. *Writing in a Bilingual Program: Habia una Vez.* Norwood, NJ: Ablex.

Goodman, K. S., and Y. Goodman. 1978. *Reading of American Children Whose Language Is a Stable Rural Dialect of English or a Language Other than English.* Washington, DC: U.S. Department of Health, Education, and Welfare.

Ramsey, P. 1987. *Teaching and Learning in a Diverse World: Multicultural Education for Young Children.* New York: Teachers College Press.

Sossa, A. 1992. "Bilingual Education Heading into the 1990s." *Journal of Education Issues of Language Minority Students* 10 (Spring): 203–12.

FUNDING CURRICULUM PROJECTS

THE greatest challenge curriculum developers often face is locating money to finance their project. We hear that money is available for such projects, but are at a loss as to how it can be accessed. Frequently, it requires as much creativity to locate financing as to generate the curriculum. This chapter includes information on three types of funding that is available for education projects:

1. Federal programs that provide money for special school projects
2. Foundations that have recently endowed education projects, programs for those with a primary language other than English, or services directed at increasing literacy
3. Foundations that identify education, including special projects, as a mission.

Not all of the projects reviewed are specifically for school-aged children; many are targeted at an adult population. Their mission, however, is similar: to educate people who are not proficient in English. It is important to keep your goal in mind when seeking funding sources. Think of other areas that are similar to yours. If you are seeking money for an English as a Second Language project for Haitian children, don't overlook foundations that have supported other Haiti projects. Also consider foundations that underwrite undertakings for other immigrant groups or for the economically disadvantaged.

When seeking a potential funding source for your project, first review any information that is available about the foundation. Look specifically at the areas of:

· Purpose: Is a mission of the foundation to provide money for education?

· Limitations: Are there specific geographic requirements? Are there some areas that are disqualified?
· Supported areas: Does the foundation provide funding for special projects?
· Grants: After reviewing the education projects that have been funded, does it appear that the organizations and projects are similar to yours?

Your search will be most useful if you also keep these questions in mind:

· Has the foundation funded projects in your subject area?
· Does your location meet the geographic requirements of the foundation?
· Is the amount of money you are requesting within the grant's range?
· Are there foundation policies that prohibit grants for the type of support you are requesting?
· Will the foundation make grants to cover the full cost of a project? Does it require costs of a project to be shared with other foundations or funding sources?
· What types of organizations have been supported? Are they similar to yours?
· Are there specific application deadlines and procedures, or are proposals accepted continuously?

This information can be found in the annual report of the foundation or in *Source Book Profiles*. Many of the larger public libraries maintain current foundation directories. If yours does not, there are Foundation Center Libraries located at:

79 Fifth Avenue
New York, NY 10003-3050
(212) 620-4230

312 Sutter Street
San Francisco, CA 94180
(415) 397-0902

1001 Connecticut Avenue, NW
Suite 938
Washington, DC 20036
(202) 331-1400

1442 Hanna Building
1442 Euclid Ave.
Cleveland, OH 44115
(216) 861-1934

Identifying appropriate foundations is the first step in your quest for money. The next step is initiating contact with the foundation, either by telephone or letter. It is a good idea to direct your inquiry to the person in charge of giving; otherwise, your letter could easily go astray. A phone call to the foundation will provide you with the necessary information.

Federal Programs that Provide Money for Special School Projects

Jacob B. Javits Gifted and Talented Students
Research Applications Division
Programs for the Improvement of Practice
Department of Education
555 New Jersey Avenue, NW
Washington, DC 20202-5643
(202) 219-2187
Provides grants for establishing and operating model projects to identify and educate gifted and talented students.

The Secretary's Fund for Innovation in Education
Department of Education
FIRST
Office of Educational Research and Improvement
Washington, DC 20208-5524
(202) 219-1496
Funds educational programs and projects that identify innovative educational approaches.

Division of State and Local Programs
Office of Bilingual Education and Minority
Language Affairs
Department of Education
330 C Street, SW—Room 5086
Washington, DC 20202
(202) 732-5700
Contact: Director
Funds projects to improve bilingual education, ESL, and English proficiency programs at all levels from preschool to adult education.

Transition Program for Refugee Children
Office of Bilingual Education and Minority
Languages Affairs
Department of Education
330 C Street, SW—Room 5086
Washington, DC 20202
(202) 732-5708
Provides funding for programs meeting the special needs of refugee children in elementary and secondary schools.

Emergency Immigrant Education
Office of Bilingual Education and Minority
Languages Affairs
Department of Education
330 C Street, SW—Room 5615
Washington, DC 20202
(202) 732-5708
Provides funding for immigrant children in grades K–12.

Division of Educational Support
Office of Elementary and Secondary Education
Department of Education
400 Maryland Avenue, SW—Mail Stop 624
Washington, DC 20202-6438
(202) 401-1342
Provides funding for projects that demonstrate effective elementary and secondary school dropout and reentry programs.

Foundations that Have Recently Endowed ESL and Literacy Projects

Mary Reynolds Babcock Foundation, Inc.
102 Reynolda Village
Winston-Salem, NC 27106-5123
(919) 748-9222

Contact: William L. Bondurant, Executive
  Director
  · $45,120 to Project Uplift for Family Literacy
  Program.
Does not support educational institutions outside
of North Carolina.

The Blandin Foundation
100 Pokegama Avenue, North
Grand Rapids, MN 55744
(218) 326-0523
Contact: Paul M. Olson, President
  · $125,500 to Grand Rapids Independent
  School District 318, Rapids Quest Program,
  to continue imaginative enrichment programs
  for Grand Rapids students.
Limited to Minnesota, with an emphasis on rural
areas.

The Boston Foundation, Inc.
One Boston Place, 24th floor
Boston, MA 02108
(617) 723-7415
Fax: (617) 589-3616
Contact: Anna Faith Jones, President
  · $15,000 to the Welcome Project for ESL
  classes at Mystic Housing Development.

California Community Foundation
606 South Olive Street, Suite 2400
Los Angeles, CA 90014
(213) 413-4042
Contact: Jack Shakley, President
Orange County:
13252 Garden Grove Boulevard, Suite 195
Garden Grove, CA 92643
(714) 750-7794
  · $15,000 to Latino Resource Organization for
  educational family program working to
  improve English literacy and develop parent-
  effectiveness skills.
Giving limited to Los Angeles, Orange, Riverside, San Bernadino & Ventura counties, CA.

The Frances L. and Edwin L. Cummings
  Memorial Fund
501 Fifth Avenue, Suite 1208
New York, NY 10017-1602
(212) 286-1778
Contact: Elizabeth Costas, Administrative
  Director
  · $10,000 to Literacy Volunteers of Westchester
  County for program to serve adult
  nonreaders and non-English speakers.

Giving primarily in metropolitan New York area,
including New Jersey and Connecticut.

The George Foundation
207 South Third Street
P.O. Drawer C
Richmond, TX 77469
(713) 342-6109
Contact: Trustees
  · $20,000 to Region Four Education Service
  Center for Adult Basic Education and ESL
  classes in Fort Bend County, TX.
Giving primarily in Fort Bend County, TX.

The George Gund Foundation
1845 Guildhall Building
45 Prospect Avenue West
Cleveland, OH 44115
(216) 241-3114
Fax: (216) 241-6560
Contact: David Bergholz, Executive Director
  · $75,552 to the Cleveland Public Schools for
  second-year support for bilingual education
  dropout prevention program.
Giving primarily in northeastern Ohio.

The Hitachi Foundation
1509 22nd Street, NW
Washington, DC 20037
(202) 457-0588
Contact: Felicia B. Lynch, Vice-President,
  Programs
  · $150,000 to Americans All for support of a
  new multicultural program in third, fifth,
  eighth, and eleventh grades of DC public
  schools.
Initial contact through letter of no more than
three pages.

The James Irvine Foundation
One Market Plaza
Spear Tower, Suite 1715
San Francisco, CA 94105
(414) 777-2244
Contact: Luz A. Vega, Director of Grants
Southern CA office:
777 South Figueroa St., Suite 740
Los Angeles, CA 90017-5430
  · $22,000 for outreach program to parents of
  Laotian children with limited English profi-
  ciency, enrolled in the Richmond Unified
  School District.

Island Foundation, Inc.
589 Mill Street
Marion, MA 02738
(508) 748-2809
Contact: Jenny D. Russell, Executive Director
· $10,000 to Officina Hispana de la Communidad for curriculum development for basic education, ESL, and job training classes.
Giving primarily in the northeastern United States. Application form required.

W. Alton Jones Foundation, Inc.
232 East High Street
Charlottesville, VA 22901
(804) 295-2134
Contact: John Peterson Myers, Director
· $70,000 to Episcopal School of New York, NY, for general school development and teacher professional development.

The Medtronic Foundation
7000 Central Avenue, NE
Minneapolis, MN 55432
(612) 574-3029
Contact: Jan Schwarz, Manager
· $12,500 to Minneapolis Public Schools to work with the community on general curriculum development.
Giving primarily in areas of company operations.

Eugene and Agnes E. Meyer Foundation
1400 Sixteenth Street, NW, Suite 360
Washington, DC 20036
(202) 483-8294
· $15,000 to the Indochinese Community Center for vocational English as a Second Language classes and job placement, targeting Amerasian and Vietnamese–African American youths, other refugees, and immigrants.

The New York Community Trust
Two Park Avenue, 24th floor
New York, NY 10016
(212) 686-0010
Fax: (212) 532-8528
Contact: Lorie A. Slutsky, Director
· $30,000 to Union Settlement Association to produce computer-based adult literacy training curriculum.
Limited to New York metropolitan area.

The Pittsburgh Foundation
30 CNG Tower
625 Liberty Avenue
Pittsburgh, PA 15222-3115
(412) 391-5122
Contact: Alfred W. Wishart, Jr., Executive Director
· $300,000 for English language skills component of Operation Exodus for Soviet Jewish resettlement.
Giving limited to Allegheny County, PA; no support to private schools.

U.S. West Foundation
7800 East Orchard Road, Suite 300
Englewood, CO 80111
(303) 793-6661
Contact: Larry J. Nash, Director of Administration
· $10,000 to Austin Technical Institute for ESL program.
Limited to states served by US WEST calling areas. Address applications to local US WEST Public Relations Office or Community Relations Team.

Foundations that Fund Education, Including Special Projects, as a Mission

Aetna Foundation, Inc.
151 Farmington Avenue
Hartford, CT 06156-3180
(203) 273-6382
Contact: Diana Kinosh, Management Information Supervisor

The Ahmanson Foundation
9215 Wilshire Boulevard
Beverly Hills, CA 90210
(213) 278-0770
Contact: Lee E. Walcott, Vice-President & Managing Director
Giving primarily in southern California.

Alcoa Foundation
1501 Alcoa Building
Pittsburgh, PA 15219-1850
(412) 553-2348
Contact: F. Worth Hobbs, President
Giving primarily in areas of company operation.

The Allstate Foundation
Allstate Plaza North
Northbrook, IL 60062
(708) 402-5502
Contacts: Alan F. Benedeck, Executive Director;
  Allen Goldhamer, Manager; Dawn Bougart,
  Administrative Assistant

American Express Minnesota Foundation
c/o IDS Financial Services
IDS Tower Ten
Minneapolis, MN 55440
(612) 372-2643
Contacts: Sue Gethin, Manager of Public Affairs,
  IDS; Marie Tobin, Community Relations
  Specialist
Giving primarily in Minnesota.

American National Bank & Trust Co. of Chicago
  Foundation
33 North La Salle Street
Chicago, IL 60690
(312) 661-6115
Contact: Joan M. Klaus, Director
Giving limited to six-county Chicago metropoli-
tan area.

Anderson Foundation
c/o Anderson Corp.
Bayport, MN 55003
(612) 439-5150
Contact: Lisa Carlstrom, Assistant Secretary

The Annenberg Foundation
St. Davids Center
150 Radnor-Chester Road, Suite A-200
St. Davids, PA 19087
Contact: Donald Mullen, Treasurer

AON Foundation
123 North Wacker Drive
Chicago, IL 60606
(312) 701-3000
Contact: Wallace J. Buya, Vice-President
No support for secondary educational institutions
or vocational schools.

Atherton Family Foundation
c/o Hawaiian Trust Co., Ltd.
P.O. Box 3170
Honolulu, HI 96802
(808) 537-6333

Fax: (808) 521-6286
Contact: Charlie Medeiros
Limited to Hawaii.

Metropolitan Atlanta Community Foundation,
  Inc.
The Hurt Building, Suite 449
Atlanta, GA 30303
(404) 688-5525
Contact: Alicia Philipp, Executive Director
Limited to metropolitan area of Atlanta and
surrounding regions.

Ball Brothers Foundation
222 South Mulberry Street
Muncie, IN 47308
(317) 741-5500
Fax: (317) 741-5518
Contact: Douglas A. Bakker, Executive Director
Limited to Indiana.

Baltimore Gas & Electric Foundation, Inc.
Box 1475
Baltimore, MD 21203
(301) 234-5312
Contact: Gary R. Fuhronan
Giving primarily in Maryland, with emphasis in
Baltimore.

Bell Atlantic Charitable Foundation
1310 North Courthouse Road, 10th Floor
Arlington, VA 22201
(703) 974-5440
Contact: Ruth P. Caine, Director
Giving primarily in areas of company operations.

Benwood Foundation, Inc.
1600 American National Bank Building
736 Market Street
Chattanooga, TN 37402
(615) 267-4311
Contact: Jean R. McDaniel, Executive Director
Giving primarily in Chattanooga area.

Robert M. Beren Foundation, Inc.
970 Fourth Financial Center
Wichita, KS 67202
Giving primarily for Jewish organizations.

The Frank Stanley Beveridge Foundation, Inc.
1515 Ringling Boulevard, Suite 340
P.O. Box 4097
Sarasota, FL 34230-4097

(813) 955-7575
(800) 356-9779
Contact: Philip Coswell, President
Giving primarily to Hampden County, MA, to organizations that are not tax-supported.

F. R. Bigelow Foundation
1120 Norwest Center
St. Paul, MN 55101
(612) 224-5463
Contact: Paul A. Verret, Secretary-Treasurer
Support includes secondary education in greater St. Paul metropolitan area.

Borden Foundation, Inc.
180 East Broad Street, 34th Floor
Columbus, OH 43215
(614) 225-4340
Contact: Judy Barker, President
Emphasis on programs to benefit disadvantaged children in areas of company operations.

The Boston Globe Foundation II, Inc.
135 Morrissey Boulevard
Boston, MA 02107
(617) 929-3194
Contact: Suzanne Watkin, Executive Director
Giving primarily in greater Boston area.

The J. S. Bridwell Foundation
500 City National Building
Wichita Falls, TX 76303
(817) 322-4436
Support includes secondary education in Texas.

The Buchanan Family Foundation
222 East Wisconsin Avenue
Lake Forest, IL 60045
Contact: Huntington Eldridge, Jr., Treasurer
Giving primarily in Chicago.

The Buhl Foundation
Four Gateway Center, Room 1522
Pittsburgh, PA 15222
(412) 566-2711
Contact: Dr. Doreen E. Boyce, Executive Director
Giving primarily in southwestern Pennsylvania, particularly the Pittsburgh area.

Edyth Bush Charitable Foundation, Inc.
199 East Welbourne Avenue
P.O. Box 1967
Winter Park, FL 32790-1967
(407) 647-4322

Contact: H. Clifford Lee, President
Giving has specific geographic and facility limitations.

The Cargill Foundation
P.O. Box 9300
Minneapolis, MN 55440
(612) 475-6122
Contact: Audrey Tulberg, Program & Administrative Director
Giving primarily in the seven-county Minneapolis–St. Paul metropolitan area.

Carnegie Corporation of NY
437 Madison Avenue
New York, NY 10022
(212) 371-3200
Contact: Dorothy W. Knoop, Secretary
Initial approach by telephone or letter.

H. A. & Mary K. Chapman Charitable Trust
One Warren Place, Suite 1816
6100 South Yale
Tulsa, OK 74136
(918) 496-7882
Contacts: Ralph L. Abercrombie, Trustee; Donne Pitman, Trustee
Giving primarily in Tulsa.

Liz Claiborne Foundation
119 West 40th Street, 4th Floor
New York, NY 10018
(212) 536-6424
Limited to Hudson County, NJ, and the metropolitan New York area.

The Cleveland Foundation
1422 Euclid Avenue, Suite 1400
Cleveland, OH 44115-2001
(216) 861-3810
Contact: Steven A. Minter, Executive Director
Initial approach should be through a letter.
Giving limited to greater Cleveland area.

The Coca-Cola Foundation, Inc.
P.O. Drawer 1734
Atlanta, GA 30301
(404) 676-2568

The Columbus Foundation
1234 East Broad Street
Columbus, OH 43205
(614) 251-4000

Contact: James I. Luck, President
Giving limited to central Ohio.

Cowles Media Foundation
329 Portland Avenue
Minneapolis, MN 55415
(612) 375-7051
Contact: Janet L. Schwichtenberg
Limited to Minneapolis area.

Dade Community Foundation
200 South Biscayne Boulevard—Suite 4770
Miami, FL 33131-2343
(305) 371-2711
Contact: Ruth Shack, President
Funding limited to Dade County, FL.

Dewitt Families Conduit Foundation
8300 96th Avenue
Zelland, MI 49464
Giving for Christian organizations.

Dodge Jones Foundation
P.O. Box 176
Abilene, TX 79604
(915) 673-6429
Contact: Lawrence E. Gill, Vice-President,
    Grants Administrator
Giving primarily in Abilene.

Carrie Estelle Doheny Foundation
911 Wiltshire Boulevard, Suite 1750
Los Angeles, CA 90017
(213) 488-1122
Contact: Robert A. Smith III, President
Giving primarily in Los Angeles area for non-tax-supported organizations.

The Educational Foundation of America
23161 Ventura Boulevard, Suite 201
Woodland Hill, CA 91364
(818) 999-0921

The Charles Engelhard Foundation
P.O. Box 427
Far Hills, NJ 07931
(201) 766-7224
Contact: Elaine Catterall, Secretary

The William Stamps Farish Fund
1100 Louisiana, Suite 1250
Houston, TX 77002
(713) 757-7313

Contact: W. S. Farish, President
Giving primarily in Texas.

Joseph & Bessie Feinberg Foundation
5245 West Lawrence Avenue
Chicago, IL 60630
(312) 777-8600
Contact: June Blossom
Giving primarily in Illinois, to Jewish organizations.

The 1525 Foundation
1525 National City Bank Building
Cleveland, OH 44114
(216) 696-4200
Contact: Bernadette Walsh, Assistant Secretary
Primarily in Ohio, with emphasis on Cuyahoga County.

The Flinn Foundation
3300 North Central Avenue, Suite 2300
Phoenix, AZ 85012
(602) 274-9000
Contact: John W. Murphy, Executive Director
Limited to Arizona.

The Edward E. Ford Foundation
297 Wickenden Street
Providence, RI 02903
(401) 751-2966
Contact: Philip V. Havens, Executive Director
Funding to independent secondary schools.

George F. & Sybil H. Fuller Foundation
105 Madison Street
Worcester, MA 01610
(508) 756-5111
Contact: Russell E. Fuller, Chairman
Giving primarily in Massachusetts, with emphasis in Worcester.

The B.C. Gamble & P.W. Skogmo Foundation
500 Foshay Tower
Minneapolis, MN 55402
(612) 339-7343
Contact: Patricia A. Cummings, Manager of
    Supporting Organizations
Giving primarily for disadvantaged youth, handicapped, and secondary educational institutions in the Minneapolis–St. Paul metropolitan area.

The Gold Family Foundation
159 Conant Street
Hillside, NJ 07205

(908) 353-6269
Contact: Meyer Gold, Manager
Support primarily for Jewish organizations.

The Haggar Foundation
6113 Lemmon Avenue
Dallas, TX 75209
(214) 956-0241
Contact: Rosemary Haggar Vaughan, Executive
   Director
Limited to areas of company operations in Dallas
and south Texas.

Gladys & Roland Harriman Foundation
63 Wall Street, 23rd Floor
New York, NY 10005
(212) 493-8182
Contact: William F. Hibberd, Secretary

Hasbro Children's Foundation
32 West 23rd Street
New York, NY 10010
(212) 645-2400
Contact: Eve Weiss, Executive Director
Funding for children, under the age of 12, with
special needs.

The Humana Foundation, Inc.
The Humana Building
500 West Main Street
P.O. Box 1438
Louisville, KY 40201
(502) 580-3920
Contact: Jay L. Foley, Contribution Manager
Giving primarily in Kentucky.

International Paper Company Foundation
Two Manhattanville Road
Purchase, NY 10577
(914) 397-1581
Contact: Sandra Wilson, Vice-President
Giving primarily in communities where there are
company plants and mills.

The Martha Holden Jennings Foundation
710 Halle Building
1228 Euclid Avenue
Cleveland, OH 44115
(216) 589-5700
Contact: Dr. Richard A. Boyd, Executive Director
Limited to Ohio.

Walter S. Johnson Foundation
525 Middlefield Road, Suite 110
Menlo Park, CA 94025
(415) 326-0485
Contact: Kimberly Ford, Program Director
Giving primarily in Alameda, Contra Costa, San
Francisco, San Mateo and Santa Clara counties in
California and in Washoe, NV. There is no
support to private schools.

W. K. Kellogg Foundation
400 North Avenue
Battle Creek, MI 49017-3398
(616) 968-1611
Contact: Nancy A. Sims, Executive Assistant,
   Programming

Donald P. & Byrd M. Kelly Foundation
701 Harger Road, #150
Oak Brook, IL 60521
Contact: Laura K. McGrath, Treasurer
Primarily in Illinois, with emphasis on Chicago.

Carl B. & Florence E. King Foundation
5956 Sherry Lane, Suite 620
Dallas, TX 75225
Contact: Carl Yeckel, Vice-President
Giving primarily in Dallas area.

Knight Foundation
One Biscayne Tower, Suite 3800
Two Biscayne Boulevard
Miami, FL 33131
(305) 539-2610
Limited to areas where Knight-Ridder newspa-
pers are published. Initial approach should be
through letter.

Thomas & Dorothy Leavey Foundation
4680 Wiltshire Boulevard
Los Angeles, CA 90010
(213) 930-4252
Contact: J. Thomas McCarthy, Trustee
Primarily in southern California, to Catholic
organizations.

Levi Strauss Foundation
1155 Battery Street
San Francisco, CA 94111
(415) 544-2194
Contacts: Bay Area: Judy Belk, Director of
   Contributions; Mid-South Region: Myra

Chow, Director of Contributions; Western Region: Mario Griffin, Director of Contributions; Rio Grande: Elvira Chavaria, Director of Contributions; Eastern Region: Mary Ellen McLoughlin, Director of Contributions
Generally limited to areas of company operations.

Lyndhurst Foundation
Suite 701, Tallan Building
100 West Martin Luther King Boulevard
Chattanooga, TN 37402-2561
(615) 756-0767
Contact: Jack E. Murrah, President
Limited to southeastern U.S., especially Chattanooga.

McDonnell Douglas Foundation
c/o McDonnell Douglas Corp.
P.O. Box 516, Mail Code 1001440
St. Louis, MO 63166
(314) 232-8464
Contact: Walter E. Diggs, Jr., President
Giving primarily in Arizona, California, Florida, Missouri, Oklahoma, & Texas.

James S. McDonnell Foundation
1034 South Brentwood Boulevard, Suite 1610
St. Louis, MO 63117
(314) 721-1532

Meadows Foundation, Inc.
Wilson Historic Block
2922 Swiss Avenue
Dallas, TX 75204-5928
(214) 826-9431
Contact: Dr. Sally R. Lancaster, Executive
    Vice-President
Limited to Texas.

The Milken Family Foundation
c/o Foundation of the Milken Families
15250 Ventura Boulevard, 2d floor
Sherman Oaks, CA 91403
Contact: Dr. Jules Lesner, Executive Director
Giving limited to Los Angeles area.

The New Hampshire Charitable Fund
One South Street
P.O. Box 1335
Concord, NH 03302-1335
(603) 225-6641
Contact: Deborah Cowan, Associate Director
Limited to New Hampshire.

The New Haven Foundation
70 Audubon Street
New Haven, CT 06510
(203) 777-2386
Contact: Helmer N. Ekstrom, Director
Giving primarily in greater New Haven and the lower Naugatuck River Valley.

Dellora A. & Lester J. Norris Foundation
P.O. Box 1081
St. Charles, IL 60174
(312) 377-4111
Contact: Eugene Butler, Treasurer
Funding includes secondary education.

The Northern Trust Company Charitable Trust
c/o The Northern Trust Company
Corporate Affairs Division
50 South LaSalle Street
Chicago, IL 60675
(312) 444-3538
Contact: Marjorie W. Lundy, Vice-President
Limited to metropolitan Chicago area.

The Principal Financial Group Foundation, Inc.
711 High Street
Des Moines, IA 50392-0150
(515) 247-5209
Contact: Debra J. Jensen, Secretary
Primarily in Iowa, with emphasis on the Des Moines area.

Z. Smith Reynolds Foundation, Inc.
101 Reynolds Village
Winston-Salem, NC 27106-5197
(919) 725-7541
Fax: (919) 725-6067
Contact: Thomas W. Lambeth, Executive Director
Limited to North Carolina. Will provide funding for special projects for K–12.

Sid W. Richardson Foundation
309 Main Street
Forth Worth, TX 76102
(817) 336-0497
Contact: Valleau Wilkie, Jr., Executive Vice-
    President
Limited to Texas.

R.J.R. Nabisco Foundation
1455 Pennsylvania Avenue, NW, Suite 525
Washington, DC 20004
(202) 626-7200
Contact: Jaynie M. Grant, Executive Director

The Winthrop Rockefeller Foundation
308 East Eighth Street
Little Rock, AR 72202
(501) 376-6854
Contact: Mahlon Martin, President
Funding primarily in Arizona, or for projects that
will benefit Arizona.

The San Francisco Foundation
685 Market Street, Suite 910
San Francisco, CA 94105-9716
(415) 495-3100
Contact: Robert M. Fisher, Director
Giving limited to the Bay Area counties of
Alameda, Contra Costa, Marin, San Francisco,
and San Mateo.

Community Foundation of Santa Clara County
960 West Hedding, Suite 220
San Jose, CA 95126-1215
(408) 241-2666
Contact: Winnie Chu, Program Officer
Limited to Santa Clara County, CA.

John & Dorothy Shea Foundation
655 Brea Canyon Road
Walnut, CA 91789
Giving primarily in California.

Harold Simmons Foundation
Three Lincoln Center
5430 LBJ Freeway, Suite 1700
Dallas, TX 75240-2697
(214) 233-1700
Contact: Lisa K. Simmons, President
Limited to Dallas area.

Sonart Family Foundation
15 Benders Drive
Greenwich, CT 06831
(203) 531-1474
Contact: Raymond Sonart, President

The Sosland Foundation
4800 Main Street, Suite 100
Kansas City, MO 64112
(816) 765-1000
Fax: (816) 756-0494
Contact: Debbie Sosland-Edelman, Ph.D
Limited to Kansas City areas of Missouri and
Kansas.

Community Foundation for Southeastern Michigan
333 West Fort Street, Suite 2010

Detroit, MI 48226
(313) 961-6675
Contact: C. David Campbell, Vice-President of
Programs
Giving limited to southeastern Michigan.

Springs Foundation, Inc.
P.O. Drawer 460
Lancaster, SC 29720
(803) 286-2196
Contact: Charles A. Bundy, President
Limited to Lancaster County and/or the town-
ships of Fort Mill and Chester, SC.

Steelcase Foundation
P.O. Box 1967
Grand Rapids, MI 49507
(616) 246-4695
Contact: Kate Pew Wolters, Executive Director
Limited to areas of company operations. Initial
contact by letter.

Strauss Foundation
c/o Fidelity Bank, N.A.
Broad & Walnut Streets
Philadelphia, PA 19109
(215) 985-7717
Contact: Richard Irvin, Jr.
Giving primarily in Pennsylvania.

Stuart Foundations
425 Market Street, Suite 2835
San Francisco, CA 94105
(415) 495-1144
Contact: Theodore E. Lobman, President
Primarily in California; applications from Washington will be considered.

T.L.L. Tempee Foundation
109 Tempee Boulevard
Lufkin, TX 75901
(409) 639-5197
Contact: M. F. Buddy Zeagler, Assistant Execu-
tive Director & Controller
Giving primarily in counties constituting the East
Texas Pine Timber Belt.

Travelers Companies Foundation
One Tower Square
Hartford, CT 06183-1060
(203) 277-4079
(203) 277-4070
Funding for school programs limited to Hartford.

Turrell Fund
111 Northfield Avenue
West Orange, NJ 07052
(201) 325-5108
Contact: E. Belvin Williams, Executive Director
Giving limited to New Jersey, particularly the northern urban areas centered in Essex County. Also giving in Vermont.

Philip L. Van Every Foundation
c/o Lance, Inc.
P.O. Box 32368
Charlotte, NC 28232
(704) 554-1421
Primarily in North Carolina and South Carolina.

Joseph B. Whitehead Foundation
1400 Peachtree Center Tower
230 Peachtree Street, NW
Atlanta, GA 30303
(404) 522-6755
Contact: Charles H. McTier, President
Giving limited to metropolitan Atlanta.

Winn-Dixie Stores Foundation
5050 Edgewood Court
Jacksonville, FL 32205
(904) 783-5000
Contact: Jack P. Jones, President
Limited to areas of company operation.

The Zellerbach Family Fund
120 Montgomery Street, Suite 2125
San Francisco, CA 94104
(415) 421-2629
Contact: Edward A. Nathan, Executive Director
Giving primarily in San Francisco Bay area.

This chapter includes a sampling of foundations that can be contacted for funding your curriculum project. By no means are these all the resources that can be tapped. Remember, think creatively! Are there any community service organizations such as the Jaycees, Lions Club, or Rotary International that can be contacted? Is there a local Community Fund that supports education projects? Ask friends and neighbors about the organizations they support. Ask if you can use their names as references—and be sure to get the names of the people to contact. Make many initial contacts, and don't be discouraged by rejections. The money is there for you; all you need is to be persistent!

References

The Foundation Directory. 1992. New York: Foundation Center.
Information about private and community grantmaking foundations in the US.

The Foundation Grants Index. 1992. New York: Foundation Center.
Provides funding patterns and other information about the most influential foundations in the US.

Government Assistance Almanac. 1992. Detroit, MI: Omnigraphics.
A comprehensive guide to federal programs that provide financial assistance.

Source Book Profiles. 1992. New York: Foundation Center.
Information on the one thousand largest U.S. foundations.

OUTLINE OF TOPICS AND SKILLS COVERED IN TEACHING ESL K–12

by Linda New Levine
Educational Consultant
Lake Katonah, New York

THERE is a great deal of diversity among public school curricula for ESL students in grades K–12. In many school districts serving a Limited English Proficiency (LEP) population, the language arts curriculum provides guidelines for instruction. In other districts, ESL teachers devise curricula based upon students' needs and published ESL texts. Still other districts have written curricula specifically for the LEP population.

Existing ESL curricula may be based upon the development of literacy skills, the development of listening and speaking skills, the development of content area information, or all three.

Because there is little uniformity in existing curricula, and because of the diversity of the population which is served by these curricula, writing a list of suggested topics and skills to be taught to the K–12 ESL population is a daunting task. I have no doubt that ESL practitioners in various parts of the country will question why certain skills and topics were included in this curriculum and others excluded.

In attempting to explain the selection and inclusion of topics and skills found here, I must explain the purpose of the curriculum as I see it. The intention of this chapter is to specify those topics and issues that are crucial components of

the ESL curriculum, separate and apart from the language arts curriculum of the school district. One of these issues is multicultural education. This topic introduces the curriculum because it provides a theoretical framework for all that follows. Other critical issues receiving explanation here include the content/language connection, the place for listening and speaking skill development within the learning package, and the problems and practices arising from the teaching of literacy skills to students who do not speak the language of the text.

I have chosen to highlight the thematic unit as the organizational structure around which this curriculum revolves. Current research and practice indicate that many ESL practitioners have begun to adopt a thematic, integrated approach to instruction and learning. This approach aligns itself nicely with the "whole language" emphasis on literacy and literature instruction in the English language arts curricula in general.

I realize, however, that not all practitioners agree on this philosophy. Many rely on a scope and sequence approach with an emphasis on specific skill development. As a result, there is an attempt to specify both thematic and skill development approaches in this curriculum. By doing so, I hope that the final product will be general enough to be of value to practitioners from all theoretical perspectives, and specific enough to provide ideas for the beginning ESL teacher in search of guidance.

As a result, there is a mixture of styles to be found in this curriculum. For example, I have included lists of thematic topics and suggested activities. The lists are accompanied by grade level designations. The grade level suggestions are to provide guidance for those teachers seeking information about what children at various grade levels can study and learn. More experienced teachers will probably find that the grade level designations are not universally applicable. For that reason, they are only suggestions, not specifications.

I have also included lists of skills by grade level. Once again, teachers in different districts may disagree with the notion of including discrete skills in an ESL curriculum at all. The skills are provided as suggestions and guidance for those teachers seeking direction. The scope and sequence are not, and were not meant to be, comprehensive. In fact, it is suggested that teachers use the Kraus *English Language Arts Curriculum Resource Handbook* to supplement this ESL curriculum in order to provide a full scope and sequence of the language arts for LEP students.

It should also be mentioned that non-English-speaking students enter the public school system at all grade levels. The initial needs of these students are similar whether they are in high school or in kindergarten. Both groups of students will need to understand the language of the school and communicate to others. Grade level designations are meaningless, therefore, when dealing with basic survival needs of students. Teachers should refer to the beginning skills listed here for K–2 students when dealing with new entrants.

I believe that it is most helpful to "spiral" curriculum for students. This means that teachers will teach the same concepts and skills to students at various times across the grade levels in an increasingly sophisticated way. Concepts and skills which are here designated for grades 3–5 may be entirely appropriate for students in middle school and high school when taught with more conceptually complex content. For this reason, again, the grade level designations are not meant to be fixed.

ESL Curriculum Topics

The ESL curricula in public school districts in the United States generally follow each district's language arts curriculum in scope and sequence. However, because educators understand that LEP students require more time to develop skills in the English language than their English-speaking peers, it is acknowledged that LEP students will not proceed at the same rate in the development of the language arts skills.

Many students in the United States are learning ESL within a bilingual setting. These students begin their language arts instruction in their native language and, at a later date, transfer their skills into the second language—English. For these students, the grade-level suggestions in the ESL curriculum may be different. In general, however, the sequence of skill acquisition will be the same.

Multicultural Education: An Overview

Access to Equity

An ESL curriculum will promote academic achievement in LEP students only to the extent that students have equal access to high quality, innovative instructional programs. TESOL International (Teachers of English to Speakers of Other Languages) has cited fourteen areas of access for LEP students through its policy statement, from the Task Force on Policy and Standards for Language Minority Students K–12, entitled "Is Your School Helping Its Language Minority Students To Meet the National Education Goals?" (In press). The access statements pertain to four broad areas of education: learning environment, curriculum, delivery of services, and assessment.

Access to Learning Environment

1. Are the schools attended by LEP students safe, attractive, and free of prejudice?

2. Is there evidence of a positive whole-school environment whose administrative and instructional policies and practices create a climate which is characterized by high expectations as well as linguistically and culturally appropriate experiences for LEP students?

3. Are teachers, administrators, and other staff specifically prepared to tailor instructional and other services to the needs of LEP students as well as being trained and qualified in their field?

4. Does the school environment welcome and encourage parents of LEP students as at-home primary teachers of their children and as partners in the life of the school? Does the school inform and educate parents and others concerned with the education of LEP students? Does the school systematically and regularly seek input from parents on information and decisions which affect all critical aspects of the education of LEP students and their schools and school districts?

Access to Curriculum

5. Do LEP students have access to special instructional programs which support the second-language development necessary for participating in the full range of instructional services offered to majority students?

6. Does the core curriculum designed for all students include those aspects that promote (1) the sharing, valuing, and development of both first and second languages and cultures among all students and (2) the higher-order thinking skills required for learning across the curriculum?

7. Do LEP students have access to the instructional programs and related services that identify, conduct, and support programs for special populations in a district? Such programs include, but are not limited to, early childhood programs, special education programs, and gifted and talented programs, as well as programs for students with handicapping conditions or disabilities, migrant education programs, programs for recent immigrants, and programs designed for students with low levels of literacy or mathematical skills, such as Chapter 1.

Access to Delivery of Services

8. Are the teaching strategies and instructional practices used with LEP students developmentally appropriate, attuned to students' language proficiencies and cognitive levels, and culturally supportive and relevant?

9. Do students have opportunities to develop and use their first language to promote academic and social development?

10. Are nonclassroom services and support services (such as counseling, career guidance, and student transportation) available to LEP students?

11. Does the school have institutional policies and procedures which are linguistically and culturally sensitive to the particular needs of ESL learners and their communities?

12. Does the school offer regular, nonstereo-typical opportunities for native English-speaking students and ESL learners to share and value each other's language and cultures?

Access to Assessment

13. Do LEP students have access to broadly based methods of assessing language and academic achievement in the content areas that are appropriate to students' age, developmental level, and level of oral and written language proficiency in the first and second languages? Are these measures unbiased and relevant? Are the results of assessments made understandable to the community from which the student comes, in the language of that community?

14. Do LEP students have access to broadly based methods of assessing special needs? Again, access is further defined by using measures that are unbiased, relevant, and understandable (TESOL In Press).

The Culturally Sensitive Curriculum

LEP students come from a variety of linguistic, cultural, and educational backgrounds. They enter the school system at varying ages, with varying levels of proficiency in their first and second languages. Schools and curricula need to accommodate the needs of this diverse population. It has already been pointed out that LEP students benefit from the following:

- a secure, caring learning environment conducive to building trust in the learner
- a whole language teaching/learning philosophy for literacy instruction
- a curriculum based upon the interests of the learners.

Other adaptations have been found helpful in effecting a culturally sensitive curriculum for LEP students.

1. Effective school curricula indicate an appreciation of cultural diversity on the part of the teacher and the school district. These curricula incorporate minority student languages and cultures in the school curriculum or both LEP and language majority students. Effective teachers of LEP students learn about the cultural backgrounds of their students. They use literature from the cultures of their students, teach content area lessons which are grounded in diversity, and provide opportunities for language majority students to learn about cultural diversity.

2. Effective school curricula include family members in the activities of the school. Parents

are used as resources for their children's learning. Teachers and parents collaborate on ways to promote the academic achievement of their children.

3. Effective curricula for LEP students appeal to a variety of learning styles. Just as English-speaking children come to school with different styles of learning, LEP students are stylistically and culturally diverse, including learners with sensory modality strength, global/analytic learners, and field-sensitive/field-independent learners.

Sensory Modality Strength. Among learners of this type are visual learners, auditory learners, and tactile-kinesthetic learners. *Visual learners* remember things they see or read. Although children from other cultures (Native American and Mexican, for example) indicate a preference for the visual learning style (Scarcella 1990, 116), most middle-American schools teach through verbal presentation. *Auditory learners* remember things they hear. Minority students with this learning style would be hard put to learn through verbal presentations they do not understand. Songs, poems, rhythmic activities, and recorded lessons may assist these learners. *Tactile-kinesthetic learners* remember things best when they manipulate materials with their hands, move their bodies, or write the material. Middle-American schools rarely support this learning modality except in the primary years. Culturally different older learners who display this learning preference will respond well to field trips, lab experiments, projects, and rote learning experiences accompanied by clapping.

Global/Analytic Learners. Global learners process information spatially. Often referred to as "top-down" learners, these students need to know and experience the big picture first, acquiring and filling in details at a later time. These learners seek patterns in new information and seek to develop relationships among facts. Chinese students, for example, demonstrate a preference for this thinking style (Scarcella 1991, 118).

Analytic learners prefer to process new information sequentially, in a linear and step-by-step fashion. Many middle Americans are thought to be analytic thinkers, processing facts instead of patterns, and many American school teachers structure learning in an analytic way.

Field-Sensitive/Field Independent Learners. Field sensitive learners enjoy working in a classroom environment where the curriculum is related and relevant to their own experiences. They enjoy working with and assisting others in groups toward a common goal, and are sensitive to the feelings and opinions of others. They rely on the guidance and modeling of the teacher. When presented with new information, they acquire it most readily when presented in a humanized story format. Many minority youngsters reflect this style, although most classrooms are not organized to accommodate it (Scarcella 1991, 120).

Field-independent learners like to work independently and enjoy competition with others. Most middle-American schools foster this learning style with a competitive approach to learning. These students enjoy dealing with new information in a discovery, trial-and-error mode. They restrict interactions with the teacher and focus on the details of the task at hand. The social environment of the learning experience is not primary for these students.

Summary

The research on diversity of learning and thinking style indicate that there is often a disparity between the home culture and the school culture of LEP children. In order to provide effective learning experiences for all children, classroom instruction and curricula must reflect the diversity of the population in the public schools.

Spencer Kagan (1992) and others have argued for the use of cooperative learning in classrooms as one way to create a more effective learning climate for all students. Kagan (1992, 2:9) cites the following benefits of cooperative learning for students:

- allows for improved comprehension of language
- allows for increased quantity and quality of language production
- allows greater access to the content curriculum
- allows increased comprehension of the content curriculum
- increases cross-ethnic friendships in the classrooms
- reduces self-segregation of minority students
- appeals to the preferred learning style of many language minority students

Integrating Content and Language Learning

Rationale

Language learning is most effective when it is a means of communicating meaningful information to children. Learning grammatical forms and structures is not meaningful to young children. However, children are naturally curious about animals, volcanoes, and the world around them. For this reason, ESL teachers suggest organizing language instruction around the content area subjects: social studies, science, mathematics, visual and performing arts, physical education, and literature.

In programs where students are not learning within a bilingual setting, it is imperative that students continue to learn content-related information while acquiring English skills in listening, speaking, reading, and writing.

Thematically integrated units of learning provide for varied language input to students, enabling them to acquire the varieties of language necessary for academic success. In addition, students are challenged cognitively through the acquisition of content information and are provided opportunities to develop learning strategies to as assist future learning.

Topic Selection

District curriculum guides in the content area subjects will provide guidance on appropriate topics. However, students may also be involved in topic selection. Student-generated topics will prove to be the most interesting to the learner. Teachers adept at integration will be able to adjust student interests to the needs of the district's curriculum mandates. The suggested topics below are based on a combination of student interest and general content focus.

Sample Thematic Units: Grades K–2

All About Me	Seasons	Friends
My Family	Reptiles	Fairy Tales
Monsters	Bears	Patterns
Apples	Same/Different	Wheels
My Community		

Sample Thematic Units: Grades 3–5

Jungle Life	Immigration	Diversity
Under the Sea	Colonial Life	Hero/ines
My State	The Prairie	My Country
Mysteries	The Tundra	
Native Americans		

Sample Thematic Units: Grades 6–8

Early Man	Empathy	War and Peace
The U.S.A.	Government	Immigration
Changes	Choices	Systems
Villains	Leadership	Symbols

Sample Thematic Units: Grades 9–12

Courage	Justice in Our Time
Success	Mysteries of Science
Transformations	America in the Future
Women in Our Time	The Individual in Society

Topic Sequencing for Cognitive Development

Cognition and language are thought to be inextricably related. The growth of a child's cognitive skills aids the development of language growth. At the same time, language development promotes a child's ability to conceptualize on a higher level. LEP students need to continue to develop cognitively while learning to speak English. ESL teachers, aware of this need for cognitive development, may structure thematic units using a hierarchy of cognitive thinking skills. The aim is to enable the child to deal with levels of thinking requiring recall and comprehension of language as well as with levels requiring the child to analyze, create, and evaluate information. Bloom's (1956) taxonomy is one cognitive structure that may be used for this purpose.

Thinking Level	Cue Words		Activities
Knowledge (Remembering previously learned material)	Observe Recall List Sort Outline	Match Define Cluster Record	Name the state. Define photosynthesis. Label the parts of a flower. List characteristics of Greek Drama.
Comprehension (Grasping the meaning)	Recognize Express Locate Paraphrase	Describe Report Tell Identify	Explain the life cycle of a butterfly. Summarize the story of . . . Identify the hero/ine. Explain how the digestive system works.
Application (Generalize: using the material in new and concrete situations)	Select Use Manipulate Sequence Organize	Imitate Dramatize Illustrate Show Demonstrate	Illustrate the setting of the story. Act out the fairy tale . . . Sequence the life cycle of a frog. Demonstrate the solution of a math problem on the board.
Analysis (Break down material so that it is more easily understood)	Examine Classify Outline Map Question	Analyze Compare Research Interpret Infer	Compare the two characters in . . . Map the best route for your vacation trip. Research the products of . . . Infer the reasons for the solution turning color.
Synthesis (Compose: putting material together to form a new whole)	Propose Plan Compose Formulate Invent	Construct Emulate Imagine Create	Construct a dinosaur that could swim and eat meat. Design a playground for our school. Propose a campaign platform. Design a contour map for an alien spacecraft landing pad.
Evaluation: (Judge: judging the value of material for a given purpose)	Compare Rank Judge Decide Rate Evaluate Predict	Criticize Argue Justify Convince Persuade Assess Value	Convince the class of the value of your product. Persuade your group to end the story your way. Decide which character is the most heroic. Evaluate the benefits of immigration. Rate the candidates for public office. Convince your elected representative of your position through a letter.

**A Sample Unit Integrating a
Content Topic and Cognitive Skill Objectives**

The sample thematic unit below is titled "Immigration." It is appropriate for students in grades 3–5 who are literate in their native languages and are developing literacy in English. This unit could be used with students after one year of exposure to English.

Listed below are a series of cognitive objectives for the unit. The objectives begin at the "knowledge" level of Bloom's hierarchy and proceed from there to higher levels.

Immigration
- recognize vocabulary relative to immigration experiences
- characterize a personal immigration experience
- organize immigration information on a graphic organizer
- interview a student to obtain immigration information
- characterize the immigration experience of another student
- compare immigration experiences
- describe the immigration experience of a historical figure
- analyze the immigration experiences studies and infer some common motivations for immigration

(Levine and Aronstam 1990, 48)

Sequencing for Language Development

In the past, the plan for language instruction followed a sequence of grammatical rules and sentence patterns. This view is widely questioned today (Stern 1983, 395). ESL teachers realize the value of learning language in content. Beginning language learners require language environments that are rich in concrete referents. They need to be able to work out the meaning of the language from the "here-and-now" context of the situation. Therefore, a good plan for sequencing instruction begins with practical experiences and language and leads to theoretical content and language. Billows describes how the learner's language is expanded from practical talk to theoretical talk by describing "four concentric spheres with the learner in the center" (Billows 1961, 9–12).

1. In the first sphere, the student uses language to describe "what the learner can see, hear, and touch directly. . . This is the classroom situation." The following activities are examples of Sphere I Talk which may be appropriate, but not limited, to the designated grade level.

Sphere I Talk: Grades K–2
　Show and Tell
　Jazz chants (Graham 1970)
　Action sequences (Total Physical Response) (Asher 1982)
　Plant seeds
Sphere I Talk: Grades 3–5
　Make models
　Science experiments
　Construct dioramas
　"Talk out" a computation problem
Sphere I Talk: Grades 6–8
　Cook
　Carpentry
　Shopping role play
　Physical education games and sports
Sphere I Talk: Grades 9–12
　Construct an engine
　Work on a computer
　Field trip to a museum
　Create a painting, jewelry, clay pot, etc.

2. In the second sphere, language centers on "what the learner knows from his own experience, his daily life, what he has seen and heard directly but cannot see or hear at the moment." This language derives from the home and the neighborhood. Learners can be reminded of these experiences through a combination of words and classroom experiences.

Sphere II Talk: Grades K–2
　Describe a family
　Remember holiday events
　Report about pets
　Describe meals
Sphere II Talk: Grades 3–5
　Remember native customs
　Recall weather-related events
　Describe a movie
Sphere II Talk: Grades 6–8
　List and illustrate a family tree
　Teach a game or a sport
　Describe a childhood memory
　Compare daily life in two different countries
Sphere II Talk: Grades 9–12
　Describing the topography of a native country
　Recalling immigration experiences
　Comparing schools in the native country and the U.S.A.
　Recalling a recipe

3. The third sphere requires language to describe what the learner "has not yet experienced directly, but what he can call to mind with an effort of the imagination, with the help of pictures, dramatization, charts and plans."

Sphere III Talk: Grades K–2

Describe a farm
List ocean animals
Describe beach activities
Talk about ghosts

Sphere III Talk: Grades 3–5

Describe the American plains
Compare a polar bear to a brown bear
Contrast a Navajo hogan to a log cabin
Explain how a volcano erupts

Sphere III Talk: Grades 6–8

Characterize Greek and Roman dress
Explain the circulatory system of a mammal
Describe the process of photosynthesis
Compare population of the United States with other countries'

Sphere III Talk: Grades 9–12

Characterize a plant cell and an animal cell
Describe the topography of Africa
Explain four simple machines
Watch a play and summarize the plot

4. The fourth sphere uses language to discuss "what is brought to mind through the spoken, written, or printed word alone, without help through visual aids." At this stage of language development, students are ready to make the transition to the mainstream language arts class.

Sphere IV Talk: Grades K–2

Recite a poem
Recall a fairy tale
Write a letter
Listen to a story without pictures

Sphere IV Talk: Grades 3–5

Read a textbook
Write a report
Cook from printed directions
Put together a model using printed directions.

Sphere IV Talk: Grades 6–8

Write a summary of a chapter
Read a story and describe the heroine
Conduct a science experiment from a written description

Sphere IV Talk: Grades 9–12

Outline a text chapter
Take notes from a lecture
Study for a test from notes
Conduct library research

A Sample Unit Integrating Content, Cognitive Objectives, and Practical and Theoretical Spheres of Talk

The Immigration Unit which is used here as a sample unit is organized to proceed from children's practical experiences to theoretical content, language, and concept. The cognitive objectives below are grouped into Spheres II, III, and IV Talk.

No Sphere I Talk introduces this unit because the children have already achieved some communicative and productive ability in English. Even at this level however, Sphere I talk is useful to children who are learning concepts that are new to them.

Sample Immigration Unit

Sphere II Talk

Objectives
1. Recognize vocabulary relative to immigration experiences.
2. Characterize a personal immigration experience.
3. Organize personal immigration information on a graphic organizer.

Activities
1. Students share pictures of family in the native country.
2. Students recall and tell each other their immigration experiences.
3. Students organize personal immigration information on a graphic organizer.

Sphere III Talk

Objectives
1. Interview a student to obtain immigration information.
2. Characterize the immigration experience of another student.
3. Compare immigration interview experiences.

Activites
1. Formulate a set of questions with which to interview students.
2. Interview the teacher.
3. Conduct student interviews.
4. Organize information on a graphic organizer.
5. Orally report interview from the graphic organizer.

6. Write a summary paragraph from the graphic organizer.
7. Illustrate the report.
8. Tell how the two experiences (personal and the other students') are the same and different.
9. Chart similarities and differences on a Venn diagram.

Sphere IV Talk

Objectives
1. Describe the immigration experience of a historical figure.
2. Analyze the immigration experiences studied and infer some common motivations for immigration.
3. Create a time line.

Activities
1. Read the life of a famous immigrant; write and answer questions about the reading.
2. Use a Venn diagram to chart similarities between the immigrant's history and the student's history, and list common experiences among all immigrants studied.
3. Organize imigrants life experiences on a time line, and write a chronological report on the life of a famous immigrant.
4. Illustrate the report of create a diorama.
(Levine and Aronstam 1990, 48–55)

Components of a Thematic Curriculum

Thematic ESL curricula contain several objectives to ensure that students are learning ina variety of areas. The majority of thematic curricula contain three categories of objectives:
• Content Area Objectives
• Language Objectives
• Learning Strategy Objectives

Content Area Objectives: a combination of the content-area goal and a cognitive skill level (see Bloom's taxonomy).
• Name the continents of the world.
• Locate the continents.
• Organize the continents into two groups: the northern hemisphere and the southern hemisphere.

• Characterize the climate of the continents in relation to their distance from the equator.
• Imagine that you were born on another continent. How would your life be different?
• Compare the pros and cons of life on two different continents and decide which lifestyle you prefer.

Language Objectives: can be described according to the grammatical form, grammatical function, sentence pattern, or all three.
Sample grammatical forms include:
• "Going to" future
• Simple present tense
• Who, What, When, Where, Why questions
• Tag questions

Sample grammatical functions include:
• Requesting
• Criticizing
• Persuading
• Commanding

Sample sentence patterns include:
• X + BE + noun phrase
• Third person plural + BE + adjective
• Verb + to + Verb
• Used to + Verb

Learning Strategy Objectives: Three categories of learning strategies are reported to be useful for LEP students (Chamot and O'Malley 1992):
• Metacognitive Strategies
• Cognitive Strategies
• Social–Affective Strategies
Chamot and O'Malley (1992, 55–56) define these strategies as follows:

Metacognitive Strategies:
1. Advance organization — Previewing the main ideas and concepts of the material to be learned, often by skimming the text for the organizing principle.
2. Organizational planning — Planning the parts, sequence, main ideas, or language functions to be expressed orally or in writing.
3. Selective attention — Deciding in advance to attend to specific aspects of input, often by scanning for key words, concepts, and/or linguistic markers.

4. Self-monitoring — Checking one's comprehension during listening or reading to checking the accuracy and/or appropriateness of one's oral or written production while it is taking place.
5. Self-evaluation — Judging how well one has accomplished a learning activity after it has been completed.

Cognitive Strategies:
1. Resourcing — Using target language reference materials, such as dictionaries, encyclopedias, or textbooks.
2. Grouping — Classifying words, terminology, or concepts according to their attributes.
3. Note taking — Writing down key words and concepts in abbreviated verbal, graphic, or numerical form during a listening or reading activity.
4. Summarizing — Making a mental, oral, or written summary of information gained through listening or reading.
5. Deduction/induction — Applying rules to understand or produce the second language or making up rules based on language analysis.
6. Imagery — Using visual images (either mental or actual) to understand and remember new information.
7. Auditory representation — Playing back in one's mind the sound of a word, phrase, or longer language sentence.
8. Elaboration — Relating new information to prior knowledge, relating different parts of new information to each other, or making meaningful personal associations with the new information.
9. Transfer — Using previous linguistic knowledge or prior skills to assist comprehension or prediction.
10. Inferencing — Using information in an oral or written text to guess meanings, predict outcomes, or complete missing parts.

Social-Affective Strategies:
1. Questioning for clarification — Eliciting from a teacher or peer additional explanation, rephrasing, examples, or verification.
2. Cooperation — Working together with peers to solve a problem, combine

information, check a learning task, model a language activity, or get feedback on oral or written performance.
3. Self-talk — Reducing anxiety by using mental techniques that make one feel competent to do the learning task.

Sample Unit Integrating Three Kinds of Objectives: Content Objectives, Language Objectives, Learning Strategy Objectives

The cognitive skill objectives have been listed in the sample Immigration Unit and grouped with their respective appropriate activities.

In this section, language objectives will be identified as appropriate to the unit. Learning stategy objectives to the specifically tught in the unit will also be identified. The many other learing stategies that could be used during the unit are not targeted for specific instruction in this unit. In actual practice, teachers will select language and learning style objectives by criteria such as (1) What do my students need to learn to be successful? and (2) What objectives are appropriate to the topic and the grade level?

Language

Objectives
1. Past tense regular and irregular verbs (e.g. immigrate, marry, die, to be born), active and passive voice
2. Learn information questions (who, what, when, where, why)
3. Sequence words of chronology (later, soon, next, first, finally)
4. Adverbial clauses of time (in 1985, after two years, etc.)
5. Compound sentences of comparison and contrast (and . . . too, also, but, how ever, although, etc.)

Activities
1. Talk about all past immigration experiences.
2. Interview another student or the teacher.
3. Ask and answer questions about a famous immigrant.
4. Tell and write about personal experiences, other students' experiences, and the experiences of a famous immigrant.
5. Tell and write about how two immigration experiences are the same and different.

Learning Strategy

Objectives
    1. Organizational planning
    2. Summarizing
    3. Questioning for clarification

Activities
    1. Organize immigration information on a graphic organizer divided into major topics.
    2. Organize information on a Venn diagram to show comparison and contrast.
    3. Create oral and written summaries of information gained through listening to student experiences or through reading about a famous immigrant.
    4. Ask information questions during an interview with another students.
    5. Ask information questions after reading about a famous immigrant.
    (Levine and Aronstam 1990, 48–55)

Listening Skills

Classroom listening skills fall into three main types:
    1. listening with attention
    2. listening with understanding
    3. listening with discrimination

Optimal Input

The process of language acquisition begins with the receptive understanding of language. In classroom situations, acquisition is enhanced when teachers provide listening situations characterized by "optimal input" (Krashen 1988, 333). Krashen cites characteristics of teacher/classroom input that aid acquisition of language:
1. Language is comprehensible
   - speak at a slower rate
   - articulate clearly
   - repeat high-frequency vocabulary
   - eliminate slang and idioms
   - use short, simple sentences
   - use objects and pictures to convey meaning
   - use facial and body gestures
   - use the blackboard and charts
   - talk about what is known to the learner
   - speak about what is happening "here and now"

2. Language is interesting and/or relevant
   - focus on topics of interest to the learner
   - design curriculum based on student input
   - design curriculum based on student age and not on language ability
   - avoid prescriptive textbooks
3. Language is not grammatically sequenced
   - focus on the meaning of the language
   - avoid teaching language rules
4. Language must be used frequently
   - provide many formal listening experiences
   - require the learner to actively respond in a nonverbal way to the listening activity
   - provide frequent listening activities, although they may be short

Grade-Level Skills

The skills that follow indicate the emphasis on teaching and learning of the skills in many districts' language arts curricula. The grade levels can be used as skill level indicators for students of any age: K-12, beginning level; 3-5, intermediate level; 6-8, upper intermediate level; 9-12, advanced level. ESL teachers will spiral these skills across grade levels according to the needs of the students. The list is not exhaustive, nor is the sequence meant to be restrictive.

Grades K–2
   - attend to teacher language
   - attend to directional language
   - attend to stories/poems/songs
   - understand word/phrase meanings
   - understand story sequence
   - understand explanations
   - discriminate letters, sounds, numerals

Grades 3–5, all of the above plus
   - attend to the main idea
   - attend to rhyme and rhythm
   - attend to specific information
   - attend to transitions: sequence, comparison, cause/effect
   - discriminate rhyme, alliteration, onomatopoeia
   - discriminate prefixes, suffixes
   - discriminate fact from opinion
   - discriminate tone
   - understand main idea
   - understand transitions
   - understand an oral presentation

Grades 6–8, all of the above plus
- discriminate emotional content
- discriminate speaker motive and point of view
- discriminate bias
- discriminate between main idea and supporting details
- discriminate theme
- understand metaphor
- understand decontextualized oral language

Grades 9–12, all of the above plus
- discriminate organizational language (signal words) for cause/effect, comparison, chronology, exposition
- understand language register (formal, informal)

Activities

These activities are listed to provide ideas for teachers. Although the activites increase in difficulty, some of the elementary activities may be appropriate at the higher grades.

Grades K–2
- directional routines requiring a physical response (Simon Says)
- Total Physical Response routines (Asher 1982)
- show and tell
- picture bingo

Grades 3–5
- directional drawing activities
- bingo
- preview questions
- listen and clap (for specific words, numbers, etc.)

Grades 6–8
- listen and write (specific prefixes, suffixes, signal words)
- dictation
- solicit information on the telephone
- note taking

Grades 9–12
- outline oral presentations
- summarize radio/television news programs
- summarize speeches

Speaking Skills

The Beginnings of Speech

LEP students begin to speak in English as they acquire receptive understanding of language. Depending on age, personality, educational background, and ethnicity, students will engage in a silent period in the classroom prior to the onset of speech. Classroom conditions that promote the development of speaking skills include:
- a secure, caring environment
- a speaker(s)/listener(s) who provides optimal input
- an interactional classroom environment characterized by small cooperative groups
- a motivation for speaking

Grade-Level Skills

LEP students enter school with limited speaking skills at all grade levels. These students begin the speech acquisition process with limited grammar and vocabulary, and gradually acquire and learn more as they progress in their language development. The skills below are labeled with function words rather than grammatical forms. This is done to indicate the types of language functions that are emphasized at different grade levels in the language arts curriculum. It should be understood, however, that students at all grade levels begin the speech process by expressing functions that are identified here as K–2 functions: naming objects, repeating utterances, etc. Therefore, the sequence of the following suggested activities is not inflexible and the grade level designations are not meant to be rigid. It is also to be expected that students will expand their vocabularies as they progress in school learning; thus, the examples of speech functions that follow are suggesons and do not represent a complete listing.

Grades K–2
- label objects
- repeat utterances
- tell a story
- describe self
- explain feelings/motivations
- recount how to do something

Grades 3–5, all of the above plus
- perform drama, poetry, choral reading, etc.
- demonstrate knowledge of grammatical rules
- read orally

- describe (outside of self)
- summarize experiences, stories, movies
- express and respond to feeling appropriately
- use a variety of appropriate registers (formal/informal)
- make an oral presentation
- express a variety of language functions (express feelings, ritualize, imagine, inform, control)

Grades 6–8, all of the above plus
- analyze literature
- participate in group discussions
- debate/defend a point of view
- question for specific information
- characterize events, people, processes
- criticize appropriately
- manipulate language with purpose (humor)

Grades 9–12, all of the above plus
- speculate on new ideas, plans, etc.
- persuade an audience
- compare with pros and cons

Activities

These speech development activites are suggestions that are appropriate, but not limited, to the sugested grade level.

Grades K–2
- singing songs
- group chants (poems, rhythmic chants, finger plays)
- dictate language experience stories
- role play stories

Grades 3–5
- give directions for a game or a demonstration
- answer questions in a quiz show
- give an oral report with visuals
- interview a family member or fellow student

Grades 6–8
- anchor a news program
- role play a scene from literature
- question a guest speaker
- debate an issue from a content area class

Grades 9–12
- persuade an audience to buy your product
- criticize the school lunch program
- compare two political systems
- tell a classmate how to get a driver's license

Reading Skills

LEP students who are already literate in a language other than English will be able to transfer the reading skills they have already acquired in the first language. For example, Spanish-speaking students who enter school in the sixth grade may have already acquired decoding skills, context skills, and comprehension skills. Even though these skills have been learned in Spanish, they will transfer to the process of reading in English. Teachers, therefore, do not need to begin the progression of reading skill development form the kindergarten level with all entering LEP students.

Students who have never learned to read in any language and are beginning to read in a second language, English, will require considerably more time to progress through the scope and sequence of the language arts reading curriculum.

The following sequence of skills and activities is based on the needs of an illiterate beginning student of English. The most effective approach to reading for the illiterate LEP student in the absence of a bilingual instructional program is one based on meaning rather than discrete skill instruction. Teaching and learning techniques that are helpful for LEP students at all grade levels include:
- the language experience approach
- shared reading
- integration of the four skill areas of listening, speaking, reading, writing
- interactional journals

Although illiterate LEP students may have a poor command of the English grammar and sound system, they do have a knowledge of the world around them. This world of meaning can be utilized in the classroom to build oral language development and reading skills through the language experience approach, whole language reading, and thematic teaching. The following chart of the four states of oral language and reading competency (Hansen-Krening 1982, 4–6) illustrates the place of meaning and discrete skill instruction within the oral language framework of the student. As students progress linguistically in English, the reading program gradually increases the emphasis upon specific decoding and comprehension skills.

Stage 1

Language Arts
- Listens to others talk
- Uses one to three words to communicate concepts
- Responds well to peer teaching
- Combines pictures with word labels
- Needs many opportunities to hear spoken language
- Needs survival language
- Learns songs and chants
- Enjoys art and can label artistic creations
- Enjoys working with rhythms
- Pantomimes

Reading
- Needs to hear stories daily
- Needs to see association between spoken/printed word
- "Reads" wordless picture books
- Listens to taped stories
- Reads word labels
- Reads own name
- Labels science experiments
- Points to locations on maps and globes
- Plays word/alphabet games

Stage 2

Language Arts
- Listens carefully, speaks in small groups
- Works with rhymes and rhythms
- Continues to rely on peers
- Needs teacher direction
- Dictates three to five word sentences
- Tells simply stories
- Writes brief invitations
- Makes code switches
- Helps write simple reports
- Gives brief oral reports telling sequence of events
- Enjoys role playing
- Uses present tense almost exclusively

Reading
- Ready for the language experience approach
- Develops sight word vocabulary
- Reads three to five word stories
- Dictates science and social studies language experience stories

- Works with simple context clues
- Sequences events
- Retells stories at recall level

Stage 3

Language Arts
- Listens/speaks purposely
- Uses language for problem solving in discussion, reporting, questioning
- Gives oral/written reports on old and new information
- Uses present/past tenses when needed
- Begins to write independently
- Expresses self spontaneously
- Debates both sides of an issue
- Distinguishes between functional and creative writing
- Performs operations with syntax
- Writes poetry
- Dramatizes
- Uses appropriate language for audience/situation

Reading
- Learns high-utility phonics
- Reads from basal readers
- Uses inferencing
- Progresses to independent reading
- Reads in the content area with advance organizers

Stage 4

Language Arts
- Anticipates audience in oral language
- Selects effective language for audience
- Labels/manipulates parts of speech
- Proofreads and edits
- Uses a variety of language genre

Reading
- Reads critically
- Identifies prejudicial language
- Predicts alternative outcomes
- Hypothesizes beyond the end of a story
- Analyses different forms and purposes of writing
- Reads independently

Grade-Level Skills

The reading skills listed here do not follow a fixed sequence of development, nor are they restricted to the designated grade level. ESL teachers may choose to spiral these skills according to student need and the nature of the reading text.

Grades K–2
- recognize letter names
- recognize high-frequency sight words
- read language experience stories
- read well-known poems, chants, rhymes
- recognize words beginning with similar consonant sounds

Grades 3–5, all of the above plus
- alphabetize, using dictionary
- read synonyms/antonyms, compound words, contractions
- identify high-frequency prefixes, suffixes, root words
- recognize the main idea and supporting facts
- sequence events
- use context clues for vocabulary meaning
- predict outcomes
- use inference

Grades 6–8, all of the above plus
- recognize persuasive devices
- develop greater skill in using affixes for word meanings
- use foreign cognates as clues to word meanings
- use reference tools: library, index, glossary, appendices
- get information from a variety of graphic sources: tables, lists, charts, graphs, time-lines, flow charts
- evaluate reading material

Grades 9–12, all of the above plus
- use a wide range of reference materials: atlas, encyclopedia, almanac, bibliography
- determine author point of view
- recognize propaganda
- read texts which are increasingly decontextualized
- expand vocabulary in the content areas

Reading across the Content Areas

Reading in specific content areas provides students with the opporunity to develop greater facility with a wide variety of vocabulary, grammatical structures, and text organization. The sample activites listed here provide ideas for teachers. The list is not exhaustive and ESL teachers will choose activites according to student learning needs, not necessarily by grade-level designation.

Grades K–2
Literature
- read story pictures
- read wordless picture books
- illustrate, pantomime, paint, or make a collage of a story
- read stories in a shared reading experience with teacher
- read predictable, patterned books
- relate self to literature
- discuss plot and/or role play
- discuss, illustrate, or impersonate characters
- illustrate or describe setting
- retell stories
- distinguish fact from fiction
- create a new ending for a story
- identify a genre (fairy tale, nonfiction)

Social Studies
- dictate and read stories about a locality: town, zoo, farm
- dictate and read stories about school and school behavior
- dictate and read stories about children in other countries
- dictate and read stories about children who lived long ago

Science
- label and read pictures relating to the five senses, parts of the body, and parts of plants.
- dictate and read the steps of a science experiment.
- dictate and read observations about nature (leaves, shadows, weather)

Grades 3–5
Literature
- read freely selected tradebooks
- read a variety of genre: biography, fiction, nonfiction, etc.
- compare/contrast two works from one genre read and discuss plot, character, setting, outcome, author point of view
- read orally to interpret character and meaning

- differentiate fact from opinion
- discern character motive

Social Studies
- contrast Pilgrim immigration to student's immigration experience
- read about the American Revolution and role play a conversation between George Washington and King George of England
- read about the geography of your state and plan a vacation with your family

Science
- read newspaper weather reports and graph the weather
- read books and poems about snow while studying the water cycle
- read books and poems about butterflies while watching a pupa make a cocoon in your classroom

Grade 6–8
Literature
- read literary classics and young adult books in a shared reading experience in your classroom
- list characteristics of characters
- compare two books with similar themes
- sequence the chronology of events in a text
- explain character motive based on plot events
- change literary form: poem to story, play to essay

Social Studies
- read about historical hero/ines and compare to hero/ines in the students' lives
- read accounts of historical events in textbooks and compare to biographical accounts of the same events
- read about the cultures of the native countries of LEP student and compare to American culture

Science
- read about a process (e.g., blood circulation) and create a poster to illustrate the concept
- correctly sequence the steps of a laboratory experiment
- read the biography of a scientist from your native country

Grades 9-12
Literature
- study the works of a significant writer
- recognize satire, irony, symbolism, imagery
- begin to employ criteria for literary criticism
- continue to use and expend the objectives from grades 6–8, when appropriate

Social Studies
- conduct research to answer a question
- read and discuss newspaper accounts of current events
- read about and compare alternative systems of government

Science
- read about biological systems and represent on a flow chart
- read newspaper accounts of environmental disasters and debate
- read about a recent scientific breakthrough and relate how it will change your life

Patterns of Text Organization

LEP students are generally introduced to a wider variety of text beginning in grade 3 (intermediate). Reading in the content areas at that grade level and beyond presents greater difficulties in comprehension. Students at this level may be reading about information that they have not personally experienced. In addition, vocabulary expands to express the specific meanings necessary for content learning. Text and tradebooks use forms of syntax and sentence structure that are not commonly heard in oral language. The language of textbooks is referred to as Cognitive Academic Language Proficiency (CALP) and is viewed as necessary for academic success in schools (Cummins 1992, 17). LEP students speak in variations of oral English that rely on the context of the situation to explicate meaning. Basic Interpersonal Communication Skills (BICS) are acquired by LEP students from the formal and informal language of the environment (Cummins 1992, 17). There is not a high degree or correlation between the acquisition of BICS and academic achievement in schools. For this reason, it is necessary for LEP students to become familiar with the world of textbooks and tradebooks. These texts are good models of CALP, and it is through reading and understanding text that LEP students will acquire the specific vocabulary, grammar, sentence patterns, and knowledge of textbook organizational patterns to become academically successful. The following patterns of textbook organization, and the words that convey and signal organizational and transitional meanings are listed below.

Patterns of Organization (Mikulecky 1985, 270–71)

1. Time Order (chronology, sequence)
   Signal words:

first	soon	later on
next	afterward	later
finally	not long after	last
in the end	eventually	at last
in the meantime	right away	dates
in the beginning	at the end	times

Organizational frames can be used to assist students further in reading and learning specific information from texts. An organizational frame is a structure, such as a graph or timeline, that sets a purpose for student learning and directs reading by visually indicating important concepts and transitions (Levine 1991, 122).

The following organizational frames are useful for the time order pattern or organization:

Timelines

John F. Kennedy

1917	Born in Massachusetts
1952	Elected to Senate for first time
1960	Elected President
1962	Cuban Missile Crisis
1963	Assassinated in Dallas, Texas

5W matirx

who	what	when	where	why

2. Comparison and Contrast (Mikulecky 1985, 272-273)
   Signal words:

faster than	yet	but
different	rather	instead
however	bigger	yet
on the contrary	similarly	like
on the other hand	as	
contrary to	in the same way	

Organizational frames that are helpful to understanding the comparison/contrast pattern are:

Comparison chart

	Hunters	Gatherers
Food Supply		
Shelter		
Division of Labor		
Social Structure		

Venn diagram

Frog   Tadpole

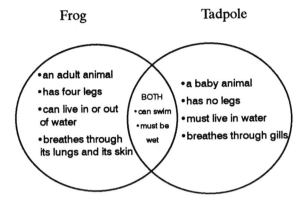

Structured overview

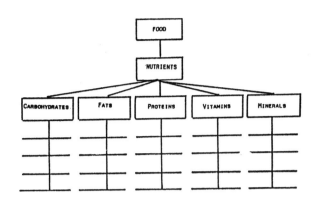

3.   Simple Listing (Mikulecky, 1985, 273-274)
    Signal words:

many	for examples	others
all	include	many
in addition	such as	a few
also		

The organizational frames useful for comprehending the simple listing pattern are:

Semantic map

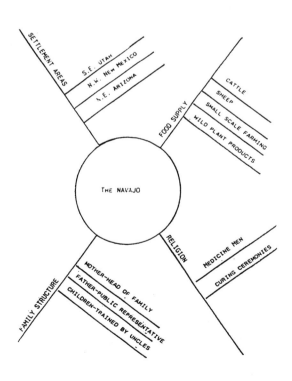

Concept ladder

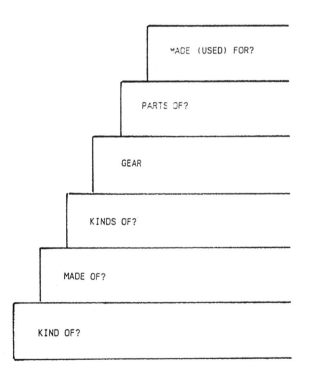

4.   Cause and Effect (Mikulecky 1985, 274-275)
    Signal words:

as a result (of)	cause (of)	lead to
result in	due to	effect of
because (of)		

Cause and effect organizational frames include:

Flowchart

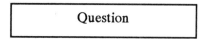

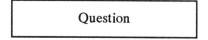

Flowchart with multiple causes

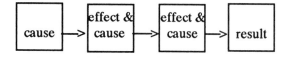

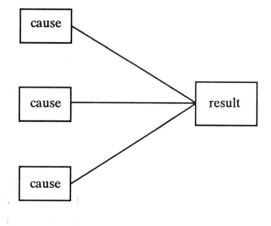

Writing Skills

The Writing Process

The revolution in writing instruction called "the writing process" is widely accepted in public schools across the United States today. Teachers of LEP students have found the process, with some modifications, to be successful with LEP students. Writing at grade-level ability is the last of the language skills to develop in LEP students. It may take many years of instruction for these students to achieve grade-level competency in writing. Nevertheless, even beginning level students can participate in the writing experience.

Hudelson (1986, 26–29) has summarized what we have learned about LEP students and the writing process:

1. Young, beginning-level LEP students can begin to compose in English before they have mastered control over the forms of the language.
2. LEP students are capable of creating different kinds of writing pieces for different purposes, especially when they are required to write in different content areas.
3. LEP students are able to revise and edit their writing even while they struggle to communicate.
4. LEP students will respond to the writing expectations of their teachers in the same way as English-speaking students.
5. Growth in writing development varies widely in LEP students, based on personality, ethnic, native language, family, and community differences.

Six Steps of the Writing Process

Enright and McCloskey (1988, 187–188) remind us of the steps of the writing process, which are helpful for LEP students. These six steps are applicable to student writers in grades K–12.

Step 1: Prewriting
   Prewriting helps students discover they have something to say; motivates them to write; helps them acquire the necessary information and content; and provides them with vocabulary, syntax, and writing structures. Helpful activities at this stage include:
   • shared experiences, such as a trip, an interview, or cooking activity.
   • the reading of literature
   • fantasy experiences, such as role playing, puppetry.
   • brainstorming of words and ideas
   • creating word webs to show relationships
   • debating different points of view

Step 2: Drafting
   In drafting, an idea from prewriting is given form. Writing is done quickly, and students are not concerned with mechanics. Invented spellings are used. Teachers can assist students by:
   • modeling the writing process for students— on charts, on the blackboard, or in a notebook.

- modeling different types of writing for students:
    1. expressive writing
    2. poetic/literary writing
    3. transactional writing

Step 3: Sharing and responding to writing:

At this stage, students seek audience feedback. The teacher creates a sense of audience in a number of ways:
- students writing together in pairs
- students writing together in large groups
- students writing together with the teacher
- large group discussion of an anonymous piece of writing on the overhead projector
- peer conference groups
- individual teacher conferences
- interactive (dialogue) journal writing

Step 4: Revising:

Students select pieces of writing to revise for quality of content and clarity of expression. The pieces are revised with a particular audience in mind. Some activities that may occur during this stage include:
- teacher demonstration of cutting/pasting techniques
- use of the word processor to make revisions
- mini-lessons on aspects of good writing, such as clarity, voice, sense of audience, sequencing, word choice, transition words, beginning and ending sentences

Step 5: Editing:

Students impose correctness on their writing in terms of the mechanics of usage and spelling. Standards will vary depending on the age of students and their language abilities . Students engage in editing activities only when the piece is going to be published for an audience. Editing activities include:
- following an editing checklist chart
- working in an editing center
- participating in an editing conference with the teacher or another student
- using a spelling dictionary or personal spelling list

Step 6: Publishing

Student writing is presented to an audience for celebration. Young students' work is occasionally published in draft form, sometimes with a reminder that the work is "in progress." Older students and more proficient students will more often revise and edit in order to publish finished pieces. Publishing can include:
- students performing a play they have written
- putting a story into the class library
- putting writing on hallway bulletin boards
- reading to another class, parent group, or over the intercom
- making a video
- making a class book, newspaper, or literary magazine

Writing across the Curriculum

LEP students need to have many opportunities to write in different content areas and for a variety of functions or purposes. In this section, five basic language functions will be integrated with content area objectives. The suggested writing activities that follow are examples of ways to integrate the development of writing functions as well as content area objectives. The activities listed are intended to promote ideas. ESL teachers may wish to select activities from a variety of grade level designations according to student need. The five functions are:
1. to express self—to express personal feelings, reactions, values, interests, or attitudes
2. to narrate—to tell a fictional story or give an account of a real event, first by dictating (as in the language experience approach), then by writing
3. to explain—to make factual information clear
4. to describe—to use words that appeal to the senses
5. to persuade—to change opinion or influence action

Grades K–2

Literature

to express self
- write a letter to a character in a story
- draw your favorite scene in a story and label it

to narrate
- write what happens in your family when you lose a tooth
- take home the class teddy bear and write down all the things s/he did on the visit

to explain
- explain how Little Red Riding Hood was fooled by the wolf
- explain why the three bears didn't eat their breakfast right away

to describe
- describe how it feels to "stick in your thumb and pull out a plum"
- describe what porridge tastes like

to persuade
- write to Goldilocks and convince her not to enter the bears' house
- list reasons why the teacher should read your book choice at reading time

Social Studies and Science
to express self

- write how it felt to immigrate to another country
- compare ways in which your native town and your new town are the same/different
- list the fruits that taste best to you
- write about your favorite season

to narrate
- write your personal immigration story
- list the different kinds of stores in your new town
- name your tadpole and tell about its daily life
- write a story about a raindrop

to explain
- explain how to cross streets safely
- tell some of the differences between a town and a city
- explain how reptiles are the same
- tell how a tadpole turns into a frog

to describe
- describe the objects in the sky at night tell how you feel on the beach in the summertime
- describe snow
- tell how objects in the Feely Box felt

to persuade
- decide whether you would rather live in the city or the suburbs and tell why
- choose a zoo animal that you think is the most dangerous and convince a friend to

agree with your choice
- list the vegetables for our class salad and convince your group to agree with your choice

Grades 3–5:
Literature
to express self
- choose a character from the story and complete the sentence: "If I were . . . I would . . . "
- write a poem about your feelings

to narrate
- write an animal fable about the class pet rabbit
- write a skit to act out in class

to explain
- rewrite a fairy tale into a news article with a headline
- write a book report

to describe
- describe what you think the character in the story looks like
- write an advertisement describing your lost pet

to persuade
- tell your friend why s/he should read your book
- write to Wilbur (*Charlotte's Web*) and convince him that he is "some pig"

Social Studies and Science
to express self
- pretend you are a Pilgrim and write a letter home
- write a poem about a holiday
- tell how you feel when it rains, snows, or is sunny
- express your reaction to a recent weather disaster

to narrate
- write a story about crossing the plains
- tell what happened at the Boston Tea Party
- write a story about the migration of a salmon
- interview a plant, tree, or flower, and tell the story

to explain
- write a report on the English colonies
- tell how Columbus traveled to the American continent
- tell how rain occurs
- tell how plants get food

to describe
- describe life in a colonial log house
- describe the food at the first Thanksgiving
- describe a hurricane
- describe the weather of the desert, tundra, or mountains

to persuade
- convince your colonial husband/wife not to emigrate
- tell reasons why your state is the best for LEP students
- choose the most important scientist and give reasons for your choice
- write letters to local representatives to begin a recycling program

Grades 6–8:

Literature

to express self
- read a biography and tell why you like the subject
- write about this class in your journal

to narrate
- write a story on the theme of "Diversity"
- write your autobiography

to explain
- write a deductive essay explaining your point of view on an issue
- explain the motivations of a fictional character or historical figure (such as Helen Keller's wild behavior as a child)

to describe
- using facts from piece of fiction, describe the setting
- write a "job wanted" advertisement for a fictional character that describes his or her talents and skills

to persuade
- view a movie version of a novel and tell which you prefer
- read two stories from your native country

and tell which is the most typical of your culture

Social Studies and Science

to express
- tell which historical figure is a hero/ine to you
- tell how you would feel as a man/woman in a hunting/gathering society
- pretend you are Galileo and defend your theory in a letter to the editor
- write how you feel about science in your learning log

to narrate
- write a fictional account of pioneer life
- write a skit about the Continental Congress
- write a myth about the Big Bang theory
- pretend you are a food molecule and write a story about your passage through the digestive system

to explain
- write a news article about an historical event
- write a character study about an historical figure
- explain the process of photosynthesis
- explain how brown-eyed parents could have a blue-eyed child

to describe
- describe General Custer for both a Native American audience and an army audience
- describe the scene and the characters at the Boston Tea Party
- describe a plant cell
- describe cellular reproduction

to persuade
- write an advertisement persuading young colonials to join the British army
- pretend you are Abigail Adams and persuade John to give women the right to vote
- write an editorial favoring a recycling program to the school newspaper
- list as many reasons as you can for continuing the space program

Grades 9–12

Literature

to express self
- write in your journal how you would have reacted if you were the character in a story

* write a love poem for Anne Frank and her boyfriend

to narrate
* write a different ending to a fiction story
* write a myth with a modern-day hero/ine

to explain
* explain some cultural differences in a story from another country
* write an essay explaining why the old man respected the fish (Hemingway's *The Old Man and the Sea*)

to describe
* locate the sensory details in the story and describe them from a first-person view
* describe the story setting as if it had taken place in modern times

to persuade
* write an argumentative essay describing the character as a hero or a coward
* persuade the hero/ine of the story not to continue making poor choices

Social Studies and Science
to express self
* express your personal reactions to the election campaign
* write a speech supporting your favorite candidate
* use a journal to tell your feelings about the AIDS crisis
* pretend you need a donor organ and write about your feelings

to narrate
* write a play script depicting an historical event
* write a fiction story about a person in a newspaper story
* write a story about a person who is addicted to drugs
* write a skit to depict a scientific process

to explain
* write an essay explaining the differences between two systems of governments
* write a letter to King George explaining why the Quartering Act is not a good idea
* research the effects of tobacco on the body
* explain the process of a science experiment

to describe
* describe what the weather is like on January 1st in your native country and compare it to the weather of your new town on that date
* describe the television appearance of a presidential candidate
* describe the appearance of quartz
* describe the appearance of vinegar as compared to water

to persuade
* write a biography of the political candidate you prefer
* give reasons why you prefer living in a representational democracy
* list reasons why acid rain is (or is not) harmful
* list reasons why your best friend should stop smoking

References

Asher, James J. 1982. *Learning Another Language through Actions: The Complete Teacher's Guidebook.* 2d ed. Los Gatos: Sky Oaks.

Billows, F. 1961. *The Techniques of Language Teaching.* London: Longman.

Bloom, Benjamin S., ed. 1956. *Taxonomy of Educational Objectives: The Classification of Educational Goals.* Handbook I: Cognitive Domain. New York: Longman, Green.

Chamot, Ana, and Michael O'Malley. 1992. "The Cognitive Academic Language Learning Approach: A Bridge to the Mainstream." In *The Multicultural Classroom: Readings for Content Area Teachers,* ed. Patricia A. Richard-Amato and Marguerite A. Snow, 39–57. London: Longman.

Cummins, James. 1992. "Language Proficiency, Bilingualism, and Academic Achievement." In *The Multicultural Classroom: Readings for Content Area Teachers,* ed. Patricia A. Richard-Amato and Marguerite A. Snow, 16–26. London: Longman.

English/Language Arts Curriculum Resource Handbook 1992. Millwood, NY: Kraus International Publications.

Enright, D. Scott, and Mary Lou McCloskey. 1988. *Integrating English: Developing English Language and Literacy in the Multilingual Classroom.* New York: Addison-Wesley.

Graham, Carolyn. 1979. *Jazz Chants for Children.* New York: Oxford Univ. Press.

Hansen-Krening, Nancy. 1982. *Language Experiences for All Students.* New York: Addison-Wesley.

Hudelson, Sarah. 1986. "ESL Children's Writing: What We've Learned, What We're Learning." In *Children and ESL: Integrating Perspectives,* ed. Pat Rigg and D. Scott Enright, 23–54. Washington, DC: Teachers of English to Speakers of Other Languages.

Kagan, Spencer. 1992. *Cooperative Learning.* N.c., CA: Resources for Teachers.

Krashen, Steve. 1988. "Providing Input for Acquisition." In *Making It Happen: Interaction in the Second Language Classroom,* ed. Patricia Richard-Amato, 330–341. White Plains, NY: Longman.

Levine, Linda New. 1991. "Organizational Frames: Integrating Language and Content." In *Issues and Innovations in ESL Teaching and Learning,* ed. Jack Gantzer and Elaine Books, 121–131. New York: New York State Teachers of English to Speakers of Other Languages.

Levine, Linda New, and Aronstam, Mona. 1990. *An Intermediate Level ESL Curriculum for the Bedford Central School District: Grades 3–5.* Bedford, NY: Bedford Central School District.

Mikulecky, Beatrice S. 1985. "Reading Skills Instruction in ESL." In *On TESOL '84: A Brave New World for TESOL,* ed. Penny Larson, Elliot L. Judd, and Dorothy S. Messerschmitt, 261–277. Washington, DC: Teachers of English to Speakers of Other Languages.

Scarcella, Robin. 1990. *Teaching Language Minority Students in the Multicultural Classroom.* Englewood Cliffs, NJ: Prentice–Hall.

Stern, H. 1983. *Fundamental Concepts of Language Teaching.* Oxford: Oxford Univ. Press.

Teachers of English to Speakers of Other Languages. In press. *Is Your School Helping Its Language Minority Students To Meet the National Educational Goals?* Washington, DC.

STATE-LEVEL CURRICULUM GUIDELINES: AN ANALYSIS

by Phillip C. Gonzales

Professor

School of Education, California State University, Dominguez Hills, Carson, California

THIS chapter provides a general over–view of state-level guidelines for English as a Second Language programs, K–12. The analysis of state guidelines is summarized by state and differences generalized by region of the country.

ESL or bilingual programs usually have their basis established by law, frequently receive supplemental funding from state sources, are monitored by state evaluators, and most often are implemented following guidelines established by state departments of education. State curriculum guidelines establish the direction, substance, and success criteria for language-based programs for Limited English Proficient (LEP) students. They help school officials decide who should be included in such programs, how to teach them, what materials to use, and when to transition them to mainstream English-only classrooms. All district-level ESL/bilingual administrators and most teachers are or should be familiar with these guidelines.

Legally, school districts with fewer than ten LEP students in any one non-English group must provide ESL services. When twenty or more students come from the same language group, ESL and bilingual services are recommended.

States vary in the manner in which they meet the needs of LEP students. In some states, programs that address these needs are grouped under the heading of Bilingual Education (which includes ESL); in others, ESL programs are included as separate concerns. In a few states, native language instruction is included in documents described for ESL programs. In a number of states, no specific reference to curriculum guidelines for ESL instruction appears in a state-mandated document. Compounding the problem is the lack of agreement of definition of terms throughout the country. Even when terminology is not specific, the range of language programs may vary from the more traditional cognitive (grammar-translation) approach and audio-lingual (repetition, pattern-drill methodology) to the more nontraditional structured immersion, whole language, or immersion approaches.

To help clarify the proliferation of terms and types of programs, this analysis begins with a discussion of the range of curricular possibilities inherent in different language development programs. This is followed by a description of the scale used in the analysis of state-level curriculum guidelines for ESL instruction. Finally, a state-by-state and region-by-region analysis and summation is provided.

Language Development Programs

There are three general categories of language development programs: direct, naturalistic, and nativistic. Each has a philosophical base, requires specified conditions for language development, has a unique look in the classroom, and has its own lesson design. Table 1 summarizes the continuum of language development programs in the states that responded.
(Phillip C .Gonzales, "Reform in Bilingual Teacher Education." Presentation of paper at National Association for Bilingual Education, Miami, Florida, 1989.)

Table 1. Language Development Programs

DIRECT	NATURALISTIC	NATIVISTIC
Language is taught directly as a prerequisite to any involvement in subject matter instruction. Language is the content of the ESL/bilingual education lesson. Focus in this type of instruction is on mastering those words, phrases or sentences presumed to be necessary prerequisites to communication. At times, instruction focuses on linguistic description of the target language as an avenue to its eventual use. Reading and writing are taught as content subjects, understanding about which is seen as preparation for their use in communication and learning. The student in this type of instruction metacognitively focuses attention on the form as well as the function of the language studied and practiced. Learning accurate use of the target language is central to its study. Teachers expect adult-like production of the language from the very beginning. They ask students for rules and patterns of acceptable usage whenever inaccurate production hinders communication.	With naturalistic language development, it is assumed that the barrier to participation in language situations is the lack of language competence. Attempts are made to recreate the conditions and circumstances that will promote language experimentation and development. In schools, students face cognitively demanding lessons which become the context for language nurturing. Students are placed in groups according to their linguistic levels. Focus is on comprehending the language used in the lesson. Within each level, teachers provide comprehensible linguistic input at a point slightly ahead of the student's known language proficiency. Accuracy in determination of proficiency is felt to be central to this type of program. Syntax is adjusted by the teacher and common vocabulary is employed in each interaction with students. Vocabulary felt necessary for understanding the lesson is taught and other difficult language is explained. This language is considered 'natural' since the language of the situation or lesson is that which receives attention. The student learns the subject matter taught when provided a linguistic environment in which he/she can participate and therefore gain access to the lesson. Students are prepared for involvement in lessons by focusing on the language he/she will encounter.	Language in these classrooms is allowed to develop as it does innately. Students are involved in linguistically demanding situations where the contexts of the content studied or situations experienced are made comprehensible. The student creates language as possible and necessary to participate in the lesson, makes sense of its message, and communicates with the teacher and peers. It is assumed that the barrier to participation in the classroom is the understanding the student has of the subject matter that is studied. With this approach, attention is focused not on the language per se but on the context in which the language is employed and the message it conveys. In the context of coming to understand this subject matter, the student is provided opportunities to hear language used appropriately and contextually and to experiment with language as s/he communicates. In these classrooms, students may either use the home language or English. The response by the teacher is always in the target language of the lesson. Essentially, language in these classrooms is acquired as it is used to learn about content and through social interactions.
CONDITIONS FOR LANGUAGE DEVELOPMENT: •students focus attention on language forms and accuracy •formal knowledge about the structure of language is seen as necessary for its learning	CONDITIONS FOR LANGUAGE DEVELOPMENT: •low affective filter-a low stress environment •comprehensible input-language adjusted to be within the listening range of the student •involvement in cognitively-demanding subject lessons •participation in activities	CONDITIONS FOR LANGUAGE ACQUISITION: •attention is on meaning and not on linguistic accuracy •language is embedded in the teaching of content •students are involved in real life situations •idiosyncratic understandings and interpretations are allowed and encouraged.

DIRECT	NATURALISTIC	NATIVISTIC
IN THE CLASSROOM	IN THE CLASSROOM	IN THE CLASSROOM
The teacher is very much in control of this classroom. The content becomes the information about the target language. The content is taught by focusing student attention on the forms and functions of that language. Accuracy in usage is emphasized. Students formally learn about the target language. They study the grammar system, prefixes and suffixes, rules about punctuation, etc. Accuracy in the application of these rules is stressed. EXAMPLE LESSONS: In language arts, students study parts of speech, construct 5-part paragraphs, and practice unaccented oral dialogues. Phonics is the mainstay of reading instruction. In social studies, students memorize the 'Gettysburg Address.' In visual/performing arts, students study musical notation and apply it as they sing. In P.E., students memorize the rules for playing baseball.	Students are perceived to lack the language necessary to handle subject matter instruction in a traditional manner. Students' language proficiencies are determined and they are grouped accordingly. Teachers prepare the homogeneously grouped students for each new lesson by focusing on the language felt necessary for successful understanding of the subject matter. The teacher controls the linguistic demands of the lessons. Word banks are common. Difficult and new vocabulary is taught prior to lessons. Grammar beyond the speaking level of the student is avoided. Readability of reading selections is controlled. And the number of concepts taught is restricted. Comprehension of the language of instruction is checked frequently. When understanding is lacking, the teacher explains, demonstrates, or uses visuals for understanding. IN THE LESSON: In all subject matter classes, students are pretaught the language of the lesson. Difficult sentences, idioms, and figurative language are explained. In language arts, students are taught comprehension and composing strategies and critical thinking which they practice as they read and write. In math, concepts from story problems are taught prior to the lesson. Student engagement is checked as they work on the calculations. In social studies, students learn a lesson about the three branches of the US Government by memorizing their names, functions, and other information. In visual/performing arts, students learn words to a new song. In P.E. students answer questions about football prior to playing the game.	Nativistic language development occurs throughout the day both at school and in the home and throughout the lifetime of the student in everyday interactions. Anytime students are assisted in understanding the 'big ideas' from content lessons or the theme from a literary reading, they are involved in nativistic instruction. Attention is to the content studied. Language development is incidental, indirect, and unconscious. Students in each situation have a partial understanding of the gist of the lesson without having to know each of the details. They focus on the general meanings they are coming to understand and not on the language that carries that meaning. Students negotiate their understandings in discussions with their peers. They discover, experiment with, and interpret ideas with them. EXAMPLE LESSONS: In literature, children read IRA SLEEPS OVER, act it out, and discuss why Ira's sister and parents made Ira reconsider whether or not to take his Teddy Bear with him when he slept over at his friend's home. In math, students apply mathematical reasoning patterns to nonmathematical situations such as advertising. In social studies, students set up and operate a model city government. In science, students plant beans and expose them to varied colors of lights. The effect of the light color is tested. In visual/performing arts, the students learn to dance the 'Hora.' In P.E., students learn to play soccer.

Types of Language Programs

1. **Cognitive** is an approach to language learning that emphasizes formal knowledge of the grammar system, rules of usage, and phonetic decoding.
2. **Audio-lingual** is language learned habitually through substitution drills, repetition, and correction. Adultlike forms of language are practiced.
3. **Foreign language** refers to studying a language in a manner that is devoid of practical application and practice in real situations. Dialogues, folklore, history, etc. may be the content used in learning the non–native language.
4. **Communicative competence** includes language that is needed to handle various situations; it is deliberately taught to students. Students create and/or memorize that language appropriate for such language-use situations as ordering in restaurants, talking to the principal, or applying for a job.
5. **Natural approach** is the method whereby language is deliberately taught as a prerequisite to lesson understanding. The vocabulary is taught with concrete understanding. The vocabulary is taught with concrete referents and movements at first, visuals later, and with verbal descriptions eventually. The lessons are contrived. An attempt is made to have these lessons emphasize the language of real classroom and community situations.
6. **Sheltered** refers to the teacher's attempt to help students learn the crucial concepts of a discipline in a protected manner. Language is adjusted to a simpler syntactical level; vocabulary is controlled; pacing of instruction is slowed; and conceptual load regulated. Remedial readinglike techniques are employed in making the language of lessons comprehensible.
7. **Structured immersion** is a program in which teachers deliberately help students come to understand prefabricated lessons and the language used to explain them. Only one language is used. Teachers plan for the active participation in lessons by speakers of a second language.
8. **Whole language** refers to giving attention to the meanings sought, interpreted, and used in understanding school lessons. Language development is seen as the by-product of whole language use in realistic and comprehensible classroom situations. Access to the content of a lesson is provided in linguistically demanding situations.
9. **Immersion** takes place in a single language environment, in which attempts are made to help the child or student make sense of situations, lessons, and experiences. Focus is on the content or topic studied. Great freedom is allowed the child seeking meaning and creating language in each lesson. Little attention is paid to the language of the lesson.
10. **Submersion** takes place in an environment in which only one language is used. The child or student is in a sink-or-swim situation in which no attempt is made to help that individual understand either the language that is heard or the situational context in which it is employed. Lessons can be both linguistically and cognitively demanding.

Analysis Scale

Questions which were asked in analyzing the state-level curriculum guidelines for bilingual/ESL programs included a survey of nine different areas—philosophy, language policy, place for subject-matter content, role of culture, development of literacy, assessment and evaluation, materials selection, classroom management, and parental involvement.

Specifically, this review explored the questions, Does the state guideline provide the following information? And if so, what is the general provision it recommends?

A. Program's language regarding instructional philosophy
   1. Clearly articulated philosophy?
   2. Description of the program's views?
   3. Instruction and assessment?
   4. Guidelines for classroom control?
B. Language policy
   1. Coherent description of the program's philosophy regarding anticipated language outcomes?
   2. Description of the approach to classroom language development appropriate for ages of students in the program?
   3. Delineation of strategies for language development to be used by teachers?

C. Place for subject-matter content
  1. Statement of commitment to subject-matter instruction?
  2. Listing of subject-matter instruction to be provided at each grade cluster?
  3. Suggestion for teaching subject-matter content to LEP students?
D. Role of culture
  1. Identification of the approach to culture?
  2. Description of cultural traits expected in teachers?
  3. Discussion of how student's background experiences, values, motivation, and learning styles as well as communicative abilities are to be accommodated by the program?
E. Development of literacy
  1. Statement of the definition of literacy recommended for the program?
  2. Discussion of how integration of the language arts will be accomplished in the program?
  3. Description of the commitment to first language literacy?
  4. Description of the decision markers for initiation of second-language literacy program?
  5. Description of ESL program, methodology, and its interrelatedness with language arts?
F. Adequate assessment and evaluation
  1. Clear description of assessment policy?
  2. Evaluation procedures?
G. Materials selection
  1. Guidelines for materials selection?
  2. Criteria for judging the merit of materials?
  3. Placement of bilingual/ESL materials in each adoption cycle?
H. Classroom management
I. Parental involvement
  1. Policy regarding the involvement of parents in educational decisions about their children?
  2. Goals to be achieved through parental involvement?
  3. Suggestions for involving parents?

Organization of the Chapter

Due to the lengthy nature of most state documents, each is summarized briefly according to the criteria listed above. To summarize the contents by region, the states submitting documents are divided into six groups as follows:

1. New England Region
   Maine
   Massachusetts
   New Hampshire
   Rhode Island

2. Middle Atlantic Region
   Maryland
   New Jersey
   New York
   Pennsylvania

3. Southeast Region
   Florida
   Georgia
   North Carolina
   Virginia

4. Central Region
   Iowa
   Louisiana
   Minnesota
   Texas

5. Mountain West Region
   Arizona
   Colorado
   Idaho
   Montana
   New Mexico

6. Pacific States Region
   California
   Oregon

New England Region

	MAINE	MASSA-CHUSETTS	NEW HAMPSHIRE	RHODE ISLAND
PHILOSOPHY	Naturalistic	Naturalistic	Direct	Nativistic
LANGUAGE POLICY	ESL required & bilingual allowed	Bilingual/ESL	5 levels of placement	Bilingual/ESL
SUBJECT-MATTER		Parallels regular curriculum	Language spirals in complexity	L1 & L2 content instruction
CULTURE	Acculturation	Two-way	Acculturation	Acculturation
LITERACY	Whole language	Integrated	Language experience & formal	Whole language
ASSESSMENT/ EVALUATION	Multiple criteria	Formal and informal	On-going & in-class	Formal and informal
MATERIALS	Minilanguage labs & technology	Cultural sensitivity	Variety	Variety
CLASSROOM MANAGEMENT	Groups & cooperative learning	Interactive		Minimal separation from English peers
PARENTS	Notification	Advisory Committee		Planning & implementation

Maine

Philosophy. This state encourages but does not require a naturalistic approach to language development in which content-area subject matter is used to teach language. Notational-functional (emphasizing lifelike situations and teaching the language to handle them) and whole language approaches are suggested. Important ideas and supporting details of the content are identified and presented as comprehensible language that can be understood by the ESL student. Oral/aural fluency precedes the introduction of English reading and writing. Children are involved in situations representative of life outside of the school.

Language policy. ESL is required for LEP students and dual language is recommended when feasible.

Role of culture. The culture and ethnic heritage of Maine is taught in at least one grade from 6th to 12th grades. The goal is not to Americanize LEP students but to validate who they are and to ensure their integration into the school community. The teacher is expected to learn about the culture and customs of the LEP students and the students are expected to learn about American culture and customs.

Development of literacy. This state encourages whole language integration of listening, speaking, reading, and writing rather than instruction of isolated skills of literacy.

Assessment and evaluation. Multiple criteria are used in evaluating LEP students, such as background information, determination of dominant language, oral language proficiency in English, level of functioning in the dominant language and in English, and the level of functioning in subject matter areas (such as mathematics, social studies, or science) in English and in the primary language. Ongoing evaluation is conducted in the language in which the student received instruction.

Materials selection. ESL classrooms should be fitted with a mini–language lab and have access to video equipment and computer technology.

Classroom management. Cooperative learning, integrated language units, and content-based ESL instruction are recommended. Maine does not have a statewide curriculum in any discipline— along with the type of ESL instruction provided, it is a local option. Buddies, community/parent volunteers, and use of language community resources are encouraged. Classroom environments should be commensurate with those provided to non-LEP students.

Parental involvement. Parents are notified of any changes in the instructional programming for their children.

Massachusetts

Philosophy. This state recommends a nativistic approach with exposure to comprehensible English as the focus. Six models of instruction are recommended: transitional use of native language at first and gradual transition to English; two-way bilingual; accelerated basic skills, intensive program to bring students up to grade level; advanced basic skills which targets older students; integrative bilingual education, to value and integrate bilingual students as a school wide resource; maintenance, to continue developing native as well as English languages throughout school experiences.

Language policy. The guidelines promote first-language instruction to continue students' progression in academic areas and as a link to English instruction. Basic active communication is addressed first; later, academic language skills receive attention. Mixing with more proficient English-speaking peers for art, music, and physical education is also recommended. The amount of time in environments where English is spoken is increased over time. With fewer than twenty students in one language in one school district, ESL is mandated. With twenty or more students of one language in one school district, transitional bilingual education is required.

Subject-matter content. This is provided initially in the first language of the student as a route to eventual success in subject-matter instruction in English. Generally, it parallels the regular school curriculum.

Role of culture. More than traditions, food, dance, and music, the guidelines stress the values and perspectives of students and their families which are recognized and considered respectfully. The program encourages ethnographic studies of students' own communities. Better human understanding is sought. Instruction draws from students' cultural/experiential knowledge base in their understanding of themselves and the social worlds that surround them. It acknowledges cultural differences and promotes two-way cultural education. Everyone contributes to increasing every classmate's awareness.

Development of literacy. All language arts skills of reading, listening, speaking and writing reinforce each other.

Assessment and evaluation. Language competence is assessed by both formal and informal means. No specific tests appear to be mandated.

Materials selection. This includes culturally sensitive materials respecting new perspectives on topics. Otherwise, no specific guidelines for material selection were provided.

Classroom management. This is organized to allow for cooperative interaction between students as well as among teachers and students. A variety of techniques is recommended: large group instruction, self-directed involvement, and small-group activities.

Parental involvement. The guidelines encourage parental and community participation and support for the school through the establishment of a Parent Advisory Committee. Parent training is promoted and cross generational interviews are planned. Parents have the right to withdraw children from inclusion in programs.

New Hampshire

Philosophy. This state encourages a direct approach to language development. The focus is on language form and analysis. Oral drill and routine practice activities are encouraged for beginning levels leading to the study of grammar, parts of speech, phonics, spelling, and writing mechanics later in the program. The program is designed to develop control over linguistic features. Opportunities are provided for language practice in social and classroom settings. Four basic ESL approaches that are recommended include the direct approach, the action/natural language method (acting out English content and structures), the cognitive/language analysis method (emphasis on analysis of language), and the language experience method (contextualized language study in real-life experiences).

Language policy. The instruction moves from survival, development of automatic control, extension and refinement of communicative situations, and application to content area study and advanced reading and composition skills. Five levels of language proficiency are identified with the fifth stage performance equivalent to language control comparable to that of same-age English-speaking peers.

Subject-matter content. All instruction spirals from introduction to refining and applying linguistic features, communication strategy and language skill, to continuously reviewing previous lessons in increasingly more complex and sophisticated ways.

Role of culture. Some attention is paid to learning the strategies, rituals, and habits of English-speaking Americans.

Development of literacy. Promotes a language experience approach which begins with accumulation and learning of sight items, progresses to writing and reading sentences and simple paragraphs with fewer and fewer errors, eventually to comprehending more complex prose. Phonics is introduced after students have attained a level of proficiency sufficient for the use of synthetic approaches to literacy.

Assessment and evaluation. An ongoing in-class assessment employs a scope and sequence of language skills, behaviors, and strategies and lists of content topics to be mastered provided in the New Hampshire curriculum guide.

Materials selection. A wide range of visual materials and action activities emphasizing language comprehension, listening, and the development of speaking skills are recommended.

Rhode Island

Philosophy. A nativistic approach is encouraged. Communication is emphasized; all domains of a language are used in each lesson; and global and whole languge activities are the basis of the ESL Core Curriculum. Learning is interactive and related to a variety of experiential learning activities such as hands-on activities, and talking, reading, and writing about a variety of real-life and academic experiences. Language is not studied, it is used in processing and applying knowledge of content. The subconscious use of language allows the student to concentrate on the content of the experience and on communicating during the experience rather than monitoring their language performance. Eventually, and with control of the language, students study language in a more formal manner. Learning and real-life experiences and situations become the context for developing skill, knowledge, and proficiency.

Language policy. The guidelines recommend placement in either a bilingual program (native-language instruction in subject areas and ESL) or ESL program for the development of English proficiency in listening, speaking, reading, and writing and for academic instruction using ESL methodology. Programs are designed for the ultimate transitioning of students into mainstream English instruction.

Subject-matter content. This includes subject matter instruction using ESL methodologies and/or in the native language. A core or global curriculum applicable to all students in Rhode Island is used in the design of the curriculum of ESL programs. Lessons are organized thematically. Language is but one of several areas of study. Cognitive strategies and skills, study skills, community knowledge, and career education are all applied to the subject-matter content being studied.

Role of culture. The goal is to develop the interpersonal and affective skills necessary for successful integration into the Anglo-American socioeconomic community and the all-English classroom.

Development of literacy. Reading, writing, speaking, and listening are integrated into the program—always emphasizing comprehension. Literacy proceeds through a global–whole language and whole word instructional experience: the students comprehend the situation or content, which leads to learn to listen and speak in the situation or about the content, which leads to learning to read and write about the situation or content with an emphasis the language and concepts experienced during the communicative or content-area situation, which leads to learning about (analyzing, abstracting, generalizing, and deducing about) the component parts and systems of the language features and forms.

Assessment and evaluation. This includes a home survey to determine primary language, tests for assessing English-language proficiencies in listening, speaking, reading and writing and appropriateness to age/grade level. Also included are standardized reading test administration, informal reports, teacher consultation, and notification of parents. Exit criteria are based on test data, teacher evaluation of proficiency, and classroom performance in academic areas measured by grades and scores. A holistic evaluation scale for examining student performance is provided and proceeds from beginning level to advanced application.

Materials selection. Students usually create their own learning materials. Encouraged is the use of recordings, films, songs and poems, literature, and other nontextbook materials.

Classroom management. Minimal separation from English-speaking peers is recommended and occurs only when necessary and only at the beginning levels. Students are encouraged to find information they want to learn; collaborating and cooperating with other ESL and standard-curriculum students occurs. The teacher guides, explains, and demonstrates how to complete activities. The teacher continuously provides input and supports group efforts at completing a task. Students collaborate in peer-pair and small task groups to learn, practice, and apply learnings. Lessons are introduced, practiced, and

developed to automaticity, extended and refined, and applied.

Parental involvement. Parents are involved in the planning and implementation of ESL/bilingual programs and given the right to question placements.

New England Region Summary

The New England region appears to be consistent with the rest of the country with an emphasis on naturalistic instruction, encouraging bilingual education and requiring ESL when necessary. The cultural component promotes a learning of those attributes necessary for adjustment and acculturation to American society. Guidelines provide for whole language literacy instruction. In most state guidelines, assessment and evaluation criteria are spelled out clearly. The lone exception to this summary is New Hampshire which encourages a direct type of language program, with formal language study and spiraling curricula. Assessment and evaluation in New Hampshire is classroom based and ongoing.

Middle Atlantic Region

	MARYLAND	NEW JERSEY	NEW YORK	PENNSYL-VANIA
PHILOSOPHY	Naturalistic	Direct	Direct	Direct/naturalistic
LANGUAGE POLICY	Meaning focus	Bilingual/ESL	ESL as content; formal knowledge	Bilingual education recommended/ ESL required
SUBJECT MATTER	Sheltered language in content areas	Bilingual -like regular program ESL focus on language	State graduation requirements; ESL as linguistic study	Vocabulary, competence in subject matter
CULTURE	Exchange and respect for difference	Dual	Acculturation	Own language & culture to learn of others
LITERACY	Integrated	Native language first; skills	Skills mastery	Skills
ASSESSMENT/ EVALUATION	Informal and diagnostic	Standardized tests	Formal	Multiple testing
MATERIALS			Commercial	
CLASSROOM MANAGEMENT	Cooperative learning/authentic collaboration		Homogeneously grouped	Age-grade appropriate classes
PARENT	Encouraged in academic areas	Advisory committee	Informed	Participation encouraged

Maryland

Philosophy. The emphasis appears to be on naturalistic approaches to language development focusing on functional usage in situations with low stress and allowing limited use of native language when English proficiency is lacking.

Language policy. The guidelines encourage learning language in social settings where teachers facilitate and encourage language experimentation and expression in situations requiring observation, hypothesizing, concluding, analyzing, summarizing, problem-solving, etc. Teacher's focus is on providing comprehensible input of language. Students practice skills of clarifying, asking for repetition, rephrasing, etc. Language correction focuses on meaning and not form.

Subject-matter content. Social learning of language occurs at first, with later applications to subject matter study. Language scaffolds are used, centering on real dialogues about authentic topics and materials. Repeated exposure to concepts occur through the varied lessons planned. Sheltered instruction is recommended which focuses student attention on the key language embedded in subject-matter. This familiarizes students with the ways in which the discourse of the discipline is organized and provides them with study skills to comprehend and apply the subject-matter being presented. Collaboration about subject matter content between the content teachers and the ESL instructors is encouraged.

Role of culture. Lessons draw on the students' prior experiences and knowledge. Students are encouraged to exchange cultural knowledge. Respect for differences is promoted.

Development of literacy. The language arts skills of listening, reading, writing, and speaking are integrated in lessons with each reinforcing the other. Writing and reading tasks focus on communication and meaning at first. Later, correctness and errors may be a consideration. Skills such as grammar or decoding are taught in meaningful, contextualized tasks where communication is the prime outcome.

Assessment and evaluation. Ongoing informal assessment of oral language and literacy performance is recommended. Diagnostic assessment for placement purposes is suggested, but specific guidelines are not provided.

Classroom management. Cooperative learning activities are recommended with students assuming responsibility for completion of tasks. Classrooms are clinical settings for student language creation and expression and for teacher interactional and interventional feedback. This environment is supportive of risk-taking necessary for language generation and experimentation. It is language- and print-rich. Students become explorers of oral and written English. The social environment is collaborative, authentic purposes are established, and opportunities for meaningful interactions are planned.

Parental involvement. Parents are encouraged to become involved in their children's academic instruction. They should be used as cultural resources, as home tutors, and as classroom teaching assistants.

New Jersey

Philosophy. Based on the assessment instruments used in evaluating program effectiveness and student placement, the major emphasis in New Jersey appears to be on a direct, or to some extent naturalistic, approach to language development.

Language policy. Students are placed in self-contained classrooms according to their level of language proficiency. Emphasis is placed on the development of English vocabulary and structures in the areas of listening, speaking, reading, and writing. ESL approaches recommended include audiolingual, community language learning, direct, grammar/translation, natural, notional/functional, silent way, and total physical response. Most of these approaches are in the category of Direct types of language programs. Most of them concentrate on the learning of language in contrived formal and analytic ways and are keyed to the skills tested by the district's language-assessment instruments. ESL is scheduled for a minimum of thirty minutes per day in elementary classrooms and a full class period at the secondary level.

Subject-matter content. Bilingual programs offer the same course of study as do monolingual programs. At the secondary level, the course of study should meet the requirements for graduation. Bilingual programs are transitional with skills developed first in the native language; later they are transferred to English. ESL emphasizes proficiency in listening comprehension, speaking, reading, and writing in English. Full participation with native English-speaking peers occurs in art, music, and physical education.

Role of culture. Instruction is recommended in bilingual programs that teach the history and culture of the native land of the parents and of the United States.

Development of literacy. This may be taught in the native language at first. In all cases transition to English reading is encouraged. A skills approach appears to be emphasized.

Assessment and evaluation. Home language is surveyed and English proficiency is determined by state-approved standardized reading tests.

Classroom management. The suggested models include pull-out, class period, in-class, high intensity, and use of resource or magnet center. No specific classroom models were provided.

Parental involvement. Parents are notified when children are placed into or exited from bilingual/ESL programs. Parent advisory committees are established for bilingual programs but not required for ESL programs.

New York

Philosophy. Direct, and to some extent naturalistic, approaches to language are promoted. Audiolingual, the silent way, and community language learning strategies are recommended and emphasize the linguistic study of vocabulary, structures, phonology, and cultural information. The central organizing principle at all levels is grammar.

Language policy. English as a Second Language is considered a specific discipline in which English is learned systematically and cumulatively, moving from concrete to abstract levels in a spiraling fashion. Attention is paid to problems in English confronted by non-native speakers as both the native language and English are frequently compared and contrasted. Oral skills are considered primary in developing communicative and linguistic competence in understanding, speaking, reading, and writing English. Listening emphasizes sound discrimination, distinguishing between syllables, words, phrases and sentences,

etc., progressing to understanding English at a nativelike level in all situations. Speaking progresses from language in social exchanges to more formal use. Grammar and vocabulary receive major attention. Reading is tied to grammar and vocabulary work at the beginning levels in controlled reading selections to mastery of less controlled reading materials later. Writing begins with sentence-level study and progresses to paragraph formation and eventually to extended-discourse composition.

Subject-matter content. High school students are expected to receive native-language or English subject-matter instruction that fulfills the state's requirements for graduation. The ESL program focuses on linguistic study primarily with some attention to language functions and contexts.

Role of culture. Teachers are expected to demonstrate cultural sensitivity toward their students. Once phonology, grammar, and vocabulary have been sufficiently learned, ESL students interact with their English-speaking peers. At this point, the ESL student studies the patterns of behavior, values, attitudes, and traditions of English-speaking Americans in order to function securely and effectively in social situations. Cultural topics at all levels emphasize the new and different cultural patterns that characterize life in the United States.

Development of literacy. Literacy is seen as the mastery of grammar and vocabulary; it includes their application to the decoding and comprehending aspects of reading. Writing is reserved for secondary school programs and is considered the last and most complex linguistic skill taught. Mastery of the conventions of punctuation, grammar, sentence construction, organization, etc., are emphasized in writing instruction.

Assessment and evaluation. Formal assessment of English proficiency is conducted and results in placement of LEP students into homogeneous, grouped ESL classes for instruction

Materials selection. Commercially produced texts and supplementary instructional materials are available for purchase.

Classroom management. Classes are homogeneously organized into four levels of linguistic competence, although individualization within each is encouraged. Mixing with native English-speaking peers occurs in such classes as music and art or during extracurricular activities.

Parental involvement. Parents are consulted during the initial placement phase and are kept informed of the student's progress throughout the ESL program. Close contact with the schools is encouraged.

Pennsylvania

Philosophy. Pennsylvania requires ESL/bilingual education but does not directly specify a philosophical stance. The tests and instructional tasks that are employed suggest an audiolingual approach at first; next there is a gradual moving to a communicative-competence approach to language education.

Language policy. ESL instruction is to be provided to all LEP students. Bilingual education is recommended whenever numbers of single-language speakers make it feasible. Daily language instruction is recommended in allotments of two to three hours for prebeginners and one hour for advanced students. Students are tracked through three levels of language competence.

Place for subject-matter content. Planned courses, including learning objectives to be achieved by students, are required in the 120 clock hours of instruction that are required. Emphasis in ESL classes is on incorporating subject vocabulary from content-area classes. Subject-matter competence is expected in native-language programs.

Role of culture. Students participate in activities utilizing their native language and culture and to increase their awareness of cultural, social, and ethnic groups that are different from their own.

Development of literacy. The initial emphasis is on aural-oral skills leading eventually and gradually to reading and writing of personal experiences with grade-level appropriate assignments.

Assessment and evaluation. The guidelines specify that multiple testing be conducted to determine native or home language proficiency and literacy, language dominance, achievement, and program placement and mainstreaming. Educational tests are specified in oral language skills, reading, achievement, and other areas. Guidelines do not specify exit criteria. In bilingual programs, testing is conducted in both English and the home language.

Materials selection. No guidelines or specific recommendations are provided.

Classroom management. Tutorial programs are allowed for small numbers of ESL students. Students are placed in age–grade-appropriate classes for instruction whenever possible with no more than a three-year differential within a group.

Parental involvement. LEP parents are encouraged to increase their participation in school/home activities, but specifics are left up to the districts.

Middle Atlantic Region Summary

The Middle Atlantic states are fairly traditional and conservative in their approach to ESL/bilingual instruction. With the exception of Maryland, most encourage a direct approach to language education. Subject-matter instruction receives attention in all guidelines and in most cases is tied to mainstream curricula. Two-way sharing of culture is encouraged. Literacy is skills-based, and assessment and evaluation is formal.

Southeast Region

	FLORIDA	GEORGIA	NORTH CAROLINA	TENNESSEE	VIRGINIA
PHILOSO-PHY	Direct	Naturalistic	Direct	Direct	Naturalistic
LANGUAGE POLICY	Formal language skills instruction	ESL as per need		ESL focus on linguistic elements	Transitional bilingual education/ESL
SUBJECT MATTER		Sheltered	Elementary language/secondary content	Language based	Related to general education
CULTURE	Acculturation	Multiculturalism		Acculturation	Acculturation
LITERACY	Skills	Language experience	Language experience/ traditional	Traditional	Whole language
ASSESS-MENT/EVAL-UATION		Informal/Formal -Monitoring of academic progress		5 levels of linguistic fluency	Formal/exit tied to achievement level
MATERIALS		Varied			Low level, high interest & other variety
CLASS-ROOM MANAGE-MENT		Cooperative learning, peer tutoring & group work		Grouping into 5 levels	Peer teaching/cooperative learning/groups
PARENT		Community resources			

Florida

Philosophy. The state guidelines recommend a direct type of language-development program that emphasizes instruction and practice in basic listening, speaking, reading, and writing study skills. Functional English survival and consumer vocabulary is taught. Grammatically correct sentence production is expected, and the students are expected to apply the conventions of standard written English, such as spelling, capitalization, punctuation, and the analysis of sentences and paragraphs. When speaking English, the student should utilize pronunciation patterns effectively. From knowledge of language and correctness of forms, instruction progresses to the use of these skills in varied tasks of reading literature and writing.

Language policy. This is not formally stated, but the guidelines encourage formal and direct instruction of language skills—presumably in either English as a second language or in the primary language.

Role of culture. Learning the culture of the United States as it relates to the students'

cultures is important. Students are expected to identify distinctive aspects of American culture expressed in literature and language.

Development of literacy. The emphasis appears to be on a skills approach to literacy.

Georgia

Philosophy. The naturalistic approach utilizing sheltered language techniques is recommended. Comprehensible input, cueing, modeling, elicitation, and chunking are suggested as ESL strategies. The focus is on making language comprehensible as a means to lesson access.

Language policy. The guidelines do not appear to provide for native language instruction. ESL instruction is provided whenever a need exists.

Subject-matter content. At beginning levels, physical education, art, and mathematics are recommended. Later, students are placed in courses that require a higher level of English proficiency, such as social studies, biology, geometry, and language arts. The content of the materials in each class are not watered down.

Survival content-area language is taught; students are involved in peer groups; learning is concrete, as are the sheltering techniques suggested for science, social studies, and mathematics. Dramatization, movement, visualization, and role playing are encouraged as language-learning procedures suggested for the arts.

Role of culture. Multiculturalism is affirmed as the schools recognize, accept, value, and promote individual diversity in a pluralistic setting. Cultural education involves more than holidays and food; it uses cross-cultural strategies to promote cross-cultural valuing. The use of multicultural literature is encouraged. Field trips, the use of community resources, and home projects are designed to develop respect for students' culture and linguistic background as English is acquired. Homework assignments that involve parents are also recommended.

Development of literacy. This includes a language experience approach to reading based on recording and reading natural language after a trip or activity. Shared reading, and formal story structure teaching are encouraged. Writing is taught as process; real-life classroom correspondence is encouraged.

Assessment and evaluation. Home language surveys and students' performances on English language proficiency tests are used for placement into and exiting from the ESL program. Monitoring of student academic progress is also undertaken.

Materials selection. Read-aloud sessions, wordless books, and short multicultural storybooks are among the nontraditional materials suggested.

Classroom management. This includes cooperative learning, peer tutoring, and collaboration in small groups. The classroom is arranged to allow students to become active, self-directed, and communicative learners.

Parental involvement. Parents are seen as partners in the schooling process. They are included as community resources, are chaperones on field trips, and are expected to work with their children on homework projects.

North Carolina

Philosophy. The Direct approach to instruction is recommended. Formal language study is conducted; and repetitive drill is suggested. The focus is on skills of the language progressing from discrimination to error-laden production, to increased control and accuracy over the language. Guides outlining the grammatical structure expectations, rules of usage, and decoding relationships, etc. that are to be taught at each skill level are provided. Comprehension and composition skills are deliberately taught as discrete lessons. Procedures for pattern drill and lists of vocabulary to be learned are also included in the guide.

Language policy. ESL and bilingual education policies are unspecified. A skills approach to language learning is promoted.

Subject-matter content. At the elementary and secondary levels, scope and sequence of skills are provided only for the language arts of listening, speaking, writing, and reading. At the secondary level, content topics are provided in biology, history, math, and competency reading.

Development of literacy. The goal is to match language experience with reading materials and language. The focus is on discrimination of English sounds, possession of listening and speaking vocabulary in English, knowledge of letters of the alphabet, sound-symbol correspondences in English, recognition of common language signals (i.e., plurals, past tense, etc.), comprehension of simple directions and ability to follow them in English, telling of stories in English, etc. Writing is believed to progress from transcription and writing legibly—with some convention and structural errors—to more and more control over the mechanics of the English-language print system.

Tennessee

Philosophy. The curriculum appears to be based on the direct approach to language development with an emphasis on linguistic discrimination, identification, and the study of sounds, letters, basic vocabulary, grammatical elements, etc. Repetition, drill, and formal language study are emphasized from the beginning.

Language policy. This separates language arts into three strands: listening and speaking, reading, and writing. The linguistic and formal aspects of language study are emphasized. Production, accuracy, and, to some extent, function are also emphasized.

Subject-matter content. A language-based approach is recommended. Linguistic structure, decoding and comprehension skills, grammar, spelling, and the mechanics of writing are included.

Role of culture. Culture is a subject to be studied and includes identification and celebration of holidays, demonstrations of the North American concept of time and the calendar, the study of cultural expectations in America, demonstrating a knowledge of acceptable community social behavior, etc. The focus is on helping the newcomer adjust to American culture.

Development of literacy. This includes the traditional formal study of reading, including skills of phonics and comprehension exercises. Writing involves a study of the alphabet, sentence construction, spelling and punctuation rules, etc., through copying at first and, later, by application to functional composing.

Assessment and evaluation. Five levels of linguistic fluency are identified.

Classroom management. Promotes grouping of students into five categories to meet needs of students.

Virginia

Philosophy. The guidelines recommend a naturalistic approach to instruction. Sheltered English procedures are employed with the content of subject-matter disciplines taught as a language lesson focusing on pronunciation and on learning the meanings of topic vocabulary. Whole language instruction focusing on global learning is also encouraged.

Language policy. Both native language transitional plus developmental (maintenance) bilingual education and ESL instruction are allowed; they concentrate on helping LEP students learn English as rapidly as possible. Five types of programs are allowed: tutorial approach, cluster or center approach, classroom ESL instruction, high-intensity language training, and bilingual education.

Subject-matter content. ESL instruction is related to and correlated with the content of the general education program in mathematics, science, language arts, etc.

Role of culture. The intent is to help ESL students adjust culturally to life in America by encouraging understanding and appreciation of the cultural diversity of the student population and encouraging ESL students to share their heritage and culture with others. No formal content is established.

Development of literacy. Literacy is developed using whole language methodologies. Language is not fragmented for study as grammatical patterns, vocabulary lists, or sound-symbol associations. Listening, speaking, writing, and reading are integrated and not taught as separate subjects.

Assessment and evaluation. Home language surveys are used in addition to proficiency tests of oral language, reading, and writing. Exit from ESL instruction occurs when the student is within one or two years of the achievement level of his or her native peers or when achievement data suggests the student will succeed in the mainstream with other English-speaking students.

Materials selection. Low-level, high-interest materials are recommended for outside reading along with simplified versions of content materials used in mainstream classes. A variety of materials including manipulatives, visual aids, and audio aids should be found in each classroom.

Classroom management. Often ESL is provided as a pull-out service. Grade placement is determined by the age of the child. ESL rarely is a full-day program. First experiences in English are in art, physical education, and mathematics. Two to four hours per day of ESL are provided for beginning and intermediate students. Peer teaching, cooperative learning, and small-group work are encouraged.

Southeast Region Summary

The Southeast Region states are fairly conservative and traditional. Direct language education programs predominate in three of the five states and naturalistic programs in the remaining two.

Acculturation is encouraged in most states with only Georgia sponsoring multiculturalism. Language experience and skills instruction are common, with only Virginia recommending whole language approaches to literacy.

Central Region

	IOWA	LOUISIANA	MINNESOTA	TEXAS
PHILOSOPHY	Direct/naturalistic	Naturalistic/ nativistic	Direct	Naturalistic
LANGUAGE POLICY	Bilingual/sheltered ESL	L1 content/English increases	ESL	Bilingual educa- tion/ESL
SUBJECT MATTER	Sheltered content instruction	Hetereogeneous/ accelerated		Language focus
CULTURE	Acculturation/Dual	Home culture value	Dual/Acculturation	Dual/Acculturation
LITERACY		Whole language	Integrated	Traditional
ASSESSMENT/ EVALUATION	Formal and con- tent knowledge	Varied formal and informal	Achievement levels compared with district norms	
MATERIALS		Challenging and dual language	Commercial and translated	
CLASSROOM MANAGEMENT		Cooperative learn- ing & peer tutoring		
PARENT			Community re- sources	

Iowa

Philosophy. A combined direct and naturalistic approach to language development is promoted. Use of the communicative approach, the cognitive approach, and the content-based approach is also recommended. The communicative approach emphasizes teaching conventional relationships between the forms and structures of the new language and their social-functioning meanings. The cognitive approach focuses on academic language and involves such practices as listening to an English statement and determining anything that might be incorrect in it. Content-based instruction (sheltered) has students learn language by using it for functional purposes. It is not taught directly, but emerges as a result of the need to communicate while performing academic activities.

Language policy. ESL classes can involve pull-out, sheltered English-content instruction, native language content-area instruction, itinerant ESL services, and tutoring. They can also be components of a bilingual program. Sheltered classes simplify vocabulary and language structures to help students overcome the language barrier in content instruction.

Subject-matter content. Sheltered content instruction is encouraged, but the specific disciplines are not identified.

Role of culture. Programs are designed to orient students to American cultural patterns and to help them participate in classroom, school, and community activities. Additionally, they further the development of a student's awareness of cultural diversity. Pride in their own bilingualism and biculturalism is promoted.

Assessment and evaluation. Initial screening includes ascertaining home language influences; English proficiency is evaluated for placement into a program; and progress is evaluated to determine proper exiting from the program. Content-area knowledge and native-language proficiency are also recommended as areas needing native-language assessment. The oral language proficiency descriptions used in informal assessment emphasize accent, grammar, vocabulary appropriateness, fluency, and comprehension.

Louisiana

Philosophy. The guidelines recommend both naturalistic and nativistic approaches to instruction. Sheltered English techniques focus on the content rather than on the form or structure of the communication. These techniques include simplified teacher talk, match of language and activities with the proficiency of students, concrete references and visuals, and the connections with previously acquired knowledge.

Language policy. Native language instruction is provided at first; the amount of subject matter taught through English is gradually increased. Language acquisition is considered the result of need and social interaction.

Subject-matter content. This includes mastery of grade-level skills. Students do not have to learn English before they receive subject-matter instruction. On the contrary, students participate successfully in a mixed-language, heterogeneous group; develop higher-level thinkings skills; and benefit from advanced course content while they are learning English. The program is not remedial in nature but promotes accelerated learning.

Role of culture. The student's culture and language are valued by the school.

Development of literacy. Whole language methodology is employed. All language arts are learned as interrelated processes acquired in the context of actual reading and writing; are not to be taught as isolated skills. Reading skills hierarchies have comprehension as their goal and should not dictate a sequence of exercises to be done out of the context of the reading process. The mechanics of writing are to be taught at the revision stage of the writing process because effective communication is the goal of writing. Reading and writing strategy instruction is provided as needed.

Assessment and evaluation. Evaluation of student progress can include: observations, anecdotal records, portfolios containing writings and other samples of student work, self-evaluations, standardized tests, results of conferences, surveys, and other informal means of data collection. A detailed list of instruction-embedded objectives that can be assessed is included in the curriculum guide.

Materials selection. Materials should include challenging, yet at times uncertain, tasks that are intrinsically interesting. Tasks are to be open-ended and instructions should be English and/or other languages as needed.

Classroom management. This includes reliance on cooperative learning and peer tutoring. Small groups of students of mixed levels of English proficiency and academic preparation take responsibility for their own learning. The classroom environment is child-centered with students working together to solve problems.

Minnesota

Philosophy. Communicative competency (direct type of language program) is encouraged and requires learning key vocabulary and building fluency in basic communication patterns. Language skill areas are to be acquired in the order of listening, speaking, reading, and writing. Pronunciation is a concern only when it interferes with meaning. In elementary school, communicative approaches to language that emphasizing achievement of functional goals are promoted. With older students, a more structural approach emphasizing discrete grammar instruction, for example, would occur.

Language policy. English instruction is recommended for at least thirty minutes per day to as much as two hours. Specialized language instruction focuses on listening comprehension, pronunciation, functional usage, vocabulary, grammar, reading, writing, spelling, and nonverbal language. Times are planned for structured interaction with English-speaking peers in nonacademic subjects, during recess, lunch, and all-school events. Models include intensive, pull-out, and in-class instruction.

Role of culture. LEP students are encouraged to share aspects of their cultural and linguistic background with other students in a way that enhances cross-cultural understanding. Mainstream classes, such as social studies, may focus on aspects of the LEP student's country. LEPs are assisted in becoming familiar with the social patterns, values, and behavioral expectations of the new country while maintaining their own value system.

Development of literacy. Reading, writing, listening, and speaking are integrated to support and reinforce each other during instruction. No specific guidelines are identified.

Assessment and evaluation. This includes home language census, English reading or English language arts achievement test or English language proficiency test—all focusing on listening, speaking, writing, and reading. Comparisons with the district's average are made in determining placement and exiting from ESL programs.

Materials selection. The guidelines recommend purchase of ESL materials to cover a range of levels; this includes comprehensive teachers' manuals. Other subject matter materials are to be adapted by ESL/bilingual teachers to make the language and content comprehensible to the students. Translated materials are allowed, if chosen judiciously.

Parental involvement. Home–school contacts and active parental participation in their children's education are encouraged. Schools are encouraged to use parents and community as cultural, volunteer, and advisory resources.

Texas

Philosophy. A naturalistic program is recommended, having a natural approach to language acquisition with some emphasis on direct instruction. Students are involved in language-use situations of a variety of types. Language is the focus of instruction and appears to be the prerequisite to functioning in content-based classes. Language study is most formalized in reading and writing activities.

Language policy. Language-use opportunities of a variety of types are provided. Lessons focus on language use through sometimes formal language study. Linguistic growth and accuracy increase

through usage and are the outcomes expected to result from activities that promote language exposure and production. Students are exposed to language-rich environments wherein they practice listening, reading, speaking, and writing in a variety of settings and with myriad speakers and listeners for a multitude of purposes. Contains provisions for primary language and for ESL instruction.

Subject-matter content. Language production is the content of instruction. Situations requiring functional and accurate use of English are provided throughout the curriculum. Reading and writing are studied as subjects. Oral language situations are deliberately established and experienced.

Role of culture. Focus on learning appropriate school behavior, recognizing, contrasting, and respecting differences among cultures, value own culture and understand relationship between language and culture.

Development of literacy. This includes traditional focus on decoding and the skills of comprehension in reading. In writing, attention in instruction is on correct grammar and accurate use of the conventions of English. The curriculum evolves to the formal study of elements in literature, study skills, and writing in a variety of modes. Accuracy in production and form is sought at all levels.

Central Region Summary

The central states are mixed in their approach to language education. Minnesota appears to be the most conservative and Louisiana the most non-traditional. Minnesota additionally is the only state that encourages ESL without directly specifying native language instruction as well. All four states support the valuing of the home culture; three states encourage acculturation as a goal.

Mountain West Region

	ARIZONA	COLORADO	IDAHO	MONTANA	NEW MEXICO
PHILOSO-PHY	Nativistic	Open	Nativistic	Direct, natural-istic, nativistic	Direct
LANGUAGE POLICY	K-12 bilingual education/ESL	Bilingual/ESL	ESL	Eclectic	Bilingual edu-cation/ESL
SUBJECT MATTER	All subject ar-eas		Content study results in lan-guage growth	Language fo-cus at first, content as possible	Local curricu-lum sequence followed/ duplication avoided
CULTURE	Dual		Multicultural	Comparative	Formal
LITERACY	Whole language		Meaning-mak-ing	Whole language	
ASSESS-MENT/EVAL-UATION	Formal and subject matter readiness	Formal and in-formal	Alignment with curriculum with standardized tests	Content area performance	Achievement and standard-ized tests
MATERIALS	Varied		Variety	Varied	
CLASS-ROOM MANAGE-MENT	Experiential		Interactive, co-operative and not tracked	Cooperative/col laborative learning	No more than 1/2 day in ESL or bilingual ed-ucation
PARENT	Parental option		Home learning		Advisory com-mittee/ permission

Arizona

Philosophy. A nativistic approach to instruction is suggested with content and language as the dual curriculum. Sheltered and structured immersion methodologies are encouraged.

Language policy. This state's policy allows native language instruction, K-12, and is designed to increase English language proficiency. Program options include transitional bilingual programs (K-6), secondary bilingual program (7-12), bilingual/bicultural program (K-12), English as a second language, and Individual Education Programs (K-12) for fewer than nine LEP students in a school district grade level. Language and content are a dual curriculum with sheltered methodologies encouraged. Content is made comprehensible by simplifying language, using concrete objects, visuals, and hands-on activities. Language arts are not separated but are inte-grated as they are used.

Subject-matter content. Academic achievement is required by law for LEP students in all subjects (K-8) required of non-LEP students and in elective and nonelective content courses required for graduation (7-12). The lessons focus on the subject matter, which is modified but not watered down.

Role of culture. Instruction includes the history and culture of Arizona and the United States as well as customs and values of both languages being taught. Classroom materials are related to the students' background knowledge and experi-ences, and encourage students to discuss the cultural dimensions of the text. Cultural interac-tions that may result in miscommunication and disharmony are part of the teachers' training. These include time and appropriate pace, standards of conduct, communication, attitudes toward work and accomplishment, relationships, use of space, authority, control, and power.

Development of literacy. The guidelines recom-mend integrating the language arts with reading and writing assistance provided from the begin-ning of the program. Authentic practice of reading and writing is encouraged. A whole language approach to literacy development is provided. Reading and writing are not taught as subjects but as processes applied to authentic materials and situations.

Assessment and evaluation. Specific language tests are identified for screening and assessment of primary home language and English proficiencies in listening, speaking, reading, and writing. Reassessment occurs every two years with all LEP students. Transition to an English-language course of study is dependent on the student's readiness to succeed based on minimum competency skills in required subjects. Reclassified students are reviewed twice during the follow-up year. Reading progress is assessed by nationally normed reading comprehension subtests of the state pupil achievement testing program.

Materials selection. Literature, concrete objects, models, films, pictures, graphs, and other visuals are suggested. Textbooks are used as a guide or a resource and are not necessarily taught from cover to cover.

Classroom management. Teachers become facilitators of language; they model its use; they encourage student risk taking and try to ensure comprehension for all students. Classrooms are seen as active, language-rich learning environments. Students are engaged in experiencing and doing rather than just listening to the teacher. Competition is discouraged and mistakes are allowed.

Parental involvement. Placement of students in bilingual or ESL programs is a parental option.

Colorado

Philosophy. This state's guidelines are wide open; individual school districts appear to determine their own approaches to ESL programs.

Language policy. Allows bilingual education moving toward English proficiency, but no specific guidelines are provided.

Assessment and evaluation. Only Colorado state-approved measures can be used. However, great latitude is allowed in the selection of tests, including parent and teacher checklists, English-language proficiency tests, and standardized tests.

Idaho

Philosophy. A nativistic approach is recommended. Students are immersed in whole language environments in which the language contexts are child-centered, literature- and activity-based, meaning-rich, talk-focused, and parent-involved. Proficiency develops as students discover, play with, and experience language while developing an awareness of how it helps them define the world around them. ESL courses of study parallel that instruction provided native speakers of English. Students actively construct

knowledge for themselves. They use cooperative problem-solving. They also learn skills in the context of real problems.

Language policy. Opportunities for language learning are provided for all children regardless of ethnicity and linguistic abilities. LEP students are to have frequent opportunities to use spoken and written language in meaningful contexts. Language proficiency develops at different rates according to the individual student.

Subject-matter content. The goals of the language arts are achieved, in part, through their being incorporated with the study of other subject areas.

Role of culture. A child's ethnic culture is to be valued and used as a bridge toward English language proficiency. Multicultural literature and subject matter are incorporated whenever possible and appropriate. Programs are committed to affirming human diversity and validating the history and culture of all ethnic groups.

Development of literacy. The goal is to integrate language arts with components of reading, writing, speaking, listening, and viewing—not to have them taught or learned in isolation. Reading is defined as meaning-making process integrating background knowledge with information sources, such as meanings, letter-sound relationships, and sentence and text structure. Writing is seen as a tool for learning, discovering, communicating, recording, and understanding all of the curriculum areas. Speaking is interactive and for communicating, expressing, and understanding information. The overall goal is to help students become thoughtful and reflective comprehenders and producers of poetic, narrative, expository, and persuasive language.

Assessment and evaluation. Assessment is aligned with the curriculum and can include standardized tests. Portfolios of student work, anecdotal records and criterion-referenced records, are part of the assessment program.

Materials selection. A wide variety of materials is recommended including but not limited to textbooks. Textbooks are used as resources. Workbooks, skills texts, or dittoes for seat work are not recommended. Trade books can replace a basal reading series. Separate texts for spelling, writing, grammar, etc, are not recommended.

Classroom management. An active, language-rich, interactive classroom is expected. Cooperative learning and peer tutoring are encouraged. Cooperative learning, reading/writing workshops, conferencing, and peer-response groups are all recommended. Tracking into ability levels is not a recommended method for grouping students.

Parental involvement. Parents are informed of the overall goals and objectives in the language arts and are given opportunities to assist learning in the school and at home. Parents are encouraged to emphasize language learning in the home.

Montana

Philosophy. Communication arts programs incorporate learning about language (direct instruction), learning language (naturalistic), and learning through language (nativistic)—all are allowed. Recommended, however, is a naturalistic approach that focuses on comprehensible input, situational activities, acceptance of errors, and provision of low-anxiety, positive, and learner-centered classes.

Language policy. The guidelines suggest that teachers apply as many of the current methodologies of language acquisition as possible in developing their own curriculum and lesson plans. An eclectic approach is urged, matching teaching style to student need and material covered. Communicative proficiency is emphasized with a focus on both interpersonal communication and the academic language of content instruction. The focus is on clear production of English. Contrasts between the primary language and English are undertaken to help students recognize changes in style, tone, and nuance inherent in translations.

Subject-matter content. The focus is on language. Initially, activities to foster interpersonal communication are introduced, and later the language of social situations is added. Content-area language lessons are designed to provide the student with the language skills necessary for successful mainstream learning.

Role of culture. The guidelines suggest using the students' cultural background in the classroom to learn English. Numerous opportunities are provided to experience mainstream culture along with exploration of and comparison with the students' own cultural traditions. Emphasis is on knowledge of the cultural characteristics of the home culture and cross-cultural influences between the home and mainstream languages. Literature representing both cultures, celebration of holidays and festivals, crafts, and appropriate second-culture etiquette and terminology are encouraged. Cultural themes are studied to develop understanding and acceptance of societal differences, enriching the appreciation of the student's own culture and its place among other world cultures. Themes such as etiquette, proxemics, gender roles, recreation, and entertainment are included.

Development of literacy. Reading and writing are introduced using the whole language philosophy. The use of native- and second-language literature is recommended. Reading and writing exercises utilize authentic contexts (menus, signs, journals, individual-generated stories, etc.)

Assessment and evaluation. Ultimately, students' progress is assessed by their performance in the content areas, including science, math, and social studies.

Materials selection. Films, classical and popular literature in all genres, culture capsules (dramatizations of cultural points of difference), newspapers, ads, and other authentic documents are used.

Classroom management. The use of cooperative and collaborative groups is recommended.

New Mexico

Philosophy. This is not stated directly but appears to emphasize the language skills needed for various grade performance as established by minimum standards. Direct instruction of orthography, syntax, lexicon, and reading content is encouraged. These approaches appear to exemplify a direct type of language program.

Language policy. The guidelimes permit primary language education, including ESL instruction. Native language instruction in subject matter is allowed; special English instruction to promote transition to English-only classrooms is also to be planned. Dual-language usage is allowed when the home-language is used as a bridge for content delivery. Language separation is recommended in the maintenance programs. At least forty-five minutes of home language content delivery daily is expected. Transition to English-only instruction should normally occur by grade four. The bilingual program and ESL instruction can continue beyond this grade with newly arrived students.

Subject-matter content. Core area content can be provided in the home language. Achievement in core areas of the curriculum is the same as that specified in the Minimum Standards for all students. Core areas include mathematics, social studies, sciences, and fine arts, and are taught in the home language of the students as needed. Duplication of instruction in two languages is to be avoided. The local curriculum sequence is followed regardless of the language being used for instruction.

Role of culture. The guidelines recommend emphasis on the history and cultures associated with the students' mother tongue. New Mexico cultures are taught in content areas in selected aspects of the curriculum. The ethnic culture is included in the areas of social studies and fine rts and is taught in English or the home language. The cultural content is taught for a minimum of thirty minutes daily.

Development of literacy. Specific methodology is not suggested. The use of standard language forms is recommended, however, for reading, writing, and linguistic development activities. Orthography, syntax, lexicon, and reading content is taught directly for a minimum of thirty minutes daily.

Assessment and evaluation. Home language and proficiency in English is determined for placement. Student performance is evaluated continuously in English reading and writing in basic skills at pertinent grade levels. Teachers and parents are surveyed in establishing the dominant language. Achievement in standardized tests in content areas and English-language skills can also be considered.

Classroom management. Students can be in a bilingual program for only less than half a day; they are in the regular program for the rest of the day.

Parental involvement. Parental wishes are honored regarding placement of the child in a bilingual program. Parental advisory committees are to be established at each bilingual/ESL school site. A parental advisory committee reviews the goals and priorities of the education program.

Mountain West Region Summary

A mixture of progressive and traditional approaches to language education is found in this region. Arizona and Idaho appear to be the most progressive; New Mexico is the most conservative. Native language instruction is encouraged in four of the states; and subject matter instruction is considered important in most. The cultural component varies considerably, ranging from formal instruction in New Mexico to a multicultural emphasis in Idaho. Whole language and meaning-making literacy programs are supported in Arizona, Idaho, and Montana.

Pacific States Region

	CALIFORNIA	OREGON
PHILOSOPHY	Naturalistic	
LANGUAGE POLICY	Sheltered ESL and bilingual education	Transitional
SUBJECT MATTER	Aligned with school's curriculum	
CULTURE	Integrated and multicultural	
LITERACY	L1 literacy leading to L2 literacy	
ASSESSMENT/ EVALUATION	Normed tests along with informal measures	District option
MATERIALS	Aligned with state frameworks	
CLASSROOM MANAGEMENT		
PARENT	Encouraged	

California

Philosophy. A naturalistic approach typifies the philosophy encouraged by this state. Programs encourage sheltered English instruction of subject-matter content. The emphasis is on life skills at first, with a focus on subject matter later. A high level of comprehensibility is encouraged in low-anxiety situations; the focus is on meaning rather than grammatical correctness. Content is communicated by adjusting the level of speech in the classroom through repetition of key words and phrases; slowing down speech; controlling vocabulary and idiomatic expressions; giving concrete examples; using body language, props, films, etc.

Language policy. This encourages home-language instruction in content areas supplemented by an ESL program.

Subject-matter content. Content-area instruction is aligned with that of the school in general. The same topics, processes, and lesson strategies considered appropriate for the various levels of instruction are found in bilingual classes and mainstream classrooms.

Role of culture. Content representing all cultures in the school district is integrated into the curriculum. Recognition, appreciation, and respect for each cultural heritage is promoted. Information from the student's culture is used as background for the new content that is studied. Subject-matter instruction is considered the forum for exploring both the differences and the commonalities in a pluralistic society. Part of learning a new language also involves becoming aware of differences in worldviews, customs, belief systems, and social conventions.

Development of literacy. Literacy is seen as an active search for meaning that can best occur in a strong primary language. Initial literacy is encouraged through the primary language. Native-language literacy is considered an assist to English literacy. An ability to understand and speak English to some extent is expected before English reading instruction can begin.

Assessment and evaluation. Normed tests—along with informal measures of reading, oral English proficiency, writing proficiency, and subject-matter preparedness—are used to determine readiness for transition to English-only instruction.

Materials selection. Subject matter materials should align with and support the state's curriculum frameworks in language arts, history/social science, mathematics, etc. ESL materials must have a communication focus and should be varied in appearance and format. Authentic speech is used throughout. Cultural features are integrated throughout the materials and are natural dimensions of the communication.

Parental involvement. Parents are included in the decision making process of schools; their involvement is encouraged by teachers frequently and clearly communicating with them in their home language.

Oregon

Language policy. This state's guidelines allow native language instruction to help students, not only to make an early and effective transition to English, but also to benefit from continuing education. The state requires special courses at each grade level, starting at grade one, to teach speaking, reading, and writing English until students can profit from classes taught in English.

Assessment and evaluation. Each school district develops a plan for identifying students whose primary language is other than English and criteria for determining when students are able to handle regular classroom instruction in English.

Pacific States Region Summary

Although limited data is available from Oregon, and none from Washington, the guidelines from California by themselves warrant analysis due to the large numbers of LEP students in this state. California appears to summarize what is occurring throughout the states in this region—its guidelines fall between the more conservative direct approach to language education to the more progressive nativistic approach. California promotes naturalistic approaches utilizing sheltered ESL techniques in subject-matter instruction. Native-language instruction is encouraged as a route to English-language development. Formal and informal measures are used in assessment and evaluation of student performance and program monitoring.

Conclusion

Even though this survey examined documents submitted by twenty-two states, it is by no means complete. Only those curricular guides and state department of education mandates that affect ESL curricula and/or bilingual education programs were examined. There may, of course, be additional documents not submitted by state departments of education that may further illuminate their philosophies, language policies, guidelines for subject-matter instruction, articulation of the role of culture, suggestions for the development of literacy, procedures for assessment and evaluation, guidelines for materials selection, recommendations for classroom management, and ideas for parental involvement.

As a generalization, there are myriad approaches and philosophies recommended throughout the country. While the naturalistic philosophical stance is the predominant approach recommended, many states continue to encourage direct instruction focusing on audiolingual or cognitive procedures. Only a handful of states are recommending nativistic language programs.

Cultural components of language programs by and large encourage acculturation and adjustment to American society. Many states support a two-way multicultural approach. A few states treat culture as subject-matter content to be taught as a separate course in school.

About half of the states recommend whole language as the approach of choice to literacy. Most of the remaining states appear to support the more traditional skills approach to literacy. States suggesting classroom management practices used cooperative learning frequently, and they suggested homogeneous grouping of students less often.

No clear-cut patterns emerge from this analysis of state guidelines for ESL curricula. No one region of the country has a monopoly on newer and more progressive approaches to language education. No one region in its entirety relies only on older, more conservative modes of language instruction.

STATE-LEVEL CURRICULUM GUIDELINES: A LISTING

THIS chapter provides bibliographic information on the state curriculum documents discussed in chapter 5. The publications are organized by state; for each state, we have provided the full address for that state's department of education, including the office to contact regarding curriculum publications (if such an office has been specified by the state department). The phone number shown is the best number to use for ordering the publications or for getting further information on the publications. We have also provided the addresses and phone numbers for states whose departments of education do not publish statewide curriculum frameworks. These states may produce curriculum materials on specific topics in English as a Second Language and in other disciplines, but they are not statewide guides as described in chapter 5.

For each publication, the listing provides the full title, document number and/or ISBN (if available), number of pages, year of publication (or reprinting), and price. Pricing is given on those publications for which Kraus had information; note that the prices shown are taken from the department's order form. Shipping and handling are often extra, and some states offer discounts for purchases of multiple copies. If a document is listed in ERIC, its ED number is shown as well.

Alabama

State Department of Education
Gordon Persons Office Building
50 North Ripley Street
Montgomery, AL 36130-3901

Division of Student Instructional Services
Coordinator, Curriculum Development/
   Courses of Study
(205) 242-8059

The Alabama State Department of Education does not produce statewide frameworks for K–12 ESL.

Alaska

State Department of Education
Goldbelt Building
P.O. Box F
Juneau, AK 99811

Division of Education Program Support
Administrator, Office of Basic Education
(907) 465-2841, Fax (907) 463-5279

The Alaska State Department of Education does not produce statewide frameworks for K–12 ESL.

Arizona

State Department of Education
1535 West Jefferson
Phoenix, AZ 85007

Education Services
Instructional Technology
(602) 542-2147

*Strategies for Teaching Limited English Proficient
Students: General ESL Strategies, Part I*
112p., 1991.

*Strategies for Teaching Limited English Proficient
Students: Content Area Strategies, Part II*
111p., 1991.

*Bilingual Programs and English as a Second
Language Programs Monitoring Guide*
140p., 1991.

Arkansas

Department of Education
Four State Capitol Mall
Room 304 A
Little Rock, AR 72201-1071

Instructional Services
Coordinator, Curriculum and Assessment
(501) 682-4558

The Arkansas Department of Education does not
produce statewide frameworks for K–12 ESL.

California

State Department of Education
P.O. Box 944272
721 Capitol Mall
Sacramento, CA 95814

California Department of Education
Bureau of Publications
(916) 445-1260

Foreign Language Framework
ISBN 0-8011-0804-7, 46p., 1989. ED 310 625.

Bilingual Education Handbook: Designing Instruction for LEP Students
ISBN 0-8011-890-x, 71p., 1990. ED 326 049.

Basic Principles for the Education of Language-Minority Students: An Overview
ISBN 0-8011-0197-2, 28p., 1982. ED 249 772.

*Individual Learning Programs for Limited English
Proficient Students: A Handbook for School
Personnel*
ISBN 0-8011-0227-8, 74p., 1984. ED 253 116.

Colorado

State Department of Education
201 East Colfax Avenue
Denver, CO 80203-1705

English Language Proficiency Unit
(303) 866-6784

English Language Proficiency Act (ELPA) Legislation, Reporting Forms and Operational Guidance
66p., 1991.

*Office for Civil Rights (OCR) Policy Update on
Schools' Obligations Toward National Origin
Minority Students with Limited-English Proficiency
(LEP Students)*
32p., November 1991.

Connecticut

State Department of Education
P.O. Box 2219
165 Capitol Avenue
State Office Building
Hartford, CT 06106-1630

Program and Support Services
Division of Curriculum and Professional
   Development
(203) 566-8113

The Connecticut State Department of Education
doesn't produce statewide frameworks for K–12
ESL.

Delaware

State Department of Public Information
P.O. Box 1402
Townsend Building, #279
Dover, DE 19903

Instructional Services Branch
State Director, Instruction Division
(302) 739-4647

Guidelines for Identification, Assessment and Placement for LEP Students
n.d.

Florida

State Department of Education
Capitol Building, Room PL 116
Tallahassee, FL 32301

Curriculum Support Services
Bureau of Elementary and Secondary Education
(904) 488-6547

Curriculum Frameworks for Grades 6-8 Basic Programs. Volume III: Language Arts Intensive English-ESOL
99p., 1990. ED 295 183.

Curriculum Frameworks for Grades 9-12 Basic and Adult Secondary Programs Language Arts Intensive English-ESOL
158p., 1990. ED 295 184.

Georgia

State Department of Education
2066 Twin Towers East
205 Butler Street
Atlanta, GA 30334

Office of Instructional Programs
Director, General Instruction Division
(404) 656-2412

English to Speakers of Other Languages Resource Guide
88p., n.d.

Hawaii

Department of Education
1390 Miller Street, #307
Honolulu, HI 96813

Office of Instructional Services
Director, General Education Branch
(808) 396-2502, Fax (808) 548-5390

Identification, Assessment and Programming System for Students of Limited English Proficiency: A Systems Manual
RS 91-0593, 29p., 1991, rev. of RS 88-4287.

Content Area Instructional Strategies for Students of Limited English Proficiency in Secondary Schools: A Sheltered Approach
RS 91-1142, 144p., 1991.

Idaho

State Department of Education
Len B. Jordan Office Building
650 West State Street
Boise, ID 83720

Chief, Bureau of Instruction/School Effectiveness
(208) 334-2165

Integrated Language Arts Course of Study, K-8
54p., 1990, 1992 (sixth printing).

Secondary English Language Arts Course of Study
34p., 1991.

Civil No. 79-1068. Idaho Migrant Council, Inc., et al. v. Board of Education

Illinois

State Board of Education
100 North First Street
Springfield, IL 62777

School Improvement Services, Curriculum Improvement
(217) 782-2826, Fax (217) 524-6125

23 Illinois Administrative Code. Title 23: Education and Cultural Resources. Subtitle A: Education.

Special Courses of Study. Part 228 Transitional Bilingual Education
5-89/9-8858/1M/#456, 17p., 1989.

Indiana

State Department of Education
Room 229, State House
100 North Capitol Street
Indianapolis, IN 46024-2798

Center for School Improvement and Performance
Manager, Office of Program Development
(317) 232-9157

Local school districts develop their own curricula, and they use regular English/language arts proficiency guides when developing ESL programs.

Iowa

State Department of Education
Grimes State Office Building
East 14th and Grand Streets
Des Moines, IA 50319-0146

Division of Instructional Services
Bureau Chief, Instruction and Curriculum
(515) 281-8141

Educating Iowa's Limited English Proficient Students
30p., 1988. ED 301 044.

Kansas

State Department of Education
120 East Tenth Street
Topeka, KS 66612-1182

The Kansas State Department of Education does not produce statewide frameworks.

Kentucky

State Department of Education
1725 Capitol Plaza Tower
500 Mero Street
Frankfort, KY 40601

Office of Learning Programs Development
Division of Curriculum Development
(502) 564-2106

The Kentucky State Department of Education is developing curriculum frameworks that local school districts may use as guides to develop their own curricula. These frameworks, which will not be state mandated, will be available in mid-September 1993.

Louisiana

State Department of Education
P.O. Box 94064
626 North 4th Street, 12th Floor
Baton Rouge, LA 70804-9064

Office of Academic Programs
Elementary Education (504) 342-3366
Secondary Education (504) 342-3404

English Language Arts Curriculum Guide for Limited English Proficient Students, Grades K-12
Bulletin 1832, 500p., 1989, rev. ed. 1991.

Maine

State Department of Education
State House Station No. 23
Augusta, ME 04333

Bureau of Instruction
Director, Division of Curriculum
(207) 289-5928

Practical Practices for ESL Teachers
133p., 1991.

Book of Solutions: Frequent Questions on Concepts, Issues and Strategies for the Education of Language Minority Children
74p., 1991 (second printing). ED 329 115 (1st ed., 1990).

Maryland

State Department of Education
200 West Baltimore Street
Baltimore, MD 21201

Bureau of Educational Development
Division of Instruction, Branch Chief,
    Arts and Sciences
(410) 333-2307

Better: English as a Second Language
83p., 1991.

Massachusetts

State Department of Education
Quincy Center Plaza
1385 Hancock Street
Quincy, MA 02169

Bureau of Equity and Language Services
(617) 770-7545

Responding to Language Minority Students: A
Handbook for Department of Education Personnel
ELMS Publication Series 1990, 24p., 1990.

Bilingual Bicultural is Two-Way Education
60p., 1976 (second printing). ED 117 272 (1st ed.,
1974).

Guidelines and Program Models in the Education
of Language Minority Students in Massaschusetts
(Chapter 71A Transitional Bilingual Education)
37p., 1991.

Common Competencies: The Promise of Linguistic/
Cultural Diversity
BELS FY91 Publication Series, 48p., 1990. ED
334 824.

Young Lives: Many Languages, Many Cultures
No.17,138-79-400-5-92-1.93-C.R., 72p., 1992.

Michigan

State Board of Education
P.O. Box 30008
608 West Allegan Street
Lansing, MI 48909

Instructional Specialists Program
(517) 373-7248

The Michigan State Board of Education does not
produce statewide frameworks for K–12 ESL
programs.

Minnesota

State Department of Education
712 Capitol Square Building
550 Cedar Street
St. Paul, MN 55101

Minnesota Curriculum Services Center
(612) 483-4442

A Resource Handbook for the Assessment and
Identification of LEP Students with Special Educa-
tion Needs
2236, 1087700, 132p., 1987.

Mississippi

State Department of Education
P.O. Box 771
550 High Street, Room 501
Jackson, MS 39205-0771

Bureau of Instructional Services
(601) 359-3778

The Mississippi State Department of Education
does not produce statewide frameworks for K–12
ESL programs.

Missouri

Department of Elementary and Secondary
Education
P.O. Box 480
205 Jefferson Street, 6th Floor
Jefferson City, MO 65102

Center for Educational Assessment, University of
    Missouri—Columbia (source for documents)
(314) 882-4694

The Missouri Department of Elementary and
Secondary Education does not produce state ESL
guidelines, but it does provide some ESL/bilin-
gual education workshops, conferences, seminars,
and materials to school districts that need help
with their ESL populations.

Montana

Office of Public Instruction
106 State Capitol
Helena, MT 59620

Department of Accreditation and
     Curriculum Services
Curriculum Assistance and Instructional
     Alternatives
(406) 444-5541

Communication Arts Curriculum Model
24p. 1990. Covers ESL and bilingual education.

*Montana School Accreditation: Standards and
Procedures Manual*
34p., 1989.

Nebraska

State Department of Education
301 Centennial Mall, South
P.O. Box 94987
Lincoln, NE 68509

The Nebraska State Department of Education
does not produce statewide ESL frameworks.

Nevada

State Department of Education
Capitol Complex
400 West King Street
Carson City, NV 89710

Instructional Services Division
Director, Basic Education Branch
(702) 687-3136

The Nevada State Department of Education is
currently developing ESL curriculum for K-12.

New Hampshire

State Department of Education
101 Pleasant Street
State Office Park South
Concord, NH 03301

Division of Instructional Services
General Instructional Services Administrator
(603) 271-2632

*Standards Series for Appropriate and Effective
Educational Programs for Limited English
Students, Module 2: Curriculum Guide*
69p., 1986.

New Jersey

Department of Education
225 West State Street, CN 500
Trenton, NJ 08625-0500

Division of General Academic Education
(609) 984-1971

*Guidelines for Development of Program Plan and
Evaluation Summary: Bilingual/ESL Programs and
English Language Services (Chapter 197, Laws of
1974 and Chapter 212 Laws of 1975 as Amended),
Fiscal Year 1991*
PTM 1000.37, 163p., 1991. ED 318 236.

New Mexico

State Department of Education
Education Building
300 Don Gaspar
Santa Fe, NM 87501-2786

Learning Services Division
Instructional Materials
(505) 827-6504

*Guidelines for Approval of State Programs—
Bilingual Education.*
11p., July 1977, rev. September 1977, August
1979.

Article 23 Bilingual Education
22-23-1, 10p., n.d.

Chapter 5 Bilingual-Cultural Education Program

New York

State Education Department
111 Education Building
Washington Avenue
Albany, NY 12234

The State University of New York
The State Education Department
Publications Sales Desk
(518) 474-3806

The New York State Core Curriculum for English as a Second Language in the Secondary Schools 86-9116, 078600, 110 p., 1983, reprinted 1986. ED 228 878.

Note: NYS curriculum for ESL in elementary schools is currently under revision. An availability date has not been set.

North Carolina

Department of Public Instruction
Education Building
116 West Edenton Street
Raleigh, NC 27603-1712

Publications Sales Desk
(919) 733-4258

English as a Second Language Curriculum Handbook, K-6
66p., Charlotte Mecklenburg School District, 1983.

English as a Second Language Curriculum Handbook, 7-12
223p., Charlotte Mecklenburg School District, 1983.

Note: These guides are used statewide for ESL programs.

North Dakota

State Department of Public Instruction
State Capitol Building, 11th Floor
600 Boulevard Avenue East
Bismarck, ND 58505-0440

Office of Instruction, Supplies
(701) 224-2272

The North Dakota State Department of Public Instruction does not currently produce a statewide ESL framework. However, the department provides technical assistance to districts, such as workshops and seminars.

Ohio

State Department of Education
65 South Front Street, Room 808
Columbus, OH 43266-0308

The Ohio State Department of Education does not produce statewide ESL frameworks.

Oklahoma

Department of Education
Hodge Education Building
2500 North Lincoln Boulevard
Oklahoma City, OK 73105-4599

School Improvement Division
Instructional Programs
(405) 521-3361

Suggested Learner Outcomes for English as a Second Language
20p., n.d.

Oregon

State Department of Education
700 Pringle Parkway, S.E.
Salem, OR 97310

Publications Sales Clerk
(503) 378-3589

ESOL Helpbook (English to Speakers of Other Languages)
15p., 29th ed., 1992.

Pennsylvania

Department of Education
333 Market Street, 10th Floor
Harrisburg, PA 17126-0333

Office of Elementary and Secondary Education
Bureau of Curriculum and Academic Services
Bilingual Education Section
(717) 787-3785

Guidelines for Educational Programs in the Commonwealth of Pennsylvania for Limited English Proficient Children
21p., 1973. ED 066 075.

Rhode Island

Department of Education
22 Hayes Street
Providence, RI 02908

Unit for Limited-English Proficient Students
(401) 277-3037

Chapter 16-54 An Act Relating to the Development of English Language Proficiency for Limited English Students
16p., 1983, reprinted 1983.

English as a Second Language Curriculum Framework
100p., n.d.

South Carolina

State Department of Education
1006 Rutledge Building
1429 Senate Street
Columbia, SC 29201

Coordinator, ESL/Bilingual Programs
(803) 734-8219

The South Carolina State Department of Education does not have mandated ESL curriculum; the department recommends using mainstream subjects to teach ESL students, i.e., content area instruction for ESL. The department also provides technical assistance to districts.

South Dakota

Department of Education and Cultural Affairs
435 South Chapelle
Pierre, SD 57501

Office of Educational Services
Elementary Curriculum (605) 773-3261
Secondary Curriculum (605) 773-4670

The South Dakota Department of Education does not produce state guidelines for ESL programs. However, the Department's Curriculum Center provides a variety of ESL resources to local districts.

Tennessee

State Department of Education
100 Cordell Hull Building
Nashville, TN 37219

Curriculum and Instruction
(615) 741-0878

Language Arts Curriculum Framework: English as a Second Language, Goals and Objectives, K-8
22p., n.d.

Language Arts Curriculum Framework: English as a Second Language, Goals and Objectives, 9-12
13p., n.d. ED 296 356.

Texas

Texas Education Agency
William B. Travis Building
1701 North Congress Avenue
Austin, TX 78701-1494

Division of Bilingual Education and Special Language Instruction
(512) 475-3555

Essential Elements: Primary Language for Bilingual Education and English as a Second Language, Prekindergarten
3p., n.d.

Essential Elements: Primary Language for Bilingual Education and English as a Second Language, Kindergarten
3p., n.d.

Essential Elements: Primary Language for Bilingual Education, Grades 1-5 and English as a Second Language, Grades 1-6
19p., n.d.

Essential Elements: English as a Second Language, Grades 7-6
4p., n.d.

Essential Elements: English for Speakers of Other Languages and English as a Second Language I, Ii, III, Grades 9-12
6p., n.d.

Utah

State Office of Education
250 East 500 South
Salt Lake City, UT 84111

Division of Instructional Services
Coordinator, Curriculum
(801) 538-7774

The Utah State Office of Education is currently developing an ESL curriculum, and is revising its policy statement on ESL/bilingual population. The new publications are scheduled to be available in 1993.

Vermont

State Department of Education
120 State Street
Montpelier, VT 05602-2703

Basic Education
Chief, Curriculum and Instruction Unit
(802) 828-3111

The Vermont State Department of Education is developing an ESL curriculum, modelled on Maine's guidelines. The new publication is scheduled to be available in 1993.

Virginia

Department of Education
P.O. Box 6-Q, James Monroe Building
Fourteenth and Franklin Streets
Richmond, VA 23216-2060

Instruction and Personnel
Administrative Director of General Education
(804) 225-2730

English as a Second Language Handbook for Teachers and Administrators
49p., 1992.

Washington

Superintendent of Public Instruction
Old Capitol Building
Washington and Legion
Olympia, WA 98504-7200

Curriculum/Student Services and
  Technology Service
Curriculum Support
(206) 753-6727, Fax (206) 586-0247

Guidelines: The Transitional Bilingual Program
n.d.

West Virginia

State Department of Education
1900 Kanawha Boulevard, East
Building 6, Room B-358
Charleston, WV 25305

Division of Instructional and Student Services
(304) 558-7805

Wisconsin

State Department of Public Instruction
General Executive Facility 3
125 South Webster Street
P.O. Box 7841
Madison, WI 53707-7841

Publication Sales
(608) 266-2188

The Wisconsin State Department of Public Instruction is developing a statewide ESL curriculum; this publication is scheduled to be available summer 1993. At present, local school districts develop their own ESL curricula as needed; they are submitted to the State Department of Public Instruction for review.

Wyoming

State Department of Education
2300 Capitol Avenue, 2nd Floor
Hathaway Building
Cheyenne, WY 82002-0050

Division of Certification, Accreditation and
  Program Services
Accreditation/Special Services Unit
(307) 777-6808

The Wyoming State Department of Education does not produce statewide frameworks for ESL programs.

TESTING AS AN ASSESSMENT TOOL

by Mark S. Patkowski
Assistant Professor
Brooklyn College, Brooklyn, New York

AS a teacher developing an English as a Second Language curriculum for your school, a major aspect of your task will be to consider and select evaluation procedures that will enhance your ESL program. Testing plays a major role in education in general, as well as in language teaching in particular. You will employ formal assessment procedures during all phases of language instruction: first, to determine the needs of your students and their appropriate placement into the program; then, to monitor their progress; and finally, to evaluate their achievement and readiness for advancement. Your assessment procedures should positively influence the learning and teaching that will take place in the program and permit you to evaluate the program's effectiveness. In addition, you will inevitably find yourself informally assessing the comprehension, speaking, reading, and writing abilities of learners whenever you interact with them.

A certain amount of controversy surrounds some testing procedures, in education in general as well as in language testing. For example, controversy exists over the well-known Scholastic Aptitude Test (SAT), which the majority of college-bound students take throughout the United States. Research shows that, in general, females do poorer than males on this standardized test. The basic purpose of the SAT is to provide some measure of the likely future academic success of the test taker; yet research

also seems to show that, in fact, females do better than males in their first two years of college, despite their lower SAT scores. This particular controversy over assessment procedures is probably among the better known to the general public; however, similar but less widely reported disputes also exist in the area of language testing. Two examples that involve specifically linguistic issues are tests designed for native speakers being administered to non-natives and excessive reliance on a single measure of ability.

Tests designed for native speakers have been misapplied to non-natives. Some decades ago, IQ tests were administered in English to immigrants who did not speak the language and, therefore, performed poorly; they were then labeled mentally defective. Much more recently, a major public university system administered a reading test designed for natives to its entire student body, which included a large proportion of non-native speakers; the test was to be a test of reading comprehension, not of reading speed. While this may have been true for natives, in one large-scale experiment with non-natives, passing rates doubled when an extra fifteen minutes were given to complete the examination. Subsequently, the university extended the test time limit for all students; yet, prior to the time extension, many ESL students were being sent into reading remediation for reasons associated with their reading speed and not their reading comprehension, because the test had been normed on a population of their native-speaking peers.

A related type of misapplication of testing procedures involves using a test that has been specifically developed for ESL students for purposes other than those intended by the test maker. For example, a test meant to assess overall English language proficiency should not be used as a diagnostic instrument to evaluate students' specific areas of strengths and weaknesses.

Excessive reliance on a single and sometimes narrow measure affects the educational careers of students. This is a major area of dispute. Is it possible to assess a student's abilities fairly and accurately on the basis of a single measure? Getting back to the SAT example, it has been found that the high school grade point average (GPA) of a student (whether male or female) is a good predictor of that student's college performance. Since the GPA is based on the student's performance in several courses over several years, the validity of this summative measure differs significantly from a score on a one-shot test.

It is interesting to note that, despite the fact that the same grades from different schools might represent different levels of student achievement, the GPA consistently turns out to be a reliable predictor of college performance. Of course, as college admission officers know, the best way to assess candidates is to examine many variables, including SAT scores, GPAs, letters of recommendation, and so on. To obtain a more authentic picture of your students' abilities, several assessment measures should be used.

A related point about using single measures to evaluate students concerns the possibility of test bias. Such bias can range from asking students from lower socioeconomic backgrounds questions based on readings about stockbrokers or polo playing to giving seemingly innocent essay topics that are taboo or embarrassing for students from different cultural backgrounds. A student could do very poorly on a particular measure for reasons unrelated to actual language proficiency.

How can you avoid these pitfalls? The chances of misapplying language tests can certainly be reduced when those giving the tests have a basic but solid understanding, not only of the fundamental principles of testing, but also of the controversies that surround them. With this in mind, the following pages will attempt to answer two broad yet fundamental questions that any educator embarking on the task of building an ESL assessment program ought to consider: (1) What is my purpose in testing? and (2) How can I best achieve that purpose?

It is only after attaining a clear idea of what you want to test that you can decide how to do the testing.

Basic Concepts and Terminology

Before being able to make a decision about what and how to test, any professional will need to understand the basic theoretical considerations that underlie any testing situation. A good way to begin is by defining and briefly discussing several of the most important terms that invariably appear in textbook discussions of testing.

We will consider seven key terms. The first three (*reliability, validity, practicality*) refer to three basic requirements of a good test; the following four (*objective, discrete-point, integrative, standardized*) refer to characteristics that may vary from test to test, depending on the test maker's approach. In addition, a few more related key terms (italicized) are also explained.

Three Requirements of a "Good" Test

Test reliability. For a test to be reliable means both that two or more examiners will assign the same score to the same paper (*rater reliability*) and that the same test taker, or two groups of matched test takers, will receive similar scores if given the test on two separate occasions (*test-retest reliability*). In the latter case, the assumption must be that no further learning has taken place between the test and retest times, and that testing conditions are essentially similar in all respects (including situational factors, such as noise or the physical layout of the testing room, and individual factors, such as the physical health or mental alertness of the examinee at the time of taking the test).

For a test to be reliable, it must yield consistent and dependable results. Test reliability is easily and precisely quantified by statistical procedures. The major commercially available language tests, such as the Test of English as a Foreign Language (TOEFL), which international applicants to many American colleges take instead of the SAT, have been thoroughly tested for reliability.

Test validity. This is the most complex, crucial, and controversial criterion of a good test. The central question of validity is whether a test really measures what it claims to measure. For example, does the SAT, which is both objectively scored (see *objective tests*, below) and quite reliable from a statistical point of view, really measure the test taker's probability of doing well academically in college (in other words, the test taker's "scholastic aptitude")? The test maker (the Educational Testing Service) holds that it does; critics have charged that the verbal section, in particular, measures not so much language proficiency as it does a form of "conventional worldliness," a knowledge of words and expressions that are used in the typical expository writing of conventional, mainstream journalism, such as that found in major newspapers and news magazines. The findings that females score lower on their SATs before going to college, yet subsequently do better than their male counterparts in their first two years in college, also raise questions about the validity of the test. Similarly, the incident involving the test of reading comprehension that turned out to have a major speed component when used with non-native students involves questions of validity.

The standard method of establishing validity of a test is by examining the relationship between the scores obtained by examinees on that test with other measures of success, such as other well-established tests (*concurrent validity*), or with actual subsequent performance (*predictive validity*). Thus, for example, the results on a test given as an exit procedure from an ESL program into the mainstream would be expected to predict fairly well the subsequent performance of those students as measured by, say, GPA. Both of these types of validity can be statistically quantified; however, the concurrent or subsequent measures selected to correlate with the test are subjective.

Other factors to be considered in assessing validity would include examining the actual content of the test, to determine whether the sample of performances being measured is truly representative of the behavior or ability being evaluated; this is usually called *face validity*. The content and approach of the test can also be examined in light of the current state of the linguistic theory field; this is called *construct validity*. These two aspects of overall validity are clearly crucial to a good test, but they can be established only on the basis of subjective judgment and cannot be quantified statistically.

In the final analysis, there is no overall, truly objective measure of validity. This means that you really need to look at various testing instruments, read about them, and perhaps even sit down and take them yourself, in order to select those that will measure students' English language skills in a way that seems reasonable and coherent to you.

Test practicality. In addition to being reliable and valid, a good test has to be practical. If a test requires that the examiner must spend two hours individually with each student, or if it is expensive or takes too long to score, a school system will probably not use it.

Four Characteristics of Tests

Most tests fall into one or more of the following categories.

Objective tests. This term is used to refer to the scoring of tests. Objective tests usually fall into the "multiple-choice-question-with-only-one-correct-answer" format and can be scored mechanically. Note that it is only the scoring itself which is objective. All tests are constructed subjectively by the test maker, and the examinee has to make subjective decisions during the test-taking process. An objective test can be biased and a poor measure of actual student proficiency (in other words, it can lack validity); again, "objective" means that you or any other examiner, or any mechanical scoring device, will arrive at the same score for any particular paper (allowance being made for occasional human error or mechanical failure). Thus, the primary advantage of objective testing is its consistency of scoring (rater reliability) and, usually, its ease of administration (practicality).

Discrete-point tests. Discrete-point tests are associated with the objective approach. The term refers to the format of the test items. The basic tenet of the discrete-point approach is that each point of language must be tested separately, that each test item must test only one aspect of language at a time. A typical discrete-point language test will divide its multiple-choice questions into grammar, vocabulary, listening, reading, and so on. Each one of these categories will be further subdivided; for example, reading might be subdivided into "getting the main idea," "making inferences," "recognizing major details," and so on.

One shortcoming of objective, discrete-point testing is that student answers may not reveal much about their true language proficiency. Most

ESL teachers have encountered students who get most or all of the answers right on an objective, discrete-point grammar quiz yet produce inaccurately the very same grammatical structures in their written or spoken language. Similarly, many college professors have had international students in their classes who apparently performed well enough on the TOEFL to be admitted but who then exhibited great difficulties in producing reasonably adequate, standard, written English.

The objective, discrete-point approach to testing has been widespread in the United States for decades, and has been applied to a broad range of subject matter. Indeed, this approach has predominated in America for over fifty years.

Integrative tests. Such tests stand in contrast to objective, discrete-point tests, and are meant to assess overall proficiency in a particular area. This is accomplished through a task that bears a reasonable resemblance to a real-life language situation; the closer this resemblance, the more *direct* the test is considered to be. Thus, a test of writing that involves an actual essay task would be considered direct, whereas one that inferred writing ability on the basis of the test taker's success in filling in blanks in a prose passage from a selection of choices would be considered indirect. The most common direct tests are essay examinations and oral interviews.

Other integrative approaches, including dictation and *cloze* tests (that is, a test constructed by taking a written passage and deleting every fifth, sixth, or seventh word), have aroused interest but are not widely used, despite some significant research support for their validity, reliability, and practicality. These are probably the easiest tests for the classroom teacher to construct, and, with simple guidelines, they may be useful for specific purposes.

Another category of integrative tests involves the *holistic* approach. The term "holistic," just like the term "objective," refers to the scoring procedure employed. In holistic testing, the examinee is asked to provide whole samples of written or oral language, rather than respond to discrete items; these samples are then evaluated in a broad manner. For example, examiners will read a student essay and then assign ratings that reflect their impression of the written work. In this approach, raters do not base their appraisals on sets of recognizable subskills but, rather, render overall judgments. Usually, essays (or interviews) are rated by two examiners, with

disagreements being resolved through a third judgment.

This may seem less "scientific" than objective testing. It would seem that different examiners would assign different scores to the same paper based on their subjective evaluations. However, like objective testing, holistic testing has been practiced in this country for decades (for example, by the Department of State's Foreign Service Institute to assess the foreign language abilities of personnel), and it gained widespread acceptance across American universities in the 1980s, particularly for the assessment of writing. The Educational Testing Service (ETS) also now offers a holistic test of writing for non-native speakers, the Test of Written English (TWE).

Furthermore, research shows that examiners can be trained to rate accurately and consistently (and thus to achieve a high level of rater reliability) and, in the case of direct interview tests, to carry out those interviews with consistency. The primary advantage of this approach lies in its greater face validity. For example, instead of making inferences about a student's ability to write on the basis of multiple-choice responses, that ability can be assessed directly by requiring the examinee to actually produce a sample of writing. The disadvantage lies in the area of practicality: the scoring takes much longer, and raters must be constantly trained, which takes time and costs money, if they are to maintain consistent standards.

It is important to note that there is no purely integrative test nor any purely discrete-point test; it is more a question of a continuum, with tests falling more toward one end or the other.

Standardized tests. Standardized tests are tests that have been extensively field tested, such as the numerous objective tests produced by the ETS, including the objective, discrete-point TOEFL and the holistic TWE. Through this field testing, ambiguities and bias in test items can be eliminated or reduced, the statistical reliability of the instrument can be ascertained, and *norms* can be established (that is, the language test can be referenced against the performance of an adequately large sample population). When a test is "normed," the scores that you obtain with your students can be compared to established scores for given populations, which may differ by social class, region, nationality, gender, and so on. This is one reason why it is inappropriate to administer to non-natives language tests (such as reading tests) that have been normed on native speakers; when this is done, the obtained scores cannot be properly interpreted.

In addition, when test makers standardize their tests, certain aspects of validity (such as concurrent and predictive validity) can also be examined statistically (but face and construct validity always remain essentially subjective judgments).

Purposes and Methods in Testing

There are several reasons for testing, and it is imperative that the test giver be clear about his or her objectives. Specifically, are you testing to place incoming students or to evaluate student progress and readiness for advancement, exemption, certification, and so on; or are you testing for instructional purposes, to "drive" the curriculum? Or are you testing for all of these purposes?

Although these purposes overlap, it is useful to examine these aspects individually. (For a comprehensive approach to developing an overall assessment program, see chapter 2.)

Testing for Placement

When testing for placement, you first need information about the students' general competence in English, to make an overall determination as to whether they should be placed into the ESL program; for those students who will be enrolled in ESL, you need more specific information to determine the level at which they should be placed. Thus, the ideal placement procedure involves a combination of proficiency, diagnostic, and achievement testing.

A proficiency test is not limited to any particular course, curriculum, or language skill (the four traditional language skills being listening, speaking, reading, and writing). Many commercially available objective tests seek to fulfill this role.

A diagnostic test provides more specific information concerning the students' areas of strengths and weaknesses. Again, many commercially available tests, even though they yield an overall proficiency score, are also subdivided into sections, such as grammar, the four language skills mentioned above, and even "discourse competence" (the ability to interact with speakers not only grammatically but also in linguistically appropriate ways).

An achievement test typically includes a sampling of the specific material covered in the classroom lessons in your program. Commercially available proficiency tests are not suitable, since they are not tied to any particular curriculum (except when you purchase a complete curriculum package with teaching and testing materials).

A good placement procedure involves a combination of tests. For example, in one ESL program, incoming students were given a standardized, discrete-point, commercially available objective test, supplemented with an in-house holistic essay exam, as well as a brief oral interview (also developed in-house). Students were then placed into the appropriate level of ESL reading, writing, conversation, and grammar classes, or even into bridge classes ("real" subject-matter classes, such as history, which were reserved for ESL students only), or specific mainstream classes that provided a hospitable and productive environment for ESL students.

Testing to Evaluate Progress and Readiness for Advancement

What is basically required to evaluate student progress and readiness for advancement is an achievement testing procedure. Essentially, this refers to teacher-prepared quizzes during the school year or semester, and teacher- or program-prepared final examinations. Such testing should include only material that has been specifically taught in class; it is important to use a varied approach in the testing and not to rely on any single measure. You may wish to experiment with current "authentic" approaches (see *New Trends in Testing*, below), such as "portfolio" evaluations of student work. Another direct and authentic approach is to allow students to take mixed programs involving both ESL and mainstream classes, and to use their performance in the mainstream as a means of assessing their progress and/or readiness to move on.

At the point of exit from the program, you may again administer a commercially available standardized proficiency test. You may even decide to evaluate all students at all levels on a yearly, program-wide basis, with a commercial test. In these cases, you should supplement whatever instrument is purchased with other means of assessment.

Using an approach that makes a student's placement into and exit from an ESL program dependent upon a single assessment measure (usually a standardized test) is counterproductive and demoralizing for the students, teachers, and program. One unfortunate and inevitable result is that some students who are clearly ready to move on are held back, even though their teachers know, based on the students' actual in-class performance, that they are ready for the mainstream. It even happens when the students have proven in bridge and mainstream courses that they can handle the rigors of the mainstream (in programs where ESL students are not restricted solely to ESL courses). Furthermore, when the same standardized test is used repeatedly, answers may be leaked, thus allowing other students to "pass" when their teachers know that they are not ready for the mainstream. These occurrences hamper the teaching process and can best be avoided by taking a broad and diversified approach to testing.

Testing To "Drive" the Program

Your testing will not only allow you to place, monitor, and promote your students, but it will also tend to provide the goals for the program's teachers and students. Tests tend to drive the curriculum; the British have even coined an acronym for this phenomenon—WYTIWYG (pronounced "witty-wig"), meaning "what you test is what you get." In the more usual technical jargon, this effect is called "backwash." If your testing has good backwash effects, it will positively influence the teaching and learning in the program, and vice versa.

Teachers frequently feel some pressure to teach to the test, and students to learn for the test. So, if the test is a standardized, discrete-point objective test, the pressure will be on to practice multiple-choice questions; if the test is a holistic essay examination that asks students to respond to questions worded according to a particular format, the pressure will be on to practice writing such essays. Thus, the testing procedure will drive educational practice at the program level.

At the individual classroom level, the individual teacher's purposes in testing will also affect the students' educational experience. A teacher can use tests negatively, for instance, to keep students busy and quiet, or by failing to return tests in a timely manner with adequate corrections and explanations. Conversely, a teacher can use testing in the classroom as a part of the overall instructional process, to provide opportu-

nities for students to improve their skills by learning from their mistakes.

Thus, if the testing in your program is varied and multifaceted, both at the program level and in the individual classrooms, there will be an incentive for teachers and students to teach, learn, investigate, explore, discover, develop, and expand their language skills in diverse and valuable ways.

Testing Procedures

To achieve your testing purpose, you must choose an appropriate assessment procedure for that particular purpose. Your selection may include tests purchased commercially or constructed in-house.

In general, commercially available tests are used for program-wide testing (for placement, progress evaluation, and exit purposes) and not for day-to-day classroom testing. In addition, you may want to supplement commercial tests with some in-house assessment procedures at the program level and use teacher-made quizzes and tests in day-to-day classroom evaluation.

Brief Review of Selected Commercially Available ESL Tests

The following review is divided into two parts: the first presents tests meant primarily for elementary and secondary school students; the second covers tests designed for high school or college students.

Tests for Elementary and Secondary School Students

The Basic Inventory of Natural Language (BINL)
CHECpoint Systems
1520 North Waterman Avenue
San Bernadino, CA 92404
(714) 888-3296

This test is a measure of oral English proficiency that focuses on natural language use and does not rely on test-taking skills. It can, therefore, be considered to have good face validity. The test, which can be used for grades K–12, is available for thirty-two languages.

During the test, which takes about ten minutes, the examinees are asked to react to pictures. Their speech is analyzed for fluency, length, and grammatical accuracy. The test manual contains the instructions on how to score the subjects' speech, but the procedure may seem a little confusing. For each grade level, students are classified as non-English-speaking, limited English-speaking, fluent English-speaking, and proficient English-speaking, according to their scores. The test was standardized on several thousand students from ages four to eighteen in California. From a statistical point of view, reliability (particularly rater reliability) and predictive validity are unproven. However, this is unfortunately true of almost all commercially available ESL tests.

The main attraction of the BINL is that you could use its elicitation techniques as a basis for developing your own test of spoken language. In addition, if there are staff members who are native speakers of some of your students' first languages, results on the BINL in those languages could be compared with results on the English BINL to establish students' language dominance.

Language Assessment Battery (LAB)
New York City Board of Education
O.E.A. Scan Center
49 Flatbush Avenue Extension, 5th floor
Brooklyn, NY 11201
(718) 596-5226/7

This test, developed by the New York City public school system in response to legal developments mandating language-appropriate education, is now widely used in New York City, New Jersey, and Connecticut. There are two versions—one in English, one in Spanish—to be used to evaluate students' language skills in grades K–12.

The test has listening, speaking, reading, and writing sections at all levels (except for kindergarten, where there is only listening and speaking). Responses are scored as correct or incorrect according to rating guidelines. The listening/speaking section that is given to grades K–2 and the speaking section for grades 3–12 are individually administered. Reading and writing sections (grades 1–12) are group administered. The test includes questions about pictures to test speaking, cloze procedures in listening and reading, and requests to write sentences with given words.

The instrument is normed on large samples of English-proficient, limited English-proficient (LEP), and Spanish-proficient students, and these norms are reported by grade. Because the test exists in two languages, it is possible to determine the language dominance of children with a Spanish language background. The test can be employed to distinguish between varying levels of language proficiency at any given point in time

and also to monitor students' progress over time. The availability of the norms makes the interpretation of scores straightforward. The test is also available in two forms, which prevents students from becoming overly familiar with it. Despite its length and complexity, this is one of the more complete language assessment instruments available for grades K–12.

Language Assessment Scales (LAS)
Linguametrics Group
P.O. Box 3495
San Rafael, CA 94912-3495
(800) 247-9436; in CA (800) 624-7373

This test is designed to measure oral skills in English or Spanish for grades 2–12. The test is administered individually and takes ten or twenty minutes. Students respond verbally to prompts, retell stories, or point to pictures. The examiner scores the test by comparing students' answers to expected answers; scoring on the story retelling is holistic. The final score places the student into one of five categories, from "no control of the language" to "fluent speaker."

The test appears to be reasonably reliable; the publishers present research results that show a good degree of rater reliability in the story task. Overall, validity seems reasonable, too; the test makers present the results of studies that compared teacher judgments with student scores on the LAS and that show general agreement between the two. However, some aspects of the test seem to lack face validity—in particular, the section of the test designed to assess the students' control of the "sounds" of the language seems irrelevant to real language use. On the other hand, the story-telling task appears useful. As with the BINL, you could use the LAS as a resource in developing your own test.

Maculaitis Assessment Program (MAC)
Jean D'Arcy Maculaitis
Alemany Press
2501 Industrial Parkway West
Hayward, CA 94545
(800) 227-2375 or (415) 227-2375

MAC is meant as a placement, diagnostic, and proficiency test for speakers of English as a second language in grades K–12. Depending on the grade level, the test takes from forty minutes to almost two hours. At the lower grade levels, the test involves listening and speaking; at later grades, reading, and then writing, are added.

Based on their scores, students are placed into one of nine categories (from low beginner to high advanced).

The test has been quite extensively standardized with student populations of various backgrounds. Thus, norms are supplied for different ethnic and linguistic populations, male and female, and across grade levels. Statistics provided by the publisher show good reliability. Statistics for predictive validity are less impressive; that is, the relationship between the score on the MAC and subsequent school grades in English was moderate at best. However, the same is true of such widely used tests as the SAT and others.

Unlike the LAB, this test does not have an alternate form, and, like the LAB, it is somewhat complex to administer and score; but it is also a very thorough instrument that can be used at all grade levels, K–12.

Quick Language Assessment Inventory
    Moreno Educational Company
    P.O. Box 19329
    San Diego, CA 92119
    (614) 461-0565

This is not really a language test but, rather, a questionnaire designed to elicit information concerning a student's language experiences at home and at school. The inventory can be administered very quickly to a child's parent or guardian (in one minute) and asks questions to determine the child's home language habits and exposure to English in and out of school. A final score is derived, and the child is then classified into one of four categories, from "mainly English speaker" to "mainly Spanish speaker."

This questionnaire provides an insufficient basis for assessing the linguistic proficiency of a child; at the same time, its focus on sociolinguistic background variables can complement linguistic information obtained through other language tests. In addition, the inventory could be useful in the initial stages of assessment, when you first meet a child and his or her parent or guardian and explain the testing procedures to them.

The Second Language Oral Test of English (SLOTE)
    Alemany Press
    2501 Industrial Parkway West
    Hayward, CA 94545
    (800) 227-2375 or (415) 887-7070

This is essentially an oral test of grammar, which evaluates the ability of ESL students of all ages and backgrounds to produce twenty standard English grammatical structures by eliciting verbal responses to pictures. The test takes about fifteen minutes and is easy to administer (which is done on an individual basis) and to score. The test, comprised of sixty items, is divided into subtests that appraise specific grammatical points, such as articles, plurals, negatives, and questions. The results give a diagnostic picture of students' abilities on the twenty specific structures in question.

Good statistics are reported for reliability and concurrent validity, but these are based on a very small sample population. This is a quick and easy instrument, but should be used only as part of a more comprehensive language assessment procedure. However, with beginning or low-intermediate students, this test could provide you with some useful information concerning your students' control of some of the basic structures of the English language. On the other hand, it is probably less useful with intermediate or advanced students.

Tests for High School and College Students

The Comprehensive English Language Test (CELT)
    McGraw-Hill Book Company
    1221 Avenue of the Americas
    New York, NY 10020
    (212) 512-4327

This is an objective, discrete-point test designed for high school and older ESL students at the intermediate and advanced levels. The test takes slightly over two hours to complete, and scoring is done with a template. There are three sections: listening, structure, and vocabulary. The first part is administered by means of a tape recording, and involves answering multiple-choice questions. The second part contains brief written dialogues with missing words; the student is offered a choice of four completions, three of which are ungrammatical. The last section also involves multiple-choice items; the vocabulary words are meant to be representative of the vocabulary that might be encountered in college-level courses.

The test has not been extensively standardized; thus, it would be difficult to judge how well your students are doing in comparison to a larger population. It would also be difficult to interpret the meaning of particular scores in terms of placement. In effect, you would have to develop your own norms (in other words, decide which scores correspond to what level in your program). Still, this test is easy to administer and score, appears reliable, and could be a good choice if you are looking for an objective test to include in your assessment procedure.

Michigan Test of English Language Proficiency
    English Language Institute
    Testing and Certification Division
    The University of Michigan
    Ann Arbor, MI 48109
    (313) 747-0456

This test of English-language proficiency contains sections on vocabulary, reading, and grammar. It is a classic, discrete-point, multiple-choice test and is meant to be used to estimate a non-native student's readiness to pursue college studies. The testing time is seventy-five minutes, and scoring is done with a stencil. The testing manual contains information concerning the interpretation of scores for placement purposes; however, the publishers present insufficient and outdated evidence concerning the norming of the test. This test has been in wide circulation at colleges throughout the United States for over twenty years; although there are many forms of it, it is possible for students to become familiar with it.

This test continues to be used quite widely at colleges even though it has not been significantly updated for years. Similarly, statistics concerning reliability and validity are outdated. Apparently, however, colleges continue to find it useful, presumably based on the in-house data that they have collected over the years. The test should be used only as one component of a broader overall assessment procedure.

Test of English as a Foreign Language (TOEFL),
Test of Spoken English (TSE), and Test of
Written English (TWE)
    Educational Testing Service
    Princeton, NJ 08541
    (609) 921-9000

These three tests are all produced by the Educational Testing Service (ETS), the major test-making institution in the country, which also brings us (in cosponsorship with the College Board, the Graduate Record Examinations Board, and others) such well-known tests as the SAT, GRE, LSAT, MCAT, and so on.

The tests are administered at special ETS testing centers and at participating colleges, universities, and institutions. These tests are essentially meant for non-native students who plan to pursue their higher education in the United States. They are probably the most widely used and most thoroughly researched ESL tests available; approximately half a million people take these tests every year across North America and in over 130 countries. The data on reliability and validity are based on very large sample populations and are statistically far more significant than those for any of the other tests that have been reviewed above. These are truly standardized tests. In addition, they are highly secure; for example, twelve new forms of the TOEFL are produced every year. In contrast, most of the commercially available tests reviewed here are available in only one or two forms, which remain the same from year to year.

The TOEFL is a standardized, objective, multiple-choice examination with three sections, each timed separately: listening comprehension, structure and written expression, and reading comprehension and vocabulary. Total test time is 110 minutes.

The listening comprehension section, administered via audiotape, presents short statements, short conversations, brief talks, and mini-lectures followed by multiple-choice items. The structure and written expression section involves completing incomplete sentences or identifying incorrect words and phrases. The reading comprehension and vocabulary section involves selecting synonyms for underlined words or phrases in sentences or answering comprehension questions that follow brief reading passages.

Prior to taking the TOEFL, examinees receive a handbook that explains the test and provides sample questions. The scores are given on a 200–800 point scale (like the SAT and GRE), and institutions determine what they consider to be passing or failing levels. Reliability is high, and studies of concurrent validity yield good results (that is, TOEFL scores tend to agree with the scores obtained on instruments that claim to measure similar abilities). TOEFL scores even show "moderate to good" levels with direct and integrative measures, though there is some dispute about the effectiveness of the TOEFL as a predictor of college GPA. The caveat here, as usual, is that excessive reliance on a single measure in making educational decisions for students is unwarranted; indeed, ETS itself warns against unwarranted reliance on the TOEFL.

The TSE is a semidirect measure of oral language and is designed for non-native adults, particularly graduate students and professionals.

The test takes approximately thirty minutes. Examinees are not interviewed directly but, rather, respond to printed and tape-recorded questions. All answers are tape-recorded and subsequently evaluated by pairs of trained raters.

As with the TOEFL, the examinee receives a handbook that explains the test and provides sample questions. The TSE begins with unscored warm-up questions to relax the testee. The scored portions of the test include reading aloud, describing a picture, completing sentences, and expressing an opinion on a controversial topic or describing a familiar object. In this way, a sufficient speech sample is elicited for rating on pronunciation and grammar. The final score is given on a 0–300 point scale, and, as with the TOEFL, institutions define for themselves what they consider to be acceptable scores.

The TWE is a direct test of writing; that is, it is an essay examination that is scored holistically by pairs of raters on a 1–6 scale. As is usual with holistic grading systems, disagreements are resolved through a third reading. The test time is thirty minutes.

This test is meant to allow the examinee to demonstrate in standard written English an ability to organize ideas and support them with examples or evidence. Compositions are expected to be 200 to 300 words long. The raters for this examination are experienced teachers of English or ESL in secondary and higher education institutions who receive extensive training. Scoring is monitored to maintain reliability.

This test was developed in response to changes in the field of language testing that have led to a greater emphasis on more integrative and direct approaches to evaluation. In addition, many, if not most, colleges were demanding that a way be found to obtain and assess actual writing samples from non-native students who wished to pursue their higher education in the United States. Similar in-house holistic writing tests have also become widespread throughout American colleges for all students, native and non-native. The backwash effect of this approach can only be positive; precollege students and teachers alike now know that writing is an important language skill that can no longer take a back seat to other skills such as reading, listening, and selecting responses from multiple-choice options.

Brief Review of Guidelines for Classroom Testing

This section will present some general principles and guidelines that you should keep in mind before you begin to develop your own ESL testing materials. I will then briefly review some selected "how-to" texts that can be consulted for thorough discussions of classroom test construction. The following four principles should be kept in mind when you plan your testing approach.

Test what you have taught. You will then be able to evaluate the extent to which students have attained your objectives. Sample the taught material fairly.

Test in a varied manner. All of the language skills should be tested (reading, writing, listening, speaking, discourse competence). Different testing approaches should be used (from the more discrete-point end of the spectrum to the more integrative). Do not make the final grade dependent on a single test or single testing approach, but use multiple testing techniques.

Test fairly and grade justly. Acquaint your students ahead of time with the testing procedures, and let them know the nature of the content on which they will be tested. Give clear and complete instructions in language that is appropriate to the students' level; supply examples. Allow sufficient time to complete the test. Make the grading straightforward and comprehensible to the students; let students know how much different sections of a test are worth in terms of the overall score.

Make the test part of the learning process. By giving your students useful feedback, you provide them with an opportunity to improve their skills. Grade and return the test on a timely basis. Do not just assign a grade; supply corrections and/or explanations, and discuss the test results with students. Use your scoring to assign greater weight to those parts of the test that most reflect the skills on which you want your students to focus.

In addition to these four overall principles, you should also bear in mind the following guidelines in developing your own tests:

Begin by specifying your objectives. Do you wish to focus on specific language skills, such as listening, speaking, reading, writing, or communicative competence? Or do you wish to focus on testing structural elements of the language, such as pronunciation, vocabulary, or grammar? Are you testing incoming students for placement, continuing students for promotion, or current students to provide feedback and encourage learning?

Choose your format and develop your items and scoring procedure. Think about how you wish to approach your task, whether from an integrative mode or from a more discrete-point approach. If you take a more integrative approach, your test items may be easier to construct, but you will have to pay extra attention to developing adequate scoring procedures. On the other hand, if you decide on the objective approach, you will discover that it is difficult to construct good multiple-choice items; however, the scoring is much easier.

Be prepared to revise the test. Ideally, you should pilot a new test or new test items on an existing test. This will allow you to analyze your items for their levels of difficulty and their ability to discriminate between different student abilities. If some items are either too easy or too hard, they are not very useful to your overall test. In addition, instructions that seemed clear to you when you wrote them may be confusing to your students and need revision. In general, there should be a reasonable "fit" between your students' scores on your test and your own assessment of their abilities.

Constructing Classroom Tests

So, given all these principles and guidelines, how does one actually go about constructing ESL tests? As mentioned earlier, there is a wide variety of actual language testing techniques available to the classroom practitioner; a brief review of some texts on classroom test construction follows.

Alderson, J., K. Krahnke, and C. W. Stansfield, eds. 1987. *Reviews of English Language Proficiency Tests.* Washington, DC: TESOL.
This publication provides an overview of some forty-seven major tests of English for non-native speakers that were developed in the United States, Great Britain, Canada, and Australia and are currently in use in those countries and throughout the world. Each entry contains a summary of the test, followed by a reviewer's appraisal. The actual reviews vary in their content and length. This is a very useful reference text and valuable information resource.

Davies, Alan. 1990. *Principles of Language Testing.* Cambridge, MA: Blackwell.
This text focuses on the concept that language testing lies at the core of language teaching. The author discusses the role of language testing in setting goals for courses and programs, for both teachers and learners. He also discusses the role

of language testing in linguistic acquisition research. The discussion focuses the reader's attention on the backwash effects of testing procedures.

Heaton, J. B. 1975. *Writing English Language Tests.* London: Longman.
This classic text is still widely used for courses in language testing for teachers. It is a practical handbook for classroom teachers and shows how to develop a wide variety of English language test items and tests. The emphasis is on objective testing, with a lot of attention paid to the construction of multiple-choice items. Other approaches (including oral interviews, dictations, and cloze procedures) are covered in less detail. There is a short chapter on interpreting test scores which introduces some basic statistical considerations.

Henning, Grant. 1987. *A Guide to Language Testing: Development, Evaluation, Research.* New York: Newbury House.
This book is also intended for teachers and teachers-in-training. The book covers an extensive range of practices and approaches in language testing. However, it also takes a strongly statistical approach; as the author acknowledges, the reader needs some acquaintance with the statistical concepts of correlation, regression, frequency distribution, and hypothesis testing. This text should be reserved for those who wish to deepen their mathematical understanding of concepts such as measurement scales, test reliability, or item analysis and item banking.

Hughes, Arthur. 1989. *Testing for Language Teachers.* Cambridge: Cambridge University Press.
This is a very practical guide for teachers. The author's purpose is to help teachers produce better tests; to that end, statistics are very largely ignored. The author's style is direct and clear, and his overall approach to teacher-made testing is definitely outside of the multiple-choice school; many interesting and valid arguments are offered to back up this point of view. There are chapters on test techniques and the testing of individual language skills which offer much practical information and many illustrations.

Jacobs, H. L., S. A. Zingraf, D. R. Wormuth, V. F. Hartfiel, and J. B. Hughey. 1981. *Testing ESL Composition: A Practical Approach.* New York:

Newbury House.
While this book is designed primarily for evaluating the written work of intermediate and advanced university students, it can be easily adapted for use with secondary school students. The testing approach is built around an "ESL Composition Profile" rating scale, and the authors show how to use such an approach in reliably evaluating student compositions. Half of the book is, in effect, a training manual on how to rate compositions, and numerous sample essays are provided for practice.

Oller, John W., Jr. 1979. *Language Tests at School.* London: Longman.
This long text (almost 500 pages) emphasizes an integrative approach (the author uses the term "pragmatic approach"). There is some theoretical discussion of the underpinnings of the discrete-point and pragmatic approaches to testing; however, there is also practical advice on how to prepare, administer, score, and interpret pragmatic tests such as dictation, cloze procedures, and various tests of written and oral language.

Underhill, N. 1987. *Testing Spoken Language: A Handbook of Oral Testing Techniques.* Cambridge: Cambridge University Press.
Intended for teachers as a basic introduction to testing spoken language, this text presents and reviews over fifty oral testing techniques. The author discusses aims, assessment procedures, marking systems, and attendant problems that raters face. The book also focuses on the need to revise and improve tests once they have been put into use.

Materials Focusing on Informal Classroom Assessment Testing

Barrs, Myra, Sue Ellis, Hillary Tester, and Anne Thomas. 1989. *The Primary Language Record.* Portsmouth, NH: Heinemann.
The PLR is a tool for assessing the day-to-day literacy learning of children in the primary grades. It is based on the idea that one main purpose of assessment (as discussed in the chapter) is to give teachers information about student learning so that they may make decisions about day-to-day teaching in their classrooms. The focus of the PLR is assessing children as they engage in using language (both oral and written) within the recurring events of the classroom. The package includes forms and checklists that teachers may use as they evaluate children's growing abilities in listening, talking, reading, and writing, as well as samples of how teachers have used them. It also includes a special appendix on bilingual children's language and literacy development.

Education Department of South Australia. 1991. *Literacy Assessment in Practice.* Urbana, IL: National Council of Teachers of English.
This volume begins by offering a framework for defining and organizing the various aspects of literacy that might be considered in literacy development. It then offers teachers a wide variety of ideas that they may use in the process of assessing their students' literacy development. The suggestions are anchored in children's ongoing life at school and are appropriate for learners from kindergarten through grade seven or eight. Although this resource was designed originally for native English speakers, the ideas are also useful in second-language settings, and the Australian public schools are quite multicultural and multilingual in population.

Genishi, Celia, and Anne Haas Dyson. 1984. *Language Assessment in the Early Years.* Norwood, NJ: Ablex.
Beginning from a social interactionist perspective of language acquisition, the authors set up a framework for assessing young children's oral and written language that is based primarily on teacher observation and description and secondarily on teacher analysis of children's oral and written language samples. The authors provide multiple examples of observational forms and records that teachers might use, as well as samples of frameworks for analysis that are based on current research in children's language acquisition. The examples that they give should provide teachers interested in developing their own forms enough guidance to be able to do so. The numerous samples of children's talk and their emerging reading and writing are a particular strength of this volume. Many of the samples feature bilingual/second-language learners. This volume would be used most appropriately for teachers working with children from preschool through third grade.

Genishi, Celia, ed. 1992. *Ways of Assessing Children and Curriculum: Stories of Early Childhood Practice.* New York: Teachers College Press.

Genishi makes her stance obvious in chapter 1 of this volume as she states, "Assessment here does not refer chiefly to standardized tests or commercially available diagnostic instruments, but to teachers' informal ways of observing and documenting development and learning" (3). In the volume, Genishi has asked six sets of early childhood (preschool through third grade) educators to describe daily life in their classroom, connecting directly the curriculum that they teach to the ongoing, often daily, assessment that they carry out. The particular strength of the volume is the richness of detail about the teaching settings. This detail contextualizes the assessment tools, making obvious the connection between what and how one teaches and what and how one assesses children's learning. Certainly, importance is given to language/literacy learning in the volume, but children are also seen as human beings, and teachers write of the need to consider children's emotional and social wellbeing and growth. One chapter in particular focuses on bilingual/second-language learners and addresses ways second grade teachers use samples of children's actual work to document changes in the learners' second language and literacy.

Goodman, Ken, Yetta Goodman, and Lois Bird, eds. 1989. *The Whole Language Evaluation Handbook.* Portsmouth, NH: Heinemann; Toronto: Irwin.
The perspective taken by this volume is that evaluation (assessment) should be about ways to know about learners and ways to revise curriculum. The contributed chapters work to provide examples of authentic assessment of learners within the contexts of their own classrooms, assessment that is rooted in documenting the learners' progress and in informing teachers about where they need to move in their work with children. Many of the chapters have been written by classroom teachers themselves, so they take on the flavor of the stories in the Genishi volume. The book includes chapters representing primary, middle grade, secondary, adult, and special education. Each section includes examples of bilingual/second-language learners.

Goodman, Ken, Lois Bird, and Yetta Goodman. 1992. *The Whole Language Catalogue: Supplement on Authentic Assessment.* Chicago: SRA.
This book is divided into three sections, each of which is full of practical suggestions for authentic,

classroom-based assessment of students' language and literacy learning. The first section concerns tools for evaluation and offers descriptions and examples of multiple ways to evaluate classroom learning, such as conferences, interviews, checklists, anecdotal records, learning logs, and portfolios. The second section considers how teachers may document student learning in naturally occurring classroom activities such as reading to children, literature study, response to literature, journal writing, writer's workshop, and thematic study. The third section provides ways for teachers and students to evaluate themselves. Contributors from around the United States and Canada have sent in examples of assessment tools that they use, and the compilers have put them together, so that examples of assessment are available on almost every page. Considerable emphasis is given to bilingual and second-language learners.

Hamayan, Else, Judith A. Kwiat, and Ron Perlman. n.d. *Assessment of Language Minority Students: A Handbook for Educators.* Arlington Heights, IL.: Illinois Resource Center.
This volume is devoted specifically to assessing the language skills of second-language learners in the public school setting. While the authors provide a bibliography of some standardized, norm-referenced measurements, the emphasis is on the kinds of assessment that individual teachers and districts might develop for their students. Multiple samples of such kinds of assessment instruments as story retelling, cloze testing in reading, dictation passages, and writing samples—as well as directions for ways to score these instruments—are provided. There is also a discussion of the importance of assessing students' abilities in their native language.

Pierce, Lorraine Valdez, and J. Michael O'Malley. 1992. *Performance and Portfolio Assessment for Language Minority Students.* Washington, DC: National Clearinghouse for Bilingual Education.
In this monograph the authors offer alternatives to standardized language and literacy assessments for language minority students, regardless of age level. They focus on two kinds of assessment, performance and portfolio, defining *performance assessment* as student demonstration of specific skills and competencies and *portfolio assessment* as the use of student work over time in a variety

of modes to show student abilities. In the area of performance assessment, they offer specific examples of ways that educators may elicit oral or written language performance and, through varied rating scales, evaluate this performance; they also include examples of self-evaluation of performance. In the area of portfolio assessment, they offer a variety of specific suggestions for organizing and using portfolios, depending on purpose and specific focus. The guidelines here should provide useful information both to individuals and to school districts wanting to utilize one or more kinds of alternative assessment in order to get a more complete picture of student learning than that afforded by standardized tests.

Rhodes, Lynn K., and Nancy Shanklin. 1992. *Windows into Literacy: Assessing Learners K-8*. Portsmouth, NH: Heinemann.
The authors of this book have worked for many years with Chapter 1 teachers and students, thinking about and designing alternatives to traditional testing, in order to assess more accurately the literacy histories and strengths and needs of Chapter 1 students, from kindergarten through middle-school levels. This handbook begins by discussing some purposes of literacy assessment and then offers a variety of assessment procedures and techniques (for example, miscue analysis, interviews, examining metacognitive aspects of literacy, and figuring out students' literacy strategies) that may be used in classrooms. There is a focus on what the authors call literacy collections which include, but are not limited to, portfolios. Although this book is based on work with native speakers of English, many of the ideas would be easily adapted to second-language learners.

Yancey, Kathleen Blake, ed. 1992. *Portfolios in the Writing Classroom*. Urbana, Il.: National Council of Teachers of English.
Portfolios have become increasingly popular as an alternative way of assessing students' writing. In this volume, classroom teachers at junior- and senior-high levels explain how they use portfolios in their own classrooms and elaborate on the ways that portfolios have changed their teaching. Various models of portfolios and ways of introducing and utilizing them are introduced in the chapters, allowing the reader to see alternatives. Although these authors are working with native English speakers, the philosophy, organizing

principles, and ways of carrying out portfolio assessment may be adapted easily to second-language settings.

New Trends in Testing

Two other issues must be considered in this discussion of testing procedures: the first concerns the current interest in authentic approaches; the second concerns developments in computer-assisted testing.

Authentic Approaches to Testing

A major preoccupation in language testing has been to make the testing more authentic. In the last decade, this preoccupation has led to the move from discrete-point to integrative testing. However, there are those who hold that even today's more direct tests, such as oral proficiency interviews and holistic essay examinations, still do not simulate truly authentic uses of language or replicate real-life language use. For example, in an oral proficiency interview, no real information is being exchanged; a natural communicative situation is not occurring. Instead, the examiner is seeking to probe the linguistic abilities of the examinee and has very little interest in the actual meaning or information contained in the examinee's verbal output. The examinee is concentrating on the structural (grammar, vocabulary, pronunciation) rather than communicative aspects of his or her speech, realizing where the examiner's true interest lies.

Faced with this dilemma, researchers have proposed that ethnographic approaches involving long-term, patient, and sympathetic observation of the examinee's authentic behavior are the solution. Such observations would need to follow systematic procedures in order to develop richer, more complex views of the developing language proficiency of language learners than can be gathered through present procedures.

This approach has penetrated the educational mainstream in the form of portfolios. For example, the New York State Commissioner of Education, Thomas Sobol, has been pushing for New York public schools to adopt far broader measures to assess students than standardized tests. Similar proposals have been made in various other states. The general approach advocated here is the portfolio approach. This means that teachers will attempt to assess students' proficiencies by establishing comprehensive profiles of their experiences and abilities through samples of work gathered over a prolonged period of time, through the completion of projects, through student self-reports and logs of activities, and by any other means available to complete this comprehensive image of the students' level and skills.

At the college level, portfolio approaches are being used experimentally with writing instruction. For example, in one class, students chose their own subjects to write about, kept a journal of personal responses to assigned texts, produced a "history" of each composition as it underwent the various stages of writing and rewriting, completed self-evaluation forms for three papers, and provided evidence of oral and written class participation. The class grade then depended on the teacher's holistic evaluations of these various materials rather than on some score obtained on a standardized test. Usually, where portfolio approaches have been incorporated on a program-wide or even institution-wide basis, evaluation of anonymously submitted student portfolios is carried out by a jury of readers. This method represents a return to teacher judgment, to involving classroom teachers in the overall assessment picture; grades are established based on collective faculty judgment.

A wide debate is raging over the feasibility and wisdom of this approach; obstacles include the fact that intensive teacher involvement with individual students is required, at a time of expanding class sizes due to fiscal constraints. In short, despite the potential high validity of this testing approach, issues of practicality in an era of dwindling resources pose major obstacles. A possible practical compromise could be to rely on a battery of more traditional tests (ranging from discrete-point to integrative) to identify students who clearly fall into passing or failing categories, and to supplement such a testing procedure with portfolio assessment for borderline cases. In other words, authentic measures probably should be gradually integrated with current testing procedures, but are unlikely to ever replace them entirely.

Computerized Language Testing

This is referred to as "computerized adaptive testing." This approach, rather than simply presenting the same test items in the same order as the equivalent paper-and-pencil test, seeks to test only long enough to obtain sufficient information to assess a respondent's ability. At this

time, computer adaptive tests are basically of the objective, multiple-choice variety, such as the TOEFL. In fact, the ETS has been developing a computerized version of the TOEFL, which demonstrates the characteristics of current tests of this nature.

Basically, an examinee is first presented with some initial test items; depending on the pattern of success and failure, the examinee is then routed through "testlets" (blocks of items) of different levels of difficulty. The respondent can backtrack to review and change answers within a given testlet. Since only items judged to be appropriate to the test taker's level are presented, the test does not take as long as the full paper-and-pencil version. Thus, testing time, fatigue, and boredom are reduced; test scores can be provided instantaneously; and test security is enhanced since two examinees are unlikely to face the same sequence of items. In addition, preliminary ETS reports show good agreement between the scores obtained on the regular and computerized versions of the TOEFL. One reported area of concern is that there is a widespread lack of computer experience among ESL students, and this could affect the validity of the procedure. In addition, computerized testing at this time is limited to a multiple-choice approach.

Program Evaluation

Another important aspect of assessment is program evaluation. Any ESL program should assess the quality of the instruction being provided and improve any areas in which weaknesses may be uncovered. In addition, as about half of the states still do not offer ESL certification to school teachers, the self-study process for ESL programs is part of the larger struggle for professional recognition.

Fortunately, TESOL has prepared extensive materials to assist ESL programs at all levels of our educational system to engage in the self-study and review process. The materials can be obtained by contacting TESOL, 1600 Cameron Street, Suite 300, Alexandria, VA 22314; (703) 836-0774. Available materials include the following:

· *Manual of Self-Study for TESOL* and *TESOL Professional Preparation Programs*
· Selected articles on selfstudy from the *TESOL Newsletter*
· *Guidelines for the Certification and Preparation of Teachers of English to Speakers of Other*

Languages in the United States
· *Statement of Core Standards for Language and Professional Preparation Programs*
· *Standards and Self-Study Questions for Elementary and Secondary Programs*
· *Standards and Self-Study Questions for Postsecondary Programs*
· *Standards and Self-Study Questions for Adult Education Programs*
· *Standards and Self-Study Questions for TESOL Professional Preparation Programs*

The purpose of the TESOL program of self-study is to result in program improvement and to allow a program to evaluate how closely it meets the standards set by the TESOL organization. The self-study process should be internally motivated and involve the faculty, staff, and administrators of a program. As described by TESOL, the four basic steps of self-study consist of the following:

Designing the Project

Determine what is to be studied. The TESOL Standards and Self-Study Questions handbook will help frame those questions. Will you focus on your program's goals, administration, instructional staffing, support services, program curriculum, program implementation, assessment procedures, or any combination of the above? You will then need to ask such questions as these:

· Are the program's objectives clearly formulated?
· Is there an administrator with appropriate training who is directly responsible for the program?
· What kind of professional development is available to the ESL staff?
· Are there adequate hours, levels, and class sizes in the program?
· How are students tested and placed?

Organizing the Study

Choose the members of the self-study committee, define tasks and roles, collect resources (including the TESOL materials), and decide on a schedule of tasks and activities.

Conducting the Study

Gather up the data, analyze records, examine opinions (of staff members, teachers, students, peers, outside consultants, outside agencies), produce written documents and a final report.

Promoting Change

A properly conducted self-study should result in a well-organized and convincingly supported final report, which should be published and widely distributed, and which should include specific recommendations for program improvement. Such a document can provide the impetus necessary to move a program forward, both in terms of its quality and in terms of the recognition that it receives from the institution of which it is a part. The self-study process must be viewed as cyclical and ongoing; your ESL program should periodically return to the self-study process in order to continually strive to meet the high standards that you and your students expect.

Conclusion

Language testing is a broad and complicated field. It is also a field that has its share of disputes and disagreements among practitioners. Nevertheless, with a good basic grasp of some fundamental principles and issues of testing, you will be able to find appropriate and effective testing procedures for your ESL program.

It is important to define your objectives clearly, to examine your options carefully, and, above all, not to rely on single measures but to test in a broad and diversified way, both to obtain more accurate assessments of your students' abilities, and to help provide your program's students and teachers with a set of appropriate goals and motivations.

Acknowledgment

The section "Materials Focusing on Informal Classroom Assessment Testing" was contributed by Sarah Hudelson, Professor of Education at The State University of Arizona.

RECOMMENDED CURRICULAR MATERIALS

by Lenora Cook
Assistant Professor
California State University, Dominguez Hills, California

OOKING at how students learn helps educators develop meaningful curricula and classroom and school structures. Over the past twenty years research findings from cognitive psychology have altered how teachers perceive learning in general and learning language in particular. This change has had a profound effect on the development of curriculum materials for teaching English as a Second Language (ESL). Grammar- and usage-based curricula that have a discrete drill-and-practice approach are being replaced by approaches that use the primary language base of the learner. Research seems to indicate that a second language is acquired in the same way as the first— through meaningful contexts in the learner's experience. The results of these investigations have led curriculum planners to rethink language-learning priorities as they develop effective curriculum materials and methodologies.

Historically, learning English or any other language as a second or alternate language has followed the direct instruction approach. This way of teaching is seen as a continuum that stresses progressively more complex "bites" of English. Using discrete lessons in vocabulary, syntax, and the vocalization of sounds to words, students acquire language in a scope and sequence that is connected neither to their lives nor to the subjects studied in a school setting. Modified direct instruction is still in use, mainly with older ESL students and those who have literacy in their native language. Materials for this approach are available from commercial publishers and are listed in this chapter only when they include the two other approaches to learning language, the naturalistic and nativistic.

The majority of materials for curriculum development in ESL are now based on two approaches to learning language or language acquisition: the naturalistic approach, sometimes called *sheltered* English or *sheltered content*; and the nativistic approach, which relies on a situational learning environment where content is embedded in experience. These curricular approaches have many similarities. Both utilize the educational and societal environment of the learner, and in both the responsibility for curriculum design becomes student-centered and flexible as teachers discover the needs and abilities of the language learner. In the naturalistic approach, which most of the recommended curriculum guides use, instruction is based on the language of the situation or lesson. This differs from the direct approach in that little formal knowledge about the structure or syntax of the language is taught; the focus for language development is participatory without correction or accuracy of form except as use inhibits understanding. Teachers design lessons that shelter or preteach needed vocabulary and that reflect the environmental and societal context of the students.

Although there are many similarities between the naturalistic and the nativistic approaches to language learning, some specific differences can been seen. In classrooms where the nativistic approach is used, the student creates and works with language as a natural outgrowth of the situation or context in which language is employed. Although the students in this environment may use either their home language or English, the teacher responds in the target language of the lesson. Because the attention is on the learner and his or her ability to understand content through the use of real-life situations, this approach causes language development or acquisition to become indirect, somewhat spontaneous, and, at times, even unconscious. The nativistic approach focuses on the use of language rather than on proficiency standards.

In an ESL classroom using the nativistic approach, the materials and the instruction come out of the learning situation of the students. For example, the students might read a piece of literature and then discuss their understandings and interpretation without specific study of vocabulary and syntactical structures found in the material. They utilize all the language arts—reading, writing, speaking, and listening—in a holistic fashion. In social studies or science—any subject area where the language arts are used to acquire information—students are given activities and materials that assist them in making the appropriate meanings from the text. Such teaching strategies are also part of native or English speakers' classrooms. The curriculum used in either the naturalistic or nativistic approach is general, evolving from the needs and interests of the students. The annotated bibliography that follows therefore contains more materials about specific activities for fostering language acquisition and fewer complete curriculum guides.

Since a review of technology-based ESL curricular materials found that, for the most part, the infusion of technology into ESL is an add-on, there are no specific curricular packages stressing language acquisition using media or computers as the primary materials. A few interactive media packages are available for single-language English classrooms; these products could easily be used in an ESL program. Teachers are encouraged to develop packages themselves by using hypertext materials such as HyperCard for the Mac and Linkway for the PC.

The use of computers in ESL classrooms has been studied with courseware reflecting the direct approach for learning vocabulary, grammatical structures, punctuation, and rhetorical formats. Much of the courseware available, especially for the secondary learner, is concentrated in this area.

No tutorial packages have been found that were designed especially for ESL students and that reflect either the naturalistic or the nativistic approach. Tool packages are available, such as word processing and publishing programs, that involve the learner in writing and illustrating from his or her own experience. Some courseware requires a speech synthesizer, which is used to vocalize illustrative choices the user makes. A list of these tool packages is included in a subsection of the bibliography.

Due to the changes in language acquisition theory and the escalating national need for courses teaching ESL in the K–12 schools, there has been a proliferation of curriculum and materials design projects during the past four years. Professional associations, school districts, universities, and teacher cooperatives have been joined in their curricular efforts by commercial publishing houses whose participation has intensified as the need for materials has grown more apparent. Many of these programs and projects utilize concepts found in language arts materials designed for the single-language English classroom.

The following is a highly selective annotated bibliography of ESL curricular guides. They represent both content-area and general language-acquisition methodologies. In their approach to language acquisition they are, in the main, nativistic, naturalistic, or a combination of the two. These materials have been selected because they meet the following criteria:

- reflective of current trends and issues in language acquisition, especially learning English as a second language
- relevant and usable by ESL practitioners, including curriculum planners, supervisors and evaluators of ESL programs, classroom teachers, teacher educators, both private and public
- accessible and obtainable easily through sources listed in each citation

The bibliography is organized according to five categories:

1. Professional resources to assist in the development of ESL Programs (K–12)—that is, resources that offer design philosophy, sample lessons, and evaluatory materials

2. ESL Program Frameworks (K–12) without sample activities or lessons
3. ESL Curricular Foundations without lessons and/or evaluatory materials
4. Other Curriculum Materials, including individual units in second language acquisition in specific content areas, relevant research studies, and a list of computer courseware tools
5. Training Materials including video programs

Many of the annotations include further references of use to curriculum planners, teachers, and teacher educators. Professional organizations, such as Teachers of English to Speakers of Other Languages (TESOL), the National Association of Bilingual Educators (NABE), the International Reading Association (IRA), and the National Council of Teachers of English (NCTE), publish monographs, handbooks, volumes, and articles pertaining to language acquisition in K–12 environments on almost a monthly basis. Many universities, such as the University of California at Los Angeles's Center for Language Education and Research, have centers for the study of language that regularly publish papers, reports, and annotated bibliographies. The National Clearinghouse for Bilingual Education and other federal, state, county, and district units also publish and distribute curricular materials on English-language acquisition.

Some of the items cited in this bibliography can be found in the database of the Educational Resources Information Center (ERIC). ERIC is an informational system sponsored by the Office of Educational Research and Improvement, within the U.S. Department of Education. ERIC documents are available on microfiche and as paper copies from the ERIC Document Reproduction Service (EDRS). Many university and regional educational libraries have the microfiche available for viewing and copying. For information about prices, contact EDRS, 7420 Fullerton Road, Suite 110, Springfield, VA 22153-2852; telephone numbers are (703) 440-1400 and (800) 443-3742. Use the ED numbers in this bibliography to identify and order documents from the EDRS. Overnight delivery and fax services are provided by EDRS for customers who need to obtain ERIC documents quickly. Parts of the annotations for these documents were drawn from *Resources in Education*, a monthly publication of the U.S. Department of Education.

Professional Resources for ESL Programs (K–12)

Arizona Department of Education. 1991. *Strategies for Teaching Limited English Proficient Students, Parts I & II.* Phoenix, AZ: Arizona Department of Education. Available from the Arizona Department of Education, Bilingual Unit, Phoenix, AZ. Approximately $4.00 per copy. Call (602) 542-3204 for information.

Both documents, parts I and II, are collections of handouts of activities appropriate to either the naturalistic or nativistic approach to language acquisition with related articles for resource. Part I deals with general K–12 ESL strategies, Part II with K–12 specific content-area ESL. In each part articles by experts in the respective fields of teaching, assessing, and implementing programs in ESL provide current research, curriculum, and implications for limited-English speakers—both as language and as content learners. In the first part a comprehensive set of handouts detail the following: current trends in ESL, including whole language theory; tips for teaching ESL students at any level; suggestions for implementing language acquisition activities in the classroom; and thirty-six guidelines to describe the environment of a literacy classroom. Part II also has a selection of handouts, including descriptions of the characteristics of content-based ESL classes across the grade and subject levels, suggestions for making content more comprehensible with a description of many sheltering techniques and activities; and a list of fifteen strategies for working with limited English proficiency (LEP) learners in content classrooms compiled from articles, school district guidelines, teacher inservice materials, and classroom observations by the author. There is an especially comprehensive listing of references, including organizations and publishers complementing each general heading in both volumes.

Fountain Valley School District. 1991. *Project G.L.A.D. A Program of Academic Excellence. Language Acquisition to Literacy in a Multilingual Setting.* ED 340 219.

Based on a Title VII project this report provides instruction and curriculum resources for infusing whole language approaches into content and language learning across the curriculum for students of ESL in upper elementary and middle school. Vocabulary-based activities predominate and are naturalistic or sheltered in approach to content vocabulary. Outlines for instructional units in science and social studies are provided as is a suggested design for general unit planning.

Freeman, Yvonne S., and David E. Freeman. 1992. *Whole Language for Second Language Learners.* Portsmouth, NH: Heinemann. ISBN 0-435-08723-1.

This book focuses on understanding how to apply whole-language strategies in classrooms where some or all of the students speak English as a second or additional language. After an introduction stating the authors' perspectives on language and learning, each of the seven chapters in the text contrasts a commonsense assumption about teaching second-language students with whole-language alternatives. Assumptions of the latter are as follows: (1) learning goes from whole to part; (2) lessons should be learner-centered; (3) lessons should have an immediate meaning and purpose for learners; (4) learning takes place in social interaction; (5) lessons should include all four modes; (6) learning should take place in the first language; and (7) faith in the learner expands student potential. Each chapter consists largely of examples from teachers who have applied whole language theory, including samples of their curricula and specific content lessons. Many practical ideas for organizing elementary classrooms are also included, as well as an extensive list of references and a complete index to citations to theories, authors, language stories, literature, writing examples, and activities.

Georgia Department of Education. 1992. *English to Speakers of Other Languages Resource Guide.* Atlanta, GA: Georgia Department of Education. The document is available from the Georgia Department of Education, Twin Towers East, Atlanta, GA 30334.

Two chapters in this document specifically deal with curricular issues in ESL. Chapter 4 contains both specific lesson designs and activities to foster second-language learning. The individual activities are mainly naturalistic in approach while the lesson designs are more nativistic, with the content embedded in the experiences provided. This seems to replicate a whole language system seen often in single or native language elementary classrooms. Each design includes a list of current resources for further reading and use. Chapter 5 concentrates on general cross-cultural guidelines and strategies that provide a multicultural perspective.

Hawaii State Department of Education. 1991. *Content Area Instructional Strategies for Students of Limited English Proficiency in Secondary Schools: A Sheltered Approach.* Honolulu, HI: Department of Education. Document RS 91-1142. Available from Office of Instructional Services, General Education Branch, Department of Education, Honolulu, HI.

The document gives an overview of the theory and practice of sheltered or naturalistic approaches in K–12 content-area instruction and provides sample lessons in social studies, mathematics, science, and literature at all grade levels. The sample lessons are set up in a common structure and are based on regular textbooks from the state's recommended list for content areas. Many of the strategies given are explained in the section on components for program design, which precedes the sample lessons. A short list of references is provided.

Peitzman, Faye, and George Gadda, eds. 1991. *With Different Eyes: Insights into Teaching Language Minority Students across the Disciplines.* Los Angeles: California Academic Partnership Program, UCLA Publishing. May be purchased from UCLA Center for Academic Interinstitutional Programs, Graduate School of Education, Gayley Center, Suite 304, Los Angeles, CA 90024-1372.

This work is a product of the California Academic Partnership Program, a cooperative effort between state schools and colleges to enhance the college preparation of students in grades 6–12; it primarily studies sheltered strategies in academic classrooms. The six chapters offer a guide to help teachers of language minority students across the disciplines gain insight in becoming reflective as well as effective teachers of ESL and their content area. Each chapter offers concrete suggestions and applications for structuring content-area activities that reflect naturalistic and nativistic theories of language acquisition. Issues in the assessment of LEP students are addressed minimally. Chapter titles include "You Have a Chance Also: Case Histories of ESL Students at the University"; "Sheltered Instruction Across the Disciplines: Successful Teachers at Work"; "Writing and Language Socialization Across Cultures: Some Implications for the Classroom"; "Helping Language Minority Students Read and Write Analytically: The Journey Into, Through and Beyond"; "Breaking New Ground: Responding to LEP Writers in Every Classroom"; and "What's Fair? Assessing Subject Matter Knowledge of LEP

Students in Sheltered Classrooms." A select bibliography of source articles and books is provided.

Peregoy, Suzanne F., and Owen F. Boyle. 1993. *Reading, Writing, and Learning in ESL: A Resource Book for K–8.* White Plains, NY: Longman. ISBN 0-8013-0844-5.

Designed to be used as a textbook for preservice or staff development, this volume is organized to correspond with chapter topics in standard reading/language arts course texts for K–8. Chapters 1 and 2 provide background information on second-language learning, mainly naturalistic and nativistic in principle. The next three chapters contain about one hundred classroom strategies in reading and writing for teaching second-language literacy with research support. These chapters are divided into the following areas: second-language learners and the writing process; reading and literature instruction for second-language learners; and reading and writing across the curriculum. The final chapter is a summary of the ideas presented in the volume. Also included is an extensive reference list.

Rigg, Pat, and Virginia G. Allen, eds. 1989. *When They Don't All Speak English: Integrating the ESL Student into the Regular Classroom.* Urbana, IL: National Council of Teachers of English. ISBN 0-8141-5693-2.

This collection of ten articles is based on the application of five principles about language learners and language learning: (1) people who are learning another language are, first of all, people; (2) learning a language means learning to do the things you want to do with people who speak that language; (3) a person's second language, like the first, develops globally, not linearly; (4) language develops best in a variety of rich contexts; and (5) literacy is part of language, so writing and reading develop alongside speaking and listening. Each article reflects those principles, focusing on practical ways—including specific examples— that they can be implemented in the elementary and secondary classroom and beyond. The final four articles focus on combining language learning and academic content (for example, mathematics, science, social studies) in the elementary and secondary schools.

Short, Deborah J. 1991. *Integrating Language and Content Instruction: Strategies and Techniques.* Washington, DC: National Clearinghouse for Bilingual Education. Program Information Guide Series. ED 338 111. U.S. Government Document ED 1.8/4: 7/2.

This work explains and illustrates three principal factors that underlie an integrated approach to teaching LEP students in grades 6–12: the use of multiple media, the enhancement of students' thinking skills, and a student-centered organization of instruction. Strategies and techniques are described for preparing for the integrated approach, including adapting naturalistic ESL techniques to the content classroom. Suggestions are offered for developing lesson plans, including a format and sample lessons.

Short, Deborah, JoAnn Crandall, and Donna Christian. 1989. *How To Integrate Language and Content Instruction: A Training Manual.* CLEAR Educational Report Series: Number 15. Los Angeles: Center for Language Education and Research. ED 305 824.

This is a guide for writing a curriculum for ESL elementary and secondary students which stresses collaboration between content-area and language-acquisition instruction. Included are a rationale for and information about curriculum integration of content material into language classes so that they accommodate LEP students. Specific strategies for integrating language and content, for adapting materials, and for developing lesson plans among all grade levels are presented in three models for implementation: sheltered classes, integrated curricula, and the whole-school approach. The suggested materials and activities reflect both naturalistic and nativistic approaches with emphasis on sheltering vocabulary within the content areas. The final section of the guide presents agendas for four staff-development workshops of varying lengths and foci. There are appendices containing subject-specific instructional strategy outlines, sample material adaptations and lesson plans, a glossary, and a rather dated list of references.

ESL Program Frameworks (K–12)

California Department of Education, Bilingual Education Office. 1990. *Bilingual Education Handbook: Designing Instruction for LEP Students.* Sacramento, CA: California State Department of Education. ISBN 0-8011-0890-X. This document is available from the Bureau of Publications, Sales Unit, California Department of Education, P.O. Box 271, Sacramento, CA 95802-0271. Approximately $4.25 per copy.

Although primarily a guide for curriculum development in primary language for bilingual programs in California, this handbook contains a section on Foreign Language and English as a Second Language Instruction in which points of concern for the ESL Program in Bilingual Education are clearly stated. Content-based second-language instruction or sheltered English instruction is explained in general terms. The section Planning the Bilingual Program contains concrete guidelines for the implementation of ESL in the content areas through strategies of using sheltered English. Characteristics of and a checklist for an effective bilingual program include the development of English literacy.

California Department of Education. 1989. *Foreign Language Framework.* Sacramento, CA: California State Department of Education. ISBN 0-8011-0804-7. This document is available from the Bureau of Publications, Sales Unit, California Department of Education, P.O. Box 271, Sacramento, CA 95802-0271. Approximately $5.50 per copy.

Chapter 6 of this guide is devoted to ESL instruction. The needs and goals of ESL programs as well as the nature of the instruction is defined, and guidelines for developing ESL curricula are introduced. The main emphasis of the chapter is the outline of a recommended program structure for ESL instruction. Chapter 7 gives the basic guidelines for considering textbooks and other instructional materials for teaching a second language. Features in communication-based activities and manipulative activities are compared in Appendix B, and a chart of competency levels from novice to distinguished in all areas of language/culture acquisition is in Appendix C.

Rivera, Charlene, and Annette M. Zehler. 1991. "Assuring the Academic Success of Language Minority Students: Collaboration in Teaching and Learning." *Journal of Education* 173(2): 52–77.

The article describes and gives a rationale for the Innovative Approaches Research Project (IARP), which focuses on developing innovative instructional and intervention models for LEP students in topic areas. The areas described include literacy, science, and math. To deal with students in elementary school, the three models presented here suggest a combination of participatory teaching and cooperative learning approaches. Although general in its application to curriculum, IARP provides goals and a design that research has found to be effective in planning lessons for LEP students. Although not explicitly stated, the models follow a mainly nativistic approach with some infusion of sheltering in the intervention model presented.

ESL Curricular Foundations

Ashworth, Mary. 1992. *The First Step on the Longer Path: Becoming an ESL Teacher.* Markham, Ontario: Pippin. Distributed in U.S. by Heinemann. ISBN 0-88751-054-X.

This is a possible course text for preservice ESL teachers K–12 or a resource text for experienced teachers. Divided into ten short chapters, with the emphasis on strategies and activities in the last six, the author uses a combination of direct and naturalistic language acquisition theories to support the activities that she has found to be effective; her theories could be put into practice easily by classroom teachers, especially those who have native and non-native speakers together in their classrooms. The author provides a list of focus questions and guiding principles to assist the reader. The questions deal with the second-language learner and his or her general and specific school environments; the guiding principles give the author's view of the second-language learner. The bibliography is organized by the chapter titles.

Crandall, JoAnn, ed. 1987. *ESL through Content-Area Instruction: Mathematics, Science, Social Studies.* Language in Education: Theory and Practice, no. 69. ED 283 387.

This work is one of the earliest comprehensive content-based ESL curriculum resources to use research on comprehensible context and communicative competence. Comprised of three essays, this publication focuses on mathematics instruction, science processes and language, and social studies. Model lessons using sheltering techniques for each content area and for situational experiences are included, as well as an extensive reference list.

Freeman, David. E., and Yvonne S. Freeman. 1991. "'Doing' Social Studies: Whole Language Lessons To Promote Social Action." *Social Education* 55(1): 29–31, 66.

This article presents a four-step model for teaching social studies that is organized around the following whole language principles: (1) lessons should proceed from whole to part; (2) lessons should be learner-centered because learning is the active construction of knowledge by students; (3) lessons should have immediate meaning and purpose for the students; (4) lessons should engage groups of students in social interaction; (5) lessons should develop both oral and written language; and (6) lessons that show faith in the learner expand students' potential. It also provides a lesson plan in illustration and gives a rationale for using whole language with second-language learners. Presented in cogent form, the article is a combination of naturalistic and nativistic activities. The reference list leans heavily on California state documents.

Garcia, Eugene. 1991. *Education of Linguistically and Culturally Diverse Students: Effective Instructional Practices.* Educational Practice Report: 1. ED 338 099.

This report reviews effective naturalistic and nativistic instructional practices taken from descriptive studies with LEP students. The common attributes in the instructional organization of the classrooms studied are presented along with some examples of implementation. Five implications from the review are presented as specific guides to curriculum: (1) any curriculum must address all categories of learning goals; (2) academic content must be related to a child's own environment and experience; (3) the more diverse the children, the more integrated the curriculum should be; (4) the more diverse the children, the greater the need for activities such as group projects; and (5) the more diverse the children, the more important it is to offer them opportunities to apply their learning in a meaningful context.

Grabe, William. 1991. "Current Developments in Second Language Reading Research." *TESOL Quarterly* 25(3): 375-406.

Although it is mainly a review of the research in second-language contexts, this article also offers information from the research for curriculum development at the secondary and adult levels of instruction. Seven guidelines for reading instruction are presented: (1) teach reading instruction in the context of a content-centered, integrated skills curriculum; (2) use a reading lab to provide individualized instruction and to practice certain skills and strategies outside the content-centered course; (3) encourage sustained silent reading to build fluency, confidence, and appreciation; (4) plan reading lessons in a pre-, during-, and postreading framework to build background knowledge, practice reading skills within meaningful texts, and engage in comprehension instruction; (5) give high priority to specific skills and strategies and practice

them consistently; (6) use group work and cooperative learning regularly to promote discussion, working with information from the reading and exploring different solutions for complex activities; and (7) use extensive concentration of silent reading to build vocabulary and structural awareness. Detailed references on reading research across content and theory areas end the article.

Johns, Kenneth M., and Connie Espinoza. 1992. *Mainstreaming Language Minority Students in Reading and Writing* (Fastback Number 340). Bloomington, IN: Phi Delta Kappa Educational Foundation. Available from Phi Delta Kappa, P.O. Box 789. Bloomington, IN 47402-0789. Approximately $1.25 per copy.

After a discussion of the barriers to language acquisition and the needs of LEP students, the major part of this monograph deals with the various approaches to creating a curriculum for ESL students using such mainstream cross-curricular strategies as student journals and cooperative learning. The authors recommend a whole-language approach to learning language and give examples of lessons using literary works, mainly at the K-4 grade level of instruction. Most of the examples are holistic and naturalistic in approach; they can be used across content areas in classrooms of students in primary grades.

Larsen-Freeman, Diane. 1991. "Second Language Acquisition Research: Staking Out the Territory." *TESOL Quarterly* 25(2): 315-50.

Primarily a review of the research done on the acquisition of a second language, this article also contains the following ten general characteristics of the learning process and of language learners, with pedagogical implications for each: (1) the learning/acquisition process is complex; (2) the process is gradual; (3) The process is nonlinear; (4) the process is dynamic; (5) learners learn when they are ready to do so; (6) learners rely on the knowledge and experience they have; (7) it is not clear from research findings what the role of negative evidence is in helping learners to reject erroneous hypotheses they are currently entertaining; (8) for most adult learners, complete mastery of the L2 may be impossible; (9) there is tremendous individual variation among language learners; and (10) learning a language is a social phenomenon. The article is useful for teachers as a guide in their curricular decision making. Lengthy research references are included.

Richard-Amato, Patricia A., and Marguerite Ann
  Snow, eds. 1992. *The Multicultural Classroom:
  Readings for Content Area Teachers.* White Plains,
  NY: Longman. ISBN 0-8013-0511-X.
This volume is described as a *sourcebook* for
teachers in multicultural classrooms. Divided into
four specific parts, the text contains articles/
chapters by major linguists and practitioners who
work in the area of language acquisition and who
study the concerns and issues of LEP students. Part
I looks at theoretical foundations, defining direct
and naturalistic approaches to language acquisition
with some reference to whole language theory in a
chapter on a conceptual framework for the integration of language and content; a separate chapter on
cooperative grouping is included. Part II specifies
cultural considerations in teaching LEP students.
Part III provides suggestions for instructional
practice, assessment, and materials for classrooms
in general with a focus on whole language and
sheltering strategies for content learning. Part IV
contains readings in specific content areas covering
the academic, art, and skills curricula. Although not
specifically stated as such, many suggestions for
practice and materials seem geared toward students
in the upper elementary and secondary schools.
References and a comprehensive index are found at
the end of the text.

Other Curriculum Materials

Adamson, Hugh Douglas. 1993. *Academic Competence. Theory and Classroom Practice: Preparing
  ESL Students for Content Courses.* White Plains,
  NY: Longman. ISBN 0-8013-0602-7.
Comprehensive in its description of how to teach
language through content in secondary and college
classrooms, this volume has a strong theoretical
(direct and naturalistic approach) and case-study
approach to curriculum design that may inhibit
novice planners. It is valuable mainly for presenting
details of the insights and experiences of ESL
students who have moved into mainstream content
courses; the book shows how curriculum planners
can use the implications of those experiences in
addition to linguistic theory. The last chapter
contains detailed activities to help ESL students
understand academic subjects taught in English.
Sixty-one additional short suggestions are included,
ranging from "Give students the first and last lines
of a text and ask them to predict the content of text
to be read" to a listening/note-taking, pair-share
activity.

Beasley, Augie, and Katherine Meads. 1991. "Print
  and Videotapes: English as a Second Language—
  The Library Media Center Connection." *School
  Library Media Activities Monthly* 7(10):32–33.
The authors describe how library media specialists
and ESL teachers work together to integrate media
into the ESL curriculum. The use of computer tools
such as word processing, graphic creation or
copying, and laser disk integration courseware is
described. Further curricular ideas for media use in
ESL classrooms are included.

Fathman, Ann K., Mary Ellen Quinn, and Carolyn
  Kessler. 1992. *Teaching Science to English
  Learners, Grades 4–8.* Washington, DC: National
  Clearinghouse for Bilingual Education. Program
  Information Guide Series. US Government
  Document ED 1.8/4: 11/992. (ED number will be
  assigned.)
The purpose of this guide is to help teachers plan,
design, and implement science concepts for ESL
students in Grades 4–8. Steps to designing science
experiences that effectively integrate language and
science content using the naturalistic approach are
presented. The sample activities, refer to weather,
animals, and plants, and are based on the text
Science for Language Learners (Fathman and
Quinn, 1989). The bibliography includes references
to language acquisition as well as science.

Goldenberg, Claude. 1991. *Instructional Conversations and Their Classroom Application.* Educational Practice Report 2. Washington, DC:
  Center for Applied Linguistics. ED 341 253.
The report describes discussion-based lessons that
create opportunities for ESL students to focus on
an idea or concept. Using the students' prior
knowledge through discussions of real-life events is
stressed. Instructional and conversational elements
for implementation across disciplines are provided.
The procedures are recommended for nonexplicit
knowledge or skill areas, such as literary or historical themes, expressive or analytic writing, as well as
complex concepts in various content areas. Most of
the procedures are appropriate for learners in
secondary schools.

Heald-Taylor, Gail. 1989. *Whole Language Strategies
  for ESL Students.* San Diego, CA: Dormac. ISBN
  0-86575-648-1.
This work contains negligible reference to the
theories and principles of either whole language or
ESL, it is a collection of activities and strategies
that are whole-language based and that seem to

promote second-language literacy. Sections are devoted to the following: creating timetables or organizing for whole language; dictated stories; literature strategies and process writing; themes, including one example (pets); and evaluation using a charted behavior inventory with a portfolio-type collection of dictations and writing samples. An extensive list of tradebooks, most of which are published in Great Britain, and a list of professional references are included at the end of the text.

McGroarty, Mary. 1989. "The Benefits of Cooperative Learning Arrangements in Second Language Instruction." *NABE Journal* (Winter): 127–43.
This article identifies some of the advantages that cooperative learning arrangements offer in second-language instruction. The following main benefits are listed along with illustrative curricular examples: (1) provides frequent opportunity for naturalistic second-language practice and negotiation of meaning through talk; (2) helps students draw on primary-language resources as they develop second-language skills; (3) offers additional ways to incorporate content areas into language instruction; (4) creates a favorable context for language development by requiring a variety of group activities and materials to support instruction; (5) allows language teachers to expand general pedagogical skills and to emphasize meaning as well as form in communication by requiring a redefinition of the role of the teacher in the classroom; and (6) encourages students to take an active role in the acquisition of knowledge and language skills and encourage themselves and each other as they work on problems of mutual interest. The article has a very general application and includes a range of references in language acquisition, grouping, bilingual education, and content- related language issues.

Padilla, Amado M., Halford H. Fairchild, and Concepcion M. Valadez, eds. 1990. *Bilingual Education: Issues and Strategies.* Newbury Park, CA: Sage. ISBN 0-8039-3639-7.
The first three parts of this work are devoted to issues, perspectives, research, program design, and evaluation in bilingual education. The largest section (part IV) has eight chapters and puts theory into practice, detailing naturalistic and nativistic strategies for both ESL and bilingual classrooms. There are articles on math and science problem solving, dialogue journal and early (first-grade) writing, and cooperative learning strategies with ESL students in heterogeneous classes. The final two chapters in the collection discuss bilingual

immersion programs and contributions from EFL. After each chapter there is a list of references pertaining to the subject(s) examined.

Peyton, Joyce K., and Leslee Reed. 1990. *Dialogue Journal Writing with Non-Native English Speakers: A Handbook for Teachers.* Washington, DC: Teachers of English to Speakers of Other Languages. ISBN 0-939791-37-4.
This work is written for new and experienced ESL teachers whose non-native-speaker students are in grades ranging in from kindergarten through high school. The authors present practical advice for the implementation and maintenance of dialogue journals in classrooms. The ten chapters focus on dialogue journal definition, benefits, initiation, maintenance, and problem solving. Profiles of four students who kept dialogue journals (first, fifth, and sixth graders) have examples of language growth over time; the prompts and teacher responses are included. Besides extensive references, an appendix on suggested further readings is provided.

Pierce, Lorraine V. 1988. *Facilitating Transition to the Mainstream: Sheltered English Vocabulary Development.* Washington, DC: National Clearinghouse for Bilingual Education. Program Information Guide Series. ED 299 826
This is a curriculum guide for vocabulary development in sheltered English; it offers practical ideas using the naturalistic approach for content-area instruction. Two units on lesson planning with lesson activities illustrate sheltered instruction in middle school in a science unit and a social studies unit. A specific lesson outline for using these units with eighth graders in a mainstream environment is provided. Adapted from a curriculum guide prepared by the Hartford Connecticut Bilingual Program's Vocabulary Development Committee, this guide focuses on facilitating the transition from ESL to mainstream classrooms with sheltered vocabulary instruction.

Pierce, Lorraine V., and J. Michael O'Malley. 1992. *Performance and Portfolio Assessment for Language Minority Students.* Washington, DC: National Clearinghouse for Bilingual Education. Program Information Guide Series. U.S. Government Document ED 1.8/4: 9. (ED number will be assigned.)
This publication describes performance assessment procedures and a portfolio assessment framework for monitoring the language development of LEP students in the upper elementary and middle

grades. The first section is a definition of the specific terms and procedures used and described in the document: alternative assessment, performance assessment, and portfolio assessment. Specific guidelines and examples for implementing performance assessment and portfolio assessment are given in the body of the document. Holistic approaches that allow for primary language as well as English to facilitate writing are stressed. There is a thorough and extensive bibliography for both the procedures described and their applicability in the language-development classroom.

Rigg, Pat, and D. Scott Enright, eds. 1986. *Children and ESL: Integrating Perspectives.* Washington, DC: Teachers of English to Speakers of Other Languages.
Composed of presentations at TESOL '85, this publication is defined by Cazden's paper "ESL Teachers as Language Advocates for Children." Besides the Cazden paper, four others are presented: "ESL Children's Writing: What We've Learned, What We're Learning"; "Reading in ESL: Learning from Kids"; "A Children's Story"; "Use Everything You Have To Teach English: Providing Useful Input to Young Language Learners." All of the papers have practical curriculum implications, although not all of them present details of the curricular guidelines. The papers refer mainly to ESL learners in elementary grades and recommend activities that follow the holistic and naturalistic approaches.

Samway, Katharine D. 1992. *Writer's Workshop and Children Acquiring English as a Non-Native Language.* Washington, DC: National Clearinghouse for Bilingual Education. Program Information Guide Series. U.S. Government Document ED 1.8/4: 10. (ED number will be assigned.)
This guide reviews the research on the writing processes of children acquiring English and presents the theory of writing as a meaning-making process; it describes how that process applies to second-language learners. A step-by-step procedure for designing and implementing a writers' workshop in the ESL classroom with suggested daily plans makes up the majority of the document. The extensive bibliography is geared primarily to native speakers of English.

Stempleski, Susan, and Paul Arcario, eds. 1992. *Video in Second Language Teaching.* Washington, DC: Teachers of English to Speakers of Other Languages. ISBN 939791-41-2.

Divided into three sections, the ten-chapter volume presents practical theoretical advice to experienced and novice teachers who use or wish to use video in their ESL classrooms. The first section, "Using Video," contains six chapters on the use of prerecorded videocassettes in specific teaching situations; sample lessons are included. The majority of this section is directed to teachers of adults, but many of the activities and suggested materials easily can be adapted for students in upper elementary and in secondary classes. The second section has a chapter on selecting videos for adult learners with criteria for selection that can be applied to videos and films for younger learners. There is also a chapter on currently available commercial video materials, which include teacher-training and staff-development packages. The third section focuses on the production of videos for second-language teaching/learning. There is a glossary of video acronyms and technical terms, a list of organizational resources, and an extensive bibliography.

Computer Tool Packages

Author, Author. School editions available for Apple computers (5.25" disks) and IBM-compatible computers (5.25" or 3.5"). Lab packs of five, networks, and site licensing are available.
A unique playwriting toolkit for students in upper elementary and secondary grades gives the user backdrops, props, characters, as well as word-processing capabilities. The user moves props and characters on-stage while entering dialogue. The play is acted out on the computer screen or can be printed. The package includes built-in outlines for traditional plays, playbill options, and a data disk with a sample play, *Jack and the Beanstalk.*

Big Book Maker. Toucan. School editions available for the Apple (3.5" or 5.25" disks), Mac, IBM-compatible computer (5.25" or 3.5"). Lab packs of five or ten and site licensing are available.
This is a series of separate courseware programs with illustrations or clip art to prompt user writing. It can be used in grades through middle school. One of the main features of this collection of programs is an easy-to-use word processor with a variety of print sizes.

Children's Writing and Publishing Center. The Learning Company. School editions available for Apple (3.5" or 5.25" disks), Mac, and IBM-compatible computers (5.25" or 3.5"). Lab packs of five or ten, site licensing, and network editions are available.

With this program the user can write and publish in various formats, including illustrated text. The pages can be automatically formatted to the user's, choice making the finished product very professional looking. Usable through middle school, this program is user-friendly to all.

Kid Works, Kid Works 2. Torrance, CA: Davidson. School editions available for Apple (3.5" or 5.25"), Mac, and IBM-compatible (5.25" or 3.5"). Lab packs of five or ten, site licensing, and network editions are available. Works with an Echo.

These are talking word processors that can be used with young language learners. The writing screen is designed like lined elementary-school paper. Users can select illustrations for their stories or draw their own. After the story is complete, users can print it out and/or listen to the computer read the story aloud.

Make-A-Book. Torrance, CA: Davidson. Available for Mac and IBM- compatible computers (5.25" or 3.5").

With this program, the user can write, illustrate, and publish his or her own books. The stories can be printed in actual book format— just print, fold, and bind. A selection of fonts and sizes is available for both fanfold, vertical, or horizontal books.

Monsters and Make Believe Plus. Toucan. School editions available for Apple (3.5" or 5.25"), Mac, and IBM-compatible computers (5.25" or 3.5"). Lab packs of five or ten, site licensing, and network editions are available. Works with an Echo. Can also be used without the synthesizer.

Designed primarily for learners in elementary school, this courseware is used to create monster-type figures in a choice of backgrounds. As a user selects a body part from the menu, the speech synthesizer voices it. The program prompts the user to write a story about the visual created. The program prints in multiple sizes, and users can hear their stories read back to them when the speech synthesizer is used.

The Writing Center. The Learning Company. Macintosh School Edition. Lab Packs and Network editions are available.

The program meets the needs of the student writer in text generation and in all areas of desktop publishing. Easy access features and flexibility in formatting, revising, and editing text combine with

a clip art library. A bilingual edition (Spanish/English) called *The Bilingual Writing Center* extends the writing and publishing characteristics of this program to include bilingual and bicultural activities in the teacher documentation.

Training Materials

The Art of Teaching ESL (Video and Leader's Guide). 1992. Reading, MA: Addison-Wesley. ISBN 0-201-19525-9. *Participant's Guides* are available (ISBN 0-201-50172-4).

This staff-development package contains nine video segments of mainly elementary classrooms in both ESL and a combination of ESL and mainstream students. Direct instructional techniques are touched upon in the video segments and activities, but the approach is primarily naturalistic. Application activities for teachers include curriculum and lesson design. The learning environments recommended for students include small-group structures, process writing, literature and whole language, and sheltered content. Tied to Addison-Wesley ESL student materials.

Los Angeles County Office of Education. 1991. *Access to English/Language Arts in Multilingual Settings.* Los Angeles, CA: The Educational Telecommunications Network. Available from Educational Materials Development Center, Los Angeles County Office of Education, 9300 Imperial Highway, Downey, CA 90242. Approximately $59.00 per package.

Part of a series of staff-development materials that reflect the principles of the *California Bilingual Handbook,* this package contains a leader's guide and videotape of a live transmission from the Educational Telecommunications Network of the Los Angeles County Office of Education (LACOE) on access to English/language arts in a multilingual classroom. A videotape is included showing teleconference hosted by Dr. Alfredo Schifini (LACOE), who interviews Dr. Alan Crawford, Dr. Marguerite Ann Snow, and Shelly Spiegel-Coleman (LACOE) as they view elementary and secondary classroom videoclips of successful English language arts programs in multilingual/ESL settings. The topics discussed during the teleconference include: (1) principles of whole language instruction as they apply to ESL; (2) effective whole language strategies for different levels of English proficiency and literacy; and (3) the support role of primary language and identification of language resources. Time is allotted for questions from those participating in the original teleconference and for answers from the panel. Activities are suggested for the leader, and a short bibliography is provided.

Los Angeles County Office of Education. 1991. *ESL in the English/Language Arts Classroom.* Los Angeles, CA: The Educational Telecommunications Network. Available from Educational Materials Development Center, Los Angeles County Office of Education, 93400 Imperial Highway, Downey, CA 90242. Approximately $59.00 per package.

The package contains a leader's guide and videotape of a live transmission from the Educational Telecommunications Network of the Los Angeles County Office of Education (LACOE) on ESL in a secondary-school English classroom. It is part of a series of staff-development materials that reflect the *California English Language Arts Framework.* Teachers view the video as part of a workshop in implementing literature experiences with secondary-school ESL students. The video contains interviews with the secondary-school ESL students about their classroom experiences, clips of actual class activities, and interviews by Dr. Mel Grubb of LACOE with Dr. Courtney Cazden and the classroom teacher, Luis Martinez. Activities are provided for the viewer/participants to guide them through a lesson plan using core materials in literature.

Peyton, Joyce K., and Leslee Reed. 1992. *Dialogue Journal Writing with Non-Native English Speakers: An Instructional Packet for Teachers and Workshop Leaders.* Washington, DC: Teachers of English to Speakers of Other Languages. ISBN 939791-39-0.

The packet contains research results, basic guidelines, helpful hints, and the experiences and sample work of teachers and students in the use of dialogue journals. Guidelines for giving workshops on writing dialogue journals, transparency masters of major points, and sample student writing across the K–12 age are found in this three-hole punched instructional packet. There is an extensive bibliography of publications about dialogue journals as well as directions for using the packet with the handbook.

Savage, K. Lynn, and Leann Howard. 1992. *Teacher Training through Videos: ESL Techniques.* White Plains, NY: Longman.

This package consists of ten videos for teachers of adult and secondary-school ESL students. Each of the videos focuses on an aspect of communicative competence or sheltering content. Actual classroom demonstrations combine with activities and approaches for staff development and/or curricular design. Sample lessons available before purchase.

IDEAS FOR SPECIAL PROJECTS

by Dorothea B. Hickey
Joan of Arc Junior High School, New York, New York

WHETHER one prefers a content-based, grammar-based, functional, or eclectic curriculum, many of the following projects and activities can be incorporated into it. ESL teachers might be in a pullout program where they see a group of students from different classes, or they might have a group from the same class. In either case, it would be beneficial to talk with the students' classroom or content area teachers to ascertain what they are doing in those classes. The ESL teacher will then be able to develop lessons around what the students are receiving in their regular classes. The vocabulary and language for the particular area will thus be strengthened, and they will be able to participate more fully in those classes. This is not meant to be an exhaustive list of sources, but merely an offering of suggestions to expand upon texts, to integrate content, or to use different modes (i.e., art, music, and drama). Not all of the materials are specifically ESL materials, but they work well or can be adapted accordingly. Many of the projects and activities can be adapted for any level or age group; therefore, where a level and grade are noted, they are not cast in stone but can be modified or expanded upon as desired. Also, whenever a level is specified, it refers to the level of proficiency in English, i.e., beginner, advanced beginner, low intermediate, intermediate, high intermediate, advanced.

I have separated the projects on the following pages according to type of activities:
Language through Content
Language through Pictures
Language through Art
Language through Drama
Language through Songs
Language through Games
Language through Holidays and Customs
Language through Multicultural Activities

Though each of the activities, for the most part, falls under a particular category, some of them might overlap categories; for example, some songs also lend themselves to drama; some of the art projects might also integrate content.

Just as our students have different learning styles, we have different teaching styles. I believe that teachers have to like and feel comfortable with the content they are presenting and the manner in which it is to be presented. Therefore, feel free to pick and choose among the activities and add to or change them as your needs dictate. Most of all, have fun!

Language through Content

As many teachers are now aware, language through content is an extremely effective means to developing and enhancing fluency. Among the books you may find helpful in teaching both language skills and content areas are several different types: those that cover a specific content area, those that cover several different subject areas, and those that can be used to supplement specific content areas. All three kinds of texts can be used in an ESL class where the teacher takes an eclectic approach. Following are some suggestions.

Earth and Physical Science, by Mary Ann
   Christison and Sharron Bassano (Reading,
   MA: Addison-Wesley, 1992), 120p.
This ESL content area text is an introduction to the subject which provides for many hands-on experiments that are sure to whet students' appetites. The chapters begin with prereading exercises in the form of questions and experiments to allow for predicting and hypothesizing in preparation for the following text. The chapters contain many illustrations, and each subtopic in a chapter is preceded by a prereading exercise and followed by a vocabulary and question review. Though the book is full of experiments, it can be supplemented with additional activities for enhancement, such as keeping a journal of observations, taking a trip to the local radio or TV station during the chapter on meteorology, or making a model of the solar system with papier-mâché, foam, or styrofoam balls. It is appropriate for junior high and high school students at the intermediate level.

Content Area ESL: Social Studies, by Dennis
   Terdy (Palatine, IL: Linmore, 1986), 169p.
This book covers United States history from the Native Americans and early settlers to the present. Each chapter begins with a prereading exercise, which is followed by two pages of text with many illustrations and photos; the chapter ends with exercises on vocabulary, comprehension, grammar, and writing. In addition, there are many maps, graphs, and charts throughout the book. This book provides a good base for understanding historical events, and the chapters can be expanded upon as desired to provide additional details or further clarification. For example, the chapter on Native Americans contains a map showing the territories of Native American tribes. Students can pick a particular tribe, do further research on it, and give a presentation to the class. The chapter on the Constitution and the Bill of Rights could be supplemented by the movie *Twelve Angry Men* and mock trials in the classroom. (See following item.) The movie *The*

Grapes Of Wrath can be shown when studying the Great Depression. This book is suitable for intermediate secondary students.

You Be the Jury, by Marvin Miller (New York:
   Scholastic, 1989), 88p.
As part of a unit on the judicial system, students could have their own trials. In *You Be the Jury*, ten cases are presented, complete with clues and evidence to be used as exhibits in the "courtroom."
   Students can take parts as defendant, plaintiff, defense attorney, prosecuting attorney, witnesses, judge, and jury. The verdict is given in the book, but the students might not want to look at it until after they have reached their own verdict. The "attorneys" will develop persuasive language so that their "clients" can win the case. The "jury" will get good practice in using English while they are "deliberating," and they will also be learning how to think about factual information and make responsible decisions. Holding mock trials creates excitement in the classroom and demonstrates to the students the importance of distinguishing between fact and opinion. To close the gap between fantasy and reality, you can contact your local district attorney's office to arrange a trip to the courthouse, and perhaps even to sit in on a trial. Many district attorneys' offices have such tours for students. This book, of which there are four editions, would be appropriate for intermediate secondary students.

Odyssey, by Victoria Kimbrough, Michael Palmer,
   and Donn Byrne (New York: Longman, 1984),
   86p.
This six-book series tells a continuing story of two teenagers and their friends and activities. The story is presented in a picture format of four or five color frames with accompanying dialogue or text next to each frame. As the books advance, the pictures decrease and the text increases. In addition to the continuing story, every other chapter is based on a subject area. Many of these chapters can be expanded into unit plans in the particular content area.
   For example, in book 1 there is a chapter describing the fictitious city in which the characters live. There is an aerial view of the city with the names of such places as churches, museums, and hotels. The students could move from this picture map of a fictitious city to making a picture map of the school neighborhood or the neighborhood in which they now live, with a description. They might also make a picture map of the

neighborhood in which they lived before coming to the United States. These activities could be further developed into a geography lesson using a map of the United States and/or of the different countries represented by students in the class.

Book 3 contains a chapter about the weather and how it is affected by the cutting down of trees. This information can be expanded into a science project on the destruction of tropical rain forests. Information about rain forests and endangered species can be obtained through local environmental organizations or from the Environmental Protection Agency in Washington, DC.

Many chapters are also conducive to developing content-area projects. This series ranges from beginner to high intermediate and would be suitable for junior high or high school students.

Helping Your Child Learn Geography (Washington, DC: U.S. Department of Education, 1990), 26p. This publication of the U.S. Department of Education addresses parents who want to begin their children's process of learning about our world, but it also suggests many activities that can be used in an ESL class. For example, there are series of activities leading to map and globe work and relating to weather in different locations. It also has a list of sources of free or inexpensive materials, as well as easy reading and picture books, many of which are stories from different cultures. This book is suitable for beginning and low intermediate elementary students.

Exploring Our World: Language Works (Cleveland, OH: Modern Curriculum Press, 1990), 32 books, 20–30p. each. This collection of books was designed to help teachers integrate science and social studies with ESL classes. It contains an A level for younger students and a B level for older students. Both levels, however, cover a range of subject matter and complexity, with 16 books in each. Each of the stories has suggested activities for prereading, critical thinking, critiquing, writing, and interdisciplinary applications. The books are each about 20–30 pages and have numerous illustrations. They cover such topics as animal habitats, conservation, feelings, and places. One of the titles, *Post Cards Home*, is a series of post cards from a grandmother to her grandchildren as she is traveling around the world; this would serve as an excellent geography project. *Tinkering* relates the activities of two children who collect all sorts of odds and ends and make things with them,

such as a dinosaur, a periscope, and a telephone network. This book would fit very well into a science project. The series provides students with content-area information as well as language practice as they work on the various projects in the books. It is appropriate for high beginner to intermediate elementary students.

All about the USA, by Milada Broukal and Peter Murphy (White Plains, NY: Longman, 1991), 92p. *All about the USA* is a reader containing thirty units of stories about American people, places, or things. The stories, written as expository pieces, are informative, historical, and sometimes quite humorous. Discussion questions following the stories stimulate exploratory thinking and can be the basis for further research on a particular subject. Many of the stories also lend themselves to cultural comparisons. The topics include such topics as hot dogs, hamburgers, and chewing gum—which you can use to inspire discussions of healthy and unhealthy eating habits. There are also biographies about Clara Barton and George Washington which can be used in a social studies project. Other stories, such as "The Joshua Tree," "The Bald Eagle," and "The Tumbleweed," bring up such topical subjects as endangered species and the environment. Thus, the stories can be used as a supplement to a social studies or science unit, or they can be a project on their own. This book is suitable for low intermediate junior high and high school students.

Language through Pictures

"A picture is worth a thousand words." Nowhere is this more true than in an ESL classroom. Beginning students especially need images to connect the world they know with the language code we use. You may want to create your own picture file—from magazines, last year's calendar, greeting cards, and parts of old posters. They can be used to develop vocabulary, write or tell a story, or practice a grammatical point. Suggestions for other sources of picture projects follow.

Picture Cards that Build Stories, by Paul Hamel and Laura Sihvonen (San Diego: Dominie, 1981). This set of forty 5½" x 8½" picture cards "tells" a story about one day in the life of an American family. Each card has a picture on one side and descriptions on the back of the card; the teacher can either elicit information about the scene from students or describe the scene to them. The descriptions are written in two forms: present and past tense, the use of which would depend on the level of the students. Each level also has a cloze exercise. The cards are reproducible so that each student can make his/her own book. They can be broken down into several themes, such as family, morning activities, school and work, and evening activities. After showing the pictures and telling the story, the students can retell the story as a language experience; the story can also be dictated for listening and writing practice. This is a very practical resource that can be used in many ways with beginning students of any age.

The Magnetic Way (Amherst, NY: Creative Edge, 1987–92).
The Magnetic Way is a kit of visual materials to be used on a large (24" x 36") magnetized board. Materials include background sheets and the small pieces to create the scene. The kit also contains plain sheets that can be used to add speech or thought bubbles, labels, or signs; these can also be used to create additional pieces by taking pictures from magazines or student drawings and pasting them onto the sheets, after which they can be cut to shape.

This program is extremely versatile and can be used with older as well as younger students. For beginners, there is the Language Development Program, which consists of four kits: "The Home," "The Community," "The Country," and "People in Action." These kits can be used to develop vocabulary, discuss daily life and experiences, tell stories, develop writing skills, and play games.

A social studies kit entitled "United States History and Geography" can help students learn about our country. In addition to the large background sheet of a topographical map, other pieces include national monuments and landmarks, as well as people such as early explorers, Native Americans, and early European settlers. These visual displays can help students develop the language to explore further the historical events of our country. Students can see, literally, such things as westward expansion as they move the pieces across the country on the board.

A science program called "Into Life Systems" provides a comprehensive study of the human body. It consists of four kits: "Getting to Know the Body," "The Head: Window to the World," "The Working Body: Engine of Life," and "Reproduction: The Wonder of Life." For each kit there are manuals designed for lower (3–8) or

upper (9–12) grades. The Reproduction manual, however, is designed for students in the middle and upper grades. Each kit contains visuals of all the parts of the body and includes light and dark skin and multicultural faces. This is an excellent way to introduce students to the vocabulary and the functions of the human body.

Picture Stories: Language and Literacy Activities for Beginners, by Fred Ligon and Elizabeth Tannenbaum, with Carol Richardson Rodgers (White Plains, NY: Longman, 1990), 121p.
The sixteen stories in this book are told through pictures. Each of the stories has ten pictures which the teacher can use to elicit information from the students, helping students to follow the story told by the pictures. There are suggested exercises such as cloze, match columns with pictures, and grammar, as well as games. The stories deal with everyday situations and are a good way of introducing students to both life and language in the U.S. This book is suitable for beginner junior high and high school students.

Language through Art Projects

Art projects are a motivating factor to many themes. They are a way to respond to content or to demonstrate an understanding of content. They can also stand on their own. Keep a supply of magazines and a box of scraps—such as fabric, yarn, wallpaper, buttons, fabric trimmings, styrofoam, and bubble packaging—to be used for projects. Following are some suggestions to get started.

Using pictures from magazines and travel brochures, traced pictures from encyclopedias and other reference books, and photos, students can make a collage of their home city or country. (Using tracing paper, trace the picture. Then, using the side of a pencil point, shade the back of the tracing. Finally, put the tracing paper, shaded side down, on oak tag or drawing paper and go over the original tracing lines; the image will be transferred onto the drawing paper. It can then be colored.) Upon completion of the collage, students can write about their country and its customs and/or give a presentation of their collage, describing and explaining the pictures.

Using travel brochures and a world map, have the students choose a place they would like to visit and find it on the map. They can then plan a trip and make a collage from the brochures and magazines. They can describe their imaginary trip in a written or oral report, including such information as distance from their home city, mode of transportation, type of clothing to pack, and things to see and do.

"Around the World in English": Students can make a collage of the countries in which English is spoken, using images that represent each country. For example, they might have pictures of a kangaroo, a pot of tea with scones, the flags of English-speaking countries, or any items that represent English to them.

Particular subject material can also be illustrated through a diorama, such as a science project on rain forests or the solar system. Most of the materials can be obtained from the home or a local variety store. To make a rain forest, for example, one could use a shoe box, various colors of yarn or ribbon, scraps of material, and construction paper or clay. Have students make trees, plants, animals, and waterfalls from these materials. Turn the shoe box on its side, and place the plants and animals inside to create a three-dimensional effect.

Dioramas can also be used for social studies projects, such as the landing of the Pilgrims or the first Thanksgiving. Students could cut pictures from a holiday coloring book or trace them from library books. Have them paste the pictures onto cardboard and stand the figures in the shoe box.

Language through Drama

Role-play very often helps to break down the emotional barriers that keep students from participating in conversations in class. They may feel more free to speak, since they are playing the part of someone else. Following are some suggestions for role-play and dramatization. In addition, students can create their own dramatizations. Writing and presenting a play for a school assembly or for parents can be an exciting project for teacher and students alike. The students can write their own play, write a script for a story or a folktale they have read or for a social studies unit, or they may use a published play.

Decision Dramas, by Barbara Radin (Studio City, CA: JAG Publications, 1992), 92p.
Twenty situations that pose a problem or conflict are presented; the students try to resolve the conflict through role play. Each student presents his/her character's viewpoint. Each situation is

followed by a writing exercise based on the situation and a dialogue of the situation for conversation practice. This type of activity gives students an opportunity to practice social language with expression and emotion. In addition to writing a script, they could create a "last scene," that is, one that might occur after the decision has been made. This book would be appropriate for the upper grades at the intermediate or advanced levels.

101 American English Idioms, by Harry Collis and Mario Risso (Lincolnwood, IL: National Textbook, 1987), 104p.
This collection is meant both to amuse and to inform. Each idiom is presented with an illustration that describes the phrase literally and an explanation or dialogue that explains its actual meaning or use. One very entertaining way of using this book is to give each pair or trio of students an idiom. They then have to mime the idiom while the other students try to guess it. Students could also write and act out a scenario for the idiom. This book would work well with intermediate and advanced students in junior high and high school.

Puppetry

While one method of presenting a play is to have the students themselves do the acting, an alternative would be to have the students make puppets to serve as actors. Hand puppets can be made quite simply by using felt squares, which can be purchased in school supply stores, craft shops, or discount stores. Students can design and decorate their puppets with paint, sequins, glitter, buttons, or fabric.

Another form of presentation is shadow puppetry, called *Wayang,* from Southeast Asia. In this process, each student makes a puppet and has a speaking and puppeteering role. The audience sees only the shadows of the puppets on a white sheet or tissue paper screen, behind which is the puppeteer maneuvering his/her puppet in front of a light. The students collaborate on the entire project, as they decide upon a topic, develop characters and plot, and write the dialogue. They can then maintain a consistency of size and style as they make their puppets. Materials needed for the puppets are oak tag, wooden dowels, clear strapping tape, needles, fishing line, and wood or cardboard.

"Shadow Puppetry" was a presentation at the 1991 New York State TESOL Annual Conference in Albany by Patricia Forton and Duane Diviney of the Ithaca City School District, Ithaca, NY. The presenters suggested the following sources for more information:

The Enchanted Caribou, by Elizabeth Cleaver (New York: Atheneum, 1985). A retelling of an Inuit tale; includes instructions for making a shadow theatre and patterns for shadow puppets.

FACES: The Magazine about People, Vol. 5: No. 6, Feb. 1989. "Important Puppets"; includes information about Turkish shadow puppets and how to make a shadow theatre.

The Rooster's Horns, by Ed Young (New York: Collins and World, 1978). Presents a Chinese folktale and includes directions and patterns for making shadow puppets and a theater.

Language through Songs

Many of us, I am sure, can remember singing popular songs, word for word, when we were youngsters. As a matter of fact, I remember my father saying to me, "Do you know your history lesson as well as you know that song?" Those words came back to me as I started to teach ESL, and I walked through the halls hearing my non-English-speaking students singing the latest rock song in English! Following are some suggestions for using music and songs in the classroom.

Jazz Chants, by Carolyn Graham (New York: Oxford University Press, 1978), 79p.
Small Talk, by Carolyn Graham (New York: Oxford University Press, 1986), 86p.
Rhythm and Role Play, by Carolyn Graham and Sergio Aragones (Studio City, CA: JAG Publications, 1991).
Jazz Chants express language in a rhythmic way in a given context. They help the student to develop stress and intonation patterns. Some chants are presented using a finger-snapping rhythm, while others have music in the background. The chants are conducive to role-play, which adds to the emphasis on expression in speaking. The chants in *Jazz Chants* focus on emotions such as pleasure and anger. Those in *Small Talk* focus on functions such as greetings, introductions, invitations, apologies, and asking for information. The chants

are repetitive, giving students ample opportunity for practice. *Rhythm and Role Play* uses chants in conjunction with picture stories, thus addressing the visual aspect also. *Jazz Chants* and *Small Talk* would be appropriate for beginners of any age group; *Rhythm and Role Play* would be appropriate for high school students at the low intermediate level and above. (All are available with audiocassettes.)

Sharing a Song, by Bob Schneider (Reading, MA: Addison-Wesley, 1987).
Sharing a Song is a music video with an accompanying book of suggested activities, as well as reproducible song and activity sheets. The music is from many genres: rock and roll, latin, calypso, rhythm and blues, gospel, and country. There are twelve songs covering different subject areas such as daily routines, school, friendship, self-awareness, and achievement. The video portion for each has two parts: one shows the author/singer in a classroom with a group of children who are talking about and singing the song; the other is a dramatization of the song. In addition to singing, the suggested activities include personal story-telling, journal writing, categorizing, role-playing, and art. The children in the video range in age from five to twelve and are of varied cultural backgrounds. The video is suitable for elementary students at the beginning and intermediate levels.

I Am Special, by Maureen McElheron (Reading, MA: Addison-Wesley, 1991).
As students learn language through songs, they can also develop the skills and behavior that are necessary for their future success. *I Am Special* is a program that covers such topics as self-esteem, grooming, responsibility, and problem solving, which are presented in songs written in the style of popular music. The author gives suggestions for activities, such as discussion, role-playing, and art, to increase awareness of ones's responsibility to self and others. *I Am Special* consists of an audiocassette with ten songs and a teacher's guide with reproducible song sheets. It is appropriate for junior high and high school students, advanced beginners and above.

Popular Music

One can also use popular music to introduce or close a project on a particular theme. If a song has a good beat and a catchy tune, and the lyrics are appropriate and understandable, you can probably use it with success. Following are a few examples of way some songs can be used.

"America," Neil Diamond: This song can be used as an introduction to a unit on immigration. Play a recording of the song, and have students pick out such words as "coming to America," "free," and "dream." They can then brainstorm on reasons why they and their families came to America.

"What a Feeling" from the soundtrack of the movie *Flashdance*: This song could open a discussion on values such as the importance of effort and commitment in accomplishing one's goals.

"Where Have All the Flowers Gone," Peter, Paul, and Mary: This song would work well in social studies units about war.

There may be other recordings of the foregoing songs by other artists; these are merely examples to give ideas for the use of songs.

Language through Games

Games can be used as a motivator, a rainy day activity, a reward, or a supplement to a project. Following are some sources of ideas for games.

Breaking Language Barriers, by Joe Wayman (Carthage, IL: Good Apple, 1985), 96p.
The sixteen projects in this book were designed to inspire sharing, thinking, and speaking. Many of the activities involve groups of students working together. Topics include "Witches, Goblins, & Ghouls," which lends itself to a Halloween unit, and "Hop to It" (about frogs) and "Rainy Days," both of which could be incorporated into a science unit. The chapters all have a fantasy/imagination activity, after which the author lists suggestions for related activities such as discussion, writing, drama, and art. All of the activities are fun and motivating, and can be used with elementary and junior high students who are advanced beginners and above.

Comics and Conversation, by Joan Ashkenas and Sergio Aragones (Studio City, CA: JAG Publications, 1985), 30p.
Comics and Conversation is a book containing twenty-two uncaptioned cartoons, ranging in length from two to nine frames. Using the shorter cartoons with beginners to develop vocabulary or the more complex cartoons with intermediate or advanced students for writing a play are some of the many suggestions the author gives for class-room activities. The pages can be reproduced for student copies or can be made into an overhead transparency. This is an extremely versatile and motivating resource and is suitable for junior high and high school students at any level.

ESL Teacher's Activities Kit, by Elizabeth Claire (Englewood Cliffs, NJ: Prentice-Hall, 1988), 271p.
This is a smorgasbord of activities for the ESL classroom. While many of the activities are geared toward younger students, others are appropriate or can be adapted for high school students. Activities include action games, seat games, songs, speaking and guessing games, as well as craft, science, and social studies projects. Some craft projects include making dough modeling compound and origami. Science projects include seed planting and making a compass. This is an excellent resource that can be used with beginner to advanced, grades K–12.

Top 20 ESL Word Games, by Marjorie Fuchs, Berenice Pliskin, and Claudia Karabaic Sargent (New York: Longman, 1991), 57p.
To provide practice and reinforcement of vocabulary and grammatical structures, *Top 20 ESL Word Games* is a book of reproducible blackline masters of such games as cloze exercises, crossword puzzles, picture puzzles, and word searches. Each of the twenty units covers a different theme, and each has four or five games on that theme. Thus, the games can be used in conjunction with a unit plan or project on that particular subject. They are appropriate for beginning junior high and high school students.

Jigsaw Puzzles

Teachers can make their own jigsaw puzzles as a lead-in to a particular topic. This can be done by pasting a picture on a piece of thin cardboard or construction paper and cutting it into puzzle pieces. Put four or five different puzzles in one envelope, and have students work together as they complete the puzzles. Working together in this way stimulates speaking, as students ask each other for help in locating pieces that belong to their particular puzzles. Students could also write a story about the process of putting the puzzle together or about the picture represented in the puzzle. With the variety of magazines available, one can find pictures on almost any subject. This activity could be used with any grade or level.

Language through Holidays and Customs

Holidays are a favorite time, and with the many different cultures represented in our classes, we have so many holidays to celebrate! Holiday projects are a good way of introducing students to American culture and of encouraging students to share their native cultures.

A Book for All Seasons, by Greta Barclay Lipson (Carthage, IL: Good Apple, 1990), 152p.
To begin, a good reference would be *A Book for All Seasons*, which lists seventy special days throughout the year. For each special day, it has background information about the day, a poem, and suggested activities. It includes Thanksgiving, Christmas, Hanukkah, the African-American festival of Kwanzaa, Valentine's Day, Arbor Day, May Day, Labor Day, and even the Statue of Liberty's birthday. Many of the days can be incorporated into a social studies or science unit or developed into a project on their own. For example, some social studies projects might revolve around Native American Indian Day, Columbus Day, Martin Luther King, Jr.'s birthday, Abraham Lincoln's and George Washington's birthdays, Black History Month, and Women's History Month Science projects might include Arbor Day and World Environment Day. As the author suggests, the material can be adapted to suit one's needs, and the suggestions can spark one's own creative energies. The activities are geared toward critical thinking, discussion, and writing, and would be suitable for intermediate to advanced junior high and high school students.

Learning about Spring and Summer Holidays, by Jeri A. Carroll and Candace B. Wells (Carthage, IL: Good Apple, 1988), 108p.
For younger students, *Learning about Spring and Summer Holidays* has various projects and activities (which are reproducible) for holidays celebrated during those two seasons. Each holiday has a story or play that tells about it, as well as further background information for the teacher. The book also includes puppets to cut out and use in the telling of the stories or in presenting plays. In addition, there are several other suggested activities for each story, including a story-picture that has write-on lines on which students can write the story in their own words. Students can compile these story-pictures to make their own book of holidays. This book is appropriate for beginner to low intermediate elementary students.

Learning about Fall and Winter Holidays, by Jeri A. Carroll and Candace B. Wells (Carthage, IL: Good Apple, 1988), 106p.
In addition to the regular holidays during the period covered by the book, there are two that are particularly relevant to ESL students: Citizenship Day, on September 12th, and United Nations Day, on October 24th. For Citizenship Day the book features a play whose characters include Alexander Graham Bell, Betsy Ross, and Martin Luther King, Jr. Each character tells what citizenship means to him or her. There are suggested activities such as making a flag or quilt, and outside activities such as a clean-up around the area. For United Nations Day the book has a play with characters from different countries; this day addresses the very timely subjects of peace and conflict resolution. Through these plays, students learn not only their responsibilities as citizens but also the language to express their understanding of citizenship. This book is appropriate for beginner to low intermediate elementary students.

ESL Teacher's Holiday Activities Kit, by Elizabeth Claire (Englewood Cliffs, NJ: Prentice-Hall, 1990), 211p.
This book contains picture stories with vocabulary, writing, and grammar exercises relating to specific holidays. For example, Thanksgiving begins with a picture story explaining the holiday itself and another picture story giving background information, beginning with the sailing of the *Mayflower*. The activity pages are reproducible and are suitable for all ages, beginning to intermediate.

Multicultural Celebrations—See below, under *Language through Multicultural Activities*

Language through Multicultural Activities

An ESL class generally contains students of many different linguistic and ethnic backgrounds. Multicultural projects are one way of helping students to better understand and appreciate each other's differences as well as their similarities.

People, by Peter Spier (New York: Doubleday, 1980), 48p.

An introduction to our multicultural society might be *People*. This is a beautifully illustrated, large (11" x 13") book that can be displayed to students as it is being read to them. The many illustrations vividly convey the message of the text, making it comprehensible to beginning students. The book stresses the individuality and uniqueness of everyone in physical appearance, clothing, religion, occupation, holidays, food, and likes and dislikes. Students could make their own books of their countries and compare the different cultures. This book would be appropriate for beginning and intermediate students of any age.

Cook and Learn, by Beverly Veitch and Thelma Harms (Menlo Park, CA: Addison-Wesley, 1981), 205p.

An important element of any culture is its food. *Cook and Learn* is a pictorial cookbook for children. It includes illustrations of the ingredients in the recipes and of needed cooking utensils, with the words written beside them. Similarly, the instructions are written simply and accompanied by illustrations. The recipes include many ethnic dishes such as pashka, Armenian meat tarts, falafel, and chi tong. The recipes are each for a single portion; thus, each child has the opportunity to participate in the preparation as well as the following feast. The cookbook is a 6" x 8½" spiral, thus making it easy to open, fold over, and stand it up at any recipe. Though some of the recipes do not require cooking, others do. If a stove is not available, a small toaster oven, an electric skillet, and/or a hot plate will suffice. The book also addresses safety and hygiene issues. Math and geography can be integrated into the cooking activity, as you teach students about measurements and the location of each recipe's country of origin. Whether students prepare a recipe for themselves or for a school fair, they are sure to delight in the process. This book is appropriate for beginner or low intermediate students of all ages.

Multicultural Celebrations, by The Children's Museum, Boston (Cleveland, OH: Modern Curriculum Press, 1992). 12 books, 20–30p. each.

For holiday or oral history projects, this series provides excellent background material. This series consists of twelve stories, in individual books, describing a particular festival or holiday of a particular culture. The stories are told from the point of view of a child in that culture and his/her family. The books are filled with beautiful color illustrations of the families and their activities. In addition to giving background information on the celebrations, these are delightful stories that sensitively introduce students to people from other cultures and their customs. Some of the cultures and holidays included in this collection are Vietnamese: the new year's festival of Tet; Russian-Jewish: the first Passover; Puerto Rican: Three Kings Day; Native American: Strawberry Thanksgiving. These books would be appropriate for advanced beginner and intermediate elementary students.

Folktales

Folktales provide another avenue for cultural sharing. Though the themes and morals prevalent in folktales were developed in different cultures long ago and over many centuries, they represent values and emotions that cross borders and span time. Therefore, students can see that many issues are common to all of us, regardless of our country of origin or when we live. Folktales are also a good lead-in to oral history projects.

Tales from around the World, by Jeanne B. Becijos (San Diego: Dominie, 1991), 88p.

This book collects twelve folktales from countries such as China, Niger, Argentina, Hungary, and the U.S. Each story begins with geography questions about its country of origin. For further background information, there is a cloze exercise on the land and the people, and a reading passage about the history of the country. There are also other prereading exercises, such as discussion questions. The story is followed by comprehension questions, as well as more thought-provoking questions. Finally, there are suggestions for follow-up activities, such as games, art projects, and writing projects. The students thus become totally involved, not only in the tale itself, but also in the country, the people, and the culture. This book would be suitable for students in the high elementary grades and above who are at the intermediate to advanced levels.

Folktales: Language Works (Cleveland, OH: Modern Curriculum Press, 1990). 17 books, 20–30p. each.

This set of seventeen folktales is for lower-level students. Each of the stories is colorfully illustrated in its own book (books are about 20–30 pages each). The accompanying guide gives suggestions for prereading, critical thinking, responding to the literature, writing, and across-the-curriculum activities. The collection includes favorites such as "Peter and the Wolf" and "The Lion and the Mouse"; lesser-known stories from Japan, Vietnam, and Africa; as well as other fables, myths, and legends. This collection is suitable for beginner to low intermediate elementary students.

Folktales of the World: The Magnetic Way
(Amherst, NY: Creative Edge, 1988).
This kit, a visual package to be used on a magnetic board, includes background scenes, people, costumes, buildings, and environmental objects from six different countries. There are also large books or individual books for each of the countries for advanced beginner or low intermediate students. This program would be appropriate for beginner to low intermediate students in all grades.

CHILDREN'S TRADE BOOKS: A GUIDE TO RESOURCES

Violet Harris

Associate Professor

University of Illinois at Urbana–Champaign, Champaign, Illinois

Think back to a time in your life when you first heard or read *The Poky Little Puppy* (Lowrey 1942), *The Little Engine That Could* (Piper 1961), *Make Way for Ducklings* (McCloskey 1941), or *The Tale of Peter Rabbit* (Potter 1989). Did you laugh and smile as the Poky Little Puppy frolicked in the grass? Perhaps you cheered as the Little Engine reached the top of the hill. Maybe you held your breath as Mr. McGregor chased Peter or as the ducklings and their mother crossed the street. Along with the pleasures of children's trade books such as these comes knowledge about language, the structures of fiction, and the world outside your home. All children, especially children enrolled in ESL classes, need similar interactions with literature.

New and restructured pedagogical philosophies and techniques, such as integrated language arts, literature-based reading instruction, and the whole language movement have placed children's trade books at the center of curricula. The growing prominence of children's trade books in schooling creates several concerns. First, how might teachers and librarians work together so that the school's collection of books expands and enhances curricula developed by teachers? Second, what resources exist that enable teachers and librarians to select those trade books that are most beneficial, given the increasing costs of books? Third, what techniques, strategies, and philosophies maximize learning and provide pleasure? These and other concerns affect the ways in which teachers and librarians share literature.

This chapter provides some answers to these questions. It includes a listing of professional organizations, resources, and trade books that are useful in ESL classrooms. The chapter is organized in terms of genre, and several examples of trade books are given for each. In addition, the chapter contains several ideas that demonstrate how teachers can create literacy interactions that spur oral and written responses, creative dramatics, and artistic activities such as music and art. Many of the books are in English, but they lend themselves to translation and can help expand children's understandings of the language. Other books are in Spanish because the majority of bilingual or translated editions are in this language. Whenever possible, books featuring other languages are included.

According to Illene Cooper, editor of children's books for *Booklist*, over 6,000 children's books are now published yearly (1992). It is nearly impossible for teachers, librarians, and administrators to read each book published. A number of resources exist that make the task of evaluation and selection less arduous. For example, the number of bookstores devoted exclusively to children's trade books increased to almost 450 in the early 1990s (Roback 1992). Many of the proprietors of these establishments are quite knowledgeable about children's trade books. If no local bookstore is available, the following professional organizations make available varied and extensive information about children's trade books and/or literacy practices.

Professional Resources

American Booksellers Association (ABA)
560 White Plains Road
Tarrytown, NY 10591
The ABA provides information about children's trade books, conducts studies, and sponsors occasional meetings.

American Library Association (ALA)
50 East Huron Street
Chicago, IL 60611
The ALA sponsors the Newbery, Caldecott, and Coretta Scott King awards for distinguished children's literature published each year. The organization also publishes books and monographs related to children's literature.

Center for Children's Books (CCB)
1512 North Fremont Street #105
Chicago, IL 60622
The CCB conducts summer institutes, occasional conferences, and publishes *The Bulletin of the Center for Children's Books*, a review journal.

Cooperative Children's Book Center (CCBC)
University of Wisconsin–Madison
4290 Helen C. White Hall
600 North Park Street
Madison, WI 53706
The CCBC maintains an examination library, sponsors biannual conferences on trends and issues in children's and young adult literature, and publishes annotated bibliographies and monographs on numerous topics.

International Reading Association (IRA)
800 Barksdale Road
P.O. Box 8139
Newark, DE 19714-8139
The IRA publishes pamphlets, monographs, books, and journals—*The Reading Teacher, The Journal of Reading*, and *Reading Research Quarterly*—that report on the latest research in literacy; members also translate research into practical classroom applications. The organization sponsors regional, national, and international conferences. The IRA publishes several lists of trade books that are favorites of teachers and children: "Children's Choices" (*The Reading Teacher*), "Young Adult Choices" (*The Journal of Reading*), and "Teachers' Choices" (*The Reading Teacher*). The organization also sponsors an award that recognizes the most distinguished first book of an author.

National Association for Bilingual Education (NABE)
Union Center Plaza
810 First Street NE, 3rd Floor
Washington, DC 20002
(202) 898-1824
NABE attempts to promote bilingual education. The group offers workshops and conferences and publishes a journal.

National Association for the Education of Young Children (NAEYC)
1834 Connecticut Avenue NW
Washington, DC 20009
The NAEYC produces numerous monographs, books, and a journal, *Young Children*, that include discussions of the evaluation and selection of literature as well as suggestions for using literature in the preschool and home.

National Council of Teachers of English (NCTE)
1111 Kenyon Road
Urbana, IL 61801
NCTE highlights, evaluates, and celebrates children's trade books in a variety of ways. Journals such as *Language Arts* and *The English Teacher* feature monthly review columns, interviews with authors and illustrators, and teaching strategies. NCTE sponsors the Orbis Pictus Award for nonfiction and the Poetry Award given to the poet for lasting contributions to poetry. Several special interest groups exist within the organization, for instance—the Children's Literature Assembly and the Hispanic Caucus.

Other professional organizations devoted to social studies and science education also recognize outstanding examples of children's trade books that augment or elaborate on essential ideas in these curricula areas.

Review Journals

Teachers, librarians, and other interested adults often require guidance when selecting trade books. Several publications review children's books on a consistent basis. A few offer suggestions for sharing the literature with children. Some routinely feature children's trade books written in other languages, especially Spanish. For example, *Horn Book Magazine* regularly features a column that reviews books written in Spanish. Many of the review journals helped forge a tradition of excellence in reviewing and criticism. These journals are found in many public, school, and university libraries:

Bulletin of the Center for Children's Books
Book Links
Booklist
Five Owls
Horn Book Magazine
Kirkus Reviews
Language Arts
New Advocate
Publishers Weekly
Reading Teacher
School Library Journal
Top of the News
VOYA (Voice of Youth Advocates)
The Web

The following journals feature occasional reviews of professional and children's trade books:

Children's Literature Association Quarterly
Children's Literature in Education
The Lion and the Unicorn

Trends, Issues, and Pedagogical Strategies

Annotated bibliographies and critical studies devoted to books about specific trends or issues such as authenticity, stereotypes, correct translations, books suitable for ESL and LEP students, and multicultural literature abound. A representative sampling of books and articles that focus on these topics, as well as teaching and learning strategies is listed below:

Cullinan, B. 1992. *Read to Me: Raising Kids Who Love To Read*. New York: Scholastic.

Cullinan, B., ed. 1987. *Children's Literature in the Reading Program*. Newark, DE: International Reading Association.
———. 1992. *Invitation To Read: More Children's Literature in the Reading Program*. Newark, DE: International Reading Association.
Freeman, E., and D. Person. 1992. *Using Nonfiction Trade Books in the Elementary Classroom*. Urbana, IL: National Council of Teachers of English.
Freeman, Y., and D. Freeman. 1992. *Whole Language for Second Language Learners*. Portsmouth, NH: Heinemann.
Goodman, K. 1986. *What's Whole in Whole Language?* Portsmouth, NH: Heinemann.
Harris, V., ed. 1992. *Teaching Multicultural Literature in Grades K–8*. Norwood, MA: Christopher-Gordon.
Jenkins, E., and M. Austin. 1987. *Literature for Children about Asians and Asian Americans*. New York: Greenwood Press.
Jett-Simpson, M., ed. 1989. *Adventuring with Books*. 9th ed. Urbana, IL: National Council of Teachers of English.
Miller-Lachman, L. 1991. *Our Family, Our Friends, Our World: An Annotated Guide to Significant Books for Children and Teenagers*. New Providence, NJ: R. R. Bowker.
Nieto, S. 1992. *Affirming Diversity: The Sociopolitical Context of Multicultural Education*. New York: Longman.
Rudman, M. 1984. *Children's Literature: An Issues Approach*. New York: Longman.
Schon, I. 1980. *A Hispanic Heritage: A Guide to Juvenile Books about Hispanic People and Culture*. Metuchen, NJ: Scarecrow Press.
———. 1988. *A Hispanic Heritage, Series II and III*. Metuchen, NJ: Scarecrow Press.
Sims, R. 1982. *Shadow and Substance: Afro-American Experience in Contemporary Children's Fiction*. Urbana, IL: National Council of Teachers of English.
Slapin, B., and D. Seale. 1988. *Books Without Bias: Through Indian Eyes*. Berkeley, CA: Oyate.
Slayer, S. 1987. *Readers Theatre: Story Dramatization in the Classroom*. Urbana, IL: National Council of Teachers of English.
Stensland, A. 1979. *Literature by and about the American Indian*. Urbana, IL: National Council of Teachers of English.
Strickland, D., and L. Morrow. 1989. *Emerging Literacy*. Newark, DE: International Reading Association.

Taylor, D., and D. Strickland. 1986. *Family Storybook Reading.* Portsmouth, NH: Heinemann.

Trealease, J. 1985. *The Read-Aloud Handbook.* New York: Penguin.

Periodicals and Newspapers

Although most major newspapers, weekly news magazines, and general and special interest periodicals no longer feature children's trade book reviews and criticism on a regular basis, some devote occasional columns or sections to the subject. *Newsweek,* for example, occasionally examines trends in children's literature such as the resurgence of folk literature and multiculturalism. *The New York Times Book Review* publishes a special section on children's trade books twice each year. *The New York Times* editors also list the picture books named "best of the year." The *Boston Globe,* in conjunction with *Horn Book Magazine,* selects best illustrators and fiction and nonfiction books each year; the awards are some of the most coveted in children's trade book publishing.

Authors and Illustrators

Children and adults often seek information about their favorite authors and illustrators. They search out answers to questions related to the author's or illustrator's life, philosophy, and listing of creative works. Several references provide valuable information. Among those recommended are the following:

Children's Literature Review. Detroit: Gale Research Company. Multiple volumes. Provides extensive critical commentary about authors as well as statements about the author's work.

Cummings, P. 1992. *Talking with Artists.* New York: Bradbury/Macmillan. Interviews with fourteen artists who have advanced children's book illustrating to higher standards of creative excellence.

Something about the Author. Detroit: Gale Research Company. Multiple volumes. Extensive information given about authors and illustrators such as biographical data, honors and awards, and professional career.

Twayne Young Authors Series. New York: Twayne Publishers. A collection of individually written critical biographies of authors who write young adult fiction, such as Walter Dean Myers.

Children's Trade Books

Research conducted over the past 25 years demonstrated the importance of teachers, librarians, and administrators acquiring knowledge about children's trade books (Cullinan 1987; Cullinan 1992; Strickland and Morrow 1989; Taylor and Strickland 1986). Children's trade books benefit children's cognitive, linguistic, social, and aesthetic development. For example, reading aloud to children daily expands their vocabularies; similarly, wide reading of trade books by children will also increase their vocabularies. Sharing trade books that represent a variety of genres provides knowledge of how stories and nonfiction are structured. For instance, historical fiction emphasizes character, setting (clothing, language, artifacts, technology, and ideas must be authentic), and plot. Many trade books contain some of the best writing and artwork; these books can serve as models for writing and can help develop visual literacy skills. Children need to know about communities, states, and nations in which they reside, as well as about other countries throughout the world. Books cannot provide the kinds of interactions offered by direct experiences, but they offer an alternative way of knowing the world as embodied in the saying, "There is no frigate like a book." Comprehension improves when children are given trade books that range from the predictable to the complex. The following sections contain discussions of books that are appropriate for ESL classes.

Picture Books

Children display particular interests in certain kinds of books at different ages. Young children (infancy through primary grades) tend to prefer books that emphasize families, children, animals, and toys; books that are short and predictable and that end unambiguously and happily. Several trade books feature these elements. A few are bilingual, primarily Spanish. Others are written in English but are easily translated and offer opportunities for acquiring new English words.

Classics

Many people think of classics as books with a particular pedigree that should introduce children to the world of Literature. Classics are simply those books that embody certain ideas, themes, or characters that are important to the culture; that appeal to generation after generation; or that are identified by critics, librarians, and parents as "the best" literature for children. The classics listed here are ones that children will enjoy hearing and reading themselves. They also lend themselves to creative dramatics. Some of these are available in Spanish translations and a few other languages.

Bemelmans, L. 1939. *Madeline.* New York: Viking. Madeline is a young girl who lives in Paris and attends a boarding school. She engages in antics that are familiar to children.

Brown, M. 1947. *Goodnight Moon.* New York: Harper. A little bunny gets ready for bed and says goodnight to many objects in the room. The repetitive and rhythmic language appeals to young listeners who can chant the phrases at the appropriate time.

Burton, V. 1942. *The Little House.* New York: Houghton Mifflin. A house passes through several seasons and years, changing from a single house in a field to a small house squeezed between buildings in a city. The house is moved and becomes happy once again in the space found in the country.

Gag, W. 1956. *Millions of Cats.* New York: Coward-McCann. A very old man and his very old wife are lonely. The wife suggests that a cat will provide some happiness. The husband agrees and searches for the perfect one. He goes out and returns with a cat, but along the way he encounters millions of cats. The repetition of some lines of text and their predictability make this one an excellent read-aloud.

Keats, E. 1962. *The Snowy Day.* New York: Viking. Peter enjoys the first snowfall of the year. He frolics and makes snow angels. The simple text and colorful collages should elicit visual and oral responses.

Lowrey, J. 1942. *The Poky Little Puppy.* New York: Western Publishing Company. Five little puppies are admonished by their mother not to dig holes as they play. One puppy always disobeys and lags behind when returning home. The puppies receive treats, but mother decides to teach the Poky Little Puppy a lesson when he does not heed her warnings.

McCloskey, R. 1941. *Make Way for Ducklings.* New York: Viking. Mr. and Mrs. Mallard have to find a new home for their expected children. They search and happen upon the public gardens of Boston. They build a nest, the ducklings are hatched, and the family must learn to live in an urban area.

———. 1948. *Blueberries for Sal.* New York: Viking Penguin. Sal and her mother are going to pick blueberries to preserve later. Sal has a pail to fill but eats her blueberries as they walk along. Imagine her surprise when she is separated from her mother and ends up following a bear.

Piper, W. 1961. *The Little Engine that Could.* New York: Platt & Munk. The hill is large and the engine is small. Will the engine make it up the hill? It has to, because children are waiting for its load of toys and treats. They do not want to be disappointed. The little engine repeats phrases such as "I think I can" that children remember and chant.

Potter, B. 1902. *The Tale of Peter Rabbit.* London: Frederick Warne. Peter and his sisters are admonished not to go into Mr. McGregor's yard. Flopsy, Mopsy, and Cottontail obey their mother, but Peter does not. Peter goes into the yard and almost becomes a pie as his father had.

Rey, M., and H. Rey. 1986. *Curious George Goes to a Costume Party.* New York: Houghton Mifflin. Adapted from the Curious George film series. Curious George is a mischievous monkey whose curiosity gets him into several humorous mishaps.

Sendak, M. 1963. *Where the Wild Things Are.* New York: Harper. Max puts on his wolf suit and is promptly sent to bed without any supper when he gets into mischief. He goes on an adventure with the Wild Things and comes back home feeling satisfied.

Seuss, Dr. 1957. *The Cat in the Hat.* New York: Random. Sally and her brother are in the house because of rain. Suddenly, their day is interrupted by a cat who appears out of no-where and performs tricks for them that result in a total mess. The fun, adventure, and language makes children laugh as the story is shared.

Contemporary Picture Books

The following books depict a range of families engaged in many familiar activities. A teacher might introduce these books in such a way that children can respond in their first language if they possess limited English skills. The teacher can share the books with individual students, in small groups, or as a whole group activity. For example, the teacher might select *Family Pictures* by C. Garza (San Francisco: Children's Book Press, 1990), which depicts the life of a young Mexican American girl growing up in Kingsville, Texas, close to the Mexican border. The family completes daily activities and special activities. The illustrations are vibrant, colorful, and folklike.

1. Decide whether to share *Family Pictures* with one student, a small group, or the whole class.
2. The text is written in Spanish and English. For those students who are not Spanish speakers, introduce the book in their languages, if possible. Ask children to draw or talk about a picture that depicts one day in their lives. You can record these comments and use them as the basis for language experience stories or students' versions of *Family Pictures*.
3. Share the book, reading in Spanish and English whenever possible. Reread sections or the entire book. Highlight the illustrations and ask students to "read" the pictures.
4. Allow children to respond to the story. You might ask such questions as, "Which picture reminded you of your family?" or "Describe a picture of you completing an activity at age 5. How would the picture look? What kinds of colors would you use?"
5. Children can work in pairs or small groups to dramatize their favorite familial activities.
6. Provide children with art materials so that they can draw pictures.
7. Children can dictate stories to accompany their pictures.
8. Share the stories with other students.

These activities should take place over several days, to allow for extensive oral language activities.

Other trade books offer similar opportunities for linking children's personal lives and experiences and integrating reading, writing, speaking, drawing, and creative dramatics. Most are in English but can be used in a number of ways. This list is not exhaustive. Search reference guides for other titles.

Barrett, J. 1989. *Willie's Not the Hugging Kind.* New York: Scholastic. Willie does not believe that it is "manly" to receive overt affection. He changes his mind when he realizes that he enjoys the comfort that hugging offers and that other boys hug as well.

Baylor, B. 1989. *Amigo.* New York: Aladdin. A little boy befriends a prairie dog and shares his secrets and dreams.

———. 1976. *Hawk, I'm Your Brother.* New York: Scribner. A boy eyes a hawk and approaches him gradually. They interact warily, with the boy imagining himself as sharing the same spirit.

Boholm-Olsson, E. 1988. *Tuan.* New York: R & S Books. Tuan goes about daily activities. He is bitten by a dog as he plays and a special medicine is needed. However, the medicine needed to prevent a serious illness is in scarce supply. Can the medicine be found in time so that he can participate in the children's festival? Set in Vietnam; some might criticize this positive portrayal of the north of Vietnam.

Brown, T. 1985. *Hello, Amigos!* New York: Henry Holt. Spend a day with a Mexican American boy as he celebrates his family. The book features photographs.

Bunting, E. 1990. *How Many Days to America?: A Thanksgiving Story.* New York: Clarion. Many immigrants share a common journey of escaping poverty or oppression. This book recreates the longing of those who seek sanctuary in the United States.

Byers, R. 1990. *Mycca's Baby.* New York: Orchard Books. A new baby nearly always causes joy; the same holds for Mycca's family. They cannot wait for the newest member of the family, because they each have something special to share.

Caines, J. 1984. *Just Us Women.* New York: Harper & Row. A young girl and her aunt take an auto trip south to visit relatives. Along the way, they stop each day to picnic, camp, frolic, or visit roadside markets.

———. 1988. *I Need a Lunch Box.* New York: Harper. A little boy notices that his older sister received a lunch box for the new school year. He feels left out until his parents realize that he wants one as well.

Casillia, R. 1991. *Con Mi Hermano/With My Brother.* New York: Bradbury. Brothers share time together.

Clifton, L. 1991. *Everett Anderson's Christmas Coming.* New York: Henry Holt. Everett cannot contain his joy as he awaits the holiday. Clifton recounts his story in the form of a poem.

Dorros, A. 1991. *Abuela.* New York: Dutton. Imagine you can fly! Rosalba and her grandmother do. They fly through the city and explore events from a new perspective.

Ets, M., and A. Labastida. 1991. *Nueve dias para navidad: Un cuento de Mexico.* 1959. New York: Viking. A tale about the nine days of celebration leading up to Christmas.

Greenfield, E. 1991. *First Pink Light.* New York: Writers and Readers. Many children will empathize with the child's desire to stay up and await a father's return from work.

Howard, E. 1988. *The Train to Lulu's.* New York: Bradbury. Two little girls visit a beloved great aunt. They look forward to the adventures that await them on their train ride, such as eating in the dining car and watching the landscape as they whisk through the area.

Johnson, A. 1989. *Tell Me a Story, Mama.* New York: Orchard. A little girl's favorite bedtime ritual is for her mother to tell a story about growing up. The girl has heard the stories so often that she pipes in with the appropriate memories and tells the stories herself.

Loh, M. 1988. *Tucking Mommy In.* New York: Orchard. Sue realizes that her mother is tired and will not have the energy to put her to bed. Mommy falls asleep, and Sue tucks her in for the night. Asian American.

Martel, C. 1976. *Yagua Days.* New York: Dial. A young boy lives in a stable, caring Latino community. The owners of the local bodega, the mailman, and other community workers are excited when he tells them he will make his first visit to Puerto Rico. The highlights of his visit to the island are meeting his multiracial extended family and sliding down the hills on yagua leaves after a rainfall.

Mora, P. 1992. *A Birthday Basket for Tia.* New York: Macmillan. Cecilia prepares a surprise gift for her aunt's ninetieth birthday. The gift is a basket filled with items symbolic of the time they spend together, such as a book, flowers, and a teacup. The story features an intergenerational Mexican American family.

Narahashi, K. 1987. *I Have a Friend.* New York: Macmillan. A boy describes his best friend, who has the ability to change shape and size. The friend disappears at night.

Ringgold, F. 1991. *Tar Beach.* New York: Crown. Cassie goes up on the roof, to "tar beach," with her family and their friends during a hot summer evening. Cassie imagines herself flying throughout the city to her favorite places.

Say, A. 1991. *The Tree of Cranes.* New York: Houghton Mifflin. A young boy does not heed his mother's advice about not playing in the water when it is cold. He gets sick, and his mother tells about her life in California as she folds origami cranes. He is enchanted by these bonsai tree decorations that are akin to those on a Christmas tree.

Surat, M. 1989. *Angel Child, Dragon Child.* New York: Scholastic. After arriving in the United States, a Vietnamese girl—Nguyen Hoa—does not fit in with the other children. She is teased about her clothing and speech. She worries about her mother who remains in Vietnam. Memories of her mother and her advice help her to cope with the situation.

Tsutsui, Y. 1987. *Anna's Secret Friend.* New York: Viking. Anna, an Asian girl, feels lonesome after her family moves to a new home in another town. Her loneliness eases as a secret friends leaves little gifts for her.

Udry, J. 1991. *What Mary Jo Shared.* 1966. New York: Scholastic. All of the children in Mary Jo's class have shared exciting things such as pets; Mary Jo wants to do something special as well. The best gift she can share is her father, a high school teacher.

Wheeler, B. 1986. *Where Did You Get Your Moccasins?* Winnipeg, Manitoba: Pemmican. All of the children in class admire a boy's new shoes. He tells them the story of how the shoes were made. Format is akin to a cumulative tale that begins over again when the teacher arrives and asks the same question.

Williams, V. 1982. *A Chair for My Mother.* New York: Greenwillow. Rosa and her grandmother and mother live together in a happy household. They must budget their money carefully. A fire destroys some of their furniture, including a favorite chair. The family saves their money, replaces the chair with a new one, and holds a celebration when it arrives.

———. 1990. *More, More, More, Said the Baby.* New York: Greenwillow. Children and an adult caretaker celebrate playtime rituals. The book is multiracial and multigenerational.

Predictable Books

These trade books help children discover how language functions. They are exposed to a variety of language forms because words, phrases, and plot episodes are repeated. The predictability enables children to guess refrains or action. Children develop a "story grammar"; they understand the structures underlying text. They also can acquire the belief that they can read because of the predictable nature of the text. Some examples follow.

Hogrogian, N. 1971. *One Fine Day.* New York: Macmillan.

Keats, E. 1971. *Over in the Meadow.* New York: Scholastic.

Martin, B., and J. Archambault. 1989. *Chicka Chicka Boom Boom.* New York: Simon & Schuster.

Omerod, J. 1986. *The Story of Chicken Licken.* New York: Lothrop, Lee, & Shepard.

Rylant, C. 1982. *When I was Young in the Mountains.* New York: Dutton.

Shaw, N. 1986. *Sheep in a Jeep.* New York: Houghton Mifflin.

Wood, A. 1984. *The Napping House.* New York: Harcourt Brace Jovanovich.

Wordless Picture Books

Wordless picture books are excellent for prompting oral and written language activities. Wordless picture books contain no text; the pictures "tell" the story. The pictures can be read in such a manner that a narrative develops. A teacher can work with students individually or in small groups in order to create an English or bilingual text to accompany illustrations. A source for additional books is Richey, V., and K. Puckett. 1992. *Wordless/Almost Wordless Picture Books: A Guide.* Englewood, CO: Libraries Unlimited, Inc.

Anno, M. 1978. *Anno's Journey.* New York: Collins-World.

———. 1978. *Anno's U. S. A.* New York: Philomel.

Briggs, R. 1978. *The Snowman.* New York: Random House.

Carle, E. 1971. *Do You Want to be My Friend?* New York: Crowell.

Crews, D. 1980. *Truck.* New York: Greenwillow.

De Paola, T. 1978. *Pancakes for Breakfast.* New York: Harcourt Brace Jovanovich.

Goodall, J. 1982. *Paddy Goes Travelling.* New York: Athenaeum.

Koren, E. 1972. *Behind the Wheel.* New York: Holt.

Mayer, M. 1967. *A Boy, a Dog and a Frog.* New York: Dial.

Omerod, J. 1981. *Sunshine.* New York: Lothrop, Lee & Shepard.

Wiesner, D. 1991. *Tuesday.* New York: Clarion. (The book contains about nine words and has many of the same features as a wordless picture book.)

Other Sources

Booklist publishes several annotated bibliographies that list books covering a range of genres. The books are translations of books written in the language of the nation or culture that will have appeal for children who share the language and culture and for others who do not. Several books appropriate for providing background information for teachers are listed in some of the bibliographies. A few of the bibliographies will list dealers from whom the books may be purchased.

Gladden, E. N. 1988. "Vietnamese Books." *Booklist* 84(17): 1479–80.

Jennings, M. 1991. "Ukrainian Books for Children." *Booklist* 88(5): 537–38.

Schon, I. 1991. "Recent Books for Young Readers Published in Mexico." *Booklist* 88(5), 535–536.

Booklinks frequently publishes annotated bibliographies that also include a summary examination of major trends, genres, and authors for a number of countries and geographic regions.

Corsaro, J. 1992. "The Caribbean." *Booklinks,* 2(1): 24–29. Annotations of books and suggested activities.

Elleman, B. 1992. "The Former Yugoslavia." *Booklinks,* 2(1): 5. A sample of the few books available that detail the literature of Yugoslavia.

Harms, J., L. Lettow, E. Strub, and D. Dale. 1992. "Russia." *Booklinks,* 1(4): 36–44. Book annotations and suggested activities.

Lewis, J. 1992. " Japan." *Booklinks,* 1(4): 24–26. An annotated bibliography that also contains a source for acquiring information about purchasing books.

Translated Books

Nieto (1992) and Barreras (1992) each argue that Latinos need to create their own literature reflecting the experiences of growing up in the United States. They argue against depending on Spanish translations of books written in English and of books about other cultures as the sole source of literature. Translated books serve a valuable function, but they do not replace the need for original literature.

Several picture books originally published in English are now available in Spanish translations. A sampling follows.

Bridwell, N. 1988. *Clifford, el gran perro colorado* (Clifford, the big red dog). New York: Scholastic.

Keats, E. 1991. *Dia de nieve* (Snowy Day). 1962. New York: Viking.

Leaf, M. 1988. *El cuento de Ferdinando* (Story of Ferdinand). 1936. New York: Puffin.

Lobel, A. 1972. *Sapo y sepo inseparables* (Frog and Toad together). Compton, CA: Santillana.

———. 1976. *Sapo y sepo un ano entero* (Frog and Toad all year). Compton, CA: Santillana.

Scieszka, J. 1992. *La verdadera historia de los tres cerditos por S. Lobo* (The true story of the three little pigs, by a wolf). New York: Viking.

Sendak, M. 1963. *Donde viven los monstruo* (Where the wild things are). Compton, CA: Santillana.

Other translated books are available from the following companies:

1100 Libros en Espanol y titulos bilingues. Para La Biblioteca—Para La Sala de clase.
Perma-Bound
Vandalia Road
Jacksonville, IL 62650
(217) 243-5451

Farrar, Straus & Giroux (Putnam Publishing Group)
19 Union Square West
New York, NY 10003
(800) 631-8571

Rhymes, Songs, and Poetry

All cultures create music and lyrics to accompany them. The rhythms and instruments differ, but the reasons for creating them are comparable. Children enjoy singing and creating sounds.

Teachers might begin with various hand-clap games such as "Pat-a-Cake" and proceed to other forms. This activity can be adapted for use in individual classes.

1. Select a range of objects that create sounds such as empty oatmeal boxes, aluminum cans, sand paper, dried gourds, musical triangles, blocks, tambourines, etc.
2. Demonstrate the ways that children can produce sounds with the instruments.
3. Distribute instruments and encourage children to play them and sing along in their first language or English.
4. Copy a simple chant, song, poem, or rhyme onto the blackboard or chart paper. Write the verse or lyrics in English and the language(s) of the children.
5. Read/sing what you have written for the children; play an instrument or encourage the children to do so. Repeat several times. Invite the children to join in and perform.
6. Group children in various formats and allow them to perform the chant, song, rhyme, or poem.

Another activity consists of writing the material on large index cards that are illustrated. Copy the children's favorites and display them in an attractive container. For example, a teacher might select several poems and songs that relate to food. Students can draw pictures of the particular foods included in the poems and songs. For example, a poem about ice cream can be copied onto a cutout of an ice cream cone. As they complete the art, the teacher can provide the English and first-language labels for the various foodstuffs on the back of the poem.

These books are quite appropriate because they contain rhymes, songs, and poems that children will enjoy for the music and the chance to dance. Consider recording some of them on tape (in English and in the language of the children) and placing them in a listening station.

Rhymes and Songs

Alexander, F. 1983. *Mother Goose on the Rio Grande*. New York: NTC.

Delacre, L. 1989. *Arroz con leche*. New York: Scholastic. Songs and poems about food.

Delacre, L. 1990. *Las navidades*. New York: Scholastic. Songs and rhymes, compiled from various Latin American countries, that relate to Christmas. The music is also provided.

Griego, M. et al. 1981. *Tortillitas para mama and other nursery rhymes* (Little tortillas for Mama). New York: Henry Holt.

Kemp, M., illustrator 1992. *Hickory, Dickory, Dock.* New York: Lodestar Books.

———. 1992. *I'm a Little Teapot.* New York: Lodestar Books.

———. 1992. *Knock at the Door.* New York: Lodestar Books.

———. 1992. *Pat-a-Cake, Pat-a-Cake.* New York: Lodestar Books.

———. 1992. *Round and Round the Garden.* New York: Lodestar Books.

———. 1992. *This Little Piggy.* New York: Lodestar Books.

Krull, K., collector and arranger. 1992. *Gonna Sing My Head Off.* New York: Knopf. A collection of 62 American folk songs. Musical arrangements for piano and guitar are also included.

Yolen, J. 1992. *Jane Yolen's Mother Goose Songbook.* New York: Caroline House/Boyd's Hills Press. A selection of 48 rhymes set to music.

Poetry

Poetry is a neglected genre. Allowing children to listen to and perform poetry can help alleviate some of the negative attitudes. However, children should not be forced to read a poem for a "correct" interpretation. Remember that response is individual, and the way in which children will interpret a poem depends on a variety of factors, such as their exposure to the genre, the manner in which it is shared, and the types of poetry selected. Research reveals that children prefer narrative poems, poems with humor, rhyming poems, and those with less obscure imagery. Read and perform a poem several times so that children can hear and feel the sounds and images. Share copies with students and encourage them to join you as you dramatize the poem. Think about using musical instruments or other objects to create musical accompaniment.

Adoff, A. 1976. *Eats Poems.* New York: Lothrop, Lee & Shepard.

———. 1986. *Sports pages.* New York: Lippincott.

———. 1988. *Flamboyan.* New York: Harcourt Brace Jovanovich.

———. 1989. *Chocolate Dreams.* New York: Lothrop, Lee & Shepard.

Bryan, A. 1992. *Sing to the Sun.* New York: Lothrop, Lee & Shepard.

Ciardi, J. 1985. *Doodle Soup.* New York: Houghton Mifflin.

Fields, J. 1988. *The Green Lion of Zion Street.* New York: Macmillan.

Giovanni, N. 1988. *Spin a Soft Black Song.* Rev. ed. New York: Farrar, Straus & Giroux.

Greenfield, E. 1989. *Nathaniel Talking.* New York: Black Butterfly Children's Books.

Hopkins, L., ed. 1982. *Circus! Circus!* New York: Knopf.

———. 1984. *Surprises.* New York: Harper.

———. 1992. *Questions.* New York: HarperCollins.

Joseph, L. 1990. *Coconut Kind of Day.* New York: Lothrop, Lee & Shepard.

Lessac, F. 1989. *Caribbean Canvas.* New York: Lippincott.

Livingston, M. 1985. *Celebrations.* New York: Holiday House.

Livingston, M., ed. 1987. *Cat Poems.* New York: Holiday House.

McCord, D. 1974. *Away and Ago: Rhymes of the Never Was and Always Is.* Boston: Little, Brown.

Merriam, E. 1981. *A Word or Two with You: New Rhymes for Young Readers.* New York: Athenaeum.

Prelutsky, J. 1984. *The New Kid on the Block.* New York: Greenwillow.

Prelutsky, J., ed. 1986. *Read-Aloud Rhymes for the Very Young.* New York: Knopf.

Pomerantz, C. 1980. *The Tamarindo Puppy and Other Poems.* (Spanish and English). New York: Greenwillow.

———. 1982. *If I Had a Paka: Poems in Eleven Languages.* New York: Greenwillow.

Silverstein, S. 1974. *Where the Sidewalk Ends.* New York: Harper & Row.

———. 1981. *A Light in the Attic.* New York: Harper & Row.

Sneve, V. 1989. *Dancing Teepees.* New York: Holiday House.

Viorst, J. 1981. *If I Were in Charge of the World and Other Worries: Poems for Children and Their Parents.* New York: Athenaeum.

Willard, N. 1986. *Night Story.* New York: Harcourt Brace Jovanovich.

Worth, V. 1987. *All the Small Poems.* New York: Farrar, Straus & Giroux.

Folk Tales

The phrases "once upon a time" and "a long, long time ago" signal to the reader the beginnings of a tale rooted in the oral tradition. These tales convey essential wisdom and entertain. Some—Bruno Bettelheim, for example—argue that children need folk tales in order to resolve basic psychological dilemmas. Folk tales are universal, and a wealth of written versions are available to children. Teachers can adapt the following technique to introduce these universal tales.

1. Select from among several commonly shared tales such as Cinderella, Snow White, Sleeping Beauty, Hansel and Gretel, Little Red Riding Hood, Rapunzel, The Three Little Pigs, Goldilocks and the Three Bears, and others. Or select a modern tale. Several versions of the tales are available as big books, which are ideal for sharing.

2. Show the pictures to students. For example, you might ask, "What does it feel like to walk in the forest as Hansel and Gretel are doing?" Or "Pretend you are the first little pig; how might you fortify your house against the wolf?"

3. Read the tale in dramatic fashion to heighten the sense of adventure or suspense.

4. Engage children by having them act out what they think will occur next.

5. Finish reading the tale and allow children to talk about other stories they have heard at home. For example, some Latino children will have familiarity with La Llorona tales.

6. Record the tales that children share and make them available in print format for use in creative dramatics or the reading corner.

7. Cinderella is a popular tale that many children enjoy. Collect several versions such as Yeh-Shin, The Rough-Faced Girl, Mufaro's Beautiful Daughters, The Brocaded Slipper, The Egyptian Cinderella, and the Disney version. Share the variants and direct students to compare and contrast the tales.

Asbjornsen, P., and J. Moe. 1991. *The Three Billy Goats Gruff*. New York: Harcourt Brace Jovanovich.

Belpre, P. 1960. *Perez and Martina*. 1932. New York: Viking. A Puerto Rican tale that follows the courtship of Perez and Martina, their marriage, and Perez's death.

Brown, M., illus. 1955. *Cinderella*. New York: Scribner.

Cauley, B. 1979. *The Ugly Duckling*. New York: Harcourt Brace Jovanovich.

———. 1986. *Puss in Boots*. New York: Harcourt Brace Jovanovich.

Climo, S. 1992. *The Egyptian Cinderella*. 1989. New York: Harper.

Garcia, R. 1987. *My Aunt Otilia's Spirits*. Emeryville, CA: Children's Book Press. Bilingual, English and Spanish.

Kellog, S. 1991. *Jack and the Beanstalk*. New York: Morrow.

Louie, A. 1982. *Yeh-shin*. New York: Philomel.

McDermott, G. 1974. *Flecha al sol: Un cuento de los indios Pueblo* (Arrow to the sun: A Pueblo Indian story). New York: Puffin.

Martin, R. 1992. *The Rough-faced Girl*. New York: Putnam.

Plume, I. 1991. *The Shoemaker and the Elves*. New York: Harcourt Brace Jovanovich.

Rohmer, H. 1982. *The Legend of Food Mountain* (La montaña del alimento). Emeryville, CA: Children's Book Press. Mexican legend that details how a red ant brought food to the world.

———. 1989. *Uncle Nacho's Hat*. Emeryville, CA: Children's Book Press. (Spanish and English). A little girl, Ambrosia, gives her uncle Ignaciao a new hat, but his old hat returns to him no matter what happens to it.

Rohmer, H., O. Chow, & M. Vidaire. 1987. *Invisible Hunters* (Los cazadores invisibles). Emeryville, CA: Children's Book Press. A legend from the Miskito Indians of Nicaragua that recounts the consequences of deception and greed.

San Souci, R. 1989. *The Talking Eggs*. New York: Dial.

Steptoe, J. 1987. *Mufaro's Beautiful Daughters*. A Zimbabwean Variant of Cinderella. New York: Lothrop, Lee & Shepard.

Vuong, L. 1982. *The Brocaded Slipper and Other Vietnamese Tales*. New York: Addison-Wesley.

Young, E. 1989. *Lon Po Po. A Chinese Variant of Little Red Riding Hood*. New York: Philomel.

Zelinsky, P. 1992. *El enano saltarin* (Rumpelstiltskin). New York: Dutton Children's Books.

Zemach, M. 1992. *La gallinita roja: Un cuento viejo* (The little red hen: An old story). New York: Mirasol.

———. 1992. *The Princess and the Froggie*. New York: Sunburst Books.

Nonfiction

Children are curious about how the world works, why some people are tall and others are short, what happens to the moon and sun, and any number of objects and phenomena. You can help them acquire a broad base of knowledge by sharing information books and biographies. You might begin by asking children what do they want to know about animals, food, the ocean, dinosaurs, or any other topics. Included in the listing are ABC, counting, and concept books. Select books that provide them with the information they need and that help them acquire additional English phrases and words.

Adler, D. 1986. *Un libro ilustrado sobre Martin Luther King, hijo* (A picture book of Martin Luther King, Jr). New York: Holiday House.
———. 1991. *Un libro ilustrado sobre Cristobal Colon* (A picture book of Christopher Columbus). New York: Holiday House.
———. 1992. *A picture book of Simon Bolivar.* New York: Holiday House.
———. 1992. *Un libro ilustrado sobre Abraam Lincoln* (A picture book of Abraham Lincoln). New York: Holiday House.
Ancona, G. 1981. *Dancing Is.* New York: Dutton.
Anno, M. 1975. *Anno's Alphabet: An Adventure in Imagination.* New York: Crowell.
Bang, M. 1983. *Ten, Nine, Eight.* New York: Greenwillow.
Barton, B. 1982. *Airport.* New York: Crowell.
Brown, R. 1987. *100 Words about Animals.* (Available in Spanish.) New York: Harcourt Brace Jovanovich.
———. 1988. *100 Words about My House.* (Available in Spanish.) New York: Harcourt Brace Jovanovich.
Carle, E. 1971. *The Grouchy Ladybug.* New York: Crowell.
———. 1974. *My Very First Book of Colors.* New York: Crowell.
———. 1974. *My Very First Book of Numbers.* New York: Crowell.
———. 1974. *My Very First Book of Shapes.* New York: Crowell.
Carrick, D. 1985. *Milk.* New York: Greenwillow.
Cole, J. 1973. *My Puppy Is Born.* New York: Morrow.
Cowcher, H. 1992. *El bosque tropical.* New York: Mirasol.
Crews, D. 1978. *Freight Train.* New York: Greenwillow.

———. 1980. *Truck.* New York: Greenwillow.
———. 1982. *Carousel.* New York: Greenwillow.
———. 1982. *Harbour.* New York: Greenwillow.
De Paolo, T. 1978. *The Popcorn Book.* New York: Holiday House.
Ehlert, L. 1989. *Color Zoo.* New York: Lippincott.
———. 1989. *Eating the Alphabet.* New York: Harcourt Brace Jovanovich.
———. 1990. *Growing Vegetable Soup.* New York: Harcourt Brace Jovanovich.
———. 1990. *Fish Eyes: A Book You Can Count On.* New York: Harcourt Brace Jovanovich.
Friedman, J. 1992. *I Speak English for My Mom.* New York: Harcourt Brace Jovanovich.
Gag, W. 1933. *The ABC Bunny.* New York: Coward.
Gibbons, G. 1987. *Trains.* New York: Holiday House.
Hoban, T. 1974. *Circles, Triangles, and Squares.* New York: Macmillan.
Hoban, T. 1985. *A Children's Zoo.* New York: Greenwillow.
———. 1987. *26 Letters and 99 Cents.* New York: Greenwillow.
Isadora, R. 1985. *I Hear.* New York: Greenwillow.
———. 1985. *I see.* New York: Greenwillow.
———. 1985. *I touch.* New York: Greenwillow.
———. 1990. *Babies.* New York: Greenwillow.
———. 1990. *Friends.* New York: Greenwillow.
Jones, F. 1992. *Nature's Deadly Creatures.* New York: Dial. Linden, A. 1992. *One Smiling Grandmother.* New York: Dial.
MacKinnon, D. 1992. *What Shape?* New York: Dial.
Rue, E. 1976. *My Nursery School.* New York: Greenwillow.
Selsam, M. 1967. *Toda clase de bebes* (All kinds of babies). New York: Scholastic.
———. 1982. *Where Do They Go? Insects in Winter.* New York: Four Winds.
Serfozo, M. 1992. *Who Wants One?* New York: Aladdin Books.

Final Comments

Children's trade books appear more frequently in all aspects of curricula and not just during story time. Teachers and librarians recognize the pleasure and educational benefits that students experience when they interact with trade books. Children in ESL classrooms need opportunities to hear, read, and play with language as they attempt to acquire fluency in English. Trade books, along with the instructional techniques associated with whole language, literature-based reading programs, and integrated language arts curricula offer some of the best opportunities for children to acquire literacy in both languages.

References

Barreras, R. 1992. "Ideas a Literature Can Grown On: Key Insights for Enriching and Expanding Children's Literature about the Mexican American Experience." In *Teaching Multicultural Literature in Grades K–8,* ed. V. Harris, 203–242. Norwood, MA: Christopher-Gordon.

Cooper, I. 1992. " Evaluating Children's Books." Panel discussion at conference sponsored by the Center for Children's Books at The University of llinois at Urbana, Illinois, October.

Nieto, S. 1992. "We Have Stories To Tell: A Case Study of Puerto Ricans in Children's Books." In *Teaching Multicultural Literature in Grades K–8,* ed. V. Harris, 171–202. Norwood, MA: Christopher-Gordon.

Roback, D. 199. "In Space, Titles, Sales, the Trend Is Still Up." *Publishers Weekly* 239 (Jan. 13): 26–31.

CURRICULUM MATERIAL PRODUCERS

T HIS chapter provides information on publishers and producers of English as a Second Language curriculum materials, textbooks, supplementary materials, software, and other items; also included are multicultural items and bilingual non-English materials. For some of the larger publishers, we have provided a listing of ESL series and book titles. For other companies, we provide a description of products. Much of the information in this chapter is based on the publishers' catalogues; for more details, you should contact the publishers directly. The addresses and phone numbers given are for the offices that will supply catalogues and other promotion material; note that these phone numbers are not for the editorial offices.

Academic Therapy Publications
20 Commercial Boulevard
Novato, CA 94949-6191
800-422-7249

Grades pre-K–12. Tests for ESL and bilingual students, supplementary curriculum materials, parent/teacher resources, remediation programs

Active Learning Corporation
P.O. Box 254
New Paltz, NY 12561
914-255-0844

High school textbooks including *The Active Reader for Writers*, reading model booklets, *Essays/Letters/Reports*, and for remedial junior high/high school, *Writing Guides* and *Writing Paragraphs*

Addison-Wesley Publishing Company
Jacob Way
Reading, MA 01867
800-447-2226

In Touch: A Beginning Communicative Course (series)
Beginning to low-intermediate. Student's books, teacher's manuals, workbooks, audiocassettes. Stresses grammar

New Dimensions (series)
Intermediate to advanced. Student's books, teacher's manuals, workbooks, audiocassettes

On Your Way (series)
Beginning to intermediate. Student's books, teacher's manuals, workbooks, audiocassettes

New Horizons in English (series)
Beginning to advanced. Student's books, teacher's manuals, workbooks, audiocassettes

Lifeskills 1, 2, and 3 (series)
Beginning to intermediate. Practice with survival

skills, grammar, reading, and writing skills. Works with *New Horizons in English*

Odyssey (series)
Beginning to high-intermediate. For secondary school students with units covering art, science, geography, and history. Student's books, teacher's manuals, workbooks, audiocassettes

Longman ESL Literacy
For the preliterate. Student's books, teacher's manuals

Other ESL texts for listening/conversation, vocabulary, pronunciation, writing, reading, grammar, business English, dictionaries, plus teacher-training videos, resource and method books. Science and math textbooks in Spanish editions

Teaching reading texts include *Happily Ever After* (series)(pre-K–grade 1), a complete literature-based early reading program with a big-books classics package, teacher's guide, supplementary materials including English and Spanish audiocassette packages, *Now Presenting: Classic Tales for Readers Theatre* (series) (elementary grades), *Story Chest* (series) (grades 1–3), *Superkids* (series) (grades K–1), *Teaching Language, Literature, and Culture* (series) (grades K–2 multicultural), *Ten Best Ideas for Reading Teachers*

Advantage Learning Systems, Inc.
210 Market Avenue
P.O. Box 95
Port Edwards, WI 54469-0095
800-338-4204

The Accelerated Reader
Grades 3–12. Software for Apple/IBM, core book list, teacher's manual, supplementary materials

Agency for Instructional Technology (AIT)
Box A
Bloomington, IN 47402-0120
800-457-4509

Grades K–12. Videocassette series, interactive videodisc/instructional software (Apple/Macintosh), and teacher's guides. For communication skills, literature, library skills

AGS
Publishers' Building
Circle Pines, MN 55014-1796
800-328-2560

Grades K–12. Diagnostic tests, supplementary programs including software for language, speech and auditory development, reading

The American Association of School Administrators
1801 North Moore Street
Arlington, VA 22209-9988
703-875-0730

Guidelines for the teaching of reading and writing

American Education Publishing
3790 East Fifth Avenue
Columbus, OH 43219
800-542-7833

Distributes materials from Creative Education, The Child's World, Listening Library, and Milliken. Books, cassettes, posters

American School Publishers
SRA School Group
P.O. Box 5380
Chicago, IL 60680-5380
800-843-8855

Grades 1–12. Supplementary programs in whole language, reading, content-area reading, test preparation, composition, grammar, writing

American Language Academy
Suite 550
1401 Rockville Pike, MD 20852
800-346-3469

Beginning through advanced, ESL and EFL students. Software for Apple/IBM, teacher's handbooks, interactive sound/graphic programs. For grammar, reading, vocabulary

Amsco School Publications, Inc.
315 Hudson Street
New York, NY 10013-1085
212-675-7000

Grammar, composition, vocabulary, literature series, textbooks, skills books and workbooks for a variety of ages. Textbooks in Spanish editions

Attanasio & Associates, Inc.
62-06 77th Place
Middle Village, NY 11379
718-565-0343

Manipulatives, audiocassettes, big books, songs for beginning readers and up

Ballard & Tighe, Publishers
480 Atlas Street
Brea, CA 92621
800-321-4332

Provides instructional programs such as *Ideas for Literature, Idea Oral Language Program Kit* and computer software for ESL vocabulary development and reinforcement

Bantam Doubleday Dell, Education and Library Division
666 Fifth Avenue
New York, NY 10103
800-223-6834

Grades pre-K–8. Multicultural literature for the whole-language classroom.

Barnell Loft
SRA School Group
P.O. Box 5380
Chicago, IL 60680-5380
800-843-8855

Pathways to Literacy
Grades 1–2. Teacher's resource books, wall charts, read-along audiocassettes. Compatible with the Barnell Loft *Phonics to Meaning* program

Phonics to Meaning
Grades pre-1–3. Student edition, teacher's edition

Grades pre-K–8. Supplementary programs for comprehension, phonics, specific skills, multiple skills, reading, spelling

Barron's Educational Series, Inc.
P.O. Box 8040, 250 Wireless Boulevard
Hauppauge, NY 11788
800-645-3476

Children's books for all ages. Study guides for English/language arts and literature

Beacon Films
(Altschul Group Corporation)
930 Pitner Avenue
Evanston, IL 60202
800-323-5448

Videocassettes and films for language arts/English, including *The Kids of DeGrassi Street Series, The Ray Bradbury Series, Storybook International Series, The Beacon Short Story Collection, Shakespeare from Page to Stage*

Berrent Publications, Inc.
1025 Northern Boulevard
Roslyn, NY 11576
800-74-LEARN

The Barnaby Brown Books (series)
Grades 2–7. Written around themes

The Literature Bridge: Connecting Reading, Writing, Listening & Speaking (series)
Grades 4–6. High interest, low readability. Anthologies, realistic fiction, social issues

See-More Books (series)
Theme reading. Stories, audiocassettes and activities

Comprehension Through Cloze (series)

Reading Success with Cloze

Whole-language resources include *Understanding What You Read* and *The Whole Language Teacher Resource Activity Book*

BGR Publishing

4520 North 12th Street
Phoenix, AZ 85014
800-892-BOOK

Grades pre-K–6. Books and materials with emphasis on whole language and multiculturalism

BLS Tutorsystems

Woodmill Corporate Center
5153 West Woodmill Drive
Wilmington, DE 19808
800-545-7766

Grades 3–12. Software for Apple/IBM, student manuals, teacher's guides, supplementary materials about career English, reading, grammar, spelling

Book-Lab

P.O. Box 7316
500 74th Street
North Bergen, NJ 07047
201-861-6763/800-654-4081

Instructional material for language delayed (ESL, bilingual, special education) learners including thematic (history, health, etc.) workbooks and textbooks

Branden

17 Station Street, Box 843
Brookline Village, MA 02147
617-734-2045

Classics, fiction, general nonfiction, microcomputer software, women's studies, and biographies

Brown Roa Publishing Media

P.O. Box 539
Dubuque, IA 52001
800-338-5578

Grades 7–12. English curriculum units, lesson plans, student handouts, tests. Topics include literature, world literature, mythology, advanced-placement English, poetry, writing, creative writing, basic and advanced composition, research, speech, thinking, reading and writing, junior high language arts, fiction/nonfiction, drama, short story, Shakespeare

Cambridge University Press

40 West 20th Street
New York, NY 10011-4211
800-872-7423

Interchange (basal series)
Beginning to high-intermediate. Student books, teacher's manuals, workbooks, audiocassettes for class and students

Communicative Grammar Practice: Activities for Intermediate Students of English
Intermediate to high-intermediate. Student book, teacher's manual

Basic Grammar in Use: Reference and Practice for Intermediate Students of English
Intermediate to high-intermediate. Student's book, answer key

Grammar in Use: Reference and Practice for Students of English
Beginning to intermediate. Student's book, answer key

From Writing to Composing: An Introductory Composition Course for Students of English
High-beginning to intermediate. Student's book, teacher's manual

Effective Reading
High-beginning to intermediate. Student's book

Titles in ESL for specific needs include *Telephoning in English, Company to Company, English for International Business & Finance*, etc., as well as professional books (e.g., *Evaluating Second Language Education, Second Language Writing, Second Language Classrooms*, and *Language Learning and Deafness*).

Chariot Software Group

3659 India Street, Suite 100C
San Diego, CA 92103
800-800-4540

Grades K–12. Macintosh educational software for English/language arts, including English grammar computer, grammar tutorials, linkword, pronunciation tutors, reading maze, *Sounds of English, Spell It Plus*

Charlesbridge Publishing
85 Main Street
Watertown, MA 02172
800-225-3214
617-926-0329

Grades K–12. Several useful series. *Charlesbridge Reading Skills Units* (series); *Dictionary Skills, Insights: Comprehension* (series); *Insights: Reading as Thinking* (series); *Networks*, a series for grades K–3 with a whole-language reading program, teacher's planning guides, anthologies, big books, small books, activity books, action packs, puppets; *Sparks for Learning*, for special needs grades K–8; *Writing and Thinking: Secondary* (series), grades 7–12, a process writing program

Chelsea Curriculum Publications
School Division, Department CUR
P.O. Box 5186
Yeadon, PA 19050-0686

Grades 4–12. Biographical and mythological literature collections with teacher's guides, literary criticism collections

Children Press
5440 North Cumberland Avenue
Chicago, IL 60656-1494
800-621-1115

Titles include multicultural folktales, *Parents as Partners in Reading* (grades preschool–4), *Our Multiethnic Heritage* (series)

Christopher-Gordon Publishers, Inc.
480 Washington Street
Norwood, MA 02062
617-762-5577

Teacher resources including *Teaching Multicultural Literature in Grades K–8, Portfolio Assessment in the Reading-Writing Classroom, Assessment and Evaluation in the Whole Language Programs*

Clark Publishing, Inc.
P.O. Box 4875
Topeka, KS 66604
913-271-8668

Junior high/high school. Softcover texts include *38 Basic Speech Experiences, Mastering Competitive Debate, Basic Drama Projects, Writing and Editing School News*

Communicad,
The Communications Academy
Box 541
Wilton, CT 06897
800-762-7464

Grades 4–12. Multimedia vocabulary and study-skills program

Communication Skill Builders
3830 East Bellevue
P.O. Box 42050
Tucson, AZ 85733
800-866-4446

Grades K–12. Culturally and linguistically diverse materials for speech and language therapy; curriculum guides, teacher's manuals, assessment forms, activity books and kits, audio and videocassettes, computer software

Compu-Teach
78 Olive Street
New Haven, CT 06511
800-448-3224

Grades pre-K–6. Software for IBM/Macintosh/Apple in reading, story composition, writing

CONDUIT
The University of Iowa
Oakdale Campus
Iowa City, IA 52242
800-365-9774

Writer's Helper, software for Windows/Macintosh/Apple/IBM-DOS for prewriting and revising and *SEEN: Tutorials for Critical Reading*, software for Apple/IBM

Contemporary Books, Inc.
Department F92
180 North Michigan Avenue
Chicago, IL 60601
800-621-1918

Look at the U.S.: A TESL Civic Series Based on the Federal Citizenship Texts (series)
Literacy to intermediate. Teaches U.S. history and government to ESL and bilingual students. Texts, teacher's guide

Choices (series)
Intermediate. Develops language skills and knowledge about U.S. society: families, health, consumerism, housing, community, rights, etc. Texts and teacher's guides

Employability and workforce education titles for levels 1–8 include *You're Hired!, Working in English, Ready to Work, Work-Wise, Skills that Work*, and *Lifeskills: Developing Consumer Competence*

Continental Press
520 East Bainbridge Street
Elizabethtown, PA 17022
800-233-0759

Grades K–12. Activity units, manipulative sets, skills series, literature-based reading, software, teacher's resource books, phonics programs, Spanish resources

Cottonwood Press
305 West Magnolia, Suite 398
Fort Collins, CO 80521
303-493-1286

Grades 5–12. Practical activity books, resource books, books, and posters for language arts classes

Creative Edge, Inc.
80 Pineview Drive
Amherst, NY 14228-2120
800-626-5052

Language Development Program
Regular edition, second language edition & early childhood edition. Includes visual overlay kits, program guide, reading, writing activity cards, teacher resource support material. Also in Spanish

Reading/Writing Link
Regular edition, second language edition & early childhood edition. Includes student books, reading, writing activity cards, teacher resource book. Also in Spanish

Creative Teaching Press
P.O. Box 6017
Cypress, CA 90630-0017
800-444-4CTP

Grades K–8. Resource guides, activity books, overhead transparencies, big-book kits, shape-book kits for teaching whole language

Creative Publications
5040 West 11th Street
Oak Lawn, IL 60453
800-624-0822

Teacher's resource books. Grades pre-K–6. Series titles include: *Themeworks, Language through Literature, Early Childhood Language, Language Arts and Problem Solving, Storytelling and Writing*

Critical Thinking Press & Software
Midwest Publications
P.O. Box 448
Pacific Grove, CA 93950
800-458-4849

Grades K–12. Remedial–average–gifted–at risk. Activity books, resource books, software, tests

Curriculum Associates, Inc.
5 Esquire Road
North Billerica, MA 01862-2589
800-225-0248
508-667-8000

Grades 2–adult education. Handbooks, workbooks, teacher's guides, software in multiculturalism, spelling, writing, language development, reading

D. C. Heath and Company
School Division
125 Spring Street
Lexington, MA 02173
800-235-3565

Texts include *Heath Reading* (series) (grades K–8), *Heath English* (series) (grades 9–12), *The Humanities: Cultural Roots and Continuities* (advanced), *Language Enrichment Program: A Companion to Heath Reading* (series) (levels R–6), *The Reading Edge: Thirteen Ways to Build Reading Comprehension* (high school advanced placement), and high school–level texts on spelling, vocabulary, writing, grammar, drama, reading fiction, poetry and literature. Social studies and math texts in Spanish editions

Dale Seymour Publications
P.O. Box 10888
Palo Alto, CA 94303-0879
800-USA-1100

Grades K–8. Teacher's source books, big books, story books and novels, activity books, self-study guides, reading kits, word games, software, teacher's resources

Dandy Lion Publications
3563 Sueldo
San Luis Obispo, CA 93401
800-776-8032

Literature, reading, poetry, and language workbooks, guides, and activity books

Davidson & Associates, Inc.
P.O. Box 2961
Torrance, CA 90509
800-545-7677

Pre-K–adult. Software for Apple/Macintosh/IBM/Tandy/Commodore, interactive (audio) programs, teacher materials in grammar, spelling, journalism, reading, ESL, foreign language

Delmar Publishers, Inc.
2 Computer Drive West
P.O. Box 15015
Albany, NY 12212-5015
800-347-7707

Early Childhood. *Growing Up with Literature, Early Childhood Experiences in Language Arts: Emerging Literacy*

Delta Systems Co., Inc.
570 Rock Road Drive
P.O. Box 987
Dundee, IL 60118-0987
800-323-8270

Publishes and distributes 6,000 ESL titles, over 4,000 foreign language titles

Didax, Inc.
One Centennial Drive
Peabody, MA 01960
800-458-0024

Preschool, elementary, special needs. Speech and language educational activities, reading-readiness materials, clearview materials, literature, topical sets/whole language, ladybird books, games

DLM
P.O. Box 4000
One DLM Park
Allen, TX 75002
800-527-4747

Grades K–12. Alternative instructional materials for early childhood, reading, writing, grammar, spelling, language development, speech, remedial/basic skills, bilingual

Econo-Clad Books
P.O. Box 1777
Topeka, KS 66601
800-255-3502

Grades pre-K–12. Literature-based and whole-language teaching materials. Literature collections, teacher's guides, teacher's resource packages, videocassettes

ECS Learning Systems, Inc.
P.O. Box 791437
San Antonio, TX 78279-1437
800-68-TEACH

Grades pre-K–12. Whole-language learning materials, language arts/English supplementary materials, writing programs, reading resources, novels units, teacher's resources, software

EDL
P.O. Box 210726
Columbia, SC 29221
800-227-1606

Reading levels 1–13 (remedial). Vocabulary, reading comprehension, fluency, and writing programs. Student books, teacher's guides and supplementary materials including audio and videocassettes, and software

Educational Activities, Inc.
P.O. Box 392
Freeport, NY 11520
800-645-3739

Grades K–adult. Software for Apple/Macintosh/MS-DOS, voice-interactive programs, support materials in English, basics, adult literacy, ESL and language impaired

Entry Publishing, Inc.
P.O. Box 20277
New York, NY 10025
800-736-1405

Reading-disabled grades 5–adult. Teacher's guides, workbooks, novels, software, audio and videocassettes, bilingual materials

Everbind Books
Marco Book Company
P.O. Box 331
Bayonne, NJ 07002-0331
800-842-4234

Junior high/high school. Collections of drama, prose and poetry, young adult literature, biography and autobiography, ethnic studies, myths and legends, teacher's guides, reference materials

Facts On File, Inc.
460 Park Avenue South
New York, NY 10016-7382
800-322-8755

Reference materials in language arts and literature, including bibliographies and dictionaries

Fearon/Janus/Quercus
500 Harbor Boulevard
Belmont, CA 94002
800-877-4283

Special education/remedial programs. Language arts, reading and writing texts, sign language texts, multicultural series, literacy tutors, guides, study guides, biographies, novels, audiocassettes, dictionaries, workbooks, magazines

Focus Media, Inc.
839 Stewart Avenue
P.O. Box 865
Garden City, NY 11530
800-645-8989

Grades pre-K–12. Software for Apple/MS-DOS/Macintosh/Commodore, support materials. In reading, writing, vocabulary, spelling, for ESL, bilingual, at-risk students

Franklin Learning Resources
122 Burrs Road
Mt. Holly, NJ 08060
800-525-9673

Hand-held electronic learning products. Spelling, dictionary companion, language master, wordmaster and encyclopedia series. Also Franklin curriculum series and secondary whole-language/writing-language arts program

Full Blast Productions
P.O. Box 1297
Lewiston, NY 14092-1297
800-268-6652

Specializing in videos and books on ESL

Gamco Industries, Inc.
P.O. Box 1862N1
Big Spring, TX 79721-1911
800-351-1404

Grades K–12. Software for Apple/MS-DOS/
Macintosh, support materials. Topics include
phonics, spelling, vocabulary, reading comprehension, writing, grammar. Social studies and science
software in Spanish editions

Glencoe/Macmillan/McGraw-Hill
P.O. Box 543
Blacklick, OH 43004-0543
800-334-7344

English Skills Series
Student editions, teacher's editions. Includes
Sentence Mechanics, Usage, Editing and Proofreading, Writing about Literature

Glencoe English (series)
Grades 7–12. Textbooks, teacher's editions,
teacher's resource book, supplementary materials

Glencoe English (series)

The Laidlaw English Series
Grades 9–12. *Composition and Grammar*, textbooks, teacher's editions, supplementary materials

Macmillan English: Thinking and Writing Processes
   (series)
Grades 9–12. Textbooks, teacher's editions,
teacher's resource book, supplementary materials
including software

PWR: Macmillan Literature Composition Software
Grades 7–12. Software, user manual, teaching notes

PWR: Macmillan English Composition Software
Grades 9–12. Software, user manual, teaching notes

English materials also include: *The Art of Writing: A
Modern Rhetoric, Business Communications, The
CORT Thinking Program, Effective Speech, Literature-Based Composition, McGraw-Hill Handbook of
English* and many literature texts. Social studies and
science texts in Spanish editions

Globe Book Company
4350 Equity Drive
P.O. Box 2649
Columbus, OH 43216
800-848-9500

Globe Anthology Series
Reading levels 5–9. A thematic literature-based
program to develop reading comprehension skills.
Texts, workbooks, teacher's manuals with tests

Globe African American Biographies

Globe Biographies (series)
Multicultural softcover texts, teacher's manuals.
Includes *Globe Hispanic Biographies, Globe World
Biographies, Globe American Biographies*

Globe Literature (series)
Grades 7–12. Textbooks, teacher's editions,
teacher's resource books, supplementary materials
including workbooks for limited English-proficient
students

The Globe Reader's Collection (series)
Reading Levels 3–8. Softcover texts, teacher's
manuals

Globe Reading Comprehension Program (series)
Reading levels 4–7. Softcover texts, teacher's
editions

Globe Writing Program
Grades 6–12. Softcover texts, teacher's editions

Globe's Adapted Classics (series)
Reading levels 3–8. 17 Softcover texts, teacher's
manuals

Communication Skills Resources. Reading Levels
4–adult. Softcover texts, teacher's manuals. Includes *Grammar and Composition for Everyday
English, Reading Road to Writing, It Happened on the
Job, Life Styles, Newspaper Workshop, Unlocking
Test Taking*, adult literacy. Social studies and science
texts in Spanish editions

Graphic Learning
61 Mattatuck Heights Road
Waterbury, CT 06705
800-874-0029

Grades K–12. Integrated language arts/social
studies programs. Student desk maps, activity
pages, teacher's guides, workbooks, supplementary
materials. Integrates geography, history, economics,

politics, sociocultural concepts, map and globe skills, language/study skills, thinking skills, ESL, bilingual

H. P. Kopplemann, Inc.

Paperback Book Service
P.O. Box 145
Hartford, CT 06141-0145
800-243-7724

Grades K–12. Multicultural, literature-based and whole-language materials, software, videocassettes, reading collections, teacher's guides, filmstrips, literature tests

Hammond Education Catalog

515 Valley Street
Maplewood, NJ 07040
800-526-4935

Grades K–12. Reading skills series. Classroom packs, softcover texts, teacher's answer key. Spanish language atlases

Hampton-Brown Books

P.O. Box 223220
Carmel, CA 93922
800-333-3510

ESL Theme Links (series)
Grades K–3. Big books, small books, teacher's guides

The Spanish Reading/ESL Connection (series)
Grades 1–4. Big books, small books, teacher's theme guide for Spanish literacy, teacher's guide for ESL

Bilingual education and multicultural titles include *¡Qué Maravilla!* and *Wonders!* (for dual-language classrooms, grades 1–4), *Rimas y Risas, Un Cuento Más* (grades pre-K–2), Spanish content-area (social studies, mathematics, science) storybooks

Harcourt Brace Jovanovich, Inc.

School Department
6277 Sea Harbor Drive
Orlando, FL 32821-9989
800-CALL-HBJ

Spotlight: An English Course
Levels 1–3. Student books, teacher's books, workbooks, cassettes, test booklet

Prism: An Intermediate Course in English
Levels 1–3. Student books, teacher's books, workbooks, cassettes, test booklet

Reading and language titles include: *Basic Drills in English Skills I–IV, Focus on Writing* (series), *HBJ Language* (series), *Imagination* (series), *Impressions* (series), *Discoveries in Reading* (series), *HBJ Lectura* (Spanish series), *HBJ Reading Program* (series), *HRW Reading: Reading Today and Tomorrow* (series). Literature titles include *Discoveries in Reading* (series for remedial reading), *HBJ Lectura* (a Spanish reading series), *HBJ Reading Program* (series), *HRW Reading: Reading Today and Tomorrow.* Science and math textbooks in Spanish editions

Harlan Davidson, Inc.

3110 North Arlington Heights Road
Arlington Heights, IL 60004-1592
312-253-9720

The Crofts Classics series contains classic works in English, American, and world literature; Goldentree bibliographies in language and literature

Heinemann Boynton/Cook

361 Hanover Street
Portsmouth, NH 03801-3959
800-541-2086

Teacher's resource books for literacy, reading, writing, literature, whole language, poetry, drama

Heinle & Heinle Publishers
20 Park Plaza
Boston, MA 02116
800-354-9706, 800-237-0053

Intercom 2000 (series)
Beginning to intermediate. An integrated core program with texts, teacher's annotated editions, tape programs and workbooks

Express English (series)
Beginning to intermediate. An integrated core program with textbooks, teacher's annotated editions, workbooks and tape program

Perspectives 2000 (series)
Intermediate. An integrated core program with video, texts, activity books, teacher's resource book, audiocassettes

The English Advantage (series)
Beginning to advanced. An integrated core program with textbooks, workbooks, teacher's editions, audiocassettes

New Arrival English (series)
Grades 6–12. Texts, audiocassettes, multilevel activity masters, picture cards. Aimed at the nonliterate, preliterate, low-literate, and at-risk students.

Voices in Literature (series)
Secondary. Comprehensive program with audiotapes, activity masters, texts and instructor's manuals

Reach Out (series)
Beginning to low-intermediate. Five levels with puzzles, songs, games, dramatics, riddles and rhymes, plus teacher's guides and student books

The Magic of English (series)
Beginning to high-beginning. Text, teacher's edition guide and teacher's edition worktext

Many other titles, from beginning to advanced, specifically geared to listening, speaking, pronunciation, vocabulary & idioms, reading, writing, grammar, and lifeskills; plus the Newbury House professional reference guides on language teaching

Holt, Rinehart, & Winston
6277 Sea Harbor Drive
Orlando, FL 32821-9989
800-225-5425

English as a Second Language

Practical English
Three-level program. Student books, instructor's manual, workbook, audiocassettes

Laugh & Learn: A Reader
Beginning through secondary

Reference Guide to English: A Handbook of English as a Second Language
Intermediate to advanced. Supplemental composition/reference text

Encounters: An ESL Reader
Organized progressively in order of difficulty

Concepts & Comments: An ESL Reader
High-beginning or low-intermediate. Designed to increase vocabulary

Getting Together: An ESL Conversation Book
High-beginning to low-intermediate. Emphasizing effective speaking

Harbrace ESL Workbook
Addresses specific needs of non-native speakers

Momentum: Developing Reading Skills
Beginning. Goal is to improve reading skills

Literature

Adventures in Literature (series)
Grades 7–12. Textbook, teacher's resource package, supplementary materials including test-generator software

African-American Literature
High school. Textbook, teacher's manual, tests

Eight Classic American Novels
High school (advanced placement). Text

Elements of Literature (series)
Grades 7–12. Textbooks, teacher's edition, supplementary materials including audiocassettes, test generator software, video series

Emerging Voices: A Cross-Cultural Reader
High school (advanced placement). Text, instructor's manual

Composition

Composition: Models and Exercises
Grades 7–12. Student edition, teacher's manual

Elements of Writing (series)
Grades 6–12. Student editions, teacher's editions, teacher's resource bank, supplementary materials including test-generator software

English Workshop
Grades 6–12. Student edition, mastery tests, teacher's answer key

From Sight to Insight: Stages in the Writing Process
High school (advanced placement). Text, instructor's manual

We Are America: A Cross-Cultural Reader and Guide
High school (advanced placement). Softcover text, instructor's manual

Language arts supplementary programs include *Acting Is Believing: A Basic Method, Learning How to Learn*. Social studies, math, and science texts in Spanish editions

Houghton Mifflin
Department J
One Beacon Street
Boston, MA 02108-9971
800-323-5663

Houghton Mifflin English Levels K–8 (series)
Grades K–8. Textbooks, teacher's editions, teacher's resources, student workbooks, supplementary materials include audiocassettes, limited English proficiency activity masters

Troubleshooter I & II (series)
Grades 7–adult. Workbooks, teacher's editions. Topics include spelling, punctuation, vocabulary, reading

National Proficiency Survey Series
Grades 9–12. Test booklets, answer sheets, manual, administrator's summary

New Directions in Reading
Grades 4–12. High-interest/low-level reading program. Student readers, teacher's guides, teacher's resource book, supplementary materials

Microcourse Language Arts
Grades 3–8. Software for students who have trouble learning by traditional methods. Topics include

sentence structure, parts of speech, mechanics, etc., and has on-line diagnostic & evaluation

Computer Software. Grades K–8. Including *First Writer, The Grolier Writer, Language Activities Courseware: Grammar and Study Skills, Microcourse Language Arts, Computer Activities for the Writing Process*. Social studies and math texts in Spanish editions

Reading/Literature

Houghton Mifflin Reading (series)
Grades K–8. Student readers, teacher's guides, teacher's resource file, supplementary materials

Houghton Mifflin Reading/Language Arts Program (series)
Grades K–8. Literary readers, teacher's guides, supplementary materials

Houghton Mifflin Reading: The Literature Experience (series)
Grades K–8. Student anthologies, theme books, read-along books, teacher's editions, teacher's resource materials, supplementary materials including audiocassettes

Houghton Mifflin Transition
Grades K–8. Limited English-proficient student program. Student readers, workbooks, teacher's guides

Programa de lectura en español de Houghton Mifflin
Grades K–6. Literature-based reading program in Spanish. Spanish trade books, teacher's guides, student workbooks, supplementary materials

Reading Resources. Grades K–8. Literature collections, book and audiocassette programs, children's books and story plans, trade-author videocassettes, reading software

Humanities Software, Inc.
408 Columbia Street, Suite 222
P.O. Box 950
Hood River, OR 97031
800-245-6737

Grades K–12. Software for IBM/Tandy/Apple/Macintosh, support materials in writing, reading, whole language

Hunter & Joyce Publishing Company
Federal Hill No. 1
R.D. 2, Box 54
Delhi, NY 13753
800-462-7483

The Hunter Writing System: Sentence Sense (series), grades 7 and above

I/CT—Instructional/ Communications Technology, Inc.
10 Stepar Place
Huntington Station, NY 11746
516-549-3000

Grades K–adult. Software for Apple/MS-DOS and support materials, filmstrips, books, activity books, audiocassettes. Topics include oral language development, visual efficiency, perceptual accuracy and efficiency, word recognition, decoding and spelling, vocabulary development, reading, comprehension skills, expressive skills, computer awareness

IBM Direct
PC Software Department 829
One Culver Road
Dayton, NJ 08810
800-222-7257

Pre-K–adult. Software for IBM, support materials, multimedia materials including CD-ROM, videodiscs, videocassettes. In reading comprehension, writing, spelling, grammar, vocabulary. Spanish program

Intellimation
Library for the Macintosh
Department 2SCK
P.O. Box 219
Santa Barbara, CA 93116-9954
800-346-8355

Grades K–12. Software for Macintosh, multimedia programs. In writing, grammar, spelling, literature

Interact
Box 997-H92
Lakeside, CA 92040
800-359-0961

Grades K–12. Simulation programs. Student guides, teacher's guides, supplementary materials including software. Topics include American literature, world literature, humanities, reading and editing skills, genealogy, poetry, media studies/mythology, public speaking, writing

International Language Institute of Massachusetts
P.O. Box 516, Sullivan Square
Nothampton, MA 01060
413-586-7569

Classroom texts including *Science for Language Learners* and *A, B, & C: Science, Mathematics, and Social Studies.*

Teacher reference texts include *Teaching Science through Discovery; Designing Group Work: Strategies for the Heterogeneous Classroom; ESL through Content-area Instruction: Mathematics, Science, Social Studies; Cooperative Learning Resources for Teachers; The Multicultural Classroom: Readings for Content Area Teachers,* and others.

International Reading Association
800 Barksdale Road, P.O. Box 8139
Newark, DE 19714-8139
800-336-READ, ext. 266

Teacher resources to enhance reading programs, current research in teaching reading and literacy development

IRI/Skylight Publishing, Inc.
200 East Wood Street, Suite 274
Palatine, IL 60067
800-348-4474

Grades K–12. Teacher's resource books, handbooks, videocassettes

J. Weston Walch Publisher
321 Valley Street, P.O. Box 658
Portland, ME 04104-0658
800-341-6094

Grades 6–adult. Literacy and nonreader education supplementary materials such as flash cards, audiocassettes, posters, life-skill materials (*Business English, Job Writing Skills*) including personal coping skills, activity packs. Teacher's resources include synopses of literature, quizzes, and tests

Jamestown Publishers
P.O. Box 9168
Providence, RI 02940
800-USA-READ

Grades K–12. Anthologies, big books (English and Spanish), readers, skills series, literature programs, comprehension programs, critical reading skills, classic author kits, reading the content fields kits including: *Best-Selling Chapters, Best Short Stories, Skills Drills, Skimming & Scanning, Spelling Power, Time Readings*

Jostens Learning Corporation
7878 North 16th Street
Suite 100
Phoenix, AZ 85020-4402
800-422-4339

Pre-K–12. Software for Apple/IBM/Tandy. In language development (available in Spanish), reading, writing

Judy/Instructo
4424 West 78th Street
Bloomington, MN 55435
800-832-5228

Grades pre-K–2. Educational materials for English/language arts, including desk tapes, sorting boxes, picture cards, puzzles, alphabet wall charts

K–12 MicroMedia Publishing
6 Arrow Road
Ramsey, NJ 07446
201-825-8888

Grades 2–12. Software for Apple/Macintosh/IBM/Tandy for writing, literature

Kendall/Hunt Publishing Company
2460 Kerper Boulevard
P.O. Box 539
Dubuque, IA 52004-0539
800-258-5622

Pegasus: Integrating Themes in Literature and Language (series)
Grades K–6. Student anthologies, books, writer's resource books, teacher's implementation guides, teacher's resource books, supplementary materials including audiocassettes

Other teaching reading and writing titles include: *Active Composing and Thinking II, Active Composing and Thinking III, Content Reading Including Study Systems (CRISS), Kendall/Hunt Spelling: Improving Spelling Performance* (series), *Kendall/Hunt Spelling: Learning To Spell*

Knowledge Unlimited, Inc.
Box 52
Madison, WI 53701-0052
800-356-2303

Teacher's guides, filmstrips, audiocassettes for poetry, journalism, composition; posters; videocassettes of literature classics, newspaper in education resource kit

Lakeshore Learning Materials
2695 East Dominguez Street
P.O. Box 6261
Carson, CA 90749
800-421-5354

Lakeshore Lifeskills (series)
Junior high/high school. Skill-building materials for reading, writing, grammar, spelling. Textbooks, workbooks, activity books, teacher's guides, software

ESL Survival Kit
Grades 1.5–3.5. Teacher's guides, workbooks, picture/word game cards, posters, dictionaries

Bilingual dictionaries include Korean/English, Cambodian/English, Vietnamese/English, Navajo/English, Japanese/English, Chinese/English, Spanish/English. Video programs include *The Natural Approach to Speaking.* There is an *Everyday*

Situations Transparency Library, and *Beginning English for Everyday Living Reproducible Activities Library* for ESL.

Laureate Learning Systems, Inc.
110 East Spring Street
Winooski, VT 05404-1837
800-562-6801

Talking software for special needs, compatible with Apple/IBM/Tandy; used for language development, concept development and processing, reading and advanced cognitive skills. Some bilingual material (French and Spanish)

Learning Links, Inc.
2300 Marcus Avenue
New Hyde Park, NY 11042
516-437-9071

Grades K–12. Literature-based study guides, individual books, whole-language sets, reading books for social studies and science, thematic units, read alouds, Spanish language books for young readers

LEGO Dacta
555 Taylor Road
Enfield, CT 06082
P.O. Box 1600
800-527-8339

Grades pre-K–12. Manipulatives, curriculum support materials. Scope and sequence includes cognitive development; transportation; animals and the environment; homes, family, and neighborhoods; problem solving and whole language; themes and project work

Literacy Volunteers of America, Inc.
5795 Widewaters Parkway
Syracuse, NY 13214
315-445-8000

Teacher and tutor resources for ESL and literacy. Texts, video guides, workshop trainer's guides, audiocassettes

Longman Publishing Group
10 Bank Street
White Plains, NY 10606
800-447-2226

Elementary. Language-experience based literacy program with manipulatives, workbooks in grammar, writing, vocabulary, reading, poetry, mythology, drama, literature, teacher's manuals

Loyola University Press
3441 North Ashland Avenue
Chicago, IL 60657
800-621-1008

Texts for grades 1–8 include *Exercises in English* (series), *Voyages in English* (series), *Writing Step-by-Step*

Macmillan/McGraw-Hill
School Division
220 East Danieldale Road
De Soto, TX 75115-9990
800-442-9685

ESL/reading

Transitional Reading Program (series)
Beginning. Student books, teacher's editions, workbooks, big book read-along stories

Transition to English (series)
Grades 2–8. Story collections, teacher's edition, theme books, Heritage Collections, audiocassettes, word & phrase books

Experiences in English Kit (series)
Grades K–8. Teacher's guide, discovery cards, writing activities, skillmasters

Reading

Connections (series)
Grades K–8. Thematic-literature units, teacher's editions, student workbooks, supplementary materials including in-service videotapes, software

Spanish Reading

Campanitas de Oro (series)
Grades R–6. Complete Spanish basal reading program. Textbooks, teacher's editions, teacher's resource packages, supplementary materials

Por el Mundo del Cuentro y la Aventura (series)
Grades R–6. Spanish basal-reading series. Textbooks, teacher's guides, workbooks

Language Arts

Language Arts Today (series)
Grades K–8. Integrated language arts program.
Textbooks, teacher's editions, teacher's resource
packages, supplementary materials including
software

McGraw-Hill English (series)
Grades K–8. Textbooks, teacher's editions,
teacher's resource packages, supplementary
materials including software

McGraw-Hill Spelling (series)
Grades 1–8. Softcover texts, teacher's editions,
teacher's resource packages, supplementary
materials including software

Merrill Spelling
Grades K–8. Textbooks, teacher's editions,
teacher's resource package, supplementary materials including software

Palmer Method Handwriting (series)
Grades K–8. Softcover texts, teacher's editions,
teacher's resource package

Social studies, math, and science texts in Spanish
editions

McDonald Publishing Company

10667 Midwest Industrial Boulevard
St. Louis, MO 63132
800-722-8080

Grades 4–9. Teaching poster sets, activity sheets,
teacher's guides, reproducible and duplicating
books for reading, writing, spelling, vocabulary

McDougal, Littell & Company

P.O. Box 8000
St. Charles, IL 60174
800-225-3809

Grades 7–12. Textbooks in composition/grammar,
(*Basic Skills in English* (series)), English (*Contem-
porary Short Stories*), Literature (*McDougal, Littell
Literature* (series)), middle school materials,
(*Language Handbook for Student Writers* (series)),

and vocabulary (*Daily Analogies* (series)). Social
studies texts in Spanish editions

MECC

6160 Summit Drive North
Minneapolis, MN 55430-4003
800-685-MECC

Grades pre-K–adult. Software for Macintosh/
Apple/MS-DOS, multimedia materials. In reading,
spelling, grammar, composition

Media Materials Publishing

Department 920301
1821 Portal Street
Baltimore, MD 21224
800-638-1010

The Essential Language Arts Program
Grades 6–12. Textbooks, workbooks, teacher's
guide, blackline masters, composition textbooks,
dictionaries, answer key, *Building Vocabulary Skills
Work Texts, Punctuation, Capitalization & Spelling
Work Text*

Special Needs Reading Resources Program
Grades 6–12. Thematic texts on solar system, travel,
scientists, statehood, presidents; teacher's guides,
vocabulary workbook, quizzes

Basic Literature Program
Grades 6-12. Textbooks, teacher's guides, blackline
masters, surveys of fiction, *Reading & Writing
Nonfiction Work Texts*

Life Skills English
Grades 6-12. Text, teacher's guide, student workbook, blackline masters, teacher's resource binder

English for the World of Work
Text, teacher's guide, workbook, blackline masters,
resource binder

Merrill

SRA School Group
P.O. Box 5380
Chicago, IL 60680-5380
800-621-0476

Grades K–12. Supplementary programs in reading,
phonics, grammar, composition, vocabulary

Micrograms Publishing
1404 North Main Street
Rockford, IL 61103
800-338-4726

Grades K–6. Software for Apple. In reading, punctuation, capitalization, grammar, spelling

The Millbrook Press, Inc.
2 Old New Milford Road-Box 335
Brookfield, CT 06804
800-462-4703

Grades K-2, 4, and 8. Reading materials, including biographies and autobiographies

Milliken Publishing Company
1100 Research Boulevard
P.O. Box 21579
St. Louis, MO 63132-0579
800-643-0008

Grades pre-K–8. Books, posters, teacher's resource guides, duplicating masters, blackline reproducibles, workbooks, filmstrips, videocassettes, whole-language resource guides

Modern
5000 Park Street North
St. Petersburg, FL 33709
800-243-6877

Grades K-12. Free loan programs, free teaching materials, media for the classroom, videos for in-service training, computer and network-based programs, interactive learning systems, and film-strips. Some in Spanish

Modern Curriculum Press
Simon & Shuster
13900 Prospect Road
Cleveland, OH 44136
800-321-3106

Basic through intermediate. *Poetry Power ESL & Concept Science—ESL/LEP* integrate ESL in other subject areas; multicultural titles include biographies of African Americans; bilingual materials in

Spanish and in English. Science textbooks in Spanish editions

Reading

The African-American Literature Collection
Softcover texts, activity sheets

Be a Better Reader (series)
Grades 4–12. Softcover texts, teacher's editions, teacher's guides

Experiencing Poetry

Foundations for Learning: Language (series)
Softcover texts, teacher's manuals, literature guides, supplementary readings, assessment kit
Life-skills resources include softcover texts, teacher's manuals and titles *Forms in Your Future* and *Writing for Life*

Reading improvement resources for reading levels 3–7 include softcover texts, teacher's manuals and titles *A Better Reading Workshop*, *The Real Stories Series*, *Open-Ended Plays* and *Open-Ended Stories*

National Resource Center for Middle Grades Education
University of South Florida
College of Education-EDU-118
Tampa, FL 33620-5650
813-974-2530

Curriculum guides, resource books, reproducible interdisciplinary units, activity books. For reading, writing, thinking skills, self-concept, study skills

National Textbook Company
4255 West Touhy Avenue
Lincolnwood, IL 60646-1975
800-323-4900

Primary & Elementary Basal Programs

Ready for English Learning System (series)
Textbooks, teacher's manuals, story cards, vocabulary cards, alphabet cards, anthology for 4 levels

Hello English Series & Learning Systems (series)
A 6-level series with teacher's manuals, audiocassettes, black-line masters books

English Experiences (also in Spanish) (series)
Textbook & teacher's manual

Activities books for elementary include: *My Book Workbook* (also in Spanish), *English All Around Us, Let's Learn about America, Creative Drama in the Classroom* (series), and learning cards

Supplementary elementary materials include: *Stepping into English Readers, Stepping into English Videos, Let's Learn English Picture Dictionary,* other dictionaries, full-color transparencies, coloring books

Junior high to adult education materials include *Everyday English,* listening/speaking titles (e.g., *Communicative American English*) and others

Titles for teaching reading to ESL students include *Advanced Beginner's English Reader, Beginner's English Reader,* as well as books on specific subjects

Titles for teaching writing to ESL students include *Practical English Writing Skills, A Complete Guide to Writing in English, Express Yourself in Written English,* and *Writing by Doing*

Literacy titles available: *Essentials of Reading & Writing English* (a series), and *Keystrokes to Literacy: Using Computers as Learning Tools for Adult Beginning Readers*

Life-skills titles are available (everyday consumer English, finding a job, etc.)

Skill Building Texts & Activity Texts

English Across the Curriculum (series)
Intermediate. Texts & teacher's manual

The English Survival Series
Beginning through advanced. Texts & teacher's manuals. Titles include *Building Vocabulary, Identifying Main Ideas, Recognizing Details, Writing Sentences and Paragraphs, Using the Context*

Everyday Spelling Workbook (series)
Beginning through intermediate. Text, audiocassettes, teacher's guide. Titles include *Basic Everyday Spelling Workbook & Practical Everyday Spelling Workbook*

Other skill-building texts include *303 Dumb Spelling Mistakes, Activities for Effective Communication through Listening, Speaking, Reading & Writing,*

Activities for English Language Learners Series, Play and Practice!, dictionaries (English and bilingual), grammar, idioms, vocabulary builders, slang and colloquial expressions books, college prep guides, English for special purposes titles (e.g., *Prevocational English, Speaking of Numbers,* etc.),

Professional Resources

Includes *The Complete ESL/EFL Resource Book, TESOL Professional Anthologies, Listening, Speaking & Reading, Grammar & Composition, The Primary & Elementary Classroom, Culture, Ideabook, Speak With a Purpose, Teaching Culture, The ABC's of Languages and Linguistics*

Bilingual/multilingual resources for Early Childhood Education include: *Nuevo Amanecer* (preschool to kindergarten reference books, learning center idea books, training video) and more (many bilingual or also in Spanish). Beginning through advanced resources include flash cards, visuals, posters, puppets, bilingual readers in Vietnamese & English, *¡Hola, Amigos! Series.* Elementary resources include *El alfabeto, Mis primeros cuentos,* and more, and readers for intermediate bilingual students include classic Spanish literature adapted for intermediate Spanish students

Bilingual classroom resources include coloring books, games in Spanish, songs, dramatizations, dances, *Christmas in Mexico,* crossword puzzles, vocabulary builders, Spanish for native Spanish speakers; in the content areas include titles in science, language arts & social studies

Spanish language development programs include: *Viva el Español, Welcome to Spanish,* and more for young people

Civilization & culture titles include collections of legends from Central & South America, Spain & Puerto Rico

Literature/writing titles include *An Anthology for Young Writers, The Art of Composition, Creative Writing: Forms and Techniques,* and more

New Dimensions in Education

61 Mattatuck Heights Road
Waterbury, CT 06705
800-227-9120

Grades pre-K–3. Language immersion and reading
readiness programs. Student readers, teacher's
editions, supplementary materials including audio-
and videocassettes

New Readers Press

Publishing Division of
Laubach Literacy International
Department 72
P.O. Box 888
Syracuse, NY 13210
800-448-8878

Laubach Way to Reading
4 levels. Skill books, teacher's manuals, readers,
checkups, audiocassettes, stories, workbooks,
crossword puzzles, software

Challenger (series)
High school (remedial). Integrated program of
reading, writing, and reasoning skills. Work-texts,
teacher's guides, supplementary materials

Newsweek Education Program

The Newsweek Building
P.O. Box 414
Livingston, NJ 07039
800-526-2595

Newsweek education program for English includes
cross-curriculum guide and free teacher's resources

Novel Units

P.O. Box 1461, Department C
Palatine, IL 60078
708-253-8200

Grades K–12. Support materials for the study of
literature; also integrated whole-language approach, including literature units, vocabulary, and
writing materials

Open Court Publishing Company

407 South Dearborn
Chicago, IL 60605
800-435-6850

The Headway Program (series)
Grades K–6. Readers, teacher's editions, workbooks, supplementary materials

Open Court Reading and Writing (series)
Grades K–6. Student workbooks, teacher's guides,
teacher resource books, supplementary materials

Special purpose programs and materials include
*Gifted and Talented Language Arts: The RISE
Program; Reading Comprehension: Catching On;
Remedial Reading: Breaking the Code; Skills Recov-
ery Program: The Reading Connection;* and supple-
mental reading kits

Orange Cherry/ Talking Schoolhouse Software

P.O. Box 390, Department S
Pound Ridge, NY 10576-0390
800-672-6002

Grades preK–8. Software for Apple/Macintosh/
IBM/Tandy, support materials, multimedia programs. For phonics, reading, vocabulary, grammar,
spelling

Oxford University Press

ESL Department
200 Madison Avenue
New York, NY 10016
800-445-9715

Secondary to adult

Crossroads (series)
Literacy to intermediate. Student books, multilevel
activity & resource packages, workbooks, teacher's
books, audiocassettes

Main Street (series)
Beginning to advanced. Student books, teacher's
books, workbooks, audiocassettes, computer disks

American Streamline (series)
Beginning to advanced. Student books, workbooks,
teacher's books, audiocassettes, lab books

On Course (series)
Secondary to adult. Student books, teacher's books, audiocassettes

Gallery (series)
High-beginning to intermediate. Student books, cassettes, teacher's guide

American WOW! (series)
Student books, workbooks, teacher's books, audiocassettes

Elementary

American Chatterbox (series)
Beginning to intermediate. Student books, workbooks, teacher's books, audiocassette

Let's Go (series)
Beginning. Student books, teacher's books, workbooks, audiocassettes

Open Sesame (series)
Beginning to high-intermediate. Student books (*Big Bird's Yellow Book, Grover's Orange Book, etc.*), teacher's books, activity books, duplicating masters, audiocassettes, pictures, dictionaries, wall charts

Supplementary materials for ESL teachers include: *The New Oxford Picture Dictionary* (bilingual in Spanish, Vietnamese, Chinese, Japanese, Cambodian, Korean, Navajo, Russian and Polish) with an activity book, bilingual edition, overhead transparencies, teacher's guide, vocabulary playing cards, and audiocassettes; other complete series for elementary ESL as well as individual titles on specific themes (e.g., *Fast Forward USA, Speaking Up at Work, Speaking of Survival*); writing and poetry titles, videos, jazz chants (English grammar, small talk, fairy tales, etc. through jazz chanting); novels; bilingual & ESL dictionaries (English-Italian, English-Chinese, English-Greek); grammar texts; English for specific purposes (e.g., business, computer science, electronics, hotel & tourist industry, etc.); journals, books for teachers, resource books, applied linguistics

Peal Software, Inc.
P.O. Box 8188
Calabasas, CA 91372
800-541-1318

Grade pre-K. Software for early acquisition of language

Peguis Publishers
520 Hargrave Street
Winnipeg, Manitoba
CANADA R3A 0X8
800-667-9673

Grades K–7. Professional books on multiculturalism and language arts including *The More-Than-Just-Surviving Handbook: ESL for Every Classroom Teacher*, McCracken, whole language, and native literature programs; readers, classroom literature

Perfection Learning
1000 North Second Avenue
Logan, IA 51546-1099
800-831-4190

Grades pre-K–12. Classic, contemporary, and multicultural literature, workbooks, posters, teacher's guides, tests, videocassettes, software

The Peoples Publishing Group, Inc.
P.O. Box 70
365 West Passaic Street
Rochelle Park, NJ 07662
800-822-1080

Students at risk. Series in practical writing, survival reading, contemporary fiction, multicultural perspective (African American, Hispanic culture and history)

Phoenix Learning Resources
468 Park Avenue South
New York, NY 10016
800-221-1274

Grades K–12. Programmed reading series, whole-language series, language skills text-workbooks, teacher's guides

Players Press, Inc.
P.O. Box 1132
Studio City, CA 91614
818-784-8918

Play anthologies, activity books, and teacher's guides for drama, clowning and mime, costume reference, make-up, technical theatre, writing

Prentice-Hall

School Division of Simon & Schuster
Englewood Cliffs, NJ 07632-9940
800-848-9500

Writing titles include *Prentice-Hall Handbook for Writers, Programmed College Vocabulary 3600, Simon and Schuster Handbook for Writers, Writing Clear Essays, Writing Skills for Technical Students, Journalism*

Grammar and composition titles include: *Developing Writing Skills, Models for Clear Writing, Prentice-Hall Grammar and Composition* (series), *Steps in Composition, Thinking and Writing about Literature*, etc.

Literature classroom resources: transparencies, computer test bank, study guides, great works library, video classics, audiocassettes, cross-curriculum ancillaries, *Myths and Their Meaning, Prentice-Hall Literature* (series)

Science texts in Spanish editions

Queue, Inc.

338 Commerce Drive
Fairfield, CT 06430
800-232-2224

Grades K–12. Software for Apple/IBM/Macintosh, support materials, multimedia materials. In ESL (titles include *The COMPress ESL Program, Ways to Read Words, Learning About Words, Reading Adventures*, etc.), creative writing, reading comprehension, writing skills, life skills, grammar, vocabulary, spelling

Regents/Prentice-Hall

113 Sylvan Avenue
Englewood Cliffs, NJ 07632
800-666-0033

Spectrum
Beginning to advanced. Student text, workbook, audio program, teacher's manual

Vistas
Beginning to intermediate. Student text, workbook, audio program, teacher's manual, visual aids

Side by Side
Beginning to intermediate. Student text, workbook, audio program, teacher's manual, visual aids

Lado English Series
Beginning to advanced. Student text, workbook, audio program, teacher's manual

Modern American English
Beginning to advanced. Student text, workbook, audio program, teacher's manual

Hopscotch
Beginning to intermediate. Student text, teacher's manual

Welcome to English
Beginning to advanced. Student text, teacher's manual

ABC New ESL Video Library
Intermediate to advanced. Student text, video, teacher's manual, visual aids

Other publications include books on vocabulary & idioms, grammar, writing, readers/reading skills, intercultural communication, speaking/conversation, pronunciation, listening skills, integrated skills, ESL literacy, survival skills, citizenship/amnesty, workplace ESL, content-area ESL, English for careers, business, science and technology, software and English for Spanish speakers

Sadlier-Oxford

11 Park Place
New York, NY 10007
800-221-5175

Grades 6–12. *Building an Enriched Vocabulary, Composition Workshop* (series), *Spelling Skills* (series), *Vocabulary Workshop Series*

St. Martin's Press

175 Fifth Avenue
New York, NY 10010
800-822-1080

Transitions
Intermediate through advanced. An interactive reading, writing and grammar text, instructor's manual

A Writer's Workbook: An Interactive Writing Text for ESL
Intermediate through advanced. Student text, instructor's manual

Exploring Through Writing: A Process to ESL Composition
Intermediate through advanced. Student text, instructor's manual

Grammar Troublespots
Low-intermediate through advanced. An editing guide for students

How English Works
A grammar handbook with readings. Student text, instructor's guide

Intermediate through advanced. Other texts and supplementary material, including reading anthologies

Santillana Publishing Co., Inc.
901 West Walnut Street
Compton, CA 90220-5109
800-245-8584

Grades K–8. Kits of student books, teacher's guides, classroom library, audiocassettes, posters in series to teach English

Elementary supplementary materials include pictures, posters, songs, big books, thematic books (e.g. *Courtroom ESL*); bilingual, multicul-tural, Spanish, reference, and professional books

Saxon Publishers
1320 West Lindsey
Norman, OK 73069
800-284-7019

Grades 6–12. Mathematics textbooks also in Spanish

Scholastic, Inc.
2931 East McCarty Street
P.O. Box 7501
Jefferson City, MO 65102-9968
800-325-6149

Spanish/ESL Titles

Wordless Big Book Units
Grades K–3. Wordless big and small books, teaching guide, audiocassette

Big Book ESL Library
Grades K–3. Big and small books, audiocassettes, ESL teaching guide, big book teaching guide

Scholastic primeros libros de lectura
Grades K–2. Big and small books, audiocassettes, activity cards, teaching guides

Sprint Reading Skills Program (series)
Grades 4–6. Developmental reading program. Skills books, story books, play books, teaching guides, supplementary materials

Vocabulary Skills (series)
Grades 1–6. Student workbooks, teacher's editions

Elementary Language Arts/Reading

Basal Breaks: Applying Reading Strategies (series)
Grades 1–6. Grade units including paperback titles, teacher's guides

Supplementary ESL/Spanish materials include *Big Books Collections* (series), *Book Center: A Whole-Language Program from Scholastic* (series), *Bookshelf* (series), *Bridges: Moving from the Basal into Literature* (series). Reading Comprehension Series includes *Reading for Information, Critical Reading, Read and Think*. Resource materials include filmstrips, magazines, activity packages, literature collections (including titles in Spanish). Special reading collections for grades K–9 include *Literature Links, Reluctant Reader Collections, Read By Reading Collection, Celebrated Books, Pleasure Reading, Sprint Libraries, Text Extenders, Multicultural Paperbacks*

Secondary Language Arts/Reading

Action 2000 (series)
Grades 7–12. Reading program for hard-to-reach students. Student anthologies, teacher's resource binders. Includes *Jobs in Your Future, Friends and Families, Making Decisions*

Project Achievement: Reading
Grades 5–12. Developmental reading program. Softcover texts, teacher's resource manuals, supplementary materials

Scope English: Writing and Language (series)
Grades 6–8. Textbooks, teacher's editions, teacher's resource binders, supplementary materials

Scope English: Writing and Language Skills (series)
Grades 9–12. Textbooks, teacher's editions, teacher's resource binders, supplementary materials

Scope Visuals (series)
Grades 7–12. Transparencies, teaching guides. Includes *Reading Comprehension Skills, Writing Skills, Word Skills, Close Reading Skills, Reference Skills, Language Skills, Career and Consumer Skills*

Social studies texts in Spanish editions

ScottForesman

1900 East Lake Avenue
Glenview, IL 60025
800-554-4411

Primary EFL/ESL

My English Book Series
Levels 1–4. Conversation books, pre-reading books, teacher's manuals

I Like English (series)
Levels 1–6. Student books, workbooks, audio books, teacher's manuals, teaching cards

Hooray for English! (series)
Student books, workbooks, songs, language cassette, teacher's manuals, posters, teaching cards

Grades K–8. Literature in collections by concepts, language patterns, world's family. Also big books

Secondary & Adult EFL/ESL

ScottForesman English (series)
Grades 7–8 and beyond. Textbooks, teacher's editions, workbooks, audiocassettes. Includes *In Contact* (beginning), *On Target* (intermediate) & *In Charge* (advanced)

English for a Changing World
Levels 1–6 (Ages 10–17). Textbooks, teacher's editions, workbooks, audio program, placement tests

English that Works
Books 1 & 2, ages teen to adult. Textbooks, instructor's editions, cultural notes, flashcards, audiocassettes

English in Tune (series)
Textbooks, teacher's editions, workbook, audio books on language and song

Cuing In
Adults, preliteracy level

Supplementary ESL materials using pictures, songs and in citizenship, communication skills and reference materials

Language arts titles include *Assignments in Exposition, College Reading and Study Skills, How to Design and Deliver a Speech, Intercultural Journeys through Reading and Writing,* and more

Literature and reading titles include *America Reads, Focus: Reading for Success* (series), *The Gateway Literature Series,* big books, readiness books, preprimer books, textbooks, teacher's editions, teacher's resource files, student workbooks, and supplementary materials including videocassettes and software

Social studies and math texts in Spanish editions

Silver Burdett and Ginn

4350 Equity Drive
P.O. Box 2649
Columbus, OH 43216
800-848-9500

World of Reading (series)
Grades K–8. Textbooks, teacher's editions, teacher's resource kits, early literacy program, supplementary materials including trade book collections, assessment materials, software, reader's journals and workbooks; interactive teaching kits of audio- and videocassettes, posters, activity guides, theme cards

World of Language (series)
Grades K–8. Textbooks, teacher editions, teacher resource file, software, primary literature program, writing and spelling activity books, classroom libraries, assessment materials, multimedia resources including audio and videocassettes

Skills Bank Corporation

15 Governor's Court
Baltimore, MD 21207-2791
800-222-3681

Software for MS-DOS/Apple/Macintosh/Tandy. In reading, language, and writing

Soft-Kat

20630 Nordhoff Street
Chatsworth, CA 91311
800-641-1057

Grades K–12. Software for language arts—reading, spelling, writing, grammar, and vocabulary

South-Western Publishing Co.
5101 Madison Road
Cincinnati, OH 45227
800-543-7972

Grades 6–12. Emphasizing communications instructional materials including texts for using computers to teach writing, *Write Now! A Process-Writing Program*, and traditional writing texts

SRA School Group
American School Publishers
Barnell Loft-Merrill-SRA
P.O. Box 5380
Chicago, IL 60680-5380
800-843-8855

Grades K–12. Supplementary programs in reading, literature, life skills, comprehension, handwriting, composition-grammar, process writing, spelling, vocabulary

Steck-Vaughn Company
P.O. Box 26015
Austin, TX 78755
800-531-5015

Reading

Developing Reading Strategies
Grades 6–12, Reading levels 2.5–6. Student workbooks, teacher's editions, classroom libraries

First-Time Phonics
Reading levels K–1. Student workbooks, picture cards, classroom library, teacher's editions

Mastering Basic Reading Skills
Grade levels 3–10, reading levels 2–7. Text-/workbooks, teacher's editions

Novel collections for special-needs students including *Short Classics, Great Unsolved Mysteries.*

Phonics and sight word programs for grades K–6 including *Building Sight Vocabulary, Power-Word Programs, Sounds, Words, and Meanings, Phonics Readers* (series), *Reading Comprehension Series, Steck-Vaughn Comprehension Skills* (series), *Steck-Vaughn Critical Thinking* (series), *Steck-Vaughn Phonics*

Language

Language Exercises (series)
Grades 1–8. Student workbooks, teacher's guides, skills books, review books

Vocabulary Connections: A Content Area Approach (series)
Grades 3–8. Softcover text-workbooks, classroom library

Writing for Competency
Grades 7–10, reading level 7. Softcover text

Whole Language

Classroom libraries include whole-language collections for primary, middle, and junior-high students; high-interest, low-level readers for middle school and secondary students; thinking, reading, comprehension, vocabulary-skills sets; hot topic sets, *The Highgate Collection* (series), *My World* (series), and big books, softcover nonfiction books, teacher's guides, Spanish editions. Science and social studies themes

Social studies texts in Spanish editions

Sundance
P.O. Box 1326
Newton Road
Littleton, MA 01460
800-343-8204

Grades pre-K–6. Early childhood materials, literature programs, developmental writing guides, thematic learning units, cross-curriculum units, classroom libraries, audio and videocassettes

SVE—Society for Visual Education, Inc.
Department JT
1345 Diversey Parkway
Chicago, IL 60614-1299
800-829-1900

Grades pre-K–9. Audio- and videocassettes, filmstrips, software, videodiscs for children's literature, reading, writing, whole-language skills

Swan Books

P.O. Box 2498
Fair Oaks, CA 95628
916-961-8778

Grades 5-12. Presents Shakespeare's plays to suit
the grade level and/or special needs of students.
Shakespeare for Young People, Shakespeare on Stage

T. S. Denison & Company, Inc.

9601 Newton Avenue South
Minneapolis, MN 55431-2509
800-328-3831

Resources for teachers to encourage reading (e.g.,
The Newbery Award, which provides information to
encourage readers, and *Launch into Literature,*
which introduces good literature)

Teacher Support Software

1035 N. W. 57th St.
Gainesville, FL 32605-4486
800-228-2871

Software covering reading and language experiences in special education, ESL, at-risk students
including multicultural experiences involving Native
Americans

Teacher Ideas Press

Attn. Department 400
P.O. Box 3988
Englewood, CO 80155-3988
800-237-6124

Teacher resource books relating to whole language,
literature across the curriculum, thinking skills;
activity books for literature, reading, storytelling,
research skills, writing, gifted and talented students

Teachers College Press

Teachers College, Columbia University
1234 Amsterdam Avenue
New York, NY 10027
800-445-6638

Resource books for training gifted and talented, for
special education, and for bilingual education

Teachers of English to Speakers of Other Languages, Inc. (TESOL)

1600 Cameron Street, Suite 300
Alexandria, VA 22314-2751
703-836-0774

Professional materials for teachers of ESL/EFL,
including reference lists, books on testing practices,
technology, and teacher preparation; student
resources for K–adult education, such as journal-
keeping guides and annotated reading lists

Thomas S. Klise Company

Old Chelsea Station
P.O. Box 1877
New York, NY 10113-0950
800-937-0092

Grades 6–12. Audio- and videocassettes, filmstrips,
records, posters, teacher's guides. In English, world
and American literature, language and writing,
grammar, fiction, poetry, drama, mythology and
fantasy

Tom Snyder Productions

90 Sherman Street
Cambridge, MA 02140
800-342-0236

Grades K–12. Software for Apple/Macintosh/IBM/
Tandy/MS-DOS, support materials, multimedia
materials for grammar and writing

Troll Associates

100 Corporate Drive
Mahwah, NJ 07430
800-526-5289

Multicultural literature (Native Americans, African
Americans, Hispanic Americans, Asian Americans), bilingual (Spanish/English), intergenerational, women in history

United Learning, Inc.

6633 West Howard Street
Niles, IL 60648-3305
800-424-0362

Grades K–12. Videocassettes, filmstrips, slides. In
reading, literature, and presentation skills

Videodiscovery, Inc.
1700 Westlake Avenue North, Suite 600
Seattle, WA 98109-3012
800-548-3472

Videodiscs, software for Macintosh/Apple/MS-DOS for reading, writing, mythology, film

Wadsworth School Group
10 Davis Drive
Belmont, CA 94002-3098
800-831-6996

College textbooks appropriate for use by college-bound, honors, or advanced placement students. Topics include reading/study skills, grammar and composition, critical thinking/writing, journalism, business English/communication, speech/forensics/communication, theatre, mass communication, telecommunication/film studies

Watten/Poe Teaching Resource Center
P.O. Box 1509
14023 Catalina Street
San Leandro, CA 94577
800-833-3389

Integrated curriculum materials, teacher's resource books, nursery rhyme strips, easels, pocket charts and stands, theme kits, big books, book/audiocassette packages, chalkboards, markboards

Weaver Instructional Systems
6161 28th Street, Southeast
Grand Rapids, MI 49506
616-942-2891

Reading Efficiency System
Software for Apple/Franklin/Radio Shack/Acorn/IBM/Atari/Commodore

English Grammar Instructional System
Grades 6 and above. Software for Apple/Franklin/Radio Shack/Acorn/IBM/Atari/Commodore

Weekly Reader Corporation
3000 Cindel Drive
P.O. Box 8037
Delran, NJ 08075

Weekly Reader Skills Books (series)
Grades pre-K–6. Reading, writing, speech, vocabulary, and library-skills workbooks, supplementary materials

Wicat
1875 South State Street
Orem, UT 84058
800-759-4228

Grades K–12. Instructional, assessment & staff development for ESL & functional literacy using MS-DOS compatibles. Software programs for capitalization, punctuation, grammar, usage and parts of speech, writing, whole-language writing activities

William K. Bradford Publishing Company
310 School Street
Acton, MA 01720
800-421-2009

Grades K–12. Software programs for reading and language arts

WINGS for Learning/Sunburst
1600 Green Hills Road
P.O. Box 660002
Scotts Valley, CA 95067-0002
800-321-7511

Grades K–college. Software for Apple/Macintosh/IBM/Tandy, multimedia materials. For reading, sequencing/categorization, handwriting, spelling, literature, writing

The Wright Group
19201 120th Ave. NE
Bothell, WA 98011-9512
800-345-6073

Grades K-6. Learning resources, with whole-language approach. For reading and writing. Includes titles in Spanish

Write Source
Educational Publishing House
Box J
Burlington, WI 53105
800-445-8613

Language arts handbooks, teacher's guides, activity books, workbooks, posters, literature collections

Zaner-Bloser
2200 West Fifth Avenue
P.O. Box 16764
Columbus, OH 43216-6764
800-421-3018

Breakthroughs: Language Development Supplements (series) (also in Spanish)
Grades 1–8. Teacher's folder with teaching notes, worksheets, and reproducible picture glossary

Day-by-Day Kindergarten Program
Cross-curriculum resource program. Teacher's resource book, student activity book, teacher's guide, supplementary materials

Developing Reading Power
Grades 1–8. Comprehension skills assessment program

Let's Read and Think (series)
Grades 1–3. Student text-workbooks, teacher's editions

Literacy Plus (series)
Grades K–8. Integrated language arts program. Teacher's guides, teacher's reference book, student reference book, student word books, trade-book collections, supplementary materials including in-service videocassettes

Supplementary materials include critical-thinking programs, guided practice books, independent readers, duplicating masters, spelling and vocabulary builders

Zephyr Press
3316 North Chapel Avenue
P.O. Box 13448-E
Tucson, AZ 85732-3448
602-322-5090

Grades K–9. Multicultural stories, whole-language source books, activity books on global awareness, audiocassettes, student books, teacher's manuals

STATEWIDE TEXTBOOK ADOPTION

EVEN states have statewide adoption of textbooks and other instructional materials for English as a second language: Arizona, California, Florida, Kentucky, New Mexico, Oklahoma, and Texas.

The policies and procedures for textbook adoption are similar in all seven states, with some minor variations.

Textbook Advisory Committee

In general, the state board of education is responsible for developing guidelines and criteria for the review and selection of textbooks and for appointing members to a textbook advisory committee. However, in a few states, the appointment of committee members is the responsibility of the governor or of the Commissioner of Education.

The textbook advisory committee is usually composed of educators, lay citizens, and parents, and can have from nine to twenty-seven appointees, depending upon the state. Membership is weighted, however, toward individuals who are educators: elementary and secondary teachers in the subject areas in which textbooks are to be adopted, instructors of teacher education and curriculum from local universities and colleges, school administrators, and school board members. Lay citizens, in order to sit on the committee, should be interested in and conversant with educational issues. An effort is made to select appointees who reflect the diversity of their state's population, and therefore decisions about appointments are often made with the purpose of having a wide representation of

ethnic backgrounds and geographical residence within the state.

Adoption Process

The textbook and instructional materials adoption process takes approximately twelve months.

Once the textbook advisory committee is formed, the members conduct an organizational meeting to formulate policy on such issues as adoption subjects and categories; standards for textbook evaluation, allocation of time for publisher presentations, and location of regional sites for such; sampling directions for publishers; and publisher contact. The committee may appoint subcommittees—made up of curriculum and/or subject specialists—to assist them in developing criteria for evaluating instructional materials.

After these procedural matters are agreed upon, the committee issues an official textbook call or "invitation to submit" to the textbook publishers. This document provides the publisher with adoption information and subject area criteria, which can either be the curriculum framework or essential skills list. Those publishers interested in having their materials considered for adoption submit their intention to bid, which shows the prices at which the publishers will agree to sell their material during the adoption period. Publishers usually bid current wholesale prices or lowest existing contract prices at which textbooks or other instructional materials are being sold elsewhere in the country.

If their bid has been accepted by the committee, the publishers submit sample copies of their textbooks for examination. The committee then hears presentations by the publishers. This meeting allows the publisher to present the texts submitted for adoption and to answer any questions the committee may have on the material. After publisher presentations, the textbooks are displayed in designated areas throughout the state for general public viewing. The committee then holds public hearings (usually two) which provide citizens with the opportunity to give an opinion on the textbooks offered for adoption. After much discussion and evaluation, the committee makes a recommendations for textbook adoption to the state board of education.

When the board of education approves the committee's recommendations, it negotiates the contract with the chosen publishers and disseminates the list of instructional materials to the school districts. The school districts will then make their textbook selections from this list. A few states also allow their school districts to use materials for the classroom that are not on the adoption list.

Textbook and Instructional Materials

There are two categories of instructional materials: basal and supplementary. Basal, or basic, materials address the goals, objectives, and content identified for a particular subject. Supplementary materials, used in conjunction with the basic text, enhance the teaching of the subject.

Instructional materials may include all or some of the following: hardcover books, softcover books, kits, workbooks, dictionaries, maps and atlases, electronic/computer programs, films, filmstrips, and other audiovisual materials.

The textbook adoption period generally runs from four to six years (California, the exception, has an eight-year contract period for K-8 only). The grade levels for adoption are usually K-12, with the following subject areas: English/language arts, social studies, foreign languages, ESL, science, mathematics, fine arts, applied arts.

Textbooks and instructional materials are ultimately judged by how well they reflect the state curriculum framework and/or essential skills objectives. Materials are rated on the following criteria: organization, accuracy, and currency of subject content; correlation with grade level requirements for the subject; adaptability for students with different abilities, backgrounds, and experiences; types of teacher aids provided;

author's background and training; physical features; and cost.

In addition, some states have social content requirements that textbooks have to meet. For instance, textbooks should be objective in content and impartial in interpretation of the subject, and should not include "offensive" language or illustrations. American values (defined as, democracy, the work ethic, free enterprise), culture, traditions, and government should be presented in a positive manner. Respect for the individual's rights, and for the cultural and racial diversity of American society, can also be addressed in the text. Finally, some states declare that textbooks should not condone civil disorder, lawlessness, or "deviance."

Kraus thanks the personnel we contacted at the state departments of education for their help in providing the states' textbook adoption lists.

List of Textbooks

Following is a compilation of the textbooks and instructional materials approved by the twenty-two states that have statewide textbook adoption. This listing is based on the relevant publications submitted to Kraus by the textbook division of the respective departments of educations.

The list is alphabetized by state; under each state, the materials are organized by grade level, if the state designates texts in this way. In some cases, supplemental material is also noted. For each textbook (and supplemental publication), the title, grade level, publisher, and copyright date are provided, as well as the termination year of the textbook's adoption period.

Arizona

Papa: Turning Points. Grades 1-2
Addison-Wesley, 1986 (Termination Year: 1992)

Yes! English for Children. Levels A-F
Addison-Wesley, 1983 (Termination Year: 1992)

Idea + Kit: Grades K-8 (also in Spanish)
Ballard, 1985 (Termination Year: 1992)

Experience in English Kit. Grades K-9
Macmillan, 1983 (Termination Year: 1992)

Reach Out: Grades 1-5
Macmillan, 1982 (Termination Year: 1992)

New Routes to English: Grades 1-6
Macmillan, 1980 (Termination Year: 1992)

Steps to English: Grades K-6
Macmillan, 1983 (Termination Year: 1992)

Pathways to English: Grades 1-6
Macmillan, 1984 (Termination Year: 1992)

Addison-Wesley ESL Series: Levels A-C
Addison-Wesley, 1989 (Termination Year: 1992)

Early Bird: Grades K-3
Charlesbridge, n.d. (Termination Year: 1992)

My World English: Levels 1-3
Steck-Vaughn, 1988 (Termination Year: 1992)

Sunshine Series: Level 1-5
Wright Group, n.d. (Termination Year: 1992)

Story Book Series: Level 1-7
Wright Group, n.d. (Termination Year: 1992)

Globe Literature: Grades 7-12
Wright Group, n.d. (Termination Year: 1992)

California

Yes! English for Children: Grades K–2
Addison-Wesley, 1983 (Termination Year: 1992)

New Horizons in English: Grades 7–8
Addison-Wesley, 1984 (Termination Year: 1992)

Teaching English Naturally: Grades K–8
Addison-Wesley, 1983 (Termination Year: 1992)

Idea + Oral Language Program: Grades K–8
Ballard & Tighe, 1985 (Termination Year: 1992)

Odyssey: A Communicative Course in English:
Grades 7–8
Longman, 1983 (Termination Year: 1992)

Steps to English: Grades 1–6
Macmillan, 1983 (Termination Year: 1992)

*The Rainbow Collection: A Natural Approach to
English as a Second Language*: Grades K–6
Santillana, 1984 (Termination Year: 1992)

*An Ant About Town: A Transitional English Reading
Program*: Grades 3–6
Santillana, 1982 (Termination Year: 1992)

English for a Changing World: Grades 7–8
ScottForesman, 1984 (Termination Year: 1992)

I Like English: Grades K–6
ScottForesman, 1985 (Termination Year: 1992)

Florida

ESOL/Intensive English, K-6

Addison-Wesley ESL: Grades K–6
Addison-Wesley, 1989 (Termination Year: 1996)

Experiences in English: Grades K–6
Macmillan, 1990 (Termination Year: 1996)

Transitions to English: Grades K–6
Macmillan, 1990 (Termination Year: 1996)

*The Santillana ESOL System for Natural Language &
Reading*: Grades K-5
Santillana, 1991 (Termination Year: 1996)

Hooray for English: Grades K–6
ScottForesman, 1989 (Termination Year: 1996)

ESOL/Intensive English, 6-8

Turning Points Series: Grades 6-8
Addison-Wesley, 1989 (Termination Year: 1996)

Prism: Grades 6-8
Harcourt, 1989/90 (Termination Year: 1996)

Spotlight: Grades 6-8
Harcourt, 1988 (Termination Year: 1996)

ESOL Listening/Speaking, Grades 9-12

Action Sequence Stories—Act II: Grades 9-12
Ballard & Tighe (Termination Year: 1996)

Real-Life English: Grades 9-12
Steck-Vaughn, 1988 (Termination Year: 1996)

Kentucky

ESL K-8

Hooray for English: Grades 1–6
ScottForesman, 1989 (Termination Year: 1998)

Hello, English: Grades 1–6
National Textbook, 1987 (Termination Year: 1998)

ESL 9-12

In Contact: Grades 9–12
ScottForesman, 1991 (Termination Year: 1998)

On Target: Grades 9–12
ScottForesman, 1991 (Termination Year: 1998)

Living in the USA: Grades 9–12
National Textbook, 1990 (Termination Year: 1998)

Intercom 2000: Grades 9–12
Heinle, 1991 (Termination Year: 1998)

Perspectives 2000: Grades 9–12
Heinle, 1992 (Termination Year: 1998)

New Mexico

IDEA+ Oral Language Program: Grades K–6
Ballard & Tighe, 1989 (Termination Year: 1997)

Action Sequence Stories: Grades 7–12
Ballard & Tighe, 1989 (Termination Year: 1997)

Oral Language Transition Program: Grades K-8
Houghton, 1989 (Termination Year: 1997)

Oxford Picture Dictionary: Grades 7–12
Jag, 1988 (Termination Year: 1997)

Begin in English Short Stories: Grades 7–12
Jag, 1992 (Termination Year: 1997)

From the Beginning—1st Reader American History:
Grades 7–12
Jag, 1990 (Termination Year: 1997)

What Next?: Grades K–2
Modern Curriculum, 1989 (Termination Year: 1997)

What's Missing: Grades K–2
Modern Curriculum, 1989 (Termination Year: 1997)

Rumplestiltskin: Grades K-2
Modern Curriculum, 1989 (Termination Year: 1997)

Elves & the Shoemaker: Grades K–2
Modern Curriculum, 1989 (Termination Year: 1997)

Three Little Pigs: Grades K–2
Modern Curriculum, 1989 (Termination Year: 1997)

Goldilocks & the 3 Bears: Grades K–2
Modern Curriculum, 1989 (Termination Year: 1997)

The English Survival Series: Grades 7–12
National Textbook, 1989 (Termination Year: 1997)

English with a Smile: Grades 7–12
National Textbook, 1992 (Termination Year: 1997)

ESL Dictionaries: Grades 7–12
National Textbook, 1994 (Termination Year: 1997)

Hello, English: Grades 3–5
National Textbook, 1987 (Termination Year: 1997)

Looking at America: Grades 7–12
National Textbook, 1985 (Termination Year: 1997)

Everyday Consumer English: Grades 7–12
National Textbook, 1989 (Termination Year: 1997)

Ready for English: Grades K–2
National Textbook, 1990 (Termination Year: 1997)

Everyday English: Grades 7–12
National Textbook, 1990 (Termination Year: 1997)

Beginner's English Reader: Grades 7–12
National Textbook, 1990 (Termination Year: 1997)

101 American Idioms: Grades 7–12
National Textbook, 1990 (Year: 1997)

Safari Grammar & Punctuation: Grades 7–12
National Textbook, 1989 (Termination Year: 1997)

303 Dumb Spelling Mistakes: Grades 7–12
National Textbook, 1990 (Termination Year: 1997)

Time: We the People: Grades 7–12
National Textbook, 1989 (Termination Year: 1997)

Express Yourself in Written English: Grades 7–12
National Textbook, 1990 (Termination Year: 1997)

Living in the USA: Grades 7–12
National Textbook, 1990 (Termination Year: 1997)

Spotlight: Grades 6–8
Holt, 1988 (Termination Year: 1997)

Prism: An Intermediate Course in English:
Grades 6–8
Holt, 1989 (Termination Year: 1997)

Superbooks - Big Books: Grades 3–6 (appropriate
for Special Education)
Santillana, 1989 (Termination Year: 1997)

Tiny Tales Readers: Grades 3–6 (appropriate for
Special Education)
Santillana, 1989 (Termination Year: 1997)

Sing It, Say It, Read It: Grades 3–6 (appropriate for
Special Education)
Santillana, 1989 (Termination Year: 1997)

The Santillana ESL System for Natural Language:
Grades K–6 (appropriate for Special Education)
Santillana, 1989 (Termination Year: 1997)

English for a Changing World: Grades 5–12
ScottForesman, 1984 (Termination Year: 1997)

My English Book Series: Grades PK–2
ScottForesman, 1987 (Termination Year: 1997)

Hooray for English: Grades 1–7
ScottForesman, 1989 (Termination Year: 1997)

Turning Points: Grades 7–10
Addison-Wesley, 1989 (Termination Year: 1997)

Addison-Wesley ESL Series: Grades K–6
Addison-Wesley, 1989 (Termination Year: 1997)

Real Writing: Grades 7–12
Dormac, 1988 (Termination Year: 1997)

The Gift of the Magi: Grades 5–12
Dormac, 1988 (Termination Year: 1997)

The Doorman: Grades 5–12
Dormac, 1988 (Termination Year: 1997)

Jealous: Grades 5–12
Dormac, 1989 (Termination Year: 1997)

Sticky Situations: Grades 7–12
Dormac, 1990 (Termination Year: 1997)

English for Life through Pictures: Grades 7–12
Dormac, 1990 (Termination Year: 1997)

Out of this World: Grades 5–12 (appropriate for
Special Education)
Dormac, 1990 (Termination Year: 1997)

Bridge Across the Americas: Grades 7–12
Dormac, 1990 (Termination Year: 1997)

In the Magic Corridor: Grades 7–12
Dormac, 1990 (Termination Year: 1997)

Ready-Go-Begin To Learn: Grades PK–1 (appropriate for Special Education)
Educational Activities, 1980 (Termination Year:
1997)

Now You're Talking!: Grades 4–AD (appropriate for
Special Education)
Educational Activities, 1987 (Termination Year:
1997)

Fearon's English Compositions: Grades 7–12 (high
risk/low level)
Fearon, 1990 (Termination Year: 1997)

Fearib's Basic English: Grades 7–12 (high risk/low
level)
Fearon, 1990 (Termination Year: 1997)

Fearon's Practical English: Grades 7–12 (high risk/
low level)
Fearon, 1990 (Termination Year: 1997)

Matchbook Five-Minute Thrillers: Grades 7–12 (high
risk/low level)
Fearon, 1988 (Termination Year: 1997)

Hopes & Dreams: Grades 7–12 (high risk/low level)
Fearon, 1989 (Termination Year: 1997)

Experiments: Grades 2–4
Childrens Press, 1990 (Termination Year: 1997)

Countries/Geography: Grades 2–4
Childrens Press, 1986 (Termination Year: 1997)

Human Body: Grades 2–4
Childrens Press, 1985 (Termination Year: 1997)

Indians. Grades 2–4
Childrens Press, 1984 (Termination Year: 1997)

Environment. Grades 2–4
Childrens Press, 1990 (Termination Year: 1997)

Oklahoma

Yes! English for Children. Grades 1–5
Addison-Wesley, 1983 (Termination Year: 1993)

Experiences in English Kit. Grades 1–6
Macmillan, 1983 (Termination Year: 1993)

I Like English. Grades 1–6
Scott, Foresman, 1985 (Termination Year: 1993)

The Riverside Oral Language Transition Complete Program. Grades 1–3
Houghton Mifflin, 1986 (Termination Year: 1993)

English Experiences. Grades 1–6
National Textbook, 1985 (Termination Year: 1993)

Easy English Activities Book. Grades 1–6
National Textbook, 1985 (Termination Year: 1993)

English All around Us. Grades 1–6
National Textbook, 1985 (Termination Year: 1993)

Hello, English. Grades 1–6
National Textbook, 1988 (Termination Year: 1993)

Turning Points. Grades 7–8
Addison-Wesley, 1986 (Termination Year: 1993)

English for a Changing World. Grades 7–8
Scott, Foresman, 1984 (Termination Year: 1993)

Odyssey Series. Grades 9–12
Longman, 1984 (Termination Year: 1993)

New Horizons in English. Grades 9–12
Addison-Wesley, 1984 (Termination Year: 1993)

New English Course. Grades 9–12
Prentice Hall, 1979 (Termination Year: 1993)

Expressways: English for Communication.
Grades 9–12
Prentice Hall, 1987 (Termination Year: 1993)

Side by Side: English Grammar through Guided Conversations. Grades 9–12
Prentice Hall, 1983 (Termination Year: 1993)

English for a Changing World. Grades 9–12
Scott, Foresman, 1984 (Termination Year: 1993)

English across the Curriculum. Grades 9–12
National Textbook, 1983 (Termination Year: 1993)

English with a Smile. Grades 9–12
National Textbook, 1984 (Termination Year: 1993)

Real-Life English. Grades 9–12
Steck-Vaughn, 1988 (Termination Year: 1993)

Texas

ESL Learning Systems Primary, Grades 1-2

Addison-Wesley ESL Primary System. Grades 1–2
Addison-Wesley, 1989 (Termination Year: 1996)

Ready for English. Grades 1–2
National Textbook, 1990 (Termination Year: 1996)

Riverside System 1—Oral Language Transition Program. Grades 1–2
Houghton Mifflin, 1989 (Termination Year: 1996)

Santillana ESL System for Natural Language & Reading Primary. Grades 1–2
Santillana, 1989 (Termination Year: 1996)

ESL Learning Systems Elementary, Grades 3-5

Addison-Wesley ESL Elementary System. Grades 3–5
Addison-Wesley, 1989 (Termination Year: 1996)

Hello, English. Grades 3–5
National Textbook, 1990 (Termination Year: 1996)

Riverside System 2—Oral Language Transition Program. Grades 3–5
Houghton Mifflin, 1989 (Termination Year: 1996)

Santillana ESL System for Natural Language & Reading Elem.: Grades 3–5
Santillana, 1989 (Termination Year: 1996)

ESL Learning Systems Middle School, Grades 6-8

Addison-Wesley ESL Middle School System. Grades 6–8
Addison-Wesley, 1990 (Termination Year: 1996)

Riverside System 3—The Oral Language Transition Program: Grades 6–8
Houghton Mifflin, 1989 (Termination Year: 1996)

ESL Learning Systems, High School, Grades 9-12

Addison-Wesley High School ESL System:
Grades 9–12
Addison-Wesley, 1990 (Termination Year: 1996)

The Spotlight/Prism Learning System: Grades 9–12
Holt, 1992 (Termination Year: 1996)

Bridge to Communication Secondary 9-12 System:
Grades 9–12
Santillana, 1992 (Termination Year: 1996)

INDEX TO REVIEWS
OF EDUCATIONAL MATERIALS

THIS index cites reviews of recently published materials for use in English as a Second Language classes, including curriculum guides, lesson plans, project books, software programs, videos, and filmstrips. The citations cover reviews from the past two years (up to August 1992), and they reflect a search of educational journals, magazines, and newsletters that would include reviews of ESL materials. The journals chosen are those that are available in teacher college libraries, in other college and university collections, and in many public libraries. They also include the major publications sent to members of the appropriate educational organizations. The review for each item can be found under the following listings:
- the title of the item
- the author(s)
- the publisher or producer/distributor
- school level (elementary, middle school, high school)
- subject (a broad subject arrangement is used)
- special medium (for "Software packages" and "Audio materials")

Abdulaziz, Helen Taylor
Academic Challenges in Reading, by Helen Taylor Abdulaziz and Alfred D. Storer (Englewood Cliffs, NJ: Prentice-Hall, 1989). Reviewed in: *TESOL Newsletter* 24, no. 4 (Aug. 1990): 25–27.

Adventures in Conversation: Exercises in Achieving Oral Fluency and Developing Vocabulary in English by Lynne Hunter and Cynthia Swanson Hofbauer (Prentice-Hall Regents, 1989). Reviewed in: *TESOL Quarterly* 26, no. 1 (Spring 1992): 156–57.

Alemany (publisher)
Here To Stay in the USA—ESL/U.S. Studies for Beginners, by Timothy Maciel and John Duffy

(Hayward, CA: Alemany, 1990). Reviewed in: *Journal of Reading* 35, no. 6 (Mar. 1992): 504–5.

Alexander, Louis G.
Longman English Grammar, by Louis G. Alexander (London: Longman, 1988). Reviewed in: *TESOL Quarterly* 24, no. 2 (Summer 1990): 309–10.

Alvarez-Martini, Martha
The Rainbow Collection, by Martha Alvarez-Martini, Evelyn Marino, Consuelo Valencia Raley, and Tracy David Terrell (Northvale, NJ: Santillana, 1984). Reviewed in: *TESOL Quarterly* 24, no. 5 (Dec. 1990): 17–18.

American Vocabulary Builder 1 & 2
by Bernad Seal (New York: Longman, 1990). Reviewed in: *TESOL Quarterly* 25, no. 4 (Winter 1991): 722–23.

Aragones, Sergio (ill.)
Comics and Conversation: Using Humor To Elicit Conversation and Develop Vocabulary, by Joan Astikenas. Reviewed in: *TESOL Quarterly* 25, no. 4 (Winter 1991): 727–28.

Astikenas, Joan
Comics and Conversation: Using Humor To Elicit Conversation and Develop Vocabulary, by Joan Astikenas. Reviewed in: *TESOL Quarterly* 25, no. 4 (Winter 1991): 727–28.

At the Door: Selected Literature for ESL Students
by Sandra McKay and Dorothy Petitt (Englewood Cliffs, NJ: Prentice-Hall, 1984). Reviewed in: *TESOL Quarterly* 24, no. 4 (Winter 1990): 736-37; *English Journal* 80, no. 8 (Dec. 1991): 26.

Audio materials
Photo Dictionary Pronunciation Workbook, audiocassette and supplementary materials (New York: Longman, 1988). Reviewed in: *TESOL Newsletter* 24, no. 5 (Oct. 1990): 23.

Benson, Beverly
Improving the Grammar of Written English: The Editing Process, by Beverly Benson and Patricia Byrd (Belmont, CA: Wadsworth, 1989). Reviewed in: *TESOL Quarterly* 26, no. 1 (Spring 1992): 161–62.

Improving the Grammar of Written English: The Handbook, by Beverly Benson and Patricia Byrd (Belmont, CA: Wadsworth, 1989). Reviewed in: *TESOL Quarterly* 26, no. 1 (Spring 1992): 161–62.

Berman, Aaron
Forestville Tales: International Folk Stories, by Aaron Berman (New York: Collier Macmillan, 1977). Reviewed in: *TESOL Quarterly* 24, no. 4 (Winter 1990): 734–35.

Bilingual Grammar of English–Spanish Syntax: A Manual with Exercises
by Sam Hill and William Bradford (Lanham, MD: University Press of America, 1991). Reviewed in: *Language Learning* 41, no. 3 (Sep. 1991): 453.

Blank, Dr. Marion
The Sentence Master, software by Dr. Marion Blank (Winooski, VT: Laureate Learning Systems, 1990). Reviewed in: *The Computing Teacher* 18, no. 4 (Dec. 1990/Jan. 1991): 53.

Bookman, Susan
Words at Work: Vocabulary Building through Reading, by Betty Sobel and Susan Bookman (New York: Collier Macmillan, 1989). Reviewed in: *TESOL Quarterly* 24, no. 3 (Fall 1990): 512–14.

Bradford, William
Bilingual Grammar of English–Spanish Syntax: A Manual with Exercises, by Sam Hill and William Bradford (Lanham, MD: University Press of America, 1991). Reviewed in: *Language Learning* 41, no. 3 (Sep. 1991): 453.

Breaking the Language Barrier: Creating Your Own Pathway to Success
by H. Douglas Brown (Yarmouth, ME: Intercultural, 1991). Reviewed in: *TESOL Quarterly* 26, no. 1 (Spring 1992): 149–52.

Brookes, Gay
Changes: Readings for ESL Writers, by Jean Winthrow, Gay Brookes, and Martha Clark Cummings (New York: St. Martin's Press, 1990). Reviewed in: *TESOL Quarterly* 24, no. 4 (Winter 1990): 737-38.

Brown, H. Douglas
Breaking the Language Barrier: Creating Your Own Pathway to Success, by H. Douglas Brown (Yarmouth, ME: Intercultural, 1991). Reviewed in: *TESOL Quarterly* 26, no. 1 (Spring 1992): 149-152.

Byrd, Donald R.H.
People Are Funny: Pictures for Practice (Book 1), by Donald R.H. Byrd and Stanley J. Zelinski III (New York: Longman, 1987). Reviewed in: *TESOL Quarterly* 25, no. 4 (Winter 1991): 727-28.

Byrd, Patricia
Improving the Grammar of Written English: The Editing Process, by Beverly Benson and Patricia Byrd (Belmont, CA: Wadsworth, 1989). Reviewed in: *TESOL Quarterly* 26, no. 1 (Spring 1992): 161–62.

Byrd, Patricia *(cont'd)*
Improving the Grammar of Written English: The Handbook, by Beverly Benson and Patricia Byrd (Belmont, CA: Wadsworth, 1989). Reviewed in: *TESOL Quarterly* 26, no. 1 (Spring 1992): 161–62.

Cambridge University Press
Clear Speech, by Judy Gilbert (Cambridge: Cambridge University Press, 1984). Reviewed in: *TESL Canada Journal* 8, no. 2 (Mar. 1991): 94.

Drama Techniques in Language Learning: A Resource Book of Communication Activities for Language Learners, by Alan Maley and Alan Duff (Cambridge: Cambridge University Press, 1982). Reviewed in: *TESL Canada Journal* 8, no. 2 (Mar. 1991): 83-84.

Grammar Practice Activities, A Practical Guide for Teachers, by Penny Ur (Cambridge: Cambridge University Press, 1986). Reviewed in: *TESL Canada Journal* 8, no. 1 (Nov. 1990): 114-6.

The Inward Ear: Poetry in the Language Classroom, by Alan Maley and Alan Duff (Cambridge: Cambridge University Press, 1989). Reviewed in: *TESOL Quarterly* 24, no. 4 (Winter 1990): 731–32.

Learning To Learn English: A Course in Learner Training, by Gail Ellis and Barbara Sinclair (Cambridge: Cambridge University Press, 1989). Reviewed in: *TESL Canada Journal* 8, no. 2 (Mar. 1991): 84.

Literature in the Language Classroom: A Resource Book of Ideas and Activities, by Joanne Collie and Stephen Slater (New York: Cambridge University Press, 1987). Reviewed in: *TESOL Quarterly* 24, no. 2 (Summer 1990): 305-6; *TESL Canada Journal* 8, no. 2 (Mar. 1991): 82.

Chamot, Anna Uhl
Language Development through Content: Mathematics Book A, by Anna Uhl Chamot and J. Michael O'Malley (Reading, MA: Addison-Wesley, 1988). Reviewed in: *Arithmetic Teacher* 38, no. 4 (Dec. 1990): 63.

Changes: Readings for ESL Writers
by Jean Winthrow, Gay Brookes, and Martha Clark Cummings (New York: St. Martin's Press, 1990). Reviewed in: *TESOL Quarterly* 24, no. 4 (Winter 1990): 737–38.

Children's Book Press
Family Pictures, by Carmen Lomas Garza, Harriet Rahmer, and Rosalma Znbizarreta (Emeryville, CA: Children's Book Press, 1990). Reviewed in: *Language Arts* 68, no. 4 (Apr. 1991): 324-25.

Claire, Elizabeth
An Indispensable Guide to Dangerous English: For Language Learners and Others, by Elizabeth Claire (Dundee, IL: Delta Systems, 1990). Reviewed in: *TESOL Quarterly* 26, no. 1 (Spring 1992): 158–59.

Claris (publisher)
Macwrite II Spanish Version, software (Santa Clara, CA: Claris). Reviewed in: *Electronic Learning* 11, no. 3 (Nov./Dec. 1991): 37.

Clear Speech
by Judy Gilbert (Cambridge: Cambridge University Press, 1984). Reviewed in: *TESL Canada Journal* 8, no. 2 (Mar. 1991): 94.

Collie, Joanne
Literature in the Language Classroom: A Resource Book of Ideas and Activities, by Joanne Collie and Stephen Slater (New York: Cambridge University Press, 1987). Reviewed in: *TESOL Quarterly* 24, no. 2 (Summer 1990): 305–6; *TESL Canada Journal* 8, no. 2 (Mar. 1991): 82.

Collier Macmillan
Crazy Idioms: A Conversational Idiom Book, by Nina Weinstein (New York: Collier Macmillan, 1990). Reviewed in: *TESOL Quarterly* 24, no. 3 (Fall 1990): 511–12.

Words at Work: Vocabulary Building through Reading, by Betty Sobel and Susan Bookman (New York: Collier Macmillan, 1989). Reviewed in: *TESOL Quarterly* 24, no. 3 (Fall 1990): 512–14.

Comics and Conversation: Using Humor To Elicit Conversation and Develop Vocabulary
by Joan Astikenas. Reviewed in: *TESOL Quarterly* 25, no. 4 (Winter 1991): 727–28.

Computation
Language Development through Content: Mathematics Book A, by Anna Uhl Chamot and J. Michael O'Malley (Reading, MA: Addison-Wesley, 1988). Reviewed in: *Arithmetic Teacher* 38, no. 4 (Dec. 1990): 63.

Conversation

Adventures in Conversation: Exercises in Achieving Oral Fluency and Developing Vocabulary in English, by Lynne Hunter and Cynthia Swanson Hofbauer (Prentice-Hall Regents, 1989). Reviewed in: *TESOL Quarterly* 26, no. 1 (Spring 1992): 156–57.

Comics and Conversation: Using Humor To Elicit Conversation and Develop Vocabulary, by Joan Astikenas. Reviewed in: *TESOL Quarterly* 25, no. 4 (Winter 1991): 727–28.

Conversation Gambits: Real English Conversation Practices, by Eric Keller and Sylvia T. Warner (Hove, England: Language Teaching, 1988). Reviewed in: *TESOL Quarterly* 24, no. 3 (Fall 1990): 510–11.

Crazy Idioms: A Conversational Idiom Book, by Nina Weinstein (New York: Collier Macmillan, 1990). Reviewed in: *TESOL Quarterly* 24, no. 3 (Fall 1990): 511–12.

Let's Talk and Talk about It, by W. Edmondson and J. House (Baltimore: Schwarzenberg, 1981). Reviewed in: *TESL Canadian Journal* 8, no. 2 (Mar. 1991): 80.

Photo Dictionary Pronunciation Workbook, audiocassette and supplementary materials (New York: Longman, 1988). Reviewed in: *TESOL Newsletter* 24 no. 5 (Oct. 1990): 23.

Talk about Values: Conversation Skills for Intermediate Students, by Irene E. Schoenberg (New York: Longman, 1989). Reviewed in: *TESOL Quarterly* 26, no. 1 (Spring 1992): 155–56.

Conversation Gambits: Real English Conversation Practices
by Eric Keller and Sylvia T. Warner (Hove, England: Language Teaching, 1988). Reviewed in: *TESOL Quarterly* 24, no. 3 (Fall 1990):510–11.

Countdown!: Taking off into Content Reading
by Alison Rice (New York: Macmillan, 1990). Reviewed in: *Language Learning* 41, no. 3 (Sep. 1991): 458.

Crazy Idioms: A Conversational Idiom Book
by Nina Weinstein (New York: Collier

Macmillan, 1990). Reviewed in: *TESOL Quarterly* 24, no. 3 (Fall 1990): 511–12.

Cummings, Martha Clark

Changes: Readings for ESL Writers, by Jean Winthrow, Gay Brookes, and Martha Clark Cummings (New York: St. Martin's Press, 1990). Reviewed in: *TESOL Quarterly* 24, no. 4 (Winter 1990): 737–38.

D. C. Heath

Read, Write and Publish, software (Acton, MA: D. C. Heath). Reviewed in: *Electronic Learning* 11, no. 1 (Sep. 1991): 42.

Davidson (publisher)

English Express, software or film/video (Torrance, CA: Davidson, 1991). Reviewed in: *Electronic Learning* 11, no. 1 (Sep. 1991): 40–63.

Delta Systems

An Indispensable Guide to Dangerous English: For Language Learners and Others, by Elizabeth Claire (Dundee, IL: Delta Systems, 1990). Reviewed in: *TESOL Quarterly* 26, no. 1 (Spring 1992): 158–59.

Dormac (publisher)

Whole Language Strategies for ESL Students, by Gail Heald-Taylor (San Diego: Dormac, 1989). Reviewed in: *TESOL Quarterly* 24, no. 2 (Summer 1990): 306–7.

Drama Techniques in Language Learning: A Resource Book of Communication Activities for Language Learners

by Alan Maley and Alan Duff (Cambridge: Cambridge University Press, 1982). Reviewed in: *TESL Canada Journal* 8, no. 2 (Mar. 1991): 83–84.

Duff, Alan

Drama Techniques in Language Learning: A Resource Book of Communication Activities for Language Learners, by Alan Maley and Alan Duff (Cambridge: Cambridge University Press, 1982). Reviewed in: *TESL Canada Journal* 8, no. 2 (Mar. 1991): 83–84.

The Inward Ear: Poetry in the Language Classroom, by Alan Maley and Alan Duff (Cambridge: Cambridge University Press, 1989). Reviewed in: *TESOL Quarterly* 24, no. 4 (Winter 1990): 731–32.

Duffy, John
Here To Stay in the USA—ESL/U.S. Studies for Beginners, by Timothy Maciel and John Duffy (Hayward, CA: Alemany, 1990). Reviewed in: *Journal of Reading* 35, no. 6 (Mar. 1992): 504–5.

Edmondson, W.
Let's Talk and Talk about It, by W. Edmondson and J. House (Baltimore: Schwarzenberg, 1981). Reviewed in: *TESL Canadian Journal* 8, no. 2 (Mar. 1991): 80.

Educational Activities (publisher)
Talk to Me, software (Freeport, NY: Educational Activities, 1990). Reviewed in: *The Computing Teacher* 18, no. 4 (Dec. 1990/Jan. 1991): 44–46.

Elementary materials
Family Pictures, by Carmen Lomas Garza, Harriet Rahmer, and Rosalma Znbizarreta (Emeryville, CA: Children's Book Press, 1990). Reviewed in: *Language Arts* 68, no. 4 (Apr. 1991): 324–25.

Forestville Tales: International Folk Stories, by Aaron Berman (New York: Collier Macmillan, 1977). Reviewed in: *TESOL Quarterly* 24, no. 4 (Winter 1990): 734–35.

Grammar Practice Activities, A Practical Guide for Teachers, by Penny Ur (Cambridge: Cambridge University Press, 1986). Reviewed in: *TESL Canada Journal* 8, no. 1 (Nov. 1990): 114–16.

Language Development through Content: Mathematics Book A, by Anna Uhl Chamot and J. Michael O'Malley (Reading, MA: Addison-Wesley, 1988). Reviewed in: *Arithmetic Teacher* 38, no. 4 (Dec. 1990): 63.

Literacy through Literature, by Terry D. Johnson and Daphne R. Louis (Portsmouth, NH: Heinemann, 1987). Reviewed in: *TESOL Quarterly* 24, no. 4 (Winter 1990): 730–31.

The Rainbow Collection, by Martha Alvarez-Martini, Evelyn Marino, Consuelo Valencia Raley, and Tracy David Terrell (Northvale, NJ: Santillana, 1984). Reviewed in: *TESOL Quarterly* 24, no. 5 (Dec. 1990): 17–18.

Read, Write and Publish, software (Acton, MA: D. C. Heath). Reviewed in: *Electronic Learning* 11, no. 1 (Sep. 1991): 42.

The Sentence Master, software by Dr. Marion Blank (Winooski, VT: Laureate Learning Systems, 1990). Reviewed in: *The Computing Teacher* 18, no. 4 (Dec. 1990/Jan. 1991): 53.

Talk to Me, software (Freeport, NY: Educational Activities, 1990). Reviewed in: *The Computing Teacher* 18, no. 4 (Dec. 1990/Jan. 1991): 44–46.

Whole Language Strategies for ESL Students, by Gail Heald-Taylor (San Diego: Dormac, 1989). Reviewed in: *TESOL Quarterly* 24, no. 2 (Summer 1990): 306–7.

Windows on Science (Spanish Edition), software (Warren, NJ: Optical Data). Reviewed in: *The Computing Teacher* 18, no. 4 (Dec. 1990/Jan. 1991): 53.

Ellis, Gail
Learning To Learn English: A Course in Learner Training, by Gail Ellis and Barbara Sinclair (Cambridge: Cambridge University Press, 1989). Reviewed in: *TESL Canada Journal* 8, no. 2 (Mar. 1991): 84.

English Express
software or film/video (Torrance, CA: Davidson, 1991). Reviewed in: *Electronic Learning* 11, no. 1 (Sep. 1991): 40–63.

English for Science
by Fran Zimmerman (Englewood Cliffs, NJ: Prentice-Hall Regents, 1989). Reviewed in: *TESOL Quarterly* 26, no. 1 (Spring 1992): 160–61.

Family Pictures
by Carmen Lomas Garza, Harriet Rahmer, and Rosalma Znbizarreta (Emeryville, CA: Children's Book Press, 1990). Reviewed in: *Language Arts* 68, no. 4 (Apr. 1991): 324–25.

Forestville Tales: International Folk Stories
by Aaron Berman (New York: Collier Macmillan, 1977). Reviewed in: *TESOL Quarterly* 24, no. 4 (Winter 1990): 734–35.

Freeman, Daniel B.
Photo Dictionary, by Marilyn S. Rosenthal and Daniel B. Freeman (White Plains, New York: Longman, 1987). Reviewed in: *TESOL Newsletter* 24, no. 5 (Oct. 1990): 22–23.

Freeman, Daniel B. *(cont'd)*
Photo Dictionary Intermediate Workbook, by
Marilyn S. Rosenthal, Daniel B. Freeman, and
Marjorie Fuchs (New York: Longman, 1989).
Reviewed in: *TESOL Newsletter* 24, no. 5 (Oct.
1990): 23.

Fuchs, Marjorie
Photo Dictionary Beginning Workbook, by
Marjorie Fuchs (New York: Longman, 1989).
Reviewed in: *TESOL Newsletter* 24, no. 5 (Oct.
1990): 23.

Photo Dictionary Intermediate Workbook, by
Marilyn S. Rosenthal, Daniel B. Freeman, and
Marjorie Fuchs (New York: Longman, 1989).
Reviewed in: *TESOL Newsletter* 24, no. 5 (Oct.
1990): 23.

Garza, Carmen Lomas
Family Pictures, by Carmen Lomas Garza,
Harriet Rahmer, and Rosalma Znbizarreta
(Emeryville, CA: Children's Book Press, 1990).
Reviewed in: *Language Arts* 68, no. 4 (Apr.
1991): 324–25.

Gilbert, Judy
Clear Speech, by Judy Gilbert (Cambridge:
Cambridge University Press, 1984). Reviewed in:
TESL Canada Journal 8, no. 2 (Mar. 1991): n.p.

Grammar
*Bilingual Grammar of English–Spanish Syntax: A
Manual with Exercises,* by Sam Hill and William
Bradford (Lanham, MD: University Press of
America, 1991). Reviewed in: *Language Learning*
41, no. 3 (Sep. 1991): 453.

*Grammar Practice Activities, A Practical Guide for
Teachers,* by Penny Ur (Cambridge: Cambridge
University Press, 1986). Reviewed in: *TESL
Canada Journal* 8, no. 1 (Nov. 1990): 114–16.

*Grammar with a Purpose: A Contextualized
Approach,* by Myrna Knepler (New York:
Macmillan, 1990). Reviewed in: *Language
Learning* 41, no. 1 (Mar. 1991): 148–49.

*Improving the Grammar of Written English: The
Handbook,* by Beverly Benson and Patricia Byrd
(Belmont, CA: Wadsworth, 1989). Reviewed in:
TESOL Quarterly 26, no. 1 (Spring 1992): 161–62.

Let's Talk and Talk about It, by W. Edmondson
and J. House (Baltimore: Schwarzenberg, 1981).
Reviewed in: *TESL Canadian Journal* 8, no. 2
(Mar. 1991): 80.

Longman English Grammar, by Louis G.
Alexander (London: Longman, 1988). Reviewed
in: *TESOL Quarterly* 24, no. 2 (Summer 1990):
309–10.

The Sentence Master, software by Dr. Marion
Blank (Winooski, VT: Laureate Learning
Systems, 1990). Reviewed in: *The Computing
Teacher* 18, no. 4 (Dec. 1990/Jan. 1991): 53.

*Grammar Practice Activities, A Practical Guide for
Teachers*
by Penny Ur (Cambridge: Cambridge University
Press, 1986). Reviewed in: *TESL Canada Journal*
8, no. 1 (Nov. 1990): 114–16.

*Grammar with a Purpose: A Contextualized Ap-
proach*
by Myrna Knepler (New York: Macmillan, 1990).
Reviewed in: *Language Learning* 41, no. 1 (Mar.
1991): 148–49.

Hamp-Lyons, Liz
*Newbury House TOEFL Preparation Kit: Prepar-
ing for the Test of Written English,* by Liz Hamp-
Lyons (New York: Harper & Row, 1989).
Reviewed in: *TESOL Quarterly* 24, no. 3 (Fall
1990): 501–6.

Harper & Row
*Newbury House TOEFL Preparation Kit: Prepar-
ing for the Test of Written English,* by Liz Hamp-
Lyons (New York: Harper & Row, 1989).
Reviewed in: *TESOL Quarterly* 24, no. 3 (Fall
1990): 501–6.

*Newbury House TOEFL Preparation Kit; Prepar-
ing for the TOEFL,* by Daniel B. Kennedy, Dorry
Mann Kenyon, and Steven J. Matthiesen (New
York: Harper & Row, 1989). Reviewed in:
TESOL Quarterly 24, no. 3 (Fall 1990): 501–6.

Heald-Taylor, Gail
Whole Language Strategies for ESL Students, by
Gail Heald-Taylor (San Diego: Dormac, 1989).
Reviewed in: *TESOL Quarterly* 24, no. 2 (Sum-
mer 1990): 306–7.

Heinemann
Literacy through Literature, by Terry D. Johnson and Daphne R. Louis (Portsmouth, NH: Heinemann, 1987). Reviewed in: *TESOL Quarterly* 24, no. 4 (Winter 1990): 730–31.

Here To Stay in the USA—ESL/U.S. Studies for Beginners
by Timothy Maciel and John Duffy (Hayward, CA: Alemany, 1990). Reviewed in: *Journal of Reading* 35, no. 6 (Mar. 1992): 504–5.

High school materials
Countdown!: Taking Off into Content Reading, by Alison Rice (New York: Macmillan, 1990). Reviewed in: *Language Learning* 41, no. 3 (Sep. 1991): 458.

English Express, software or film/video (Torrance, CA: Davidson, 1991). Reviewed in: *Electronic Learning* 11, no. 1 (Sep. 1991): 40–63.

English for Science, by Fran Zimmerman (Englewood Cliffs, NJ: Prentice-Hall Regents, 1989). Reviewed in: *TESOL Quarterly* 26, no. 1 (Spring 1992): 160–61.

Comics and Conversation: Using Humor To Elicit Conversation and Develop Vocabulary, by Joan Astikenas. Reviewed in: *TESOL Quarterly* 25, no. 4 (Winter 1991): 727–28.

Grammar Practice Activities, A Practical Guide for Teachers, by Penny Ur (Cambridge: Cambridge University Press, 1986). Reviewed in: *TESL Canada Journal* 8, no. 1 (Nov. 1990): 114–16.

Improving the Grammar of Written English: The Editing Process, by Beverly Benson and Patricia Byrd (Belmont, CA: Wadsworth, 1989). Reviewed in: *TESOL Quarterly* 26, no. 1 (Spring 1992): 161–62.

Improving the Grammar of Written English: The Handbook, by Beverly Benson and Patricia Byrd (Belmont, CA: Wadsworth, 1989). Reviewed in: *TESOL Quarterly* 26, no. 1 (Spring 1992): 161–62.

Interactive Techniques for the ESL Classroom, by Connie L. Shoemaker and F. Floyd Shoemaker (Rowley, MA: Newbury House, 1991). Reviewed in: *Language Learning* 41, no. 4 (Dec. 1991): 635–36.

Longman American Structural Readers: Horizontal Readers, by various authors (New York: Longman). Reviewed in: *TESOL Quarterly* 24, no. 4 (Winter 1990): 733.

Macwrite II Spanish Version, software (Santa Clara, CA: Claris). Reviewed in: *Electronic Learning* 11, no. 3 (Nov./Dec. 1991): 37.

Outsiders: American Short Stories for Students of ESL, by Jean S. Mullen (Englewood Cliffs, NJ: Prentice-Hall, 1984). Reviewed in: *TESOL Quarterly* 24, no. 4 (Winter 1990): 735–36.

When They Don't All Speak English: Integrating the ESL Student in the Regular Classroom, ed. by Virginia G. Allen and Pat Rigg (Urbana, IL: NCTE, 1989). Reviewed in: *The Reading Teacher* 45, no.4 (Dec. 1991): 327.

Write Soon!: A Beginning Text for ESL Writers, by Eileen Prince (New York: Macmillan, 1990). Reviewed in: *Language Learning* 41, no. 3 (Sep. 1991): 455.

Hill, Sam
Bilingual Grammar of English–Spanish Syntax: A Manual with Exercises, by Sam Hill and William Bradford (Lanham, MD: University Press of America, 1991). Reviewed in: *Language Learning* 41, no. 3 (Sep. 1991): 453.

Hofbauer, Cynthia Swanson
Adventures in Conversation: Exercises in Achieving Oral Fluency and Developing Vocabulary in English, by Lynne Hunter and Cynthia Swanson Hofbauer (Prentice-Hall Regents, 1989). Reviewed in: *TESOL Quarterly* 26, no. 1 (Spring 1992): 156–57.

House, J.
Let's Talk and Talk about It, by W. Edmondson and J. House (Baltimore: Schwarzenberg, 1981). Reviewed in: *TESL Canadian Journal* 8, no. 2 (Mar. 1991): 80.

Hunter, Lynne
Adventures in Conversation: Exercises in Achieving Oral Fluency and Developing Vocabulary in English, by Lynne Hunter and Cynthia Swanson Hofbauer (Prentice-Hall Regents, 1989). Reviewed in: *TESOL Quarterly* 26, no. 1 (Spring 1992): 156–57.

Improving the Grammar of Written English: The Editing Process
by Beverly Benson and Patricia Byrd (Belmont, CA: Wadsworth, 1989). Reviewed in: *TESOL Quarterly* 26, no. 1 (Spring 1992): 161–62.

Improving the Grammar of Written English: The Handbook
by Beverly Benson and Patricia Byrd (Belmont, CA: Wadsworth, 1989). Reviewed in: *TESOL Quarterly* 26, no. 1 (Spring 1992): 161–62.

An Indispensable Guide to Dangerous English: For Language Learners and Others
by Elizabeth Claire (Dundee, IL: Delta Systems, 1990). Reviewed in: *TESOL Quarterly* 26, no. 1 (Spring 1992): 158–59.

Interactive Techniques for the ESL Classroom
by Connie L. Shoemaker and F. Floyd Shoemaker (Rowley, MA: Newbury House, 1991). Reviewed in: *Language Learning* 41, no. 4 (Dec. 1991): 635–36.

Intercultural (publisher)
Breaking the Language Barrier: Creating Your Own Pathway to Success, by H. Douglas Brown (Yarmouth, ME: Intercultural, 1991). Reviewed in: *TESOL Quarterly* 26, no. 1 (Spring 1992): 149–52.

Johnson, Terry D.
Literacy through Literature, by Terry D. Johnson and Daphne R. Louis (Portsmouth, NH: Heinemann, 1987). Reviewed in: *TESOL Quarterly* 24, no. 4 (Winter 1990): 730–31.

Keller, Eric
Conversation Gambits: Real English Conversation Practices, by Eric Keller and Sylvia T. Warner (Hove, England: Language Teaching, 1988). Reviewed in: *TESOL Quarterly* 24, no. 3 (Fall 1990): 510–11.

Kennedy, Daniel B.
Newbury House TOEFL Preparation Kit; Preparing for the TOEFL, by Daniel B. Kennedy, Dorry Mann Kenyon, and Steven J. Matthiesen (New York: Harper & Row, 1989). Reviewed in: *TESOL Quarterly* 24, no. 3 (Fall 1990): 501–6.

Kenyon, Dorry Mann
Newbury House TOEFL Preparation Kit; Preparing for the TOEFL, by Daniel B. Kennedy, Dorry Mann Kenyon, and Steven J. Matthiesen (New York: Harper & Row, 1989). Reviewed in: *TESOL Quarterly* 24, no. 3 (Fall 1990): 501–6.

Knepler, Myrna
Grammar with a Purpose: A Contextualized Approach, by Myrna Knepler (New York: Macmillan, 1990). Reviewed in: *Language Learning* 41, no. 1 (Mar. 1991): 148–49.

Language Acquisition
Breaking the Language Barrier: Creating Your Own Pathway to Success, by H. Douglas Brown (Yarmouth, ME: Intercultural, 1991). Reviewed in: *TESOL Quarterly* 26, no. 1 (Spring 1992): 149–52.

Drama Techniques in Language Learning: A Resource Book of Communication Activities for Language Learners, by Alan Maley and Alan Duff (Cambridge: Cambridge University Press, 1982). Reviewed in: *TESL Canada Journal* 8, no. 2 (Mar. 1991): 83–4.

English Express, software or film/video (Torrance, CA: Davidson, 1991). Reviewed in: *Electronic Learning* 11, no. 1 (Sep. 1991): 40–63.

English for Science, by Fran Zimmerman (Englewood Cliffs, NJ: Prentice-Hall Regents, 1989). Reviewed in: *TESOL Quarterly* 26, no. 1 (Spring 1992): 160–61.

Here To Stay in the USA—ESL/U.S. Studies for Beginners, by Timothy Maciel and John Duffy (Hayward, CA: Alemany, 1990). Reviewed in: *Journal of Reading* 35, no. 6 (Mar. 1992): 504–5.

An Indispensable Guide to Dangerous English: For Language Learners and Others, by Elizabeth Claire (Dundee, IL: Delta Systems, 1990). Reviewed in: *TESOL Quarterly* 26, no. 1 (Spring 1992): 158–59.

Interactive Techniques for the ESL Classroom, by Connie L. Shoemaker and F. Floyd Shoemaker (Rowley, MA: Newbury House, 1991). Reviewed in: *Language Learning* 41, no. 4 (Dec. 1991): 635–36.

The Inward Ear: Poetry in the Language Classroom, by Alan Maley and Alan Duff (Cambridge: Cambridge University Press, 1989). Reviewed in: *TESOL Quarterly* 24, no. 4 (Winter 1990): 731–32.

Language Acquisition *(cont'd)*

Language Development through Content: Mathematics Book A, by Anna Uhl Chamot and J. Michael O'Malley (Reading, MA: Addison-Wesley, 1988). Reviewed in: *Arithmetic Teacher* 38, no. 4 (Dec. 1990): 63.

Learning To Learn English: A Course in Learner Training, by Gail Ellis and Barbara Sinclair (Cambridge: Cambridge University Press, 1989). Reviewed in: *TESL Canada Journal* 8, no. 2 (Mar. 1991): 84.

Literacy through Literature, by Terry D. Johnson and Daphne R. Louis (Portsmouth, NH: Heinemann, 1987). Reviewed in: *TESOL Quarterly* 24, no. 4 (Winter 1990): 730–31.

People Are Funny: Pictures for Practice (Book 1), by Donald R.H. Byrd and Stanley J. Zelinski III (New York: Longman, 1987). Reviewed in: *TESOL Quarterly* 25, no. 4 (Winter 1991): 727–28.

Photo Dictionary Beginning Workbook, by Marjorie Fuchs (New York: Longman, 1989). Reviewed in: *TESOL Newsletter* 24, no. 5 (Oct. 1990): 23.

Photo Dictionary Intermediate Workbook, by Marilyn S. Rosenthal, Daniel B. Freeman, and Marjorie Fuchs (New York: Longman, 1989). Reviewed in: *TESOL Newsletter* 24 no. 5 (Oct. 1990): 23.

Photo Dictionary Pronunciation Workbook, audiocassette and supplementary materials (New York: Longman, 1988). Reviewed in: *TESOL Newsletter* 24, no. 5 (Oct. 1990): 23.

The Rainbow Collection, by Martha Alvarez-Martini, Evelyn Marino, Consuelo Valencia Raley, and Tracy David Terrell (Northvale, NJ: Santillana, 1984). Reviewed in: *TESOL Quarterly* 24, no. 5 (Dec. 1990): 17–18.

When They Don't All Speak English: Integrating the ESL Student in the Regular Classroom, ed. by Virginia G. Allen and Pat Rigg (Urbana, IL: NCTE, 1989). Reviewed in: *The Reading Teacher* 45, no. 4 (Dec. 1991): 327.

Whole Language Strategies for ESL Students, by Gail Heald-Taylor (San Diego: Dormac, 1989). Reviewed in: *TESOL Quarterly* 24, no. 2 (Summer 1990): 306–7.

Windows on Science (Spanish Edition), software (Warren, NJ: Optical Data). Reviewed in: *The Computing Teacher* 18, no. 4 (Dec. 1990/Jan. 1991): 53.

Language Development through Content: Mathematics Book A
by Anna Uhl Chamot and J. Michael O'Malley (Reading, MA: Addison-Wesley, 1988). Reviewed in: *Arithmetic Teacher* 38, no. 4 (Dec. 1990): 63.

Language Teaching
Conversation Gambits: Real English Conversation Practices, by Eric Keller and Sylvia T. Warner (Hove, England: Language Teaching, 1988). Reviewed in: *TESOL Quarterly* 24, no. 3 (Fall 1990): 510–11.

Laureate Learning Systems
The Sentence Master, software by Dr. Marion Blank (Winooski, VT: Laureate Learning Systems, 1990). Reviewed in: *The Computing Teacher* 18, no. 4 (Dec. 1990/Jan. 1991): 53.

Learning To Learn English: A Course in Learner Training
by Gail Ellis and Barbara Sinclair (Cambridge: Cambridge University Press, 1989). Reviewed in: *TESL Canada Journal* 8, no. 2 (Mar. 1991): 84.

Let's Talk and Talk about It
by W. Edmondson and J. House (Baltimore: Schwarzenberg, 1981). Reviewed in: *TESL Canadian Journal* 8, no. 2 (Mar. 1991): 80.

Literacy through Literature
by Terry D. Johnson and Daphne R. Louis (Portsmouth, NH: Heinemann, 1987). Reviewed in: *TESOL Quarterly* 24, no. 4 (Winter 1990): 730–31.

Literary Portraits: An Anthology of Modern American Prose and Poetry for Students of English
by J. Donnie Snyder (New York: Macmillan, 1989). Reviewed in: *TESOL Quarterly* 24, no. 4 (Winter 1990): 738–39.

Literature in the Language Classroom: A Resource Book of Ideas and Activities
by Joanne Collie and Stephen Slater (New York: Cambridge University Press, 1987). Reviewed in: *TESOL Quarterly* 24, no. 2 (Summer 1990): 305–6; *TESL Canada Journal* 8, no. 2 (Mar. 1991): 82.

Longman
American Vocabulary Builder 1 & 2, by Bernad Seal (New York: Longman, 1990). Reviewed in: *TESOL Quarterly* 25, no. 4 (Winter 1991): 722–23.

Longman American Structural Readers: Horizontal Readers, by various authors (New York: Longman). Reviewed in: *TESOL Quarterly* 24, no. 4 (Winter 1990): 733.

Longman English Grammar, by Louis G. Alexander (London: Longman, 1988). Reviewed in: *TESOL Quarterly* 24, no. 2 (Summer 1990): 309–10.

Longman Preparation Course for the TOEFL, by Deborah Phillips (New York: Longman, 1989). Reviewed in: *TESOL Quarterly* 24, no. 3 (Fall 1990): 516–17.

People Are Funny: Pictures for Practice (Book 1), by Donald R.H. Byrd and Stanley J. Zelinski III (New York: Longman, 1987). Reviewed in: *TESOL Quarterly* 25, no. 4 (Winter 1991): 727–28.

Photo Dictionary, by Marilyn S. Rosenthal and Daniel B. Freeman (White Plains, New York: Longman, 1987). Reviewed in: *TESOL Newsletter* 24, no. 5 (Oct. 1990): 22–23.

Photo Dictionary Beginning Workbook, by Marjorie Fuchs (New York: Longman, 1989). Reviewed in: *TESOL Newsletter* 24, no. 5 (Oct. 1990): 23.

Photo Dictionary Intermediate Workbook, by Marilyn S. Rosenthal, Daniel B. Freeman, and Marjorie Fuchs (New York: Longman, 1989). Reviewed in: *TESOL Newsletter* 24, no. 5 (Oct. 1990): 23.

Photo Dictionary Pronunciation Workbook, audiocassette and supplementary materials (New York: Longman, 1988). Reviewed in: *TESOL Newsletter* 24, no. 5 (Oct. 1990): 23.

Talk about Values: Conversation Skills for Intermediate Students, by Irene E. Schoenberg (New York: Longman, 1989). Reviewed in: *TESOL Quarterly* 26, no. 1 (Spring 1992): 155–56.

Louis, Daphne R.
Literacy through Literature, by Terry D. Johnson and Daphne R. Louis (Portsmouth, NH: Heinemann, 1987). Reviewed in: *TESOL Quarterly* 24, no. 4 (Winter 1990): 730–31.

Maciel, Timothy
Here To Stay in the USA—ESL/U.S. Studies for Beginners, by Timothy Maciel and John Duffy (Hayward, CA: Alemany, 1990). Reviewed in: *Journal of Reading* 35, no. 6 (Mar. 1992): 504–5.

McKay, Sandra
At the Door: Selected Literature for ESL Students, by Sandra McKay and Dorothy Petitt (Englewood Cliffs, NJ: Prentice-Hall, 1984). Reviewed in: *TESOL Quarterly* 24, no. 4 (Winter 1990): 736–37; *English Journal* 80, no. 8 (Dec. 1991): 26.

Macmillan
Countdown!: Taking off into Content Reading, by Alison Rice (New York: Macmillan, 1990). Reviewed in: *Language Learning* 41, no. 3 (Sep. 1991): 458.

Grammar with a Purpose: A Contextualized Approach, by Myrna Knepler (New York: Macmillan, 1990). Reviewed in: *Language Learning* 41, no. 1 (Mar. 1991): 148–49.

Write Soon!: A Beginning Text for ESL Writers, by Eileen Prince (New York: Macmillan, 1990). Reviewed in: *Language Learning* 41, no. 3 (Sep. 1991): 455.

Macwrite II Spanish Version
software (Santa Clara, CA: Claris). Reviewed in: *Electronic Learning* 11, no. 3 (Nov./Dec. 1991): 37.

Maley, Alan
Drama Techniques in Language Learning: A Resource Book of Communication Activities for Language Learners, by Alan Maley and Alan Duff (Cambridge: Cambridge University Press, 1982). Reviewed in: *TESL Canada Journal* 8, no. 2 (Mar. 1991): 83–84.

The Inward Ear: Poetry in the Language Classroom, by Alan Maley and Alan Duff (Cambridge: Cambridge University Press, 1989). Reviewed in: *TESOL Quarterly* 24, no. 4 (Winter 1990): 731–32.

Marino, Evelyn
The Rainbow Collection, by Martha Alvarez-
Martini, Evelyn Marino, Consuelo Valencia
Raley, and Tracy David Terrell (Northvale, NJ:
Santillana, 1984). Reviewed in: *TESOL Quarterly*
24, no. 5 (Dec. 1990): 17–18.

Matthiesen, Steven J.
*Newbury House TOEFL Preparation Kit; Prepar-
ing for the TOEFL,* by Daniel B. Kennedy, Dorry
Mann Kenyon, and Steven J. Matthiesen (New
York: Harper & Row, 1989). Reviewed in:
TESOL Quarterly 24, no. 3 (Fall 1990): 501–6.

Middle school materials
Countdown!: Taking off into Content Reading, by
Alison Rice (New York: Macmillan, 1990).
Reviewed in: *Language Learning* 41, no. 3 (Sep.
1991): 458.

English Express, software or film/video (Torrance,
CA: Davidson, 1991). Reviewed in: *Electronic
Learning* 11, no. 1 (Sep. 1991): 40–63.

Forestville Tales: International Folk Stories, by
Aaron Berman (New York: Collier Macmillan,
1977). Reviewed in: *TESOL Quarterly* 24, no. 4
(Winter 1990): 734–35.

*Grammar Practice Activities, A Practical Guide for
Teachers,* by Penny Ur (Cambridge: Cambridge
University Press, 1986). Reviewed in: *TESL
Canada Journal* 8, no. 1 (Nov. 1990): 114–16.

Interactive Techniques for the ESL Classroom, by
Connie L. Shoemaker and F. Floyd Shoemaker
(Rowley, MA: Newbury House, 1991). Reviewed
in: *Language Learning* 41, no. 4 (Dec. 1991): 635–
36.

*Language Development through Content: Math-
ematics Book A,* by Anna Uhl Chamot and J.
Michael O'Malley (Reading, MA: Addison-
Wesley, 1988). Reviewed in: *Arithmetic Teacher*
38, no. 4 (Dec. 1990): 63.

Literacy through Literature, by Terry D. Johnson
and Daphne R. Louis (Portsmouth, NH:
Heinemann, 1987). Reviewed in: *TESOL
Quarterly* 24, no. 4 (Winter 1990): 730–31.

Macwrite II Spanish Version, software (Santa
Clara, CA: Claris). Reviewed in: *Electronic
Learning* 11, no. 3 (Nov./Dec. 1991): 37.

The Rainbow Collection, by Martha Alvarez-
Martini, Evelyn Marino, Consuelo Valencia
Raley, and Tracy David Terrell (Northvale, NJ:
Santillana, 1984). Reviewed in: *TESOL Quarterly*
24, no. 5 (Dec. 1990): 17–18.

Read, Write and Publish, software (Acton, MA:
D. C. Heath). Reviewed in: *Electronic Learning*
11, no. 1 (Sep. 1991): 42.

The Sentence Master, software by Dr. Marion
Blank (Winooski, VT: Laureate Learning
Systems, 1990). Reviewed in: *The Computing
Teacher* 18, no. 4 (Dec. 1990/Jan. 1991): 53.

Windows on Science (Spanish Edition), software
(Warren, NJ: Optical Data). Reviewed in: *The
Computing Teacher* 18, no. 4 (Dec. 1990/Jan.
1991): 53.

Write Soon!: A Beginning Text for ESL Writers, by
Eileen Prince (New York: Macmillan, 1990).
Reviewed in: *Language Learning* 41, no. 3 (Sep.
1991): 455.

Mullen, Jean S.
*Outsiders: American Short Stories for Students of
ESL,* by Jean S. Mullen (Englewood Cliffs, NJ:
Prentice-Hall, 1984). Reviewed in: *TESOL
Quarterly* 24, no. 4 (Winter 1990): 735–36.

National Council of Teachers of English (publisher)
*When They Don't All Speak English: Integrating
the ESL Student in the Regular Classroom,* ed. by
Virginia G. Allen and Pat Rigg (Urbana, IL:
NCTE, 1989). Reviewed in: *The Reading Teacher*
45, no. 4 (Dec. 1991): 327.

Newbury House (publisher)
Interactive Techniques for the ESL Classroom, by
Connie L. Shoemaker and F. Floyd Shoemaker
(Rowley, MA: Newbury House, 1991). Reviewed
in: *Language Learning* 41, no. 4 (Dec. 1991): 635–
36.

O'Malley, J. Michael
*Language Development through Content: Math-
ematics Book A,* by Anna Uhl Chamot and J.
Michael O'Malley (Reading, MA: Addison-
Wesley, 1988). Reviewed in: *Arithmetic Teacher*
38, no. 4 (Dec. 1990): 63.

Outsiders: American Short Stories for Students of ESL
by Jean S. Mullen (Englewood Cliffs, NJ:
Prentice-Hall, 1984). Reviewed in: *TESOL
Quarterly* 24, no. 4 (Winter 1990): 735–36.

People Are Funny: Pictures for Practice (Book 1)
by Donald R.H. Byrd and Stanley J. Zelinski III
(New York: Longman, 1987). Reviewed in:
TESOL Quarterly 25, no. 4 (Winter 1991): 727–28.

Petitt, Dorothy
At the Door: Selected Literature for ESL Students,
by Sandra McKay and Dorothy Petitt
(Englewood Cliffs, NJ: Prentice-Hall, 1984).
Reviewed in: *TESOL Quarterly* 24, no. 4 (Winter
1990): 736–37; *English Journal* 80, no. 8 (Dec.
1991): 26.

Phillips, Deborah
Longman Preparation Course for the TOEFL, by
Deborah Phillips (New York: Longman, 1989).
Reviewed in: *TESOL Quarterly* 24, no. 3 (Fall
1990): 516–17.

Photo Dictionary
by Marilyn S. Rosenthal and Daniel B. Freeman
(White Plains, NY: Longman, 1987). Reviewed
in: *TESOL Newsletter* 24, no. 5 (Oct. 1990): 22–
23.

Photo Dictionary Beginning Workbook
by Marjorie Fuchs (New York: Longman, 1989).
Reviewed in: *TESOL Newsletter* 24, no. 5 (Oct.
1990): 23.

Photo Dictionary Intermediate Workbook
by Marilyn S. Rosenthal, Daniel B. Freeman,
and Marjorie Fuchs (New York: Longman,
1989). Reviewed in: *TESOL Newsletter* 24, no. 5
(Oct. 1990): 23.

Photo Dictionary Pronunciation Workbook
audiocassette and supplementary materials (New
York: Longman, 1988). Reviewed in: *TESOL
Newsletter* 24, no. 5 (Oct. 1990): 23.

Prentice-Hall
Academic Challenges in Reading, by Helen Taylor
Abdulaziz and Alfred D. Storer (Englewood
Cliffs, NJ: Prentice-Hall, 1989). Reviewed in:
TESOL Newsletter 24, no. 4 (Aug. 1990): 25–27.

At the Door: Selected Literature for ESL Students,
by Sandra McKay and Dorothy Petitt

(Englewood Cliffs, NJ: Prentice-Hall, 1984).
Reviewed in: *TESOL Quarterly* 24, no. 4 (Winter
1990): 736–37; *English Journal* 80, no. 8 (Dec.
1991): 26.

*Outsiders: American Short Stories for Students of
ESL*, by Jean S. Mullen (Englewood Cliffs, NJ:
Prentice-Hall, 1984). Reviewed in: *TESOL
Quarterly* 24, no. 4 (Winter 1990): 735–36.

Prentice-Hall Regents
*Adventures in Conversation: Exercises in Achieving
Oral Fluency and Developing Vocabulary in
English*, by Lynne Hunter and Cynthia Swanson
Hofbauer (Prentice-Hall Regents, 1989).
Reviewed in: *TESOL Quarterly* 26, no. 1 (Spring
1992): 156–57.

English for Science, by Fran Zimmerman
(Englewood Cliffs, NJ: Prentice-Hall Regents,
1989). Reviewed in: *TESOL Quarterly* 26, no. 1
(Spring 1992): 160–161.

Prince, Eileen
Write Soon!: A Beginning Text for ESL Writers, by
Eileen Prince (New York: Macmillan, 1990).
Reviewed in: *Language Learning* 41, no. 3 (Sep.
1991): 455.

Pronunciation
Clear Speech, by Judy Gilbert (Cambridge:
Cambridge University Press, 1984). Reviewed in:
TESL Canada Journal 8, no. 2 (Mar. 1991): 94.

Rahmer, Harriet
Family Pictures, by Carmen Lomas Garza,
Harriet Rahmer, and Rosalma Znbizarreta
(Emeryville, CA: Children's Book Press, 1990).
Reviewed in: *Language Arts* 68, no. 4 (Apr.
1991): 324–25.

The Rainbow Collection
by Martha Alvarez-Martini, Evelyn Marino,
Consuelo Valencia Raley, and Tracy David
Terrell (Northvale, NJ: Santillana, 1984).
Reviewed in: *TESOL Quarterly* 24, no. 5 (Dec.
1990): 17–18.

Raley, Consuelo Valencia
The Rainbow Collection, by Martha Alvarez-
Martini, Evelyn Marino, Consuelo Valencia
Raley, and Tracy David Terrell (Northvale, NJ:
Santillana, 1984). Reviewed in: *TESOL Quarterly*
24, no. 5 (Dec. 1990): 17–18.

Schwarzenberg (publisher)
> *Let's Talk and Talk about It*, by W. Edmondson and J. House (Baltimore: Schwarzenberg, 1981). Reviewed in: *TESL Canadian Journal* 8, no. 2 (Mar. 1991): 80.

Science
> *Windows on Science (Spanish Edition)*, software (Warren, NJ: Optical Data). Reviewed in: *The Computing Teacher* 18, no. 4 (Dec. 1990/Jan. 1991): 53.

Seal, Bernad
> *American Vocabulary Builder 1 & 2*, by Bernad Seal (New York: Longman, 1990). Reviewed in: *TESOL Quarterly* 25, no. 4 (Winter 1991): 722–23.

The Sentence Master
> software by Dr. Marion Blank (Winooski, VT: Laureate Learning Systems, 1990). Reviewed in: *The Computing Teacher* 18, no. 4 (Dec. 1990/Jan. 1991): 53.

Shoemaker, Connie L. and F. Floyd
> *Interactive Techniques for the ESL Classroom*, by Connie L. Shoemaker and F. Floyd Shoemaker (Rowley, MA: Newbury House, 1991). Reviewed in: *Language Learning* 41, no. 4 (Dec. 1991): 635–36.

Sinclair, Barbara
> *Learning To Learn English: A Course in Learner Training*, by Gail Ellis and Barbara Sinclair (Cambridge: Cambridge University Press, 1989). Reviewed in: *TESL Canada Journal* 8, no. 2 (Mar. 1991): 84.

Slater, Stephen
> *Literature in the Language Classroom: A Resource Book of Ideas and Activities*, by Joanne Collie and Stephen Slater (New York: Cambridge University Press, 1987). Reviewed in: *TESOL Quarterly* 24, no. 2 (Summer 1990): 305–6; *TESL Canada Journal* 8, no. 2 (Mar. 1991): 82.

Snyder, J. Donnie
> *Literary Portraits: An Anthology of Modern American Prose and Poetry for Students of English*, by J. Donnie Snyder (New York: Macmillan, 1989). Reviewed in: *TESOL Quarterly* 24, no. 4 (Winter 1990): 738–39.

Sobel, Betty
> *Words at Work: Vocabulary Building through Reading*, by Betty Sobel and Susan Bookman (New York: Collier Macmillan, 1989). Reviewed in: *TESOL Quarterly* 24, no. 3 (Fall 1990): 512–14.

Software packages
> *English Express*, software or film/video (Torrance, CA: Davidson, 1991). Reviewed in: *Electronic Learning* 11, no. 1 (Sep. 1991): 40–63.

> *Macwrite II Spanish Version*, software (Santa Clara, CA: Claris). Reviewed in: *Electronic Learning* 11, no. 3 (Nov./Dec. 1991): 37.

> *Read, Write and Publish*, software (Acton, MA: D. C. Heath). Reviewed in: *Electronic Learning* 11, no. 1 (Sep. 1991): 42.

> *The Sentence Master*, software by Dr. Marion Blank (Winooski, VT: Laureate Learning Systems, 1990). Reviewed in: *The Computing Teacher* 18, no. 4 (Dec. 1990/Jan. 1991): 53.

> *Talk to Me*, software (Freeport, NY: Educational Activities, 1990). Reviewed in: *The Computing Teacher* 18, no. 4 (Dec. 1990/Jan. 1991): 44–46.

> *Windows on Science (Spanish Edition)*, software (Warren, NJ: Optical Data). Reviewed in: *The Computing Teacher* 18, no. 4 (Dec. 1990/Jan. 1991): 53.

Speech
> *Talk to Me*, software (Freeport, NY: Educational Activities, 1990). Reviewed in: *The Computing Teacher* 18, no. 4 (Dec. 1990/Jan. 1991): 44–46.

Storer, Alfred D.
> *Academic Challenges in Reading*, by Helen Taylor Abdulaziz and Alfred D. Storer (Englewood Cliffs, NJ: Prentice-Hall, 1989). Reviewed in: *TESOL Newsletter* 24, no. 4 (Aug. 1990): 25–27.

Talk about Values: Conversation Skills for Intermediate Students
> by Irene E. Schoenberg (New York: Longman, 1989). Reviewed in: *TESOL Quarterly* 26, no. 1 (Spring 1992): 155–56.

Weinstein, Nina
Crazy Idioms: A Conversational Idiom Book, by Nina Weinstein (New York: Collier Macmillan, 1990). Reviewed in: *TESOL Quarterly* 24, no. 3 (Fall 1990): 511–12.

When They Don't All Speak English: Integrating the ESL Student in the Regular Classroom
ed. by Virginia G. Allen and Pat Rigg (Urbana, IL: NCTE, 1989). Reviewed in: *The Reading Teacher* 45, no. 4 (Dec. 1991): 327.

Whole Language Strategies for ESL Students
by Gail Heald-Taylor (San Diego: Dormac, 1989). Reviewed in: *TESOL Quarterly* 24, no. 2 (Summer 1990): 306–7.

Windows on Science (Spanish Edition)
software (Warren, NJ: Optical Data). Reviewed in: *The Computing Teacher* 18, no. 4 (Dec. 1990/ Jan. 1991): 53.

Winthrow, Jean
Changes: Readings for ESL Writers, by Jean Winthrow, Gay Brookes, and Martha Clark Cummings (New York: St. Martin's Press, 1990). Reviewed in: *TESOL Quarterly* 24, no. 4 (Winter 1990): 737–38.

Word processing
Macwrite II Spanish Version, software (Santa Clara, CA: Claris). Reviewed in: *Electronic Learning* 11, no. 3 (Nov./Dec. 1991): 37.

Words at Work: Vocabulary Building through Reading
by Betty Sobel and Susan Bookman (New York: Collier Macmillan, 1989). Reviewed in: *TESOL Quarterly* 24, no. 3 (Fall 1990): 512–14.

Words for Students of English: A Vocabulary Series for ESL, Vols. 1–8
by H. D. Rogerson (Pittsburgh: University of Pittsburgh Press, 1988–1990). Reviewed in: *TESOL Quarterly* 25, no. 4 (Winter 1991): 725.

Write Soon!: A Beginning Text for ESL Writers
by Eileen Prince (New York: Macmillan, 1990). Reviewed in: *Language Learning* 41, no. 3 (Sep. 1991): 455.

Writing
Changes: Readings for ESL Writers, by Jean Winthrow, Gay Brookes, and Martha Clark Cummings (New York: St. Martin's Press, 1990). Reviewed in: *TESOL Quarterly* 24, no. 4 (Winter 1990): 737–38.

Improving the Grammar of Written English: The Editing Process, by Beverly Benson and Patricia Byrd (Belmont, CA: Wadsworth, 1989). Reviewed in: *TESOL Quarterly* 26, no. 1 (Spring 1992): 161–62.

Literature in the Language Classroom: A Resource Book of Ideas and Activities, by Joanne Collie and Stephen Slater (New York: Cambridge University Press, 1987). Reviewed in: *TESOL Quarterly* 24, no. 2 (Summer 1990): 305–6; *TESL Canada Journal* 8, no. 2 (Mar. 1991): 82.

Read, Write and Publish, software (Acton, MA: D. C. Heath). Reviewed in: *Electronic Learning* 11, no. 1 (Sep. 1991): 42.

Write Soon!: A Beginning Text for ESL Writers, by Eileen Prince (New York: Macmillan, 1990). Reviewed in: *Language Learning* 41, no. 3 (Sep. 1991): 455.

Zelinski, Stanley J., III
People Are Funny: Pictures for Practice (Book 1), by Donald R.H. Byrd and Stanley J. Zelinski III (New York: Longman, 1987). Reviewed in: *TESOL Quarterly* 25, no. 4 (Winter 1991): 727–28.

Zimmerman, Fran
English for Science, by Fran Zimmerman (Englewood Cliffs, NJ: Prentice-Hall Regents, 1989). Reviewed in: *TESOL Quarterly* 26, no. 1 (Spring 1992): 160–61.

Znbizarreta, Rosalma
Family Pictures, by Carmen Lomas Garza, Harriet Rahmer, and Rosalma Znbizarreta (Emeryville, CA: Children's Book Press, 1990). Reviewed in: *Language Arts* 68, no. 4 (Apr. 1991): 324–25.

KRAUS CURRICULUM DEVELOPMENT LIBRARY CUSTOMERS

THE following list shows the current subscribers to the Kraus Curriculum Development Library (KCDL), Kraus's annual program of curriculum guides on microfiche. Customers marked with an asterisk (*) do not currently have standing orders to KCDL, but do have recent editions of the program. This information is provided for readers who want to use KCDL for models of curriculum in particular subject areas or grade levels.

Alabama

Auburn University
Ralph Brown Draughton Library/Serials
Mell Street
Auburn University, AL 36849

Jacksonville State University
Houston Cole Library/Serials
Jacksonville, AL 36265

University of Alabama at Birmingham
Mervyn H. Sterne Library
University Station
Birmingham, AL 35294

*University of Alabama at Tuscaloosa
University Libraries
204 Capstone Drive
Tuscaloosa, AL 35487-0266

Alaska

*University of Alaska—Anchorage
Library
3211 Providence Drive
Anchorage, AK 99508

Arizona

Arizona State University, Phoenix
Fletcher Library/Journals
West Campus
4701 West Thunderbird Road
Phoenix, AZ 85069-7100

Arizona State University, Tempe
Library/Serials
Tempe, AZ 85287-0106

Northern Arizona University
University Library
Flagstaff, AZ 86011

University of Arizona
Library/Serials
Tuson, AZ 85721

Arkansas

Arkansas State University
Dean B. Ellis Library
State University, AR 72467

Southern Arkansas University
The Curriculum Center
SAU Box 1389
Magnolia, AR 71753

*University of Arkansas at Monticello
Library
Highway 425 South
Monticello, AR 71656

University of Central Arkansas
The Center for Teaching & Human Development
Box H, Room 104
Conway, AR 72032

California

California Polytechnic State University
Library/Serials
San Luis Obispo, CA 93407

California State Polytechnic University
Library/Serials
3801 West Temple Avenue
Pomona, CA 91768

California State University at Chico
Meriam Library
Chico, CA 95929-0295

*California State University, Dominguez Hills
Library
800 East Victoria Street
Carson, CA 90747

California State University at Fresno
Henry Madden Library/Curriculum Department
Fresno, CA 93740

California State University at Fresno
College of the Sequoia Center
5241 North Maple, Mail Stop 106
Fresno, CA 93740

California State University at Fullerton
Library Serials BIC
Fullerton, CA 92634

California State University at Long Beach
Library/Serials Department
1250 Bellflower Boulevard
Long Beach, CA 90840

*California State University at Sacramento
Library
2000 Jed Smith Drive
Sacramento, CA 95819

California State University, Stanislaus
Library
801 West Monte Vista Avenue
Turlock, CA 95380

*La Sierra University
Library
Riverside, CA 92515

Los Angeles County Education Center
Professional Reference Center
9300 East Imperial Highway
Downey, CA 90242

National University
Library
4007 Camino del Rio South
San Diego, CA 92108

San Diego County Office of Education
Research and Reference Center
6401 Linda Vista Road
San Diego, CA 92111-7399

San Diego State University
Library/Serials
San Diego, CA 92182-0511

*San Francisco State University
J. Paul Leonard Library
1630 Holloway Avenue
San Francisco, CA 94132

San Jose State University
Clark Library, Media Department
San Jose, CA 95192-0028

*Stanford University
Cubberly Library
School of Education
Stanford, CA 94305

*University of California at Santa Cruz
Library
Santa Cruz, CA 95064

Colorado

Adams State College
Library
Alamosa, CO 81102

University of Northern Colorado
Michener Library
Greeley, CO 80639

Connecticut

*Central Connecticut State University
Burritt Library
1615 Stanley Street
New Britain, CT 06050

District of Columbia

The American University
Library
Washington, DC 20016-8046

*United States Department of Education/OERI
Room 101
555 New Jersey Avenue, N.W., C.P.
Washington, DC 20202-5731

*University of the District of Columbia
Learning Resource Center
11100 Harvard Street, N.W.
Washington, DC 20009

Florida

*Florida Atlantic University
Library/Serials
Boca Raton, FL 33431-0992

Florida International University
Library/Serials
Bay Vista Campus
North Miami, FL 33181

Florida International University
Library/Serials
University Park
Miami, FL 33199

Marion County School Board
Professional Library
406 S.E. Alvarez Avenue
Ocala, FL 32671-2285

*University of Central Florida
Library
Orlando, FL 32816-0666

University of Florida
Smathers Library/Serials
Gainesville, FL 32611-2047

*University of North Florida
Library
4567 St. Johns Bluff Road South
Jacksonville, FL 32216

*University of South Florida
Library/University Media Center
4202 Fowler Avenue
Tampa, FL 33620

University of West Florida
John C. Pace Library/Serials
11000 University Parkway
Pensacola, FL 32514

Georgia

*Albany State College
Margaret Rood Hazard Library
Albany, GA 31705

Atlanta University Center in Georgia
Robert W. Woodruff Library
111 James P. Brawley Drive
Atlanta, GA 30314

*Columbus College
Library
Algonquin Drive
Columbus, GA 31993

Kennesaw College
TRAC
3455 Frey Drive
Kennesaw, GA 30144

University of Georgia
Main Library
Athens, GA 30602

Guam

*University of Guam
Curriculum Resources Center
College of Education
UOG Station
Mangilao, GU 96923

Idaho

*Boise State University
Curriculum Resource Center
1910 University Drive
Boise, ID 83725

Illinois

Community Consolidated School District 15
Educational Service Center
505 South Quentin Road
Palatine, IL 60067

Illinois State University
Milner Library/Periodicals
Normal, IL 61761

Loyola University
Instructional Materials Library
Lewis Towers Library
820 North Michigan Avenue
Chicago, Illinois 60611

National–Louis University
Library/Technical Services
2840 North Sheridan Road
Evanston, IL 60201

Northeastern Illinois University
Library/Serials
5500 North St. Louis Avenue
Chicago, IL 60625

*Northern Illinois University
Founders Memorial Library
DeKalb, IL 60115

Southern Illinois University
Lovejoy Library/Periodicals
Edwardsville, IL 62026

*University of Illinois at Chicago
Library/Serials
Box 8198
Chicago, IL 60680

University of Illinois at Urbana—Champaign
246 Library
1408 West Gregory Drive
Urbana, IL 61801

Indiana

Indiana State University
Cunningham Memorial Library
Terre Haute, IN 47809

Indiana University
Library/Serials
Bloomington, IN 47405-1801

Kentucky

Cumberland College
Instructional Media Library
Williamsburg, KY 40769

*Jefferson County Public Schools
The Greens Professional Development Academy
4425 Preston Highway
Louisville, KY 40213

Maine

University of Maine
Raymond H. Fogler Library/Serials
Orono, ME 04469

Maryland

*Bowie State University
Library
Jericho Park Road
Bowie, MD 20715

*University of Maryland
Curriculum Laboratory
Building 143, Room 0307
College Park, MD 20742

Western Maryland College
Hoover Library
2 College Hill
Westminster, MD 21157

Massachusetts

*Barnstable Public Schools
230 South Street
Hyannis, MA 02601

Boston College
Educational Resource Center
Campion Hall G13
Chestnut Hill, MA 02167

Bridgewater State College
Library
3 Shaw Road
Bridgewater, MA 02325

Framingham State College
Curriculum Library
Henry Whittemore Library
Box 2000
Framingham, MA 01701

Harvard University
School of Education
Monroe C. Gutman Library
6 Appian Way
Cambridge, MA 02138

*Lesley College
Library
30 Mellen Street
Cambridge, MA 02138

*Salem State College
Professional Studies Resource Center
Library
Lafayette Street
Salem, MA 01970

Tufts University
Wessell Library
Medford, MA 02155-5816

*University of Lowell
OLeary Library
Wilder Street
Lowell, MA 01854

*Worcester State College
Learning Resource Center
486 Chandler Street
Worcester, MA 01602

Michigan

*Grand Valley State University
Library
Allendale, MI 49401

*Wayne County Regional Educational Services
Agency
Technical Services
5454 Venoy
Wayne, MI 48184

Wayne State University
Purdy Library
Detroit, MI 48202

*Western Michigan University
Dwight B. Waldo Library
Kalamazoo, MI 49008

Minnesota

Mankato State University
Memorial Library
Educational Resource Center
Mankato, MN 56002-8400

Moorhead State University
Library
Moorhead, MN 56563

University of Minnesota
170 Wilson Library/Serials
309 19th Avenue South
Minneapolis, MN 55455

Winona State University
Maxwell Library/Curriculum Laboratory
Sanborn and Johnson Streets
Winona, MN 55987

Mississippi

Mississippi State University
Mitchell Memorial Library
Mississippi State, MS 39762

University of Southern Mississippi
Cook Memorial Library/Serials
Box 5053
Hattiesburg, MS 39406-5053

Missouri

Central Missouri State University
Ward Edwards Library
Warrensburg, MO 64093-5020

Missouri Southern State College
George A. Spiva Library
3950 Newman Road
Joplin, MO 64801-1595

Northeast Missouri State University
Pickler Library/Serials
Kirksville, MO 63501

Southwest Baptist University
ESTEP Library
Bolivar, MO 65613-2496

Southwest Missouri State University
#175 Library
Springfield, MO 65804-0095

*University of Missouri at Kansas City
Instructional Materials Center
School of Education
5100 Rockhill Road
Kansas City, MO 64110-2499

University of Missouri at St. Louis
Library
St. Louis, MO 63121

Webster University
Library
470 East Lockwood Avenue
St. Louis, MO 63119-3194

Nebraska

Chadron State College
Library
10th and Main Streets
Chadron, NE 69337

University of Nebraska
University Libraries
Lincoln, NE 68588

University of Nebraska at Kearney
Calvin T. Ryan Library/Serials
Kearney, NE 68849-0700

*University of Nebraska at Omaha
Education Technology Center/Instructional
 Material
Kayser Hall, Room 522
Omaha, NE 68182-0169

Nevada

*University of Nevada, Las Vegas
Materials Center—101 Education
Las Vegas, NV 89154

*University of Nevada, Reno
Library (322)
Reno, NV 89557-0044

New Hampshire

Plymouth State College
Herbert H. Lamson Library
Plymouth, NH 03264

New Jersey

Caldwell College
Library
9 Ryerson Avenue
Caldwell, NJ 07006

Georgian Court College
Farley Memorial Library
Lakewood, NJ 08701

Jersey City State College
Forrest A. Irwin Library
2039 Kennedy Boulevard
Jersey City, NJ 07305

*Kean College of New Jersey
Library
Union, NJ 07083

Paterson Board of Education
Media Center
823 East 28th Street
Paterson, NJ 07513

*Rutgers University
Alexander Library/Serials
New Brunswick, NJ 08903

St. Peters College
George F. Johnson Library
Kennedy Boulevard
Jersey City, NJ 07306

Trenton State College
West Library
Pennington Road CN4700
Trenton, NJ 08650-4700

William Paterson College
Library
300 Pompton Road
Wayne, NJ 07470

New Mexico

University of New Mexico
General Library/Serials
Albuquerque, NM 87131

New York

*BOCES—REPIC
Carle Place Center Concourse
234 Glen Cove Road
Carle Place, NY 11514

*Canisius College
Curriculum Materials Center
Library
2001 Main Street
Buffalo, NY 14208

Fordham University
Duane Library
Bronx, NY 10458

Hofstra University
Library
1000 Hempstead Turnpike
Hempstead, NY 11550

*Hunter College
Library
695 Park Avenue
New York, NY 10021

*Lehman College
Library/Serials
Bedford Park Boulevard West
Bronx, NY 10468

*New York University
Bobst Library
70 Washington Square South
New York, NY 10012

*Niagara University
Library/Serials
Niagara, NY 14109

Queens College
Benjamin Rosenthal Library
Flushing, NY 11367

St. Johns University
Library
Grand Central and Utopia Parkways
Jamaica, NY 11439

State University of New York at Albany
University Library/Serials
1400 Washington Avenue
Alany, NY 12222

State University of New York College at Buffalo
E. H. Butler Library
1300 Elmwood Avenue
Buffalo, NY 14222

State University of New York College at Cortland
Teaching Materials Center
Cortland, NY 13045

State University of New York College at Oneonta
James M. Milne Library
Oneonta, NY 13820

Teachers College of Columbia University
Milbank Memorial Library/Serials
525 West 120th Street
New York, NY 10027

North Carolina

*Appalachian State University
Instructional Materials Center
Belk Library
Boone, NC 28608

Charlotte–Mecklenburg Schools
Curriculum Resource Center
Staff Development Center
428 West Boulevard
Charlotte, NC 28203

*East Carolina University
Joyner Library
Greenville, NC 27858-4353

North Carolina A&T State University
F. D. Bluford Library
Greeensboro, NC 27411

North Carolina State University
D. H. Hill Library
Box 7111
Raleigh, NC 27695-7111

University of North Carolina at Chapel Hill
Davis Library/Serials
Campus Box 3938
Chapel Hill, NC 27599-3938

University of North Carolina at Charlotte
Atkins Library
UNCC Station
Charlotte, NC 28223

University of North Carolina at Wilmington
William M. Randall Library
601 South College Road
Wilmington, NC 28403-3297

*Western Carolina University
Hunter Library/Acquisitions
Cullowhee, NC 28723

Ohio

Bowling Green State University
Curriculum Center
Jerome Library
Bowling Green, OH 43403-0177

Miami University
Library
Oxford, OH 45056

*Ohio State University
2009 Millikin Road
Columbus, OH 43210

University of Akron
Bierce Library/Serials
Akron, OH 44325

*University of Rio Grande
Davis Library
Rio Grande, OH 45674

*Wright State University
Educational Resource Center
Dayton, OH 45435

Oklahoma

Southwestern Oklahoma State University
Al Harris Library
809 North Custer Street
Weatherford, OK 73096

*University of Tulsa
McFarlin Library
600 South College
Tulsa, OK 74104

Oregon

Oregon State University
Kerr Library/Serials
Corvallis, OR 97331-4503

Portland State University
Library/Serials
Portland, OR 97207

University of Oregon
Knight Library/Serials
Eugene, OR 97403

Pennsylvania

*Bucks County Intermediate Unit #22
705 Shady Retreat Road
Doylestown, PA 18901

*Cheyney University
Library
Cheyney, PA 19319

East Stroudsburg University of Pennsylvania
Library
East Stroudsburg, PA 18301

Holy Family College
Grant and Frankford Avenues
Philadelphia, PA 19114

*Indiana University of Pennsylvania
Media Resource Department
Stapleton Library
Indiana, PA 15705

Kutztown University
Curriculum Materials Center
Rohrbach Library
Kutztown, PA 19530

La Salle College
Instructional Materials Center
The Connelly Library
Olney Avenue at 20th Street
Philadelphia, PA 19141

Lock Haven University of Pennsylvania
Library
Lock Haven, PA 17745

*Millersville University
Ganser Library
Millersville, PA 17551-0302

*Pennsylvania State University
Pattee Library/Serials
University Park, PA 16802

*Shippensburg University of Pennsylvania
Ezra Lehman Library
Shippensburg, PA 17257-2299

*Slippery Rock University
Bailey Library
Instructional Materials Center
Slippery Rock, PA 16057

University of Pittsburgh
Hillman Library/Serials
Pittsburgh, PA 15260

West Chester University
Francis H. Green Library
West Chester, PA 19383

Rhode Island

Rhode Island College
Curriculum Resources Center
600 Mt. Pleasant Avenue
Providence, RI 02908

South Dakota

Northern State University
Williams Library
Aberdeen, SD 57401

University of South Dakota
I. D. Weeks Library
414 East Clark
Vermillion, SD 57069

Tennessee

Tennessee Technological University
Library
Cookeville, TN 38505

Trevecca Nazarene College
Curriculum Library
Mackey Library
33 Murfreesboro Road
Nashville, TN 37210-2877

*University of Tennessee at Chattanooga
Library/Serials
Chattanooga, TN 37403

*University of Tennessee at Martin
Instructional Improvement
Gooch HallRoom 217
Martin, TN 38238

*Vanderbilt University
Curriculum Laboratory
Peabody Library
Peabody Campus, Magnolia Circle
Nashville, TN 37203-5601

Texas

Baylor University
School of Education
Waco, TX 76798-7314

East Texas State University
Curriculum Library
Commerce, TX 75429

*East Texas State University
Library
Texarkana, TX 75501

*Houston Baptist University
Moody Library
7502 Fondren Road
Houston, TX 77074

*Incarnate Word College
Library
4301 Broadway
San Antonio, TX 78209

*Sam Houston State University
Library
Huntsville, TX 77341

*Southern Methodist University
Fondren Library
Dallas, TX 75275-0135

Stephen F. Austin State University
Library/Serials
Box 13055 SFA Station
Nacogdoches, TX 75962

Texas A&M University
Library/Serials
College Station, TX 77843-5000

*Texas Tech University
Library
Lubbock, TX 79409

Texas Womans University
Library
Box 23715 TWU Station
Denton, TX 76204

University of Houston—University Park
University of Houston Library
Central Serial
4800 Calhoun
Houston, TX 77004

University of North Texas
Library
Denton, TX 76203

*University of Texas at Arlington
Library
702 College Street
Arlington, TX 76019-0497

University of Texas at Austin
General Libraries/Serials
Austin, TX 78713-7330

University of Texas at El Paso
Library
El Paso, TX 79968-0582

*University of Texas—Pan American
School of Education
1201 West University Drive
Edinburg, TX 78539

Utah

Utah State University
Educational Resources Center
College of Education
Logan, UT 84322-2845

Vermont

University of Vermont
Guy W. Bailey Library/Serials
Burlington, VT 05405

Virginia

Longwood College
Dabney Lancaster Library
Farmville, VA 23909-1897

*Regent University
Library
Virginia Beach, VA 23464-9877

University of Virginia
Alderman Library
Serials/Periodicals
Charlottesville, VA 22901

*Virginia Beach Public Schools
Instruction and Curriculum
School Administration Building
2512 George Mason Drive
Virginia Beach, VA 23456

Washington

Central Washington University
Library/Serials
Ellensburg, WA 98926

University of Puget Sound
Collins Library
Tacoma, WA 98416

University of Washington
Library/Serials
Seattle, WA 98195

Washington State University
Library
Pullman, WA 99164-5610

Western Washington University
Wilson Library
Bellingham, WA 98225

Wisconsin

University of Wisconsin—Eau Claire
Instructional Media Center
Eau Claire, WI 54702-4004

University of Wisconsin—Madison
Instructional Materials Center
225 North Mills
Madison, Wisconsin 53706

University of Wisconsin—Oshkosh
F. R. Polk Library
Oshkosh, WI 54901

University of Wisconsin—Platteville
Library
One University Plaza
Platteville, WI 53818-3099

University of Wisconsin—Whitewater
Learning Resources
Whitewater, WI 53190

Wyoming

*University of Wyoming
Coe Library
15th and Lewis
Laramie, WY 82071

AUSTRALIA

Griffith University
Library
Mount Gravatt Campus
Nathan, Queensland 4111

CANADA

The Ontario Institute for Studies in Education
Library
252 Bloor Street West
Toronto, Ontario M5S 1V6

Queens University
Education Library
McArthur Hall
Kingston, Ontario K7L 3H6

*University of New Brunswick
Harriet Irving Library/Serials
Fredericton, New Brunswick E3B 5H5

University of Regina
Library/Serials
Regina, Saskatchewan S4S 0A2

University of Saskatchewan
Library
Saskatoon, Saskatchewan S7N 0W0

University of Windsor
Leddy Library/Serials
Windsor, Ontario N9B 3P4

*Vancouver School Board
Teachers Professional Library
123 East 6th Avenue
Vancouver, British Columbia V5T 1J6

HONG KONG

*The Chinese University of Hong Kong
University Library
Shatin, N.T.

KOREA

*Kyungpook National University
Department of Education
Taegu 702-701, Korea

THE NETHERLANDS

National Institute for Curriculum Development
(Stichting voor de Leerplanontwikkeling)
7500 CA Enschede

APPENDIX:
CURRICULUM GUIDE REPRINT

CURRICULUM developers can often find ideas and models by studying curriculum guides from state departments of education and school districts. In this chapter, we have reprinted the following material:

Content Area Instructional Strategies for Students of Limited English Proficiency in Secondary Schools: A Sheltered Approach. 1991. Honolulu: Hawaii State Department of Education.

The guide is reprinted in its entirety except for pages 69–78 and 115–24, which contain material copyrighted by authors or publishers other than the Hawaii State Department of Education but which can be obtained by contacting Hawaii.

Part I discusses the theoretical underpinnings of the sheltered approach and goes on to enumerate teacher and student behaviors connected with this approach. Part II focuses on the critical elements involved in the sheltered appraoch and discusses at length teaching methodology and strategies. This section ends with ideas for integrating language and academic skills. Part II presents lesson preparation and classroom management for sheltered instruction and includes sample lessons in social studies, science, mathematics, and literature. Appendixes 1–4, which conclude the guide, consist of record-keeping examples for teachers, coaching guidelines, and examples of webbing.

Readers of this *Handbook* may notice that Hawaii was not included in chapter 5, *State Curriculum Guidelines: An Analysis.* Hawaii's guide, here reprinted, was received too late for inclusion. We apologize for any inconvenience, but hope readers will appreciate its reprinting.

To obtain a complete copy of this guide, contact the Hawaii State Department of Education, P.O. Box 2360, Honolulu, HI 96804.

CONTENT AREA INSTRUCTIONAL STRATEGIES FOR STUDENTS OF LIMITED ENGLISH PROFICIENCY IN SECONDARY SCHOOLS

A SHELTERED APPROACH

Office of Instructional Services/General Education Branch • Department of Education • State of Hawaii
RS 91-1142 • December 1991

The Honorable John Waihee
Governor, State of Hawaii

BOARD OF EDUCATION

Dr. Mitsugi Nakashima, Chairperson
Debi Hartmann, First Vice-Chairperson
William A.K. Waters, Second Vice-Chairperson

Rev. Darrow L.K. Aiona   Betty Lou Miura
Margaret K. Apo   Ronald Nakano
Karen Knudsen   Charles Norwood
Denise Matsumoto   Sivia Sasa
Francis R. McMillen   Meyer M. Ueoka
Randal Yoshida

Charles T. Toguchi, Superintendent of Education
Dr. Herman M. Aizawa, Deputy Superintendent

Dr. Philip J. Bossert, Assistant Superinendent
Office of Information & Telecommunication Services

Donald Nugent, Assistant Superintendent
Office of Personnel Services

Alfred Suga, Assistant Superintendent
Office of Business Services

Liberato C. Viduya, Jr., Assistant Superintendent
Office of Instructional Services

Shirley Akita, District Superintendent
Kauai District Office

Linda Y. Chung, District Superintendent
Leeward District Office

Dr. Alan Garson, District Superintendent
Hawaii District Office

James Y.S. Kim, District Superintendent
Honolulu District Office

Robert B. Lee, District Superintendent
Central District Office

Lokelani Lindsey, District Superintendent
Maui District Office

Sakae Loo, District Superintendent
Windward District Office

9/91

CONTENT AREA INSTRUCTIONAL STRATEGIES FOR STUDENTS OF LIMITED ENGLISH PROFICIENCY IN SECONDARY SCHOOLS

A SHELTERED APPROACH

This book was developed by the Hawaii Bilingual/Bicultural Education Project through funds provided under Title VII, of the Elementary and Secondary Education Act of 1965, as amended, Grant #G008710501. The opinions expressed herein do not necessarily reflect the positions or policy of the U.S. Office of Education, and no official endorsement by the U.S. Office of Education should be inferred.

FOREWORD

A culturally responsive educational system takes into account the language, experience and cultural background of the students. This background forms the basis for new knowledge, new experiences, attitudes and skills that are necessary for a learner in a multicultural society.

As part of this effort to be responsive to the educational needs of students of limited English proficiency (SLEP) in our public schools, the Department has developed, through its ESEA Title VII Bilingual Education Projects, instructional materials which supplement the regular texts and materials used in the classroom.

This volume was designed to provide assistance in instruction for teachers when their classes consist of students representing different language or ethnic groups. It is hoped that through the use of this book with sample lessons on sheltered English instruction in the content areas, teachers will be able to help their SLEP learn the core content subjects more effectively and rapidly. Teachers are encouraged to use the sheltered English instruction model in developing their own teaching plans.

Although this material is intended primarily for teachers serving students of limited English proficiency, the material may be used by other teachers whose students can benefit from sheltered instruction.

Charles T. Toguchi
Charles T. Toguchi, Superintendent

ACKNOWLEDGEMENTS

Appreciation is extended to Dr. Margarita Calderon, University of Texas at El Paso who developed the basic materials and to Eduardo Calderon who formatted them. Special thanks are given to project Resource Teachers who wrote additional sample lesson plans and field-tested the lessons:

Margarita Adair
Socorro Deguzman
Susan Hamada
Kathryn Heath
Felisa Lindsey
Patricia Park
Eulanda Strong

Thanks are also extended to regular classroom teachers who worked with the materials (Lynne Lee and Mary Cathy Barnes).

The materials were revised and edited by Winona Chang and Josephine D. Pablo.

TABLE OF CONTENTS

iv

OVERVIEW

Due to the diversity of language groups in Hawaii schools, it is not uncommon to have more than five different language or ethnic groups represented in a classroom. When it is not possible to have a bilingual teacher or aide for each of the language groups, the Sheltered Approach is an alternative to help Students of Limited English Proficiency develop academic language proficiency essential in insuring their success in mainstream classrooms. The use of the Sheltered Approach provides the transition between native language instruction or English as a Second Language (ESL) and mainstream English. However, the Sheltered Approach or "sheltered subject matter teaching" is not a substitute for but a supplement to bilingual education or ESL. In sheltered subject matter teaching, SLEP learn content area subjects in a comprehensible and meaningful manner. Studies have shown that sheltered subject matter teaching results in subject matter learning as well as impressive amounts of language acquisition.

This handbook for sheltered instruction is organized in three parts. The first is a theoretical rationale for the Sheltered Approach and a listing of sheltered and cooperative instruction behaviors. The second part includes the critical elements of the Sheltered Approach, and the components for a program design. The third section contains a brief presentation of lesson preparation and classroom management for sheltered content instruction. This is followed by sample lessons in social studies, science, mathematics, and literature.

Good teaching by all teachers for limited English proficient students is possible. This handbook is an attempt to make that a reality.

1

Part I

THEORIES And PRACTICES

Of The

SHELTERED INSTRUCTIONAL APPROACH

- Theories of the Sheltered Approach

- Teacher and Student Behaviors in Sheltered and Cooperative Instruction

3

THEORIES And PRACTICES Of The
SHELTERED INSTRUCTIONAL APPROACH

What is the Sheltered Approach?

The Sheltered Approach is an approach to teaching English as a second language (ESL) which uses English as the medium for providing content area instruction. It provides content area instruction to SLEP while emphasizing development of their English language skills (Savitt 1985, Krashen 1985, Parker 1985, Guzman 1986).

Why is the Sheltered Approach important?

Using the Sheltered Approach to teach content area subjects is a means of making the transition between instruction in the native language and instruction in mainstream (native-like) English. When native language instruction is not available, sheltered content instruction, along with English language development instruction, must be the first step for SLEP at the beginning level of English proficiency.

Research indicates that in addition to making course content accessible to SLEP, sheltered instruction also plays an important part in the acquisition of English by these students.

When is the Sheltered Approach used?

The Sheltered Approach, a concept relatively new to American schools but one which has been in use in Europe for over thirty years, is a response to two problems in the teaching of SLEP.

The first problem is that of transition from native language instruction to English-only instruction in academic subject areas. Students in bilingual programs who received content area instruction solely in their first language and English as a second language instruction had difficulty when moved abruptly into all-English classrooms. It became apparent to educators that these children needed a transitional period during which their content area instruction would be in English, but in an adapted form of English appropriate to their level of language proficiency. This adapted form became known as "Sheltered English."

The research of Jim Cummins[1] proved what classroom teachers of SLEP knew from experience: subjects which involved considerable cognitive demand, such

---

[1] ("The Role of Primary Language Development in Promoting Educational Success for Language Minority Students" in Schooling and Language Minority Students: A Theoretical Framework. Office of Bilingual Bicultural Education, California State Department of Education. Los

as social studies and science, are more difficult for SLEP than subjects which are more concrete (art, music, crafts).

An ideal bilingual program, based on Stephen Krashen's adaptation of Cummins' Model of Language Proficiency, was thus developed and provided an intermediate phase between first language content area instruction and mainstream content area instruction. Figure 1 is a model of such a program.

MODE OF INSTRUCTION			
English Proficiency	Native Language	Sheltered Approach	Mainstream English
Beginning	Language Arts, Math, Science, Social Studies	ESL, PE, Art, Music	
Intermediate	Language Arts, Science, Social Studies	ESL, Math, Science	Art, Music, PE
Advanced	Language Arts	Language Arts, Math, Science, Social Studies	Art, Music, Math, Science, Social Studies
FLUENT	Language Arts (direct instruction or via content areas)		Language Arts, Art, Music, PE, Math, Science, Social Studies

Figure 1

This model permits beginning level SLEP to start receiving instruction in English in subjects which use a greater degree of experiential rather than expository presentation. Experiential learning involves observation, firsthand experience, demonstrations, imitation; in general, doing things. Expository learning, on the other hand, involves receiving new information through listening to the teacher, discussion and reading. Subjects which require expository learning are taught in the student's native language.

Angeles; Evaluation, Dissemination and Assessment Center; California State University Los Angeles; 1981, p. 39).

6

Meeting the linguistic and academic needs of SLEP from diverse language groups is the <u>second problem</u> that triggered interest in the Sheltered Approach. The influx of Southeast Asian and Middle Eastern refugees in recent years brought languages, such as Vietnamese, Cambodian, Laotian, Hmong, Mien, and Farsi, to our schools. Bilingual teachers, instructional assistants and materials are often difficult, if not impossible, to locate for such languages. Class size and other programmatic constraints may also preclude the provision of daily first language instruction. In cases where native-language instruction is not possible, sheltered instruction is the logical starting point for SLEP.

By providing content area instruction in a sheltered mode, two goals are accomplished simultaneously. Students keep up with grade-level content subjects, and their proficiency in the kind of English used in the classroom improves. Often, ESL instruction tends to focus on language and language forms rather than on communication. In a sheltered class, language proficiency develops from using the new language in an informal manner to accomplish tasks.

Sheltered English instruction cannot substitute for the benefits derived from a full bilingual instructional program where science, math and other subjects are taught in the students' primary language. However, sheltered English instruction does make subject matter more accessible to students in multiple-language classrooms where bilingual programs are difficult to implement.

Before we describe the sheltered instruction process, some background on second language acquisition is needed.

Second Language Acquisition.

The research upon which the Sheltered Approach is based comes primarily from the work of three specialists: Jim Cummins of the Modern Language Center of Ontario, who has published extensive research on bilingual education; Stephen Krashen of the University of Southern California, an outstanding authority in the field of second language acquisition; and Michael Long of the University of Hawaii, who has developed a means of evaluating teacher-pupil interaction.

Language Acquisition: Two Types

Two elements of Cummins' (1981) research are critical to understanding sheltered instruction: BICS and CALP. Cummins has shown that while minority language students may quickly develop Basic Interpersonal Communication Skills (BICS), which is the ability to carry on everyday conversations, this kind of proficiency does not indicate an equivalent level of Cognitive Academic Language Proficiency (CALP). He points out that "too often language minority children are judged capable of receiving instruction along with English-only children on the basis of their fluency in BICS. Consequently, the SLEP are mainstreamed when their CALP is insufficiently developed." (Cummins, 1981)

For language minority students, there are two distinct types of difficulty in terms of school subjects. One is how much of a cognitive demand the subject has, and the other is how abstract the subject is. Cummins represents this dual system of difficulty by means of a quadrant as shown in Figure 2.

A MODEL OF LANGUAGE PROFICIENCY

COGNITIVELY UNDEMANDING
(EASY)

	A	C	
	Tasks	**Tasks**	
	• ESL/TPR	• Telephone Conversations	
	• Art, Music, PE	• Reading notes on Bulletin Board	
	• Following oral directions	• Written directions (no diagrams or examples)	
	• Face-to-face conversations	• Computer tests	
	• Viewing exhibits		
CONTEXT EMBEDDED (CLUES	• Computer graphics		CONTEXT REDUCED (FEW CLUES)
	B	D	
	Tasks	**Tasks**	
	• Actual demonstrations	• Writing compositions	
	• AV assisted lessons	• CTBS, SAT, CAP tests	
	• Math computations	• Reading/writing	
	• Science experiments	• Math concepts and applications	
	• Social Studies projects	• Explanations of new abstract concepts	
	• Mapping (cognitive)	• Lectures with few illustrations	
	• Role playing	• Workbooks, Worksheets	
	• Discussions	• Computer applications	
	• Computer graphics with simple texts		

COGNITIVELY DEMANDING
(DIFFICULT)

Developed by Dennis Parker and Margarita Calderon, Ph.D.

Figure 2

8

By crossing the two continuum lines, Cummins created four quadrants (A, B, C, and D), each with samples of the kinds of tasks involved. The tasks in quadrant "A" are easy in both senses. Conversely, those in quadrant "D" are difficult in both senses. Thus, there is a natural progression of appropriate kinds of tasks for sheltered instruction (A to B to C to D) which should parallel a student's development in English proficiency.

Acquisition vs. Learning

Krashen's (1981) work centers on the difference between language learning and language acquisition. He characterizes language learning as that which has typically taken place in foreign language classes and which results in knowledge about the language rather than in competence of communicating in that language. Language acquisition, he says, is a natural process which takes place when the "affective filter" (the psychological barrier caused by fear of having to perform) is not activated. When subject area content is presented to SLEP in a comprehensible manner, they acquire language proficiency by "doing something" in the language rather than by studying its elements. Thus, language acquisition may be seen as an unconscious development of proficiency while language learning is a conscious process which promotes correctness rather than builds proficiency.

In acquisition activities, the affective filter, which shuts off comprehensible input when a person feels nervous or threatened, is not activated because attention is focused on the content of the activity rather than on the language forms being used. To reduce the effects of the affective filter, preproduction level students should be permitted a "silent period" during which they develop listening comprehension without any requirement to perform orally in the new language. By learning content in a sheltered mode, students can both keep up with the subject matter and accelerate their acquisition of English.

Acquisition through Negotiation

Michael Long's research (1984) deals with the results of different kinds of teacher-pupil and pupil-pupil interaction. He proposes that by modifying questioning strategies so that more open questions (many answers possible) and referential questions (those to which the teacher does not already know the answer) are posed, pupils who have begun to use English will have the opportunity to negotiate meaning. The negotiation of meaning process, he points out, is an essential part of second language acquisition.

Michael Long recommends that "two-way" tasks be used in sheltered activities. These are tasks in which each student in a group has some part of the information needed for the group to complete its assessment. Since each member has information that no other member has, the students must negotiate meaning among themselves to complete the group assignment. This informal use of the new language, however awkward it may be in form, is a critical part of the language acquisition instruction commonly used in language development classes. The best types of two-way tasks are those structured through Cooperative Learning methods and techniques. A way of integrating Cooperative Learning and Sheltered Instruction is outlined in the following pages.

What sheltered instruction is <u>not</u>.

Sheltered instruction does not mean *watering down* of the curriculum, content of the subject matter, objectives or achievement goals. On the contrary, sheltered instruction is an opportunity for *making sure* that SLEP keep up to par with complex concepts and the amount of subject matter that *all* students need to master in the secondary schools.

OUTLINE Of
SHELTERED And COOPERATIVE INSTRUCTIONAL
TEACHER And STUDENT BEHAVIORS

I.   Goals and Benefits

    A.   Improves student self-image, student behavior, and academic achievement.

    B.   Provides a context for student interaction, negotiation for meaning, and contextual clues.

    C.   Provides context for higher order thinking and metacognition in learning to process social skills and academic content.

    D.   Promotes cultural democracy, respect for individual differences whether cultural, racial, religious or life-styles.

    E.   Helps students develop social skills for the complexity and changes needed in the work place with emphasis on processing information and working collaboratively with others.

    F.   Improves leadership development opportunities and develops independent learners (internal locus of control).

    G.   Enhances classroom climate.

II. Teacher Behaviors and Classroom Management

Management in the classroom is critical. Management is used to set up the proper environment for learning language, social and academic skills. The goal of a well-managed classroom is that students learn to manage themselves.

The teacher's role in the classroom is helping students to develop the social skills necessary for collaborating with others, as well as to gain content information processing skills. By developing collaborative skills, students gain a valuable set of skills for life and for tomorrow's workplace, and at the same time, students improve in academic achievement.

    A.   Research on L_2 (Second Language) Acquisition (Krashen, 1981; Long, 1983; Calderon et al, 1982) identifies teacher behaviors and classroom organizational structures that help LEP students process information. A list of these behaviors follows:

11

1. Provide comprehensible input by helping students focus on the message, meaning and task to be accomplished.

2. Provide contextual clues through the use of visuals, realia, props, and manipulatives for introducing all lessons.

3. Use audio clues to guide comprehension.

4. Use body language and gestures to explain vocabulary and concepts.

5. Adapt classroom speech by using shorter, simpler sentences, clear pronunciation, controlled vocabulary, redundancy and expansions.

6. Provide many opportunities for SLEP to interact with other students. Students should constantly communicate and negotiate for meaning with peers of different levels of English proficiency and different ethnic groups.

7. Provide ample opportunities for SLEP to ask many questions in the classroom, negotiate for meaning, and to clarify their understanding.

8. Model always the linguistic and social behaviors desired for each particular task.

9. Model the metacognitive processing skills of debriefing; lead discussions on thinking processes for arriving at conclusions, the inquiry processes, hypotheses formation and testing, and other learning strategies.

10. Organize lessons to include advance organizers, components for developing, applying and checking for understanding. By the close of each lesson, students should be able to produce the desired academic behaviors. Students should debrief their learning and thinking process, as well as their social behavior for each activity.

B. Johnson and Johnson (1983) identify five major steps in teaching cooperative skills:

Step 1. Helping students see the need for the skills.
(1) Display posters, bulletin boards, seating arrangements and other evidence to show that the teacher considers the skills to be important. (2) Communicate to students why mastering the skills is important. (3) Validate the importance of skills

12

by giving communication groups two grades: one for achievement and one for appropriate use of targeted communication/social skills.

Step 2. Ensuring that students understand what each skill is.
(1) Work with students to generate specific phrases and behaviors that express the skill. (2) Demonstrate, model, and have students role play the skill. (3) Teach only one or two skills at a time.

Step 3. Setting up Practice Situations.
(1) Assign specific roles to group members, such as reader, encourager, summarizer, and time keeper. (2) Announce that the specific skill will be observed and counted.
(3) Practice fun cooperative activities that are nonacademic but which develop team-building skills.

Step 4. Ensuring that students process their use of skills.
(1) Model the processing behaviors desired. (2) Provide time, about 10 minutes, for processing at the end of each activity. (3) Provide a set of procedures to follow and model the communication. (4) Provide opportunities for positive feedback among group members on the processing activity.

Step 5. Ensure that students persevere in practicing the skills.
As with any skill, there will be a period of slow learning, then rapid improvement, followed by a leveling off, then more improvement, and so forth. Students have to practice communication skills long enough to reach the first plateau, or leveling off, and integrate these skills into their active behavioral repertoire. This requires sustained practice over long periods of time.

The goal for all cooperative learning is to reach a stage where teachers can structure a cooperative lesson and have students automatically engage in high level communication skills while achieving their academic learning goals.

13

Part II

PROCESSES And PROCEDURES

For

SHELTERED INSTRUCTION

- Critical Elements
- Components for Program Design:
  Methodology
  Teaching Strategies
  Integration of Language and Academic Skills

15

CRITICAL ELEMENTS

An often-quoted statement about the Sheltered Approach is that it is "just good teaching;" that is, it is a process whereby the teacher determines the capabilities of a group of students and then finds ways to take them from that level of capacity to the desired level. But Sheltered Approach is not "just good teaching," it incorporates elements of effective teaching. To provide instruction which is comprehensible on the one hand and still parallel with mainstream course goals and objectives on the other involves much more than simply having teachers adjust their style of presenting lessons. Other factors need to be considered:

A. Sheltered classes or lessons should be part of a clearly defined and articulated program designed to bring SLEP from whatever entry level they are at to a level of proficiency which will permit them to function as fluent English proficient students.

B. Sheltered lessons should provide growth in cognitive academic proficiency and should have the same basic content and objectives as mainstream lessons.

C. Sheltered lessons should provide growth in the acquisition of English through comprehensible input and contextualization.

D. Sheltered lessons should provide growth in the acquisition of study skills and social skills to permit students to become functional in today's society.

E. Sheltered lessons should promote among SLEP a positive self image and a positive attitude toward learning.

COMPONENTS FOR PROGRAM DESIGN

Sheltered classes or lessons should be part of a clearly defined and articulated program designed to bring SLEP from wherever they are upon entry to a level of proficiency which will permit them to function as fluent English proficient students.

Principles in designing a sheltered program include:

A. Standardized tests designed for native speakers are appropriate for SLEP only when the students have reached the advanced fluency stage. Initial assessment should be done with instruments for measuring non-native students' skills in listening, speaking, reading, and writing. In addition, some means of determining students' educational background is necessary.

17

B. The following factors are listed in order of importance as considerations for placing students for sheltered instruction:

1. Cognitive readiness for the course content.

2. Level of English proficiency.

3. Age or grade level.

Student placement is perhaps the most critical and difficult area of providing sheltered instruction because it requires so much change and flexibility on the part of teachers and administrators. But if the first two factors are not given priority in grouping SLEP, the teacher of sheltered instruction will not have a target level of English and conceptual proficiency for which lessons can be adapted. Students with the least proficiency will then not receive parallel and comprehensible instruction.

C. Students with minimum levels of education and/or first language literacy should receive first priority for available bilingual resources. Bilingual instructional assistants should be available to assist with sheltered lessons.

D. Proficient bilingual students should be encouraged to serve as peer tutors during sheltered lessons. Cooperative Learning techniques should also be used to set up interactive classroom structures.

E. Sheltered Approach teachers need continuous training and support in order to implement effective sheltered instructional programs.

1. Sheltered instruction teachers should coach and support one another. Because sheltered English is a new and uncharted field, peer coaching is particularly necessary. Just as early settlers had to rely on each other and cooperate in the absence of organizational support systems, such teachers have little access to references and guidelines for assistance and must assist one another for feedback, direction and continuous self-improvement.

2. Sheltered instruction teachers as specialists should collaborate with bilingual teachers, ESL teachers, mainstream teachers, and administrators to seek continuous program improvement. A program for SLEP, however small, should not be regarded as a separate element attached to the regular curriculum, like a dinghy trailing a yacht, but as an integral part of the total school program. SLEP are entitled by law to equal educational opportunity, but to make that equal opportunity a reality requires adjustments and changes in every aspect of the school. The teacher using the Sheltered Approach can and must provide guidance in this process.

3. These teachers should provide policy-makers with recommendations and suggestions necessary for program adaptation and program quality.

4. Teachers using sheltered instruction should continue to receive inservice training on sheltered techniques in their content area (math, science, social studies, etc.) at least one day every other month. Research has also proven that teachers need to meet with peers at least every other week in study groups to work out problems and share successes in classroom implementation.

METHODOLOGY

Sheltered Approach lessons should provide growth in cognitive academic proficiency and should have the same basic content and objectives as mainstream lessons.

A. The first step in adapting a lesson to a sheltered mode is to determine and list its basic content and objectives.

B. The teaching strategies below can be used for introducing content and achieving objectives. These strategies can be combined in many ways into unit lesson plans.

C. These plans should focus first on building students' listening comprehension skills and should incorporate two-way task activities to encourage student negotiation of meaning. As much as possible, classroom activities should involve students doing things, rather than simply listening to the teacher or reading textbooks.

D. As the plans are implemented, the teacher should use both formal and informal means of assessing students' progress to determine how successful the sheltered instruction has been and to revise plans accordingly.

E. In implementing sheltered instruction, teachers are urged to use the guidelines and sample checklists for peer-coaching (included as Appendices 1 and 2) to help one another work toward desired teacher behaviors that promote sheltered instruction.

TEACHING STRATEGIES

Sheltered lessons should provide growth in the acquisition of English through comprehensible input and contextualization.

19

A. Vocabulary Building

Language proficiency develops when significant needs and purposes for communication are fulfilled. Thus, classroom activities should involve using English as a means or a tool to perform various functions and to communicate meaning rather than focusing on the language itself.

While vocabulary acquisition is an important part of any subject area lesson, Sheltered Approach lessons should stress comprehension of oral or written vocabulary prior to production (i.e., use of vocabulary in speaking and writing) and should keep vocabulary learning within the context, not in isolated lists.

Vocabulary building is one of the most important factors to consider in Sheltered Instruction, or for that matter, in any instructional activity. Without a shared language there can be no teaching or learning taking place.

The most urgent need for SLEP is to acquire rapidly a sufficiently large enough vocabulary in order to understand the content of the instructional unit and to be able to express ideas and feelings, as well as to master the material. Therefore, time needs to be set aside for vocabulary building before and during each lesson. Although, at first, teachers may feel that they cannot afford to spend time on vocabulary building, they will soon realize that it pays huge dividends if they do, and that there are major student losses if they don't. Ironically, even fluent speakers of English suffer when vocabulary and background building are not conducted. But one of the major reasons why SLEP progress so slowly or fail in the content courses is because the classroom teacher does not spend enough time on vocabulary building.

Time Frame for Vocabulary Building

1. At the beginning of each chapter, one class period should be devoted to:

   - Tapping students' prior knowledge of the subject.
   - Previewing material to be studied – key concepts, chapter headings, advance organizers for sub-topics.
   - Introducing the necessary vocabulary.

2. Vocabulary building activities should be interspersed throughout the week's activities in order to ensure comprehension and progress.

3. Students should be tested on key vocabulary terms at the end of the chapter, unit or study.

Techniques

Special techniques for vocabulary building include:

- Using gestures, body language and visuals, such as pictures, drawings on the board, and actual objects.
- Pointing to these visuals to clarify meaning.
- Labeling drawings and pictures to help students make the connection between oral and written English.
- Using the students' ideas as the starting point and elaborating on them to clarify meaning. This allows the students to contribute to the meaning process and enhances their self-esteem when their ideas are accepted.
- Repeating incorrect utterances correctly in an unexaggerated manner and encouraging the students to assimilate the correct structure without their feeling embarrassed or being criticized.
- Incorporating role-playing activities to allow students to learn new concepts and language through personalized, physical activities which anchor knowledge of the new vocabulary.

Strategies/Activities

In order to help students acquire a large vocabulary within a short period of time, vocabulary instruction needs to go beyond the teaching of isolated words. **Repeating words, orally or in writing, that are not understood prevents students from accessing background knowledge or setting the new words in an understandable context.** Vocabulary development must be tied to the development of concepts. When words are introduced in ways that activate existing knowledge, students make important connections between old and new information and become aware of how the new words fit within their semantic repertoire.

Previewing the selection

Vocabulary is first introduced in context as the teacher previews what is to be studied. The teacher can point to pictures in the book and to paragraphs where the words are found. The class can discuss the headings, while the students and teacher scan the pages together. Skimming to determine the main ideas or scanning to find specific details of interest can be very effective pre-reading activities. Previewing helps learners understand rapidly what they are about to hear or read in the new lesson. Previewing questions also can be very helpful.

21

Think-Aloud (Metacognition)

When an important procedure (science experiment) or a sequence (life-cycle) is part of understanding a key concept and vocabulary, the teacher says aloud the sequence or procedure while actually performing it. The teacher also says aloud any thinking or decision-making s/he is doing during that procedure. This metacognitive behavior can be taught to the students as a thinking skill. Students can learn to develop a plan to solve problems and can, therefore, describe their actions step-by-step before implementing it to solve a problem. When the plan does not succeed, the students can retrace their steps to investigate another way to solve the dilemma.

Meaningful Sentences

On large chart paper, the teacher lists words with spaces between for writing definitions and meaningful sentences. As students offer definitions and sentences, the teacher writes them down. Meaningful sentences should give everyone a good "mind movie" of what the word is all about. In a lesson to construct meaningful sentences, the teacher-student discourse might go something like this:

Teacher: Who can give me a meaningful sentence with the word <u>octopus</u>?

Student: The octopus is big and ugly.

Teacher: Tell me more about the octopus. Remember, a meaningful sentence should describe the word somewhat. If we took out the word octopus, we would have a sentence such as "The _____ is big and ugly" and we can substitute words such as truck, monster, building, etc. in the blank space. If we can replace the word with so many other words, then that is **not** a meaningful sentence. That does not give a good "mind movie" of what an octopus is for someone who has never seen one. So let's try again.

Student: How about, "The octopus has eight legs"?

Teacher: Can we also say, "The spider has eight legs"?

Student: Can we say, "The octopus wrapped its eight legs around the swimmer and pulled him to the bottom of the sea"?

Teacher: That's better. That tells us the octopus is big, lives in the water, and has eight legs. What else could we add?

22

Mapping

Semantic maps are also very effective in building vocabulary. Completing semantic webs, or maps, engages students in a mental activity which activates prior knowledge and provides new words for talking about that knowledge.

At first, the teacher needs to model on the board techniques for mapping and webbing. When the teacher takes students through a webbing activity, they see graphically the labels used to express key concepts and the attributes or characteristics of those concepts.

In creating their own semantic map, students might work with a topic that appears in the center of the map and verbalize words associated with the topic. The words are recorded around the topic. Mapping, spoking or webbing can be created at various levels of complexity. (See Appendix 3 for examples.) Students should be encouraged to draw simple pictures to accompany their written words.

Grouping

This technique is similar to webbing. By classifying or reclassifying, not just content concepts and vocabulary, but also any language material into meaningful units, it will make the material easier to remember because it reduces the number of discrete elements. Groups can be based on the type of word, such as all nouns or verbs; topic (words about weather); practical function (things on the lab table); linguistic function (apology, request, demand, denial); dissimilarity or opposition (friendly/unfriendly; dangerous/safe). These words and their meanings can be placed on color-coded cards to represent the different groups.

Imagery

Visual images may be the most potent device to aid recall of verbal material. A large proportion of learners have a preference for visual learning. Relating new language to concepts can be done through meaningful visual imagery, either in the mind or by drawing. The students can be asked to picture in their minds or make a "mind movie" of an object, a set of locations for remembering a sequence of words or expressions, or a mental representation of the letters of a word.

Sounds

Students can be asked to identify a familiar word in their own language that sounds like the new word. This is the auditory link. Then, the students generate an image of some relationship between the new word and a familiar one. This is the visual link. Both links must be meaningful to the learners. For example, they can use a familiar word to remember something abstract by associating it with a picture of something concrete that sounds like that word (<u>Minnesota</u> imagined as a mini-soda).

Physical Response

Students should physically act out a new expression (pouring in the liquid; closing the lid), or meaningfully relate a new expression to a physical feeling or sensation (freezing, cold, warm, lukewarm). With abstract social studies concepts (such as trial, the accused, attorney) students should role-play a trial where lawyers' and the judge's words are scripted out, rehearsed, and role-played.

Highlighting

Learners sometimes benefit by highlighting vocabulary or key concepts with the help of other students or as a whole group with the teacher. This strategy emphasizes the major points in a dramatic way: through color, <u>underlining</u>, CAPITAL LETTERS, Initial Capitals, BIG WRITING, **bold writing**, *stars*, boxes, circles, and so on. Students can invent their own highlighting devices.

Word Banks

An additional tool is to have students create their own word banks on index cards with the key word on one side and the definition on the other. The cards can be kept in a box, in envelopes, or on a ring. Rings with word cards can be hanging from the ceiling where students work in teams.

Learning Logs

Another option is to have students write down the words and their definitions or meaningful sentences in daily Learning Log entries. The logs are used throughout the unit as personalized dictionaries and writing tools. Learning Logs can become language learning notebooks in which students record assignments given by the teacher; their own goals and objectives for learning the topic; words the students hear or read and want to learn by asking someone or look up in the dictionary;

summaries of what they read or heard; records of errors they want to work on and the reasons they think they are making those errors; strategies that are helping them learn.

When the teacher probes and builds meaning jointly with the student, the student will remember that meaning and the words much better.

Once all the words have been discussed and identified with this procedure, the chart paper is taped on the wall where students can see it during activities that require the use of those words.

Color-Coded Co-op Cards (CCCC)

This is a cooperative learning activity (described in Appendix 5) for helping students master new vocabulary. Students are teamed in groups of four, so that two pairs can work together. First, they are given a pre-test which consists of matching the new words with their definitions. Students are then given color-coded cards, each one receiving a stack of index cards in one color. The students make word banks by writing each word they missed on the front of the card and its definition on the back. By giving each student a different color, they can keep track of their word banks as they drill each other in pairs. Each time a word is mastered, the card is placed on the table. Otherwise, it is placed in the back of the deck being held in the partner's hand. After all the cards have been stacked on the table, a post-test is given. Students grade their tests and continue studying the words they missed.

Midway through the lesson, another practice test is given, with more time for pair-practice. A final vocabulary test is given at the end of the unit.

Roundtable and Write-Around

These two strategies (described in the appendix) can be used to review vocabulary, spelling, and sentence writing. They can be used at the beginning or end of a class period for 5 or 10 minutes.

B.   Teacher Speech

The teacher using the Sheltered Approach must speak in a manner that is appropriate to the proficiency level of the students. All of us have the ability to adjust our speech to different listeners. We do not speak to children or non-native speakers in the same manner that we use for employers or when addressing a group of native English-speaking adults. Our ability to adjust depends upon our sensitivity and experience. The

25

teacher of sheltered lessons, through experience and conscious development of sensitivity, can become adept at communicating with students of different levels of English proficiency by utilizing such techniques as:

1. A slower, but not unnatural, rate of speech.

2. Clear enunciation.

3. Simpler and shorter sentences.

4. More repetition, rephrasing, clarifying, restatements, and redundancy.

5. Controlled vocabulary and idioms.

C. Contextualization

Context-reduced (abstract) lesson contents should be contextualized so as to become comprehensible to SLEP.

1. Make abstraction more concrete by using "here and now" examples which are easily understood.

2. Provide visual reinforcement or verbal input through:

    a. Pantomime, gestures, facial expressions.

    b. Props, models, realia.

    c. Pictures, blackboard sketches.

    d. Films, filmstrips, videotapes, slides, transparencies.

    e. Demonstrations.

    f. Hands-on and interactive tasks.

3. Break down complex tasks into simpler steps with specific instructions as in Total Physical Response (TPR) activities ("look at the map on page 105. Put one finger on Rome. Put another finger on London...")

D. Checking for Understanding

Verification of comprehension should be carried out frequently during a lesson.

1. "Wh____" questions (who, what, where, etc.)

26

2. "Proof" questions (How do you know that?)

3. "Idiot" questions (So, the head of the United States is called a king, right?)

4. Confirmation checks (Do you mean ...?)

E. Background Knowledge

The teacher should activate the students' prior knowledge and help structure advance organizers by having an informal discussion about a topic before teaching its details. Webbing and graphing as a total group help students bring out what they already know and begin the mental predicting process.

F. Error Correction

To prevent students from withdrawing and thus shutting off comprehensible input, the teacher should minimize stress created by forcing oral production or linguistic correctness too early.

1. The teacher should recognize that language errors are a necessary part of second language acquisition.

2. The teacher should concentrate on the message students communicate, not the correctness of the message (function before form).

3. When correction is done, the teacher should use the restatement form:

Student: I don't got a pencil.
Teacher: Oh, you don't have a pencil, Here is one.

4. The teacher should help students overcome the "all or nothing" attitude toward comprehending oral or written English and change it to "get as much as you can."

G. Student Interaction Opportunities

The teacher should use interactive activities as much as possible.

1. The teacher should frequently interrupt him/herself with questions to the students.

2. Frequent and short group activities should be used to encourage communication among students.

27

a. Groups of mixed languages provide practice in communicating in English.

b. Groups of the same language permit students to assist one another on lesson content.

3. A variety of interactive activities should be planned.

a. Cooperative learning

b. Peer tutoring

c. Games

d. Projects in which students work in groups to create a specific product.

4. Interdependent dialog between the teacher and the students should be used frequently.

a. Dialog in which meaning is negotiated rather than simply transmitted. The difference is essentially that of discussion versus lecture or instructions.

b. Referential rather than display questions. In the former, the teacher seeks new information ("What do you think this looks like?"), while in the latter, the teacher already knows the answer ("Where is the animal's beak?").

c. Personalized rather than impersonal conversation ("Let's say that Juan has to buy 3 quarts of milk, and each quart costs 52¢...").

H. Textbook Selection/Adaptation

Texts must be made comprehensible to students. There are three major ways to accomplish this:

1. A simplified text. In some cases it is possible to locate a text which is simpler than the one used for a mainstream class and which still contains the same basic content. This kind of text is ideal for the parallel sheltered lesson. Often such texts will be richer in illustrative material but will not have the same degree of detail as the mainstream text.

2. A supplementary workbook. Some publishers have devised sheltered workbooks to accompany specific mainstream texts. A simplified summary of the content of the mainstream text is accompanied by extensive clear illustrations and activities appropriate for SLEP.

3. Teacher adaptation. In this case, the teacher uses the mainstream text as an aid to classroom instruction rather than something that students study at home. The teacher may rewrite the lesson using simpler structure and vocabulary. In class, the teacher draws heavily on the illustrative material in the text, supplementing with oral summary and a variety of techniques for making the content comprehensible. The teacher paraphrases the text and uses many checks to ensure comprehension. The use of American idioms and clever language structures like puns is avoided.

   a. Mapping, Webbing, Graphic Organizers

   The teacher uses pre-reading strategies to motivate thinking, activate prior knowledge, and develop curiosity and enthusiasm. The technique of webbing involves putting a key word in the center of the blackboard. Students are asked to brainstorm other words which that key word brings to mind. As the teacher writes these words down, she/he organizes them into categories. Once this process of categorization has been learned, it can be applied to text chapters or lessons, first done in class as a total class activity and then working toward an individual independent activity.

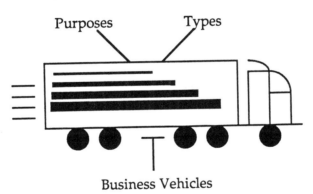

Business Vehicles

   b. Oral to Written Format

   The teacher summarizes a section of the text orally in a manner that is comprehensible to the students and through questioning and discussion verifies student comprehension. The teacher then

29

reads the section aloud. Group activities are assigned in which students must refer to the text. As lessons progress, students become less and less dependent upon summaries and more capable of working with the text independently.

c. Graphic Summaries

The teacher presents the essential information of a section or chapter to the students in a graphic form, using charts, diagrams, maps, graphs, timelines, etc. This material (on handouts) is used to explain the content and as a source for student activities. As students progress through the text, the illustrative material becomes increasingly less complete, and students use the text to fill in missing parts.

INTEGRATION OF LANGUAGE AND ACADEMIC SKILLS

Sheltered lessons should provide growth in the acquisition of the 3 Rs through science, math or social studies.

A. Listening Comprehension

The ability to comprehend oral messages is essential for success not only in the second language, but education in general. In order to succeed in the mainstream English classroom, the student must be able to understand the teacher's directions and explanations, as well as the information that fellow students share. Acquiring good listening skills is essential to developing fluency in English.

Understanding comes from familiarity with the key words and the context. In most cases, the student needs to understand about 75% of the utterance for it to be comprehensible. The student relies on what she/he already knows and on the context of the message to get the meaning.

Teachers can help in the process by incorporating structured listening comprehension activities into the curriculum. Two of the more common listening comprehension activities are Total Physical Response and the Name Technique.

<u>Total Physical Response</u>

Commands are given first to the whole class to execute. Later, after competence has been built up, commands are addressed to individuals. No verbal response is required when using TPR. Comprehension is checked by seeing if students can do what they have been instructed to do. While TPR is often an activity for beginning-level students, it has been used successfully in sheltered lessons to teach such diverse concepts as the planetary system, the forces that drew countries into World War I, and geometry.

Name Technique

This technique is used in presenting new vocabulary. The teacher will need examples or pictures of the concrete vocabulary items being taught. The words are introduced to the students, and then the object or pictures are given to different students. The teacher checks comprehension by asking such questions as: "Who has the leaf?" "Who has the stem?" "Who has the picture of the king? or "Who has the picture of the peasant?"

B.   Speaking

It is important that SLEP not be rushed into speech production. Speech, as well as the other language skills, should be allowed to develop naturally. First attempts at speech will not be perfect, and emphasis should not be placed on correcting them. Emphasis should be placed on the meaning.

To facilitate the student's acquisition of English, the level of questions the teacher asks can be varied to meet the proficiency level of the students. The following examples of questions are given in order of difficulty:

- Who has the square? Who has the circle? Who has the triangle?

  Questions such as these require that the students simply name the person holding the object.

- Is this the square? Is this the circle? Is this the triangle?

  Questions such as these require only a "yes" or "no" answer from the student.

- Is this a square or a triangle? Is this a triangle or a square?

  Here students must identify the correct object by choosing and saying its name.

- What is this?

  Students must identify and say the name of the object.

Only when students have enough familiarity with the subject and enough proficiency in English should they be expected to answer higher-level questions.

C. Writing

Writing is an essential literacy skill which is usually considered to be more difficult to master than listening, speaking or reading. It is not, however, one that needs to be delayed until students have perfected other language skills.

Writing is a process. There are various components to the process: prewriting (getting the ideas), composing (putting the ideas together on paper), revision (reworking what has been written so that it makes sense to those who will read it), and postwriting (publishing). While it may appear to be a linear process, this is not necessarily the case. Writers may begin with prewriting activities, write, and then go back to prewriting activities. The steps can vary with individual writers and can vary from writing task to writing task.

Just as initial attempts at speech produce "imperfect" language, so will initial (and often advanced) attempts at writing result in error-ridden language. Again, the emphasis should be on the message the student is trying to give, not on the form. Or in the case of the science project, it is the understanding of the concept that is important, more than the correctness of the written passage.

The teacher can assist students in becoming good writers by:

• Providing a variety of good reading material.

• Engaging students in a variety of prewriting activities before expecting students to write about a subject (i.e., discussion, brainstorming, outlining, drawing, etc.)

• Setting a purpose and an audience for all writing activities.

• Responding to what the student has written.

• Allowing students to develop, share, and discuss their writing with others.

D. Reading

To increase the student's understanding of the reading material, the teacher should begin with the language the student already knows by using a Language Experience Approach to reading. In this approach, the teacher elicits information from students about the subject, transcribing what they say. Their words become their first reading material on the subject. Because they will be reading what they already know how to say, success in reading the written word is assured.

Before being transitioned into the mainstream classroom, however, the SLEP will need to know how to read a mainstream textbook. The "how" is emphasized because reading is a process of the reader interacting with the text that he/she reads. Reading is not just knowing the vocabulary words and structures used in the reading material. The teacher can help enhance the comprehension of reading in English by:

- Discussing the title of the reading selection.

- Discussing any pictures, graphs, charts, maps, etc.

- Discussing the context of the reading (time, place, reasons, etc.)

- Setting a purpose for the reading.

- Setting up questions or predictions about the reading.

- Making similar readings available in the student's first langauge.

- Previewing the content, concepts and key ideas of the reading in the students' first language or in Sheltered English.

- Bringing the students' prior knowledge of the topic to the surface.

- Shortening the reading assignment for SLEP by selecting key paragraphs instead of whole sections or chapters.

- Before distributing duplicated materials, the teacher may have the SLEP use highlighters to mark important items. For example, yellow may be used to point out important information; pink to highlight key vocabulary; turquoise for sections that must be read and learned.

- Using cooperative learning techniques such as The Bilingual Cooperative Integrated Reading and Composition (CIRC) developed for SLEP populations (Calderon, Hertz-Lazarowitz, Tinajero, 1991).

E. Cooperative Learning

Cooperative learning is a strategy to increase motivation and retention, help students develop a positive image of self and others and to provide a vehicle for critical thinking, problem solving, and collaborative social skills.

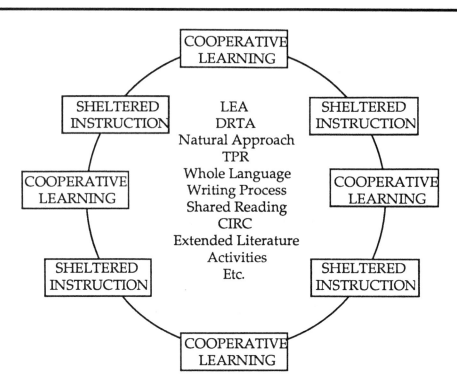

Teaching methods, such as Language Experience Approach (LEA), Directed Reading Thinking Activities (DRTA), Total Physical Response (TPR), Cooperative Integrated Reading and Composition (CIRC) and others as listed above can be easily integrated into sheltered instructional practices and cooperative learning structures. Some sample teaching techniques are also listed below.

SAMPLE SHELTERED-COOPERATIVE INSTRUCTIONAL STRATEGIES AND ACTIVITIES	
1. Brainstorming	2. Team Name, Logo, Etc.
3. Expert Jigsaw	4. Group Product
5. Roundtable	6. Cooperative Integrated Reading and composition
7. Color Coded Coop Cards	8. Tea Party
9. Numbered Heads Together	10. Heads Together/Group Discussion
11. Learning Logs	12. Focused Free Write

34

13.	Write Around	14.	Language Experience Approach
15.	Poster Reports	16.	Tear Ups
17.	Story Mapping	18.	Story Related Activity
19.	Line-Ups, Line Ups, Line Ups	20.	Talking Before Thinking
21.	Tee-Shirt Worksheet	22.	Drama Jigsaw

These teaching techniques can be used as anticipatory sets or opening activities, for combining with several other techniques, for reviewing, for assessment, for debriefing or processing critical learning skills and social skills, and for bringing closure to a lesson unit. See next page for a brief description of the techniques/strategies and groupings.

Brainstorming

A group discussion technique of short duration that contains these elements: spontaneous, rapid contributions, non-judgmental, all ideas accepted, and open-ended.

After an idea is presented, no explanations are given or required. Far-out, unusual contributions are accepted. Within the short period, quantity is important, and so, silence is avoided.

The recorder or recorders write all ideas down.

Color-Coded Co-op Cards (CCCC)

After a lecture, audio-visual presentation, reading of a text, or doing an experiment, students can work together to master the concepts or vocabulary through CCCC. The steps are:

1. Give a pretest.

2. Students create color-coded cards on the words or problems each one missed. Each student on the team has a different color card.

3. Students tutor each other with the cards. Tutors hold up the card. The tutee reads the question (answer is seen by tutor only). The tutee attempts to answer. If the answer is correct, the card is "won back" by the tutee; if not, it is placed on the bottom of the deck to be repeated. When the tutee wins back all his or her cards, the tutor and tutee roles are switched.

4. Students take a practice test.

5. Repeat the practice and testing if necessary.

6. Give final test, scoring, recognition.

Cooperative Integrated Reading and Composition (CIRC)

This is generally a paired activity. After the pre-reading motivation or introduction is presented, students predict what the selection is about from the title. Then pairs read to each other (ear-to-ear) and work on questions from the teacher or text. Pairs then write a literary response: poem, essay, narrative, as a summary of the activity.

Cooperative Review

The day before an exam, students in groups make up review questions. They take turns asking the other groups the questions. The group asking the question gets a point for asking the question. The group initially called on receives a point if members can add any important information to the answer. Or, the teacher brings in the questions. You can also combine Numbered Heads Together with Cooperative Review: the teacher or students ask the review question. Then, time is allocated for group discussions of the answer. After a brief "Heads Together" time, a number is called, 3, 2, 4, or 1. Students with the corresponding numbers have the opportunity to come up with the right answer. A second number is called after a correct answer is provided, and another student can earn a point for his or her team by adding additional material to the original correct answer. If the teacher feels there is still important information to be brought out, a third number may be called, and so on.

Group Discussion

When students are sitting in groups, a teacher can ask at various times during a lecture or presentation that the students discuss the meaning of something, why something works, or how a problem might best be solved. This very simple cooperative learning structure can complement a traditional lesson and provide a way to check for understanding. The group work can vary from a few minutes to a full class session.

Group Investigation

Group Investigation is designed to provide students with broad and diverse learning experiences which are different from the acquisition of predetermined facts and skills. Research has revealed that Group Investigation is particularly effective in increasing higher level cognitive abilities among students (Sharan and Hertz-Lazarowitz, 1980).

Step 1: Identifying the Topic and Organizing Pupils into Research Groups

Students are grouped into heterogeneous groups and they choose the specific inquiry topics.

Step 2: Planning the Learning Task

Group members or pairs determine subtopics for investigation. Groups decide what and how to study. They set the goals of learning.

37

Step 3: Carrying out the Investigation

Multi-lateral communication is stressed as students communicate with collaborators, teacher, other groups, and other resource persons. Students gather information, analyze and evaluate the data, and reach conclusions.

Step 4: Preparing the Final Report

The investigation culminates in a product: a report, event or summary. Students organize, abstract and synthesize information. Groups decide on content and the format of their presentation; a steering committee of group representatives coordinates the work of groups.

Step 5: Presenting the Final Report

Exhibitions, skits, debates, and reports are acceptable formats, as is inclusion of class members not in the group.

Step 6: Evaluation

Assessment of higher level learning is emphasized, including applications, synthesis, and inferences. Teachers and students may collaborate on evaluation; the steering committee may work with the teacher in creating the exam.

Heads Together

This is a catchy title for a group activity. Team members "put their heads together" to perform various tasks, e.g.,

Find words that are synonyms.

Create a sentence using as many words from the vocabulary list as they can.

Write more mathematical examples or problems.

Develop a plan to study or make a product.

Categorize.

Summarize.

Select or create a team name, song or cheer, logo, banner.

38

Jigsaw

The original Jigsaw method was developed to place students in situations of extreme interdependence. To do so, each student was provided with only part of the academic materials, but was evaluated on how well he or she could master the whole unit. Each student on a team, therefore, had but one piece of the jigsaw puzzle, but needed to complete the whole picture. Details are provided by Aronson, et al. (1978) and Aronson & Goode (1980). The elements of Jigsaw include:

Team-Building and Communication Training

Extensive team building includes role-playing, brainstorming, and specially designed group activities.

Study Group Leader

The importance of a group leader is stressed. Group leaders are selected by the teacher and receive special training. They organize the group, keep the group on task, serve as group/teacher liaison, model productive social and academic behaviors, and help resolve conflicts.

Teams

Teams range in size from three to seven members; five or six-member teams are recommended. Teams are heterogeneous with regard to ability level, racial, linguistic proficiency, sex characteristics, and personality factors such as assertiveness. Besides the leader, other roles may include reporter, recorder/artist, timekeeper, and encourager.

Expert Group

Each team member reports to an expert group composed of members from other teams who have been assigned the same expert topic. Students meet in their expert groups to exchange information and master the material. All the experts may make a graph or web to show their own teams. Then the experts return to their home teams and take turns teaching their teammates about their own topics.

Individual Assessment and Reward

Students take individual tests or quizzes covering all of the material of the learning unit. There may be no group score or grade, or there may be team scores that are determined by summing the improvement over the earlier performance by each member.

Language Experience Approach

A strategy that uses oral language for teaching skills in listening, speaking, reading, and writing. The communication cycle begins with the student's own out-of-school experiences which become the subjects for language learning activities.

The student dictates something to a literate person who writes down the words verbatim so that the student can see how the words spoken look when written down. This written piece is then used to teach the student reading.

Learning/Writing Logs/Diaries

Individual logs document students' reactions to events and lessons and are particularly useful if entries interpret what has happened.

After students receive new information, they are given a question or topic which would prompt them to demonstrate an understanding of the content. They may restate main ideas, suggest new ideas and details, add their personal reactions, recall experiences, or record thoughts.

Line-ups, Line-ups, Line-ups

This group activity may be used to list items in some order, such as:

1. Slowest to fastest
2. Largest to smallest
3. Cheapest to most expensive
4. Shortest to tallest
5. Lightest to heaviest
6. Birth dates of the students
7. Alphabetizing names, spelling words
8. Concepts, categories, characteristics
9. Chronological order of events
10. Sequencing
11. Numerical order
12. Closest to farthest
13. Longest to shortest
14. Least to most

Numbered Heads Together

Numbered Heads Together is basically a variant of Group Discussion. The important thing is having only one student represent the group but not

40

informing the students in advance who the group representative will be. That twist insures total involvement of all the students.

First, students number off in their group. Then, a question is given. The groups next put their heads together, discuss the answer, and make sure all group members know the answer. After this group-preparation period, the teacher calls out a number. All students with that number raise their hand. The teacher then calls on one of these group representatives to answer the question. Each correct answer generates points for that team.

Poster Reports

Students summarize the content in groups and make a poster highlighting the important facts through illustrations and writing.

Reader's Theater

Students read a story, play or poetry aloud, assigning certain parts to different groups or pairs of students. This is a variation of choral reading.

Roundtable

Roundtable can be used for team building, for review, and for brainstorming. The steps are as follows:

1. Students sit in a circle.

2. Only one pencil and one piece of paper are allowed per table.

3. The paper must circulate and everyone *must* have a turn in writing an answer.

4. Teams race to obtain as many correct answers as possible for questions such as:

    a. Write as many words as you can from the words "Valentine's Day."

    b. Write as many pairs of numbers as you can that add up to 21.

    c. Write as many characteristics of the Natural Approach as you can.

    d. Write as many names of U.S. Presidents as you can.

5. Teams score (count) their correct answers and trade papers with the group next to them to verify correct answers.

41

6. The team score is placed on the blackboard.

Team	Trial 1	Trial 2
A	15	
B	16	
C	12	

7. Teacher interviews the most successful group and identifies strategies that worked.

8. There is another trial. But, before the race begins, instruct the teams to take 30 seconds to discuss the strategy they will use. Next, give the problem the same time allotment they had for the first problem (1 or 2 minutes).

9. Continue to debrief and point out effective strategies for each consecutive trial.

Story Mapping

There are many ways to do story maps in teams. One way is to let each student draw and write a few words about one event or one character. Then all the pages are stapled together. A cover and title page are added to make it into a book.

Story Related Writing

Students .write a story similar to the one they had read, but can invent new characters, events or ending. They use as much as possible the vocabulary and writing style from the story they had first read.

Talking Before Thinking

This is a brainstorming variation to help team members focus on a topic for investigation or writing.

Team members number off. The teacher calls out a number and that student in each team selects an item appropriate to the lesson.

All team members take turns talking about that item:

- What they know about it.

- What they would like to find out about it.

42

- What they want to learn.

The recorder takes notes in three columns: What We Know, What We Want to Know More, and What We Can Learn.

Team members must all talk, think, and talk some more; be very positive, and contribute to the three categories.

Tea Party

A lot of space is needed for this activity. First, divide the class into two groups. Both groups form 2 concentric circles in the middle of the room, facing each other. Give them a sheet with questions that they can answer jointly, in 1 or 2 minutes for each question. After they have answered the first question, have the outer circle move one step to the right so they are facing a new partner. They are given again 1 or 2 minutes to answer the second question, and thus, they continue moving to other partners until they answer all the questions.

You many vary the way questions are asked. The outside circle may ask all the questions and the inner one answers. Then, there is a shift where the inner circle asks the questions and the others answer. Another way is to call the outside circle "odd" and the inside "even." The questions so numbered will be asked by the matching circle and the other circle answers. This method alternates the questioners and responders.

Afterwards, debrief, check for correct answers, and discuss the process of learning through this activity.

Another configuration is to form two or four long lines instead of circles.

Team or Group Product

Groups are instructed to assign roles to each member (writer, artist, presenter, time keeper, coach, team leader, etc.). Give time allocations for each event (reading: 5 minutes; discussion: 10 minutes; mural: 10 minutes; presentation: 3 minutes each group). Products can be a mural, a learning center, an essay, a poem, a worksheet, a presentation with visuals, a dramatization, etc.

Tear-Ups

Each team will tear 2 sheets of differently colored construction paper into creative pieces. The members will study the pieces and imagine what figures the pieces represent. The team will write a group story and paste the

43

pieces beside the story portions that match. The teams will share their stories.

Tee Shirt Worksheet

Each student draws a tee shirt on a large sheet of construction paper. Within the outline of the tee-shirt, the student will draw pictures of favorite hobbies on a sleeve and what that student plans to do after graduation on the other sleeve. Other drawings on the "shirt" may include favorite singer, TV program, snacks, movie, family outing, etc.

Students then exchange tee-shirts and collect autographs from each other.

Unstructured Team Practice and Coaching

After a class lecture or reading of a new assignment, students may be assigned to groups or pairs and given time for mastering the new material.

Write Around

The class has a general area as a focus. The teams meet and each member writes an opening sentence on a sheet of paper and then passes it to the right. The sheets are passed until each story or summary is completed. It is then returned to the originator who writes a conclusion and makes corrections.

The teams select their best story and a reader to share it with the rest of the class.

Part III

SAMPLE LESSONS

For

SHELTERED INSTRUCTION

- Lesson Preparation and Classroom
  Management Steps for Lesson Design
- Social Studies Lessons
- Mathematics Lessons
- Science Lessons
- Literature Lessons

45

LESSON PREPARATION And CLASSROOM MANAGEMENT
For SHELTERED CONTENT INSTRUCTION

A. **CONTENT OBJECTIVE(S)**

1. Study the selection, paying attention to the following points: readability for the majority of your students; text features; text structures; main points; students' familiarity with or lack of prior knowledge of the topic.

2. Decide what are the essential concepts in the selection.

3. Determine the requisite concepts or background information that the students need to understand.

4. Set the content objectives for the unit. Be thinking about the evaluation techniques to be used and the acceptable mastery levels.

B. **LANGUAGE OBJECTIVES**

1. Decide the language objectives.

2. Decide on the vocabulary items that must be pretaught. Try to limit the lexical items to those absolutely necessary for understanding.

C. **LEARNING STRATEGIES OBJECTIVES**

Decide on the learning strategy objective(s). Select the learning or higher order thinking strategies for the lesson.

D. **MATERIALS AND TEACHER TOOLS**

Develop the teacher input component for the lesson. Organize the steps to make the lesson comprehensible. Determine the teaching materials and the realia needed. Decide how context clues already in the text will be used.

E. **CLASSROOM STRUCTURES**

Determine grouping and total class activities. Plan activities for pairs, triads, teams of 4 or 5. Decide ways to place students into teams: random or predetermined assignments.

47

F. PROCEDURES

ANTICIPATORY SET

1. Develop an anticipatory set for the unit. Plan the strategy for stating the objectives to the students. Predetermine the experiences you will provide as background knowledge about the unit. Select the activities which can be used to tap prior background/experiences. Organize the vocabulary activities, including a timetable.

2. Chamot and O'Malley (1987) recommend the following activities for initiating a lesson:

    a. Brainstorming

        • Activation of prior knowledge
        • Development of critical thinking skills
        • Academic language development

    b. Concrete Activities

        Physical Action
        • Listening to and following oral directions
        • Kinesthetic involvement

        Using Manipulatives
        • Making concrete representations of math concepts
        • Demonstrating a science process

    c. Vocabulary Development

        • Games or Puzzles
        • Writing sentences to contextualize new words

    d. Advance Organization

        • Overview of topic to be presented
        • Why topic important
        • Objectives of the lesson

3. Establish the social setting. Select social rules to ensure that there is a climate for developing academic, social, and learning skills. Decide the roles for each team member. Plan to remind other students to respect differences in language, culture and experiences.

INSTRUCTION

1. Review the principles for sheltering instruction in this handbook. Review TIPS FOR LESSON DELIVERY at the end of the LESSON PREPARATION section.

2. Select the method(s) for teacher directed instruction or student cooperative group instruction. Plan for days 1, 2, 3, 4, and 5. Estimate the time students will need to accomplish their group tasks. Decide when you need to teach, reteach, test and retest.

3. Determine the:

   Amount of text to be read
   Purpose(s) for reading
   Comprehension skill(s) to be taught
   Text features to be highlighted
   Group practice related to the input, the main concept(s), and
      objective(s)
   Amount of verbal interaction in group practice
   Evaluation of group practice
   Follow-up of students not comprehending

4. Decide on your classroom structure and the order:

   Whole group webbing activity
   Cooperative learning activity
   Teams and their sizes (5, 4, or 3 members)
   Assigning roles to team members
   Social rules for the day
   Steps to accomplish the task

STUDENT PRACTICE

Use the objective(s) to determine the kinds of student practice needed, individual and/or team.

The following suggestions for this phase are made by Chamot and O'Malley. For developing skills in Learning Strategies, the following should be practiced in teams: advance organization, organizational planning, elaboration, grouping, and transfer.

CLOSURE EVALUATION

1. Select the strategy to determine what the students have accomplished, how they feel, and what they have learned by the end of the class.

2. The following activities serve as both closure and evaluation of a day's work:

   a. Teacher Directed

   - Debrief by asking:

     What did you like about this lesson? What are three important messages? What does this have to do with ...?

   - Administer a brief test.
   - Require a sharing of group products.
   - Give a final test.

   b. Student Directed

   - Check and correct each other's answers.
   - Discuss steps, strategies used.
   - Discuss team members' roles, contributions, potential problems.
   - Use self-observation checklists and debriefing.
   - Keep learning logs.

REVIEW THE LESSON AS A WHOLE

1. Check on whether the lesson was actually sheltered.

2. Analyze whether a fairly accurate time frame was given for each activity.

3. Check to see that the handouts and worksheets have been all designated, written, duplicated.

4. Make sure the wall charts (instructions, social rules, etc.) have been designed and made.

TIPS FOR LESSON DELIVERY

1. Preview with linguistic information by going over pertinent vocabulary, phrases, idioms, and structures before a lesson or reading. Provide a simplified reading as prelude to the unmodified version.

2. Preview with extralinguistic information in discussing a topic, picture, title, author, the purpose, etc., before a reading or lesson.

3. Use simplified or modified input-controlled vocabulary, idioms, utterance length and complexity, pace, pronunciation, voice volume, repetitions, emphasis, etc.

4. Use here-and-now focus-talk about things in the present context; use present marked verbs.

5. Include many contextual clues – visuals, realia, manipulatives, activities, situations, kinetics, etc.

6. Use repetition, restatements or paraphrases of previous utterances.

7. Do comprehension checks by asking questions to determine if the listener has understood what has just been said or displayed.

8. Include two-way activities where meaning is negotiated between information equals; each party has information or skills (ability which the other one needs to complete a task or purpose).

9. Encourage extensions (semantic) where a speaker picks up on what another has just said and elaborates on or adds to the meaning.

10. Have students practice expansions (structural) by repeating an incorrect utterance correctly. Expansions may function as confirmation checks. (May or may not be attended to by the listener).

11. Teach students to apply confirmation checks when one party asks a question of another who has just spoken, in order to confirm exactly what is thought to have just been said.

12. Use clarification requests during which a listener asks the speaker to clarify, elaborate on, or restate in some way what has just been said.

13. Establish a low anxiety climate and focus on the SLEP's intended meaning rather than on language errors.

51

14. Display an interest in and use of home culture by accepting different approaches and written home language terms in place of English terms.

52

LESSON PLANS
SOCIAL STUDIES LESSON #1

CHAPTER 18 - SCIENTIFIC REVOLUTION AND ENLIGHTENMENT (<u>A History of the World</u>, by Marvin Perry, Houghton Mifflin Co., 1985)

PART I
Scientists Develop a New View of Nature, pp. 401-407.

LESSON DURATION: 5 class periods

A.   CONTENT OBJECTIVES

Same as for all students, as written in teacher's manual or district curriculum. Specifically:

• How scientists developed a new view of nature (1550-1750).

• The type of reform enlightenment that thinkers sought.

B.   LANGUAGE OBJECTIVE

The teacher will teach or check for prior knowledge of the following concepts and terminology:

anatomy	enlightenment	microscope
artists	experiments	motion
banned	forbidden	patrons
circulation of blood	geocentric theory	posed problems
classification system	gravity/inertia	reason
contradict	heliocentric theory	Renaissance
controversy	hypothesis	revolving/rotating
corpses	in proportion to	satellites
demonstrations	interpreting data	scholars
discoveries	logical	scientific revolution
dissecting	masterpieces	scientific study
drawing conclusions	mathematical order	shaped by
earthly/spiritual	measurements	skeletons
elements	medieval belief	sweeping changes
ellipse	medieval view	system
encourage	method	telescope

53

C. LEARNING STRATEGIES

Advance organization, scientific inquiry, organizational planning, grouping, classification.

D. MATERIALS NEEDED

Manipulatives or pictures: the universe, the world; human anatomy, blood circulation; microscope and samples; a telescope; chart paper; color markers, colors, color-coded coop cards.

E. CLASSROOM STRUCTURES

Cooperative teams of 4 or 5 students. Students must select a (1) time keeper; (2) recorder/artist; (3) reporter; (4) team leader; and (5) encourager.

The teacher will see that every table has one high achiever/fluent English speaker, a low achieving/limited English speaker, and two or three average students or intermediate speakers of English.

For every activity there must be interdependence among all team members which is why the roles are so important. The encourager must make sure that everyone participates and contributes. The team leader makes sure that everyone is on task.

F. PROCEDURE

Class #1

Students are in cooperative teams of four or five. The teacher's introduction includes <u>activating prior knowledge</u> - brainstorming, spoking, hypothesis forming, using manipulatives.

The teacher will drop a sheet of paper and an apple from the same height and ask the students to describe what happened.

<u>Spoking or webbing technique for brainstorming</u> (10 minutes)

All answers will be recorded on a large chart, using a spoking or webbing technique. Each spoke is a "hypothesis." The chart paper is saved for proving each hypothesis at the end of the chapter.

This exercise would indicate how much the students know about gravity/inertia, experimentation, hypothesis, etc., the whole scientific inquiry process.

54

The teacher explains the objectives and reasons the topic is important. For example: The next three days the class will learn about the years when people began to study the world, the stars, the human body, and everything in nature in an organized way. This was an important period in history because it was the beginning of great scientific experiments and a new look at government, education, and the way people lived in society. They asked themselves a lot of questions and thought of many solutions just as you did with the paper and apple. This was the beginning of scientific experiments much like the ones today -- going into space, studying the bottom of the ocean, discovering a cure for cancer.

INSTRUCTION

<u>Heads Together</u>: (2 minutes)

The students are asked to think of other scientific projects and discoveries. They are to put their heads together and think of two or three important discoveries, recent or in the past, that are of great importance today. Each team will take one minute to discuss and agree on one discovery only to share.

<u>Paired Reading</u>: (3 minutes)

Next, the students will turn to page 401 to read the introduction. Students will:

1. Read the introduction silently or aloud in pairs.

2. Discuss in pairs what the introduction says and give two examples as to why that period in history is important today.

<u>Expert Jigsaw</u>: (10 minutes)

In their teams, students will number off #1 through #4. If there is a fifth student in the group that student can twin with any 1-4 student. Students will re-form as groups of the same number. Projects for the expert groups are:

TABLE 1.   Medieval thinkers see the earth as the center of the universe. Medieval thinkers accept Aristotle's views. Copernicus proposes a sun-centered universe.

TABLE 2.   Galileo proves his observations by experimentation. Galileo studies the stars and planets, and supports Copernicus' theory.

TABLE 3.   Kepler discovers laws of planetary motion, and Newton describes an orderly universe.

TABLE 4.   Several advances in natural sciences are made.

Next, each group reads and discusses its own topic. HOMEWORK is assigned: Read pages 401-407. Students are told to return to the same tables tomorrow to continue working on their projects.

Class #2

Students go to Tables 1-4 to continue studying their assigned pieces of the jigsaw. At each table is a set of pictures with word labels or the real objects (realia) which refer to the concepts each group is studying. For instance, a microscope, a skeleton or pictures of human anatomy and blood circulation are given to Table 4; the planets and earth to Table 1; the universe, the sun, the telescope to Tables 2 and 3, and so on. All the pictures or manipulatives that the teacher can gather are distributed to the tables. Have a set of Color Coded Coop Cards with the necessary vocabulary for each team. Students can define the words or they can be already defined and ready for drill and application. Charts, poster paper, or newsprint and colors or markers are available for student use.

In addition, when they arrive, the students will find at their table a worksheet that explains their tasks as follows:

For the class period, Expert Groups are to:

1.   Continue discussion and outlining of key concepts.

2.   Identify unfamiliar vocabulary, define and learn the new words.

3.   Use pictures/manipulatives to discuss the beliefs of the scientists being studied. (20 minutes)

4.   Draw a picture of the beliefs or discoveries that students are studying.

5.   Create Expert's Posters for teaching the information and terminology to home groups. (20 minutes)

As the groups work on their assignments, the teacher first walks around monitoring as the activities get off the ground, clarifying questions about the task, adding information if necessary, and making sure every team is on target.

After the first 20 minutes, the teacher meets with each team for five minutes to:

1. Review its outline.

2. Discuss its approach to the task.

3. Correct misinterpretations of a role.

4. Intervene in any group processing activity that might stifle the final product.

As student groups proceed with their tasks, the teacher continues to monitor the activity, stopping to facilitate a process when asked.

HOMEWORK ASSIGNMENT: Finish poster or re-read pp. 402-407.

Class #3

Students are still in their Expert Groups. They will need about 10 minutes to wrap things up: finish sharing posters, new additions, corrections, etc.

Next, students are to return to their home teams and begin instructing their peers. Each student has 10 minutes to report and answer questions. Other students in the group will take notes and ask questions after each student's report. The timekeeper must keep careful time.

HOMEWORK ASSIGNMENT: Review notes.

Class #4

Students are with their home teams. They have 15 minutes to answer the questions on p. 407 or any other questions the teacher has selected to test the students on. After the questions are answered, the teacher conducts a Group Review to check the answers and to give all students the opportunity to review and learn all the material. (20 minutes)

GROUP REVIEW

This is the day before the exam! First, students number off from 1-4 (or 5). Then, a team member calls out the question. Time is given for group discussions on the answer and to make sure all group members know the answer. After this group-preparation period, the team member calls out a number, such as 3. All students with that corresponding number raise their hands. The team member asking the question selects the team that is to answer. Only number 3 can answer that question. Each correct answer generates points for that team.

Students in groups take turns asking the other groups the test review questions. The group asking the questions gets a point for asking the question. When the group called upon answers the question, it gets a point for the correct answer or a correct portion of the answer. Another group can answer or add the missing information and get a point.

The important thing is calling only one student to represent the group but not informing the students in advance who the group representative will be. That twist insures total involvement of all students.

CLOSURE

Pull out the Paper and Apple spoking hypothesis chart made during Class #1. Have students put their heads together and discuss which hypotheses were proven to be true and which were not.

Close by summarizing the "scientific study" process.

Class #5: TEST

PART II
Enlightenment Thinkers Seek Reforms, pp. 407-413.

LESSON DURATION: 4 class periods

A. **CONTENT OBJECTIVES**

Same as for all students.

B. **LANGUAGE OBJECTIVE**

Make sure SLEP know the correct interpretation or cultural definitions for:

aristocratic	fame	law
atheists	fanaticism	possession
civilized	government	power
corruption	honor	religion
deists	human behavior	revolutionary
economics	intolerance	security

C. **LEARNING STRATEGIES**

Reading and study skills, cooperation, clarification, summarizing.

D. **MATERIALS NEEDED**

Wall Chart or student copies of the SQ3R steps. Color Coded Coop Cards for new vocabulary words and their definitions.

E. **CLASSROOM STRUCTURE**

Same cooperative teams of 4 or 5 students. Roles are switched: timekeeper becomes recorder, recorder becomes reporter, etc.

Previous reporters are reminded to help the new reporters, and everyone is to help each other with their new roles.

F. **PROCEDURES**

Class #1

CLASSROOM STRUCTURE

Whole class for explanation of SQ3R. Then students are to continue working in the same teams.

ACTIVATE PRIOR KNOWLEDGE (5 minutes)

Review the 5 scientific study steps from **PART I** with a graphic organizer as students contribute the information:

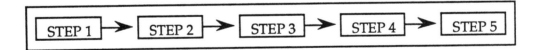

STATE OBJECTIVES AND WHY TOPIC IS IMPORTANT (1 minute)

The next three days will be spent in studying how the people in the "Age of Reason" tried to improve society, government and humanity through the use of reason. Students start this section by doing a survey of the information in **PART II** of the chapter, asking and answering questions and discussing the information.

INSTRUCTION (5 minutes)

The teacher will present the group technique called SQ3R. These are the steps and Social Rules for the lesson:

S Q 3 R   METHOD

DESCRIPTION:

The following method was developed by Francis P. Robinson for Reading/Study Skills. It is called the SQ3R METHOD (Survey, Questions, Read, Recite, Review) and consists of five steps.

1. SURVEY

    Survey the selection to be read by glancing over the headings, illustrations, italicized words, etc., in 2 or 3 minutes. Construct an outline of the ideas in your mind -- chapter title, headings, subheadings, introductory paragraphs, summary, important ideas, maps, graphs, illustrations.

2. QUESTION

    Look at the first main heading and turn the heading into a question. For example: The heading might be "People Working Together." Ask: How do people work together? Does a job get done faster when people work together?

3. READ

    Read to find the answers to your questions. This requires an active search for the answer on the part of the reader.

4. RECITE

    Now look away from the book and recite the answers to your questions. Use your own words and name an example, if applicable. If you can do this, you know what is in that section. If you cannot, glance over the section again.

5. REVIEW

    Review the selection by reconstructing an outline in your mind of the selection. Try to recall important ideas and their relationships. Also try to think of applications of the ideas learned. If gaps exist in your memory, go back over the selection.

In a group, adapt SQ3R by:

1. Writing down questions and answers.

2. Making sure everyone has answers to all questions.

3. Making sure everyone knows the information on the pages of the selection.

Students will have 20 minutes to do pages 407-410 (end with "philosophers write for the encyclopedia.")

DEBRIEF (5 minutes)

Every team shares one question and answer.

Class #2

Students will continue with SQ3R and debriefing at the end of the period. Students are to learn the material on pages 410-413.

HOMEWORK ASSIGNMENT: Read pages 407-413.

Class #3

The teacher will have activities to review the vocabulary (25 minutes) and share final outlines (25 minutes).

1. A vocabulary pre-test is given.

2. Students learn the words they missed through a Color Coded Coop Card activity.

3. A post-test is administered.

4. Teams are to come up with one outline. The outline is placed on a chart or the chalkboard for teams to compare outlines.

HOMEWORK ASSIGNMENT: Study outline and notes.

Class #4

The students will do a paper-pencil test (25 minutes) and learn how the information can be transferred (25 minutes).

1. The test is given and papers collected.

2. The whole class will review the correct answers together.

3. The students will then describe how the information they studied the past two weeks applies to their lives today. Teams will have 10 minutes to discuss and summarize their ideas. Then, all teams share those ideas.

LESSON PLANS
SOCIAL STUDIES LESSON #2

UNIT 7 - THE WORLD OF THE MIDDLE AGES (Civilizations of the Past: Peoples and Culture, by Jack Abramowitz and Kenneth A. Job, Modern Curriculum Press, 1981)

LESSON DURATION: 10 class periods

A. CONTENT OBJECTIVES

Same as specified in the Teacher's Guide. Emphasis is on how people lived and what this period means in the history of humankind.

B. LANGUAGE OBJECTIVE

The teacher will teach or check for prior knowledge of the following:

architecture	crafts	fief	Middle Ages
barter	Crusades	heraldry	minstrels
charity	Dark Ages	Islam	monasteries
chivalry	diocese	Judaism	nobles
Christianity	divine right	justice	serfs
civilization	fallow	manor	tournaments
commerce	feudalism	medieval	vernacular

C. LEARNING STRATEGIES

Vocabulary building (meaning from context), organizing (from question and answer pattern), inferring.

D. MATERIALS NEEDED

Textbook	Filmstrip Series (The Middle Ages, National Geographic Society, 1983)
Realia	Chart paper, markers, crayons
Pictures	Student worksheets
	Current news articles from magazines or newspapers

E. CLASSROOM STRUCTURE

Whole class, pairs, and cooperative teams of five each:

Recorder/Note Taker	Task Master/Team Leader
Timekeeper	Reporter
Encourager	

F.   PROCEDURES

Class #1

The teacher will conduct a whole class discussion on the prospect of AIDS being a worldwide epidemic, comparing this possibility with the plagues of the 6th and 14th centuries, when several hundred millions died in Europe and Asia. The teacher then leads into the name given to the first part of this historical period, the Dark Ages. The new unit covers the period before the first plague until after the second epidemic. Students take a pretest and view the filmstrip series that introduces the unit. A followup discussion should cover the key concepts from the filmstrip.

The teacher gives students the Vocabulary Overview Guide (See Appendix 2, page 137) or has them turn to those sheets in their notebooks and cover the assigned material in Sections A and B. Section C is assigned as homework to accompany the next homework, pp. 168-9.

Students are to do <u>SQ3R</u> technique in preparation for doing homework.

Class #2: Cooperative Teams

Each cooperative team will work on one or two of these questions for a report.

Team I: What kind of government did the ancient Romans have?
Team II: Name three ways in which the government affected the lives of the people.
Team III: What happened to the ancient Romans in the 5th century A.D.? Describe the people who caused this.
Team IV: How did Europe change after the 5th century A.D.?
Team V: Why have historians given the period between 450 and 850 A.D. its special name?
Team VI: What religion became important during this period and why?
Team VII: Name three ways in which the people's everyday lives changed when Rome was no longer in power.

Team members: Team leader
                        Recorder/Reporter
                        Timekeeper/Encourager
                        Checker/Praiser

After fifteen minutes, the teams are to report. The students listening will have their note-taking sheets ready with the key topics listed:

1. Roman government
2. Life in ancient Rome
3. Fall of Rome
4. Changes in Europe
5. The Dark Ages
6. Christianity
7. Changes in people's lives

If there are serious misunderstandings being communicated to the students, corrections are done at the conclusion of the reports. The students then return to their teams and exchange note sheets and help each other with the key points.

Homework: Read pp. 170-1.

Class #3

Team reports not completed on Day #2 will be given. The review of note-taking by team members and by whole class will follow after all reports are done. Students need to see that this note-taking skill is helpful in every subject.

If the students have completed the planned activities for Class #2, they will continue with the lesson for pages 170-1. The whole class recalls what they already know about modern governments. The teacher writes their responses on the board:

Type of Government	Titles of Leaders	Names of Countries

Next, the cooperative teams will make charts on the question: Why were the governments of the Middle Ages said to look like a pyramid? Each team works with a sheet of chart paper and crayons, etc. At the end of 20 minutes, each team leader shows the class the team's chart with a short explanation. All the pyramids are put on the board.

The teams will reassemble and read pp. 172-3 silently. Each team leader will then go to pick out a question for his/her team to answer:

1. What was a manor?
2. Why was a manor mostly self-sufficient?
3. Where did the working people live?
4. What did the serfs and peasants do in the manor?
5. What was the work of the nobles (men and women)?
6. What kinds of food crops did the people raise?
7. What kind of work schedule did the common people have?
8. (Add a "How" or "Why" question).

The teams' reporters will share each team's answer with the whole class. Since everyone has also read the same pages, the other teams must ask the reporters questions, i.e., questioning the answer given or asking for more information.

A scoreboard is used for debriefing at the end of the class.

Class #4/5: Pairs , Teams

Have pairs do No. 1 on p. 174, "Remembering What We Have Read," and No. IV on p. 175. The pairs then can check with the answer sheet on the teacher's desk and mark their own scores.

Next, the teams will do No. II on p. 174, and No. V on p. 175. Half of the teams will do the picture on the left, and the other half the right picture. The left-hand picture teams will take Question No. V, 1 and the right-hand picture teams will do No. V, 2. At the end of 20 minutes, all left-hand picture teams meet and all right-hand picture teams get together to share common and different observations. One reporter must be ready to report from the combined left teams and one to report on the combined right report.

Class #5/6

The two general reporters will be giving their reports this day. The class will be doing note-taking. The students will focus on the major topics: The Left Picture, The Right Picture, Life During the Middle Ages; A. The Life of a Serf; B. Society and Class in the Middle Ages.

Homework: Pages 176-9.

Class #6/7

Expert Jigsaw Technique

Students are assigned to one of four groups:

GROUP 1 - <u>FOOD</u> - What kinds of foods were eaten during the Middle Ages? When did the people eat? What were some of the customs connected with eating? Were there special foods eaten on special occasions? Why were there foods that were not eaten? Do people today eat the same foods?

GROUP 2 - <u>SHELTER</u> - Where did the people live? What was their shelter made of? How did the homes of the rich people differ from those of the poor? What was the purpose of each part of the castle (moat, drawbridge, etc.)? What system of sanitation was there?

GROUP 3 - <u>CLOTHING</u> - What kind of clothing did men and women wear? What were their clothes made of? What did the children wear? How did the poor and the rich dress? Were there special costumes worn for special occasions?

GROUP 4 - <u>RECREATION</u> - What did the people do during their non-working times? Did the rich and the poor do the same things? When did both groups of people get together to do things? Did the children go to school?

Each team should consist of:
    Team leader
    Coach/Encourager
    Secretary/Reporter
    Artist
    Researcher

The teams will meet and discuss their topics. Students are told that they are responsible for presenting their information to the other students and to answer any questions they might have on each team's topic.

The teams are encouraged to find outside resources to take to class the next day. They should plan on some visual aids to liven up their reports.

Class #7/8

Students go into their cooperative teams to continue working on their presentations. Every team member is encouraged to have a role in the presentation.

The following should be available to the students:

1. Chart paper
2. Marking pens, crayons, colored pencils
3. Props and pictures borrowed from the lending library at the Honolulu Academy of Arts

Tell the teams that every expert group should:

1. Continue discussing its section of the reading.
2. Identify all the unfamiliar vocabulary.
3. Draw scenes or create manipulatives or props to use in the class presentation.
4. Select vocabulary words for the whole class to study.

While the students are working, the teacher circulates among the teams to give assistance as needed. Instructional direction should also be given.

Class #8/9

Students organize their note-taking sheets to record key ideas from each team of experts. Each expert team has 10-15 minutes for its presentation and 5 minutes or longer for questions from the other students. The teacher should also be prepared to ask questions for clarification. Time is spent on the vocabulary words prepared by the teams.

Class #9/10

Reports of the expert teams are finished. Key ideas are reviewed and the presentations evaluated with discussions on what the students liked best about each report and how to improve the next expert jigsaw experience. Points are given for each report.

Class #10/11

The students are given cards with questions based on the reports and key concepts from the reading assignments. The Tea Party is continued until all the students have had a chance to answer each question.

LEARNING TO COMMUNICATE MATHEMATICALLY

Mathematics discourse, especially written discourse, presents considerable difficulties for many students, particularly students of limited English proficiency. The language register of mathematics includes unique features of vocabulary, syntax (sentence structure), semantic properties (truth conditions), and discourse (text). (Crandall, 1987).

VOCABULARY

Mathematical vocabulary is composed of meanings appropriate to the communication of mathematical ideas, the understanding of mathematical concepts and the expression of these ideas and structures. Therefore, SLEP need a mathematical vocabulary which includes words such as :

divisor	denominator	quotient
coefficient	equal	rational
irrational	column	table
power	variation	imaginary

In addition to isolated vocabulary items, the mathematics register uses special vocabulary to create complex strings of words or phrases which are often combined to form new concepts. For example, even the simple phrase "a quarter of the apples" can be a complex mathematical term which can be problematic to LEP students (Crandall, 1987). Other terms are:

least common multiple   negative exponent

Many LEP students are not yet aware that **addition** can be signaled by any of these words:

add	plus	and
sum	combine	increased by

or that **subtraction** can be signaled by these words:

subtract from	minus	difference
decreased by	less	less than
take away		

Certain mathematical key words with prepositions can be very confusing for LEP students. For example:

4 multiplied by 10	4 increased by 10
4 divided by 10	4 divided into 10
4 multiplied by itself	x exceeds two by seven

Mathematical symbols can be verbalized in various ways. For example "*a*" may be expressed as:

the square of "*a*"	the second power of "*a*"
"*a*" squared	"*a*" to the second power

Students must learn to relate symbols such as <, >, [ ] and ( ) to mathematics concepts or processes and then translate these into everyday language in order to express the mathematical ideas embedded in the symbols. For example: $3(x + 10) - 4x = (-6 + x) (-5)$ is a structure that SLEP need ample time and practice to verbalize and process.

Commas and periods play different roles in different countries. In several countries, commas are used to separate whole numbers from decimal parts while decimal points are used for this purpose in the United States. Our teachers may need to make this clear to students who are familiar with the comma used for separating whole numbers and fractions.

SYNTAX

Since mathematics is a study of relationships, comparative structures are an essential and recurring part of mathematical discourse. The following are difficult structures for LEP students to master:

greater than/less than	as in	all numbers greater than 4
n times as much	as in	Mary earns five times as much as I do. Mary earns $60,000. How much do I earn?
as ... as	as in	Joseph is as old as Maria
-er than	as in	Melia is 6 years older than Mai. Melia is 20. How old is Mai?
numbers used as nouns (rather than adjectives)	as in	Twenty is five times a certain number. What is the number?
passive voice	as in	10 (is) divided by 2 X *is defined* to be equal to zero. When 10 *is added* to a number the result is 43.

The lack of one-to-one correspondence between mathematical symbols and the words they represent poses considerable difficulty for LEP students. The following are some common <u>errors</u> to anticipate:

Eight divided by 2   is translated $2 \div 8$

The square of the
quotient of a and b   is translated $(a \text{ and } b)^2$

The number a is 5 less
than the number b   is translated $a = 5 - b$

Logical connectors are words or phrases which carry out the function of marking a logical relationship between two or more basic linguistic structures. Some connectors include *if ...then, if and only if, because, that is, for example, such that, but consequently, and either ...or.* (Kessler, Quinn, and Hays, 1985). SLEP must know which situation is signaled--similarity, contradiction, cause and effect or reason and result, chronological or logical sequence. They have to know where logical connectors appear in a sentence (at the beginning, middle, or end of a clause), and they must be aware that some connectors can appear in only one position, while others can appear in two or all three positions, and that change in position can signal a change in meaning. For example:

For every real number *a* there is a unique real number *-a*, such that
$a + (-a) = 0$ and $(-a) + a = 0$

If *a* is a positive number, then *-a* is a negative number; if *a* is a negative number, then *-a* is a positive number; if *a* is 0, then *-a* is 0.

The opposite of *-a* is *a*; that is, $-(-a) = a$.

SEMANTICS AND INFERENCES

The referents of variables are particularly difficult for SLEP. Variables stand for the *number* of persons or things, *not* the persons or things themselves. The following classic word problem illustrates this point.

There are five times as many students as teachers in the math department. Write an equation that represents this statement.

Many students will write $5s = t$, which follows the literal word order of the natural language sentence. The correct equation is $5t = s$. This kind of reversal error is common among students when they have been taught one-to-one correspondence between word and symbol. Experienced with such word

81

problems, they incorrectly expect that all problems can be solved in the same manner.

BUILDING MATHEMATICAL COMMUNICATIVE COMPETENCE

The first objective of sheltered math instruction is to ensure that students have a basic understanding of the relationship between what is spoken and what is written. A mathematics book contains vocabulary, syntax, symbols, diagrams, charts, and graphs that are not commonly used in other books. It is very difficult for SLEP to express this content in words. Therefore, math teachers need to stress the use of oral language by having students verbalize all operations in sentences, summarize, repeat, paraphrase, read aloud, work together, and discover their own ways of making sense of the written words and communicating the meaning of those words to one another. **Mathematical thinking, mediated by linguistic processes, is a prerequisite for mathematics achievement.**

The most effective math instruction for SLEP is typically presented through cooperative learning activities, individual tasks and tutorial sessions that use manipulatives, graphics, and other hands-on concrete experiences that clarify and reinforce meaning. Activities should involve listening comprehension, verbal production, reading and writing of the language features identified for the particular math lesson.

LESSON PLANS
MATHEMATICS LESSON #1

Chapter 1 — PAPER AND PENCIL COMPUTATION, (<u>Practical Mathematics:</u> <u>Consumer Applications</u>, by Marguerite Fredrick, Robert Postman, Steven Leinwand, and Laurence Wantuck. Holt, Rinehart & Winston, 1989.)

This textbook is organized to provide students with meaningful activities, easily adaptable to sheltered instructional techniques and strategies. The focus should be on preteaching vocabulary in two sets: 1) the words necessary to understand the content of the lesson, and 2) the words used to explain the lesson. The following are tips for sheltering the lesson.

USING THE CHAPTER OPENER

Preteach/review:
- ordinary numbers
- how numbers are used in various sports

COOPERATIVE LEARNING

Have teams come up with a team name and a team banner or cheer as a Team Building Activity.

WARM-UP

Review math addition vocabulary in this manual.

INTRODUCTION

Model each process; then have students work together on 2 or 3 examples for each skill.

ASSIGNMENTS

Distribute the **Practice Exercises** for students to work independently. Then they check their answers with their teammates. Have students exchange papers with another team to check their answers as they are called out. Ask for number of correct answers and record them as team scores.

FOLLOW-UP ACTIVITY

Conduct activity as stated in the book. Be sure each team member has an assigned role: recorder, map reader, adding pro, checker, time keeper/encourager.

WARM - UP

Model subtraction process and naming/labeling each step of an option

INTRODUCTION

Have students use a spoking technique to brainstorm the uses of subtraction:

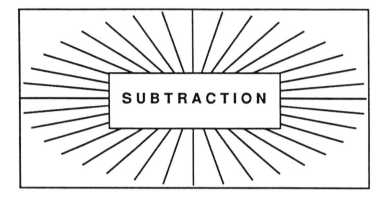

Students will also review the vocabulary in this manual dealing with subtraction. If necessary, repeat the review steps.

ASSIGNMENTS

Assign equal numbers of exercises to each team. Find a pattern to assign the problems so that each team has problems from levels 1, 2 and 3. For example, Team 1 does problems #1, 5, 10, 15, 20, 25, 35, 37 and Team 2 does problems # 2, 6, 11, 16, 21, 26, 31, 38, etc.

FOLLOW-UP ACTIVITY

Conduct cooperative learning activities as suggested but assign roles to everyone in the team.

WARM-UP, INTRODUCTION AND INSTRUCTION, FOLLOW-UP ACTIVITY

Preteach vocabulary for multiplication listed in this manual, then teach the lesson as suggested in pages 6 and 7, using pictures and chalkboard to go over each step meticulously.

Make Concept Cards with index cards in sets of four for each of the teams as follows:

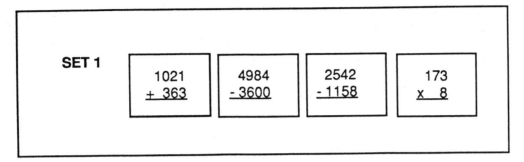

All four answers equal <u>1384</u>. Instruct students to do the operations and to get up and find their 3 partners and form new teams.

Ask teams to select a team name and to work in their teams to complete correctly as many of the 48 problems as possible.

Ask students to do word problems together. Then, instruct them and develop 2 similar word problems. Students should exchange those 2 problems with another team, solve and return them to the team for checking and grading.

DIVIDING WHOLE NUMBERS AND DECIMALS

ROUNDTABLE. Give one copy of the Practice Page 4 to each team. Do a Roundtable (as described in the appendix) for 5 minutes. Have teams exchange papers, check completed problems and return sheets to teams. Record scores and debrief. Ask students to share strategies and discuss strategies for improving the next round. Conduct the Roundtable again for another 5 minutes or longer if needed.

LESSON DURATION: 4 class periods

A. **CONTENT OBJECTIVES**

Same as specified in the Teacher's Guide. Emphasis is on estimating and calculating various quantities.

B. **LANGUAGE OBJECTIVE**

The teacher will teach or check for prior knowledge of the following:

estimate	gal.	less than
products	mi.	how much more
quotients	d.	weekday/weekend
wages	wk.	about how many/much
tips	ad	usually
per		

C. **LEARNING STRATEGIES**

Learning to estimate; comprehension; solving word problems.

D. **MATERIALS NEEDED**

Textbook	Index cards
Newsprint	Worksheet
Markers	

E. **CLASSROOM STRUCTURES**

Whole class, cooperative teams of 3 or 4.

F. **PROCEDURES**

Class # 1

Warm-up (10 minutes)

The teacher will lead the class discussion on the practical value and uses of estimation. Then the teacher instructs on the steps of estimation.

Roundtable (25 minutes)

Cooperative teams of 3-4 students will use the Roundtable strategy and do the practice exercises (p. 12). Each student will complete one problem before passing the worksheet to the next student. Other team members may tutor and assist the student if needed.

When time is called, teams exchange worksheets while the teacher calls out the correct answers and team scores are recorded. During the debriefing, students share the strategies used and how to improve the next Roundtable.

Another Roundtable is held for the remaining problems (to #46). Scores are recorded again.

Instruction (15 minutes)

For the rest of the period, the teacher teaches the 5-Point Checklist* so that every student understands. A technique is to verbalize the entire thought process as the problem is solved, step by step. The teacher can help the students identify all the important words in the problem. A diagram may be made to help the students understand the problem.

Use Exercise #47 as a model:

Tuna sandwiches sell for ⁽²⁾ ($2.85.) ⁽¹⁾<u>About how much will 5 tuna sandwiches cost?</u>

(3) Estimate: "About how much do they cost?"
(4) Multiply to find the answer: 5 x $3.00 = $15.00.
(5) $15.00 ÷ $3.00 = 5 sandwiches.

Class # 2

Warm-up (5 minutes)

Select 5-10 problems from Class #1. Hand the problems (written on index cards) to different students to do on the board, so that roll can be taken.

Numbered Heads Together (15 minutes)

Teams will do Practice Sheet 14, #1-12. The teacher will call teams by name and the number of the student to give the answer.

---

* 1. Understand the question. Underline it.
  2. Find the needed information. Circle it.
  3. Plan what to do. Find the action.
  4. Choose the operation. Find the answer.
  5. Check back. Compare the facts.

Jigsaw (25 minutes)

Students will use Problems #13-16 on Practice Sheet 14. Expert teams will use the 5-Point Checklist and write out the problem on newsprint to share.

Debrief (5 minutes)

Debrief on problems solved. If any were not solved, discuss reasons.

Class # 3

Warm-up (10 minutes)

Review 5-Point Checklist. Students meet in teams and do Numbered Heads Together on Problems #17-20.

Team Product (30 minutes)

Each group will next do a Team Product. The teams will write 3 similar word problems, each on an index card. The teams will exchange cards and solve the problems.

Debriefing (10 minutes)

Debrief on how the problems were solved.

Class # 4

Warm-up (5-10 minutes)

Teach or review these terms:

less than	usually	weekdays
weekends	how much more	payroll

Numbered Heads Together (25 minutes)

Teams will work on Practice Sheet #16, each doing No. 1-8 by discussing the problems — using the 5-Point Checklist.

Independent Work (10 minutes)

Hand out the bottom half of Practice Sheet #16 to each student. This will serve as a quiz for checking on individual student achievement.

Debrief (5-10 minutes)

MATHEMATICS LESSON #2

Chapter I — READING ALGEBRA, Words into Symbols: Sentences. (Algebra I, by Mary Dolciani, Richard Swanson and John Graham, Houghton Mifflin, 1986.), pages 40-47.

LESSON DURATION: 5 class periods

A. CONTENT OBJECTIVES

1. Translate numerical relationships stated in words into mathematical sentences.
2. Translate mathematical sentences into numerical relationships.
3. Same as those on pages 17 and 30.

B. LANGUAGE OBJECTIVE

The teacher will teach or check for prior knowledge of the following concepts:

mathematical sentence	equation
inequality	satisfy
open sentence	solution or root of an open sentence
solve an open sentence	graph of an open sentence
set-builder notation	solution set
side of an equation	side of an inequality
sum of	more than
less than	when...the result is

C. LEARNING STRATEGIES

Ability to infer meaning from algebraic relationships expressed in words and symbols.

D. MATERIALS NEEDED

Index cards (10 per team)
Color-Coded Coop Cards (Use four colors, one color per student in team. For each color you will need 16 cards, one for each language objective). Write vocabulary item on the front of the card and its definition on the back. Alternative: students can develop their own CCC Cards.

E. CLASSROOM STRUCTURES

Cooperative learning teams of four. Some activities will be conducted in pairs.

89

F.   INSTRUCTIONAL PROCEDURES

Class # 1

Modeling (10 minutes)

Students are in cooperative teams of four. The teacher's introduction is providing a <u>model</u> of the process to be learned. The teacher will write three mathematical sentences on the chalkboard and elicit responses to questions about what the students observe.

Heads Together (10 minutes)

Do a Heads Together using a fourth example so that each team practices writing a mathematical sentence.   (5 minutes)

Confirm teams' answers with total class.   (Another 5 minutes)

Color Coded Co-op Cards (20 minutes)

Give pre-test on the 16 language items. Add more items if needed. (5 minutes)

Have students pair up for Color Coded Co-op Card practice of the items they missed. (10 minutes)

Give post-test. It's OK if they still missed a few definitions. (5 minutes)

Talking Roundtable. (10 minutes)

Begin oral exercises on the bottom of page 40. Have students number off from 1 to 4 and instruct them to use a Roundtable procedure to ensure each one practices translating a word sentence into a mathematical sentence. The students will probably only complete half of the problems.

Class #2

CLASSROOM STRUCTURE

Talking Roundtable (5 minutes)

Begin with the Roundtable activity for review and warm-up   Students can begin with the second half of the problems from page 40.

90

Jigsaw (15 minutes)

Assign each team a set of problems from pages 41-42, #1-24. Ask students to answer the problems together by first making sure each one works on one or two problems, and then checking and verifying each other's answers.

Sharing (20 minutes)

When the teams finish their assigned problems, they appoint a reporter to write the answers on the board. When his/her team's turn comes, the reporter will read the question and the answer.

Knowledge (10 minutes)

The students check to see that they have all 24 answers correct. They discuss any difficulties, clarify questions and make sure that they all understood the procedures, in order to be ready for tomorrow's quiz.

Class #3

Numbered Heads Together (25 minutes)

Use eight or nine problems from the set on pages 40-41, No. 1-15, and do a numbered Heads Together quiz. (Check the end of this section for steps to the teaching strategy.)

Word Problem Cards (25 minutes)

In preparation for this activity, select a variety of problems, from No. 1-38 on pages 41-43. Remove key words, phrases, whole pieces of information, and/or the problem question. Write or type each problem with the gaps on an index card. If you laminate your cards, be sure to leave enough space for the left-out portion.

In class, explain this cloze procedure to the students. Have them fill in the blanks with whatever they think will make sense in the problem. Then have the students solve the problem after the information is added. Give each team four or five cards.

Class #4

Creative Word Sentences (35 minutes)

Have the teams develop two word sentences similar to the ones they had worked on previously. Have the teams solve the word sentences. Then, each team is to write the word sentences on separate index cards. The teams will then exchange cards, solve each other's word sentences, and verify answers with the original card developers.

Vocabulary Test and Practice (15 minutes)

Have students use their CCC Cards to review language items and other necessary vocabulary again. Give a test.

Class #5

Preparation for a Tea Party (25 minutes)

Have the teams develop a Tea Party worksheet, using the Chapter Summary and Review on pages 44 and 45. Assign each team a different section of the summary, so that the concepts, vocabulary, etc., will not be duplicates of other teams'.

Tea Party (25 MINUTES)

Conduct a Tea Party using the worksheets developed by the teams. This will be a practice for the final test.

LESSON PLANS
SCIENCE LESSON #1

CHAPTER 13 - HEAT (Experiences in Physical Science, by Michael Magnoli, et al.,
Laidlaw Brothers, 1985.)

LESSON DURATION: 10 class periods

A. CONTENT OBJECTIVES

Same as those on T69-T73.

B. LANGUAGE OBJECTIVE

The teacher will be sure that students know the following:

calorie	density	insulation
chemical reaction	electric heaters	measure
condensing	expand	radiating
conduction	fossil fuels	range
container	friction	solar energy
contract	fuel	substances
convection	generator	temperature
degree	heat	volume

C. LEARNING STRATEGIES

Grouping, inferencing, organizing, graphing

D. MATERIALS NEEDED

Objects recommended by the text.

Pictures	Chart paper	Water containers
Thermometers	Paper clips	

E. CLASSROOM STRUCTURES

Whole class and cooperative teams of four.

Each group must include one student with top grades in science, one that is
SLEP, one who has low grades in science, and one average student.
Students are reminded that both the final product and each member's
contribution will be graded.

F. PROCEDURES

Class #1

Students are instructed to rub their hands and asked how their hands feel. Next, each is given a paper clip and told to straighten it and bend the wire back and forth ten times. The teacher demonstrates the procedure and everyone counts aloud. Then the students are asked to touch their cheek with the wire. They are asked how the wire feels.

Next, the class discusses other ways in which heat is also produced. Pictures of different types of fires, solar energy and other examples are shown.

The class then discusses why heat is important. Answers are written on the board.

The teacher asks: What is energy? Then, he/she draws spokes from the main idea and asks for things that work. For example:

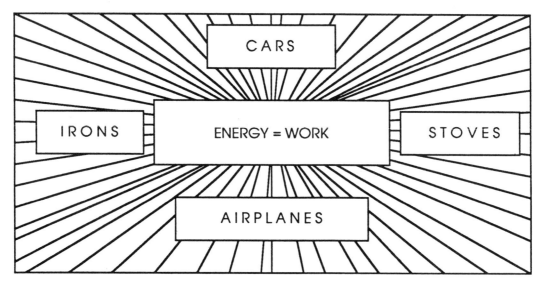

The objectives of the lesson are discussed. A connection to the careers suggested at the end of the unit is made. (1 minute)

Jigsaw

Each team will be assigned one of the following topics/activities:

1. Heat or temperature   p. 252-253
2. Measuring temperature   p. 253
3. Measuring heat energy   p. 254
4. Solar energy   p. 256-257
5. Heat from fuels   p. 257
6. Chemical and nuclear reactions   p. 257-258
7. Heat from friction   p. 258

Each team is to present an experiment (suggested by the book, or the teacher, an encyclopedia, etc.) and present it to the class during the week (10-15 minute presentation). Students have $2\frac{1}{2}$ class periods to prepare. They should also draw charts or make outlines with important information that other students need to know before, during or after the presentation.

For the rest of this class period, students will begin reading and organizing their approach to their presentation.

Class #2

Demonstration (10 minutes)

The teacher demonstrates for the students how to conduct an experiment by doing the one on page 255.

After the experiment, each team (or 2 teams) is given the four questions listed on page 255 (answers on T70). Teams are given 10 minutes to come up with their answers and read them to the total class.

Jigsaw (10 minutes)

The students are given the remaining 10 or so minutes to do more planning on their experiment, and on role and task assignments. Each group is closely monitored. Announce that they will have one more class period to finish.

Class #3

Students use the whole period to finish preparing for their presentation/ demonstration. The teacher checks their notes and procedures and makes sure that they have everything they need.

Class #4

The first four or five teams present. The other teams are instructed to read the question that pertains to each presentation and to take notes during the presentation. At the end of each presentation the students will have five minutes to write the answers to the questions on their Team Worksheet.

Class #5

The rest of the teams present and remaining questions on the Team Worksheet are answered. The 10 questions should address some particular theme, topic, problem, or highlight that emerged during this unit.

Class #6

An individual test can be given on the 10 questions, or the Cooperative Review or Tea Party activity can be used to give the teams additional points.

Class #7

Now that the students know the Jigsaw process and have experienced the benefits of peer cooperation, they continue to learn cooperating skills and the Jigsaw process. The additional projects in HEAT AND MATTER AND HOW HEAT TRAVELS pages 259-264 are assigned to the teams.

1. Each team can be assigned a topic.

2. Each team will have 10-15 minutes to present an experiment.

3. All students are expected to read the related passages before each presentation (homework assignments).

4. All students will fill in the answers to their Team Worksheet #2.

Classes #8 & 9

Teams perform their experiment in front of the class. All other students answer their Worksheet.

Class #10

The teacher selects 10 questions from both Worksheet to do a Tea Party. There is a debriefing of the content and process of the Jigsaw and the Tea Party as closure.

TEAM WORKSHEET #1

1.   Explain the difference between heat and temperature.

2.   Describe how temperature is measured.

3.   Name two commonly used temperature scales and tell how they differ.

4.   Describe how heat is measured.

5.   Name two standard units of heat.

6. List some major sources of heat energy.

7. Describe how heat is generated from various sources.

8. Explain what a renewable heat source is and give examples.

9. Define the term "friction."

10. Describe some ways in which the sun's energy can be used in the home.

98

TEAM WORKSHEET #2

1.   What do the terms "expand" and "contract" mean?

2.   How is density affected by heat?

3.   What happens to a liquid at its freezing point?

4.   What happens to a liquid at its boiling point?

5.   How does heat travel?

99

6. What causes heat to move through a solid?

7. How does radiation differ from convection?

8. Explain what is meant by "insulation."

9. What causes winds?

10. How do people keep their houses warm when it is very cold in the winter?

LESSON PLANS
SCIENCE LESSON #2

CHAPTER 20 - BIRDS AND MAMMALS (Biology, by Irwin L. Slesnich, et al., Scott, Foresman and Co., 1980.)

LESSON DURATION: 9 class periods

A. CONTENT OBJECTIVES

Same as chapter objectives on page 475 and any other concept that the SLEP might need help in to successfully master the unit material.

B. LANGUAGE OBJECTIVE

The teacher will check for prior knowledge of the bold print words and words in italics from the text plus:

characteristics   nervous
circulatory   oxidation
digestive   placental
ectothermic   reproductive cycle
endothermic   respiratory
environmental adaptability shivering
mammals   skeletal
marsupial

C. LEARNING STRATEGIES

Use of graphic organizers for comparing/contrasting, describing and explaining; grouping; classification; social skills for working in pairs and small teams.

D. MATERIALS NEEDED

Pictures   Chart paper or newsprint
Index cards for CCCC   Learning Log booklets.

E. CLASSROOM STRUCTURE

Total class lecture (teacher) and discussion (students and teacher) for the warm-up activities, for previewing information before each day's activity. See attached pages for a sample of adapted material.

Pairs and teams should consist of mixed ability (1 high, 1 medium, 1 low) in content as well as in English proficiency.

F. PROCEDURES

Class #1

The class studies the objectives and discusses the first paragraph on page 475.

The teacher gives an introduction (10 minutes) of the information on pages 476-477. Pictures on the board or picture cards are used to ensure that information is comprehensible to all SLEP.

The teacher models how the graphic organizing technique is done by asking students to help with a web on the board using the information on page 477 as in the example in Appendix 3.

A debriefing is done with the students. Guide questions may be: What category did we start with first? Where did you find the information for the subcategories? What was discussed next? Where did you find that information?

Class #2

1. A preview of the information on pages 478-485 is done using visuals, manipulatives, etc. (10 minutes)

2. Expert teams are organized. Instructions are given on how to conduct an Expert Jigsaw. Each team is to do a webbing on each of the following categories: (20 minutes)

   a. Bird digestion system
   b. Bird reproduction system
   c. Bird nervous system
   d. Bird feathers

   e. Bird respiratory system
   f. Bird skeletal system
   g. Bird circulation system
   h. Bird plumage

Class #3

All students in each Expert team finish copying the group web. They practice talking about it, then return to their home teams to teach their teammates (5 minutes each student) and to discuss, learn and copy the webs made by the other experts. (30 minutes)

The experiment on page 486 is set up. Pairs of students are supposed to keep their daily observations of the development of the embryo in their Learning Log. Drawings and key words are acceptable for SLEP. Emphasis is on content and concept accuracy, not on language errors.

Class #4

The information on mammals (pages 488-496) is previewed with pictures, realia, and/or drawings. (10 minutes)

The teacher explains the comparison-contrast graphic organizer process and has the teams fill in the information. (10 minutes) Teams are monitored as they proceed to fill the information in the grid. There are four blank spaces for the information they can find.

	Egg Laying Mammals	Marsupials	Placental Mammals	Bird
Skeletal				
Reproductive				
Nervous				
Respiratory				
Digestive				
Circulation				
Muscle				
Skin				
Vision				
Brain				
Teeth				

103

Class #5

The completed graphs may be displayed on the walls and students will describe the process they use to complete their assignment and point out any additional information that they find. (Debriefing)

KWL (Know, Want to Find Out, Learn) activity is introduced next. The teams are to answer the Review questions on pages 477, 485, 496 and 498 by using KWL in teams. This procedure examines and builds upon students' prior knowledge of topics.

For each review question students discuss the answer. They will analyze their work and the recorders will write:

1. What they already know,
2. What they still do not, and
3. What they still need to learn through further reading or research.

The KWL Example Worksheet is on page 96. The teams can develop their own grids.

Students are to maintain their individual Learning Logs. The teacher will spot check the logs.

Class #5

Students may continue working on their KWL. There should be resource books or library privileges if the students wish to research some of their questions.

A debriefing should be covered.

Learning Logs are again spot checked.

Class # 7 and 8

Color Coded Coop Cards are used for learning the test questions on page 499. The Student Leader in each team is instructed to make sure that <u>all</u> students in the team are tutored until they master all the questions. The procedures for Color Coded Coop Cards are as follows:

Color Coded Coop Cards (CCCC)

After a lecture, audio-visual presentation, reading of a text, or doing an experiment, students can work together to master the concepts or vocabulary through CCCC. The steps are:

a.   The students take a pre-test.

b.   Students create color-coded cards for the words or problems each student missed. Each student on the team has a different color card.

c.   Students tutor each other with the cards. Tutors hold up the card. The tutee reads the question (answer is seen by tutor only). The tutee attempts to answer. If the answer is correct, the card is "won back" by the tutee; if not, it is placed on the bottom of the deck to be repeated. When the tutee wins back all her/his cards, the tutor and tutee switch roles.

d.   Students take a practice test.

e.   The practice test is repeated if necessary.

f.   The students take the final test. Recognition is given for best papers.

Closure is done through debriefing.

105

K W L EXAMPLE WORKSHEET

K	W	L
What We Know	**What We Want to Find Out**	**What We Learned and Still Need to Learn**
Black widow spiders have six legs.	How many baby spiders are born at the same time?	The black widow spider eats her husband and sometimes her babies.
Black widow spiders eat other insect.	Do black widow spiders hurt people?	They live in all parts of the United States.
Black widow spiders eat other spiders.	Why are they called Black Widow Spiders?	They have a red or yellow hourglass shape on their abdomen.
Black widow spiders are dangerous to people.	What is a widow?	
Black widow spiders have special markings.		
Black widow spiders kill their babies.		
Black widow spiders do not live here.		

SAMPLE OF ADAPTATION

Chapter 20 - Birds and Mammals (Biology, by Irwin Slesnick, et al., Scott, Foresman and Co., 1980.)

Page 476, The Trait of Warm-bloodedness

On a cold morning, a raccoon stalks its prey--a frog. It is likely to catch the frog, too, because the frog moves more slowly in cold weather than in warm weather. The raccoon has no such disadvantage--it moves at its usual pace, no matter what the weather.

Birds and mammals are warm-blooded, or endothermic. They are known as endotherms. Warm-blooded animals, such as raccoons, remain warm even when the temperature around them changes. The body temperature of frogs and other ectothermic, or cold-blooded, animals rises when the weather is hot and drops when the weather is cold. They are known as ectotherms.

In endotherms as in ectotherms, body heat is produced when food and oxygen are combined in the cells. The oxidation, or burning, of food produces energy and heat. However, when an endotherm is exposed to cold, the rate of heat production goes up, and its body temperature remains constant.

Endotherms have good body insulation--feathers, fur, or fat. Their protective covering helps slow the loss or gain of body heat to or from the environment.

A Suggested Adaptation of the Text

One cold morning, a raccoon is slowly, carefully following an animal to catch for food--a frog. The raccoon will catch the frog, because cold weather makes the frog move slowly. The frog moves faster in warm weather.

The weather will not do the same thing to the raccoon who moves at the same speed when the weather is hot or when the weather is cold.

Raccoons are called mammals. Birds and mammals are warm-blooded, or endothermic. These animals are called endotherms. Endotherms are warm-blooded, such as raccoons. Warm-blooded animals stay warm even when the air around them becomes cold.

The body temperature of frogs and other ectothermic, or cold-blooded animals, changes to match the temperature of the air around them. When the weather is hot, the temperature of the cold-blooded animals rises. When the weather is cold, their body temperature drops. Cold-blooded animals are called ectotherms.

In all animals, both endotherms and ectotherms, body heat is made when food and oxygen are joined in the body cells. The <u>oxidation</u>, or burning, of food in the body makes energy and heat. But when an endotherm is outside in cold weather, the body produces more heat to keep it at the same temperature.

Every endotherm has a good body cover--feathers, fur, or fat. This body cover helps to keep the heat of the body from leaving too fast and helps to keep the body from becoming too hot.

LESSON PLANS
LITERATURE LESSON #1

CONTENT: Greek Mythology

The Shining Stars: Greek Legends of the Zodiac, McLeish, Kenneth, N.Y.: Cambridge University Press, 1981.

Book of Greek Myths, D'Aulaire, Ingri and Edgar, N.Y.: Doubleday & Co., Inc., 1962.

Activities with Myths, Karl, Nancy, O'Fallon, MO.: Book Lures, Inc., 1983.

LESSON DURATION: 23 Classroom Periods

A. **CONTENT OBJECTIVES**

1. Help students learn major Greek myths which have influenced literature, art, and architecture throughout history.

2. Explain the need to know the basis of allusions made by authors and educated men and women.

3. Teach students about the basic components in narratives.

4. Facilitate students' learning of how to do research and formulate alternatives.

B. **LANGUAGE OBJECTIVES**

1. The teacher will teach or check for prior knowledge of the following terms and concepts:

zodiac	12 main Greek gods/goddesses
astronomy	12 Zodiac signs
myth/mythology	Mount Olympus
constellation	Greece/Greek
characters	Europe
personality	peninsula
physical appearance	islands
problem	climax
solution	feature articles
editorials	

2. Help students use words, sentence patterns and the conventions of written and oral language appropriately.

LEARNING STRATEGIES

Grouping, webbing, brainstorming, predicting, note taking, organizing, oral activities, learning logs, poster reports and publishing.

C. MATERIALS NEEDED

Trade Picture Books on Greek Stories
Vocabulary cards/index cards
Worksheets from Activities with Myths
Construction paper, typing paper, art supplies
Computer copies of zodiac signs
Film: "Clash of the Titans"

D. CLASSROOM STRUCTURES

Whole class, cooperative teams of three, individual

E. INSTRUCTIONAL PROCEDURES

Classes #1 & 2

Conduct a whole class discussion on zodiac signs. If your SLEP are from Asia, have them share the oriental zodiac with the class. The oriental zodiac is a 12-year instead of a 12-month cycle.

Discuss the meaning of the words zodiac, myth, constellation and develop understanding of these concepts.

Each team receives a set of zodiac pictures from the computer program, Print Shop.

Each team makes a pie graph depicting the Greek zodiac signs and dates.

Class #3

Introduce the basic historic facts about the country of Greece.

Each team meets as a group to predict what each zodiac sign means before hearing the stories.

Read the first story, "The Horn of Plenty" (Capricorn). Students take individual notes. Then students free write about the story in their Learning Logs.

110

Class #4

The whole class brainstorms how characters are developed in a story, emphasizing physical appearance and personality traits.

Review and paraphrase the basic components of a story: introduction, problem, climax, solution and ending.

Teams meet to decide what the problem, climax and solutions are in the story about the Capricorn sign. One team member records on a chart.

Classes #5 & 6

Expert Jigsaw. A member from each team will form a new expert team. The teacher gives each team 2-3 short zodiac stories on the remaining eleven stories. The teams read the stories and then select 5-8 key vocabulary words and decide on what the problems, climaxes, and solutions are for each story.

Then the experts go back to their original teams. All the team members share the above information and record the data on the same chart.

Class #7

Randomly select members from each team to answer literal questions about characters, vocabulary words, and story components. Give the team a score based on the performance of its team member.

Class #8

Introduce to the whole class the names of the twelve main Greek gods/goddesses. Introduce the concept of the importance of Mount Olympus and of mythology/legend.

Have students take notes.

Class #9

Expert Jigsaw. Form 3-4 new teams. Each team will be assigned a short list of the gods/goddesses to make charts with the following information:

God/Goddess   Symbols   Characteristics

Each team reads short summaries about the main gods/goddesses. Then all report back to the whole class.

Have students record the information. All members are responsible for all the information.

Class #10

Give each team the worksheet, "Olympus Crest." The team completes the crest on the team's favorite god/goddess. The team pretends to be that god or goddess, using the first person language.

Team members then share this with the whole class. The crest will be displayed in the classroom. (See attachment).

Class #11

Each student receives the worksheets: "Take-a-message" and "Horoscopes" (2 pages). These are individual writing assignments to be completed in class. (See attachment). Recall the lesson on the zodiac and have students read the horoscope sheets. Assist in paraphrasing and use sheltered language.

Classes #12 & 13

Distribute the attached, "The Twelve Labors of Heracles." Form new teams. Have the teams read the complete story and discuss the labors. Explain that Heracles is also known as Hercules. Each team selects which labor it would like to work on.

Each team then makes an 8-panel comic poster using bubbles for the dialogue. These posters will be shared orally and displayed on the bulletin board.

Class #14

Distribute the worksheet, "Mythology Tic-Tac-Toe," as an individual writing assignment. (See attachment). Be sure there are sufficient copies of the myths for each student to use for this assignment.

Class #15

Review the differences between facts and opinions and between feature articles and editorials. (Students already should have worked on these components). Assign "Theseus Slays the Minotaur." Have teams organize to complete the assignment as (1) a factual account, (2) an editorial, and (3) a feature story.

Brainstorm. Brainstorm with the class and do a webbing about problems in the world today.

Direct teams to write an editorial to the school newspaper identifying a major problem today, i.e., AIDS, pollution, overpopulation, arms race or drugs and write it as though Zeus were in a time capsule and were visiting us today. (See worksheet).

Class #16

Assign each team a different area: zodiac signs, gods/goddesses, monsters, mythology vocabulary and make up twenty-five trivia cards. One side of the card has the question and the other side the meaning/answer. (See Mythical Monsters as model).

Review the cards to sort out any duplications. Prepare the questions and answers for a Tea Party.

Class #17

Teams participate in a trivia board game using the teams' vocabulary cards. Teams will be given bonus points based on their game scores.

Classes #18 & 19

Provide typing paper, construction paper and art supplies. Each team makes a booklet, using materials already covered in class plus creative items such as "new myths" a team may want to write.

Upon completion, teams share the booklets orally and keep them on display for a week.

Booklets:
Zodiac Book
Gods/Goddesses Book
Mythology Dictionary

Class #20

Tea Party. Have students (or yourself) develop a tea party review of all the materials in preparation for a final test.

Class #21

Administer unit test: literal questions, inferences, and essay question, "Why is Greek Mythology Important Today?"

Classes #22 & 23

Show film, "Clash of the Titans" as a culminating activity.

LESSON PLANS
LITERATURE LESSON #2

CONTENT: Philippine Literature

FOOTNOTE TO YOUTH (<u>Asian-Pacific Literature</u>, Volume 3, Hawaii Department of Education, 1981.) pp. 73-80.

LESSON DURATION: 9 Classroom Periods

A. **CONTENT OBJECTIVES**

   1. Assist students to comprehend a story studied for its narrative and cultural contents.

   2. Help students deduce the theme of this didactic narrative and how it might affect themselves.

B. **LANGUAGE OBJECTIVES**

   The teacher will check for prior knowledge or teach the following according to each homework assignment:

   <u>Assignment 1</u>

footnote	emerged	stature	youth
carabao	prodded	salmon	furrows
virility	unhitched	burrowed	cursorily
hesitant	clammily	desirable	climacteric
insolent			

   <u>Assignment 2</u>

tensed	*batalan*	self-consciousness	smudged
unvarnished	relieved	obliquely	partake
expectantly	*kundiman*	pitied	decrescent
vigorously	diseased	feeble	petroleum
dentist			

   <u>Assignment 3</u>

intense	impatient	essay	troublous
clamor	confused	uncomfortable	exacting
absorbed	uttering	indifference	immensely
gazing	sourly	asserted	inflexible
knuckles	confined	fidgeted	resented
tatay	permission	impassioned	*inay*

125

<u>Assignment 4</u>

sweltering	contradicting	profusely	saw-horse
compress	calloused	tyranny	terribly
rebuking	embarrassed	whispered	paternity
awe	guilty	*camiseta*	

<u>Assignment 5</u>

beckoned	punish	pierced	thrust
traced	stray	tremulous	wisp
parched	demonstrative	ascended	swelling
mercilessly	*sawali*	smarted	*papag*
hilot			

<u>Assignment 6</u>

successive	suitor	dreamfully	shapeless
querulous	humiliated	interminable	fulfill
wisdom	laundering	forsaken	

<u>Assignment 7</u>

flustered	marriage	triumph	muttered
resentment	wistfully	fluttering	objections
extremely	descended	acridly	*itay*

LEARNING STRATEGIES

Grouping, webbing, brainstorming, journal writing, poster reports, oral activities, prediction, note taking

MATERIALS NEEDED

Cloze worksheets
Index cards
Learning Logs
Chart paper

CLASSROOM STRUCTURES

Whole class
Cooperative learning teams of four or five
Pairs
Individual

F. **INSTRUCTIONAL PROCEDURES**

Class #1

1. Explain what didactic literature is and its purpose. Introduce the story and its setting. (15 minutes)

2. Conduct whole class discussion with **Webbing** and have a hypothesis formed on what "Footnote to Youth" means. (20 minutes)

3. Assign first reading: p. 73 to top of p. 74. Students will do pretest on Assignment 1 vocabulary list.

Class #2

1. Pairs review vocabulary and use **CCCC** strategy on words missed. (15 minutes)

2. Do Cloze exercise, using **Numbered Heads Together.** (10 minutes)

3. Have students write an entry in their logs: "I Know Someone Like Dodong (or Teang)." (15 minutes)

4. Assignment reading, p. 74 (six paragraphs). Review language items for Assignment 2. (10 minutes)

Class #3

1. Hand out Cloze Worksheet 2 for **Numbered Heads Together** activity. (10 minutes)

2. Hold a brainstorming session on the possible emotions felt by Dodong, his mother and father. Put student contributions on a chart. (10 minutes)

3. Heads Together teams review language objectives assigned in Class #2. (20 minutes)

   Select 5 words for an individual test. Present the definitions and have students write the correct words. Have team members correct the quiz. Do **CCCC** for those words missed and drill on the cards.

4. Assign reading, p. 74 (from paragraph 7) to the middle of p. 75. Present language objectives for Assignment 3. (10 minutes)

Class #4

1.   Pairs in teams work on Cloze Worksheet 3 and reform as a whole team to check on their answers. (15 minutes)

2.   Individual Learning Log entries will be based on "How My Family Makes Big Decisions." (15 minutes)

3.   Teams meet, share log entries, and select one to share with the class. (10 minutes)

4.   Assign reading from middle of p. 75 to end of page. Language items for Assignment 4 are handed out. (5 minutes)

Class #5

1.   Teams hold discussion on the main idea of the reading. The follow-up whole class discussion will be on why Dodong is embarrassed. (15 minutes)

2.   Language objectives are done as a whole class. Students take notes and break into teams to review and adjust note-taking on the vocabulary as **Heads Together**. (10 minutes)

3.   Individuals do Cloze Worksheet 4 and hand in the completed lesson for grading. (5 minutes)

4.   Assign reading of p. 76 to the double space. Discuss language items for Assignment 5. Go over the ethnic words listed. (20 minutes)

Class #6

1.   Introduce the topic of preparation for marriage: What couples need to know and what skills they should acquire. In a class of two or more ethnic groups, divide the students into ethnic teams and have a group product on Essential Marriage Skills, those specific to one gender and those needed by both.

Each team will identify the traditional, culturally-oriented skills and the recent skills needed for living in America. The product might be a chart or a series of drawings to cover:

Essential Marriage Skills

Wife	Husband	Both

If there is only one ethnic group in the class, the teams may be assigned to cover the skills of the wife, husband, and both. This can be an Expert Jigsaw activity with one large chart made for the whole class by each Expert Group.

If there is time left in the period, discuss what Dodong's skills are and what skills he lacks. What do the students foresee as problems in his life?

Assign reading from the bottom portion of p. 76 to top half of p. 77. Language items are in Assignment 6.

Class #7

1. Individual Work (10 minutes)

    Students independently complete Cloze 6. Then they meet in teams to correct the exercise.

2. **Heads Together** (25 minutes)

    Students remain in their teams and answer this question:

    > Why did Dodong separate the two ideas of (1) Youth and Love and (2) Life?

    The teams must be prepared to explain what the difference is between the two concepts. Each team will share its conclusions with the whole class.

3. **Group Discussion** (10 minutes)

    The teacher leads the class into assumptions about Dodong's anger and Teang's unhappiness.

4. The last homework assignment is to finish the story. The language lesson is Assignment 7.

129

Class #8

1. **Pairs** (10 minutes)

    Students in pairs review the language homework. Then a quiz is given on the items. Scores will be for each member of the pairs.

2. **Learning Log** (20 minutes)

    Each student tapes into his/her log a copy of Cloze Worksheet 7, completes the Cloze and checks with the text. Then, the students will enter a personal interpretation as to why the father feels very sorry for his son. What could the father have done to prevent this situation? What lesson can they (the students) learn from this?

3. **Group Discussion** and Debriefing (20 minutes)

    The class will look at its hypothesis formed eight lessons ago and determine whether the hypothesis was proven. The next major questions are: What is the lesson being taught by the story? How does this lesson affect the students in the class? What cultural implications are seen in the lesson? Should the practice(s) continue? Why or why not?

Class #9

Allow students to meet in ear-to-ear pairs to review before the test. Administer a vocabulary test of key words from the entire narrative.

CLOZE WORKSHEETS

Cloze Worksheet 1

The sweetish, earthly (smell) comes from the many fresh (furrows) broken into the (earth or ground). Dodong is (seventeen), has (pimples) on his face, and dark (down) on his upper lip. Teang has straight, glossy (hair), a small brown (face), and small black (eyes).

Cloze Worksheet 2

Field work makes Dodong (dirty), and so, he goes to a (creek) to take a (bath). Dodong goes (home) and eats a (supper) of (fish) and (rice). He does not eat the (ripe bananas).

Cloze Worksheet 3

Dodong's father has a (toothache). When Dodong tells him about (marrying) Teang, his father is (silent) at first. Dodong's father's (eyes) have a strange helpless (light).

Cloze Worksheet 4

Teang is giving (birth) to their (first) child. Dodong feels (afraid) of the (house) and of (Teang) and also feels (queer). He is going to be a (father). He realizes that he is (young).

Cloze Worksheet 5

After the birth of his first child, Dodong feels more (embarrassed) and (guilty). He even feels like (crying) and wants somebody to (punish) him. He sees (Teang) asleep and wants to (touch) her, but he feels (embarrassed). He asks for his (son).

Cloze Worksheet 6

For (six) years in a row, a new (child) comes along. Dodong gets (angry) with himself sometimes, but (Teang) does not (complain). She sometimes (cries) and (wishes) she did not (marry).

One of the (questions) Dodong wants to ask is why (Life) does not fulfill all of (Youth's dreams).

Cloze Worksheet 7

When (Blas) is eighteen years old, he tells (Dodong) that he wants to (marry). Dodong feels (helpless) and cannot do (anything). Dodong even feels very (sad) and (sorry) for (Blas), his (son).

132

REFERENCES

Calderon, M. (1986-88) <u>Multilingual Teacher Training Institute Manuals</u> on <u>Whole Language Approaches and Cooperative Learning</u>, Santa Barbara, CA: MTTI.

Calderon, M. (1986-88) <u>Multilingual Trainer of Trainers Institute Manuals on ESL and Sheltered Instruction</u>. Santa Barbara, CA: MTTI.

Calderon, M., Rathmell G., Younglove, C., and W.B. Olsen, J. (1987) <u>Sheltered Instruction</u>. Santa Barbara, CA: MTTI.

Chamot, A., and O'Malley, M. (1987) <u>The Cognitive Academic Language Learning Approach</u> (CALLA)

Cummins, J. (1981) The Role of Primary Language Development in Promoting Educational Success for Language Minority Students. In <u>Schooling and Language Minority Students: A Theoretical Framework</u>. Office of Bilingual Education, California State Department of Education, Los Angeles, CAP: EDAC.

Jones, B.F., Palincsar, A.S., Ogle, D.S., and Carr, E.G. (1987) <u>Strategic Teaching and Learning: Cognitive Instruction in the Content Areas</u>. Arlington, VA: ASCD.

Krashen, S. (1981) Bilingual Education and Second Language Acquisition Theory. In <u>Schooling and Language Minority Students: A Theoretical Framework</u>. Office of Bilingual Education, California State Department of Education. Los Angeles, CA: EDAC.

Long, M. (1984) Native speaker/non-native speaker conversation and the negotiation of comprehensible input. In <u>Applied Linguistics</u>, Vol. 4, No. 2. pp. 126-141.

While you observe the sheltered lesson, check off the examples of sheltering techniques and then jot down a word or two to describe what part of the lesson accomplished it.

	Observed	Indication
1. Focus on message, meaning, task		
2. Use of visuals		
3. Use of realia, props, manipulatives		
4. Use of audio clues		
5. Use of body language		
6. Slower speech		
7. Clear pronunciation		
8. Shorter, simpler sentences		
9. Controlled vocabulary		
10. Restatement, examples, synonyms		
11. Repititions		

Adapted from Monterey MTTI, Dennis Parker, and Margarita Calderon, <u>MTTI Manuals</u>.

Appendix 1

Vocabulary Overview Worksheet

Chapter Title: _____

(category title)	(category title)
(target word)	(target word)
a. (clues	a. (clues)
b. (definitions)	b. (definitions)

Appendix 2

137

COACHING GUIDELINES

SAY WHAT YOU SAW . . . .

rather than what you thought/felt about it.

    a. Teacher behaviors: actions, discourse, gestures, activities, etc.

    b. Student behaviors: reactions, focus of attention, performance, etc.

    c. Lesson characteristics: format, activities, content, pace, etc.

ASK QUESTIONS . . . .

rather than make recommendations.

    a. Why do you feel that way?

    b. How would you do that differently?

    c. What do you mean?

    d. Is that what you expected?

    e. Which of these is the easiest/most difficult for you?

ESTABLISH THE FOCUS FOR THE NEXT SESSION:

    a. What teacher or student behaviors will be the focus of the next observation?

    b. What lesson characteristics or components do you want to pay the most attention to the next time?

    c. The items of focus should be specific, concrete, and limited in number.

Appendix 3

139

Welcome to the Wonderful World of Webbing

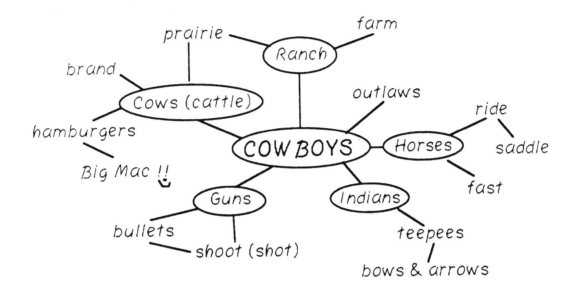

Michael Power, MRC-14

Appendix 4

141

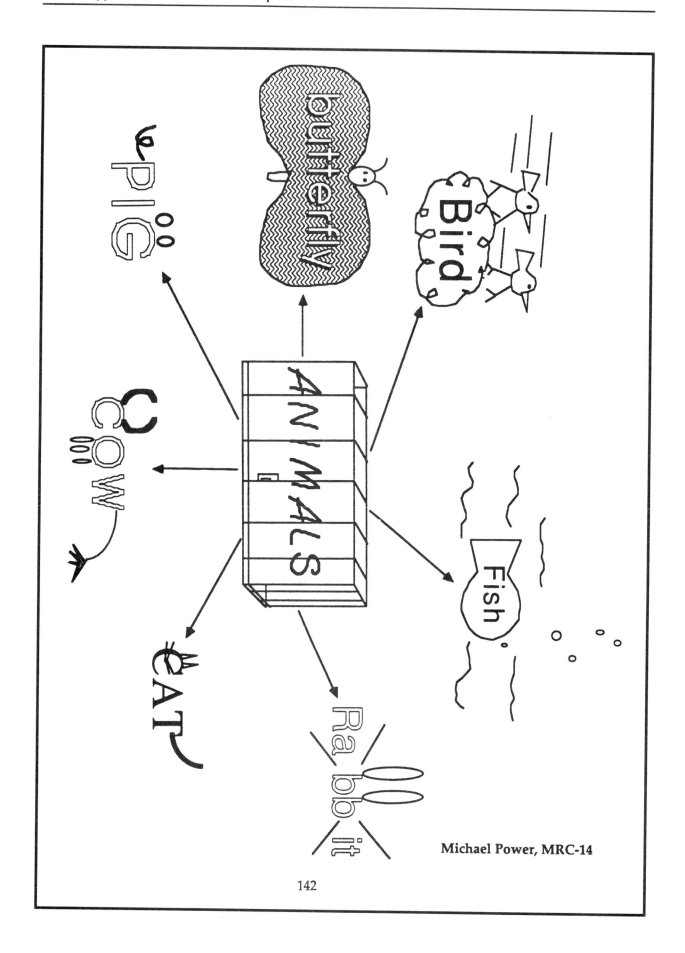

Michael Power, MRC-14

142

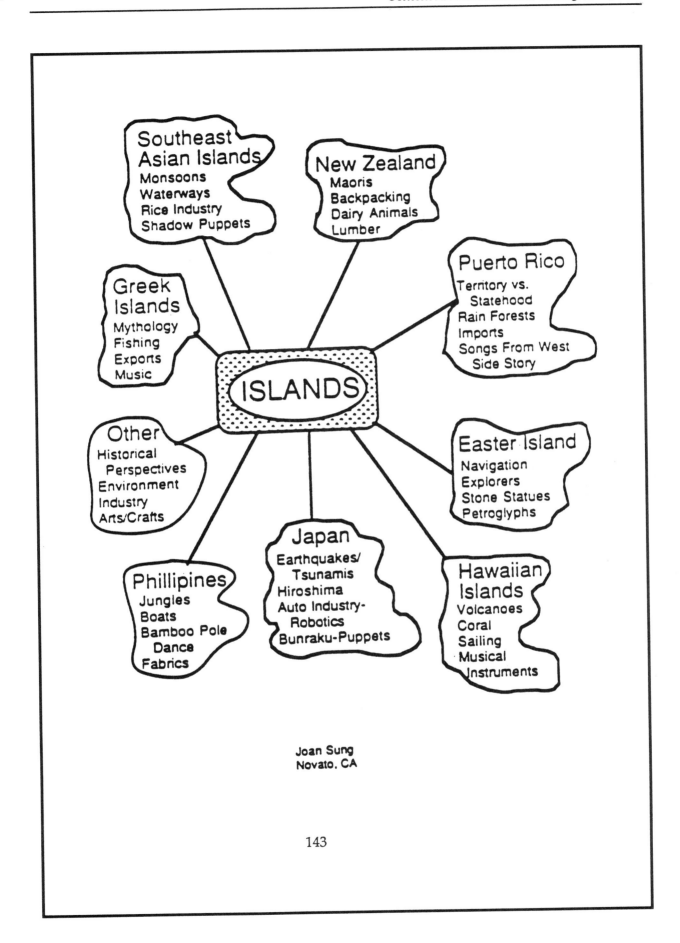

Joan Sung
Novato, CA

143

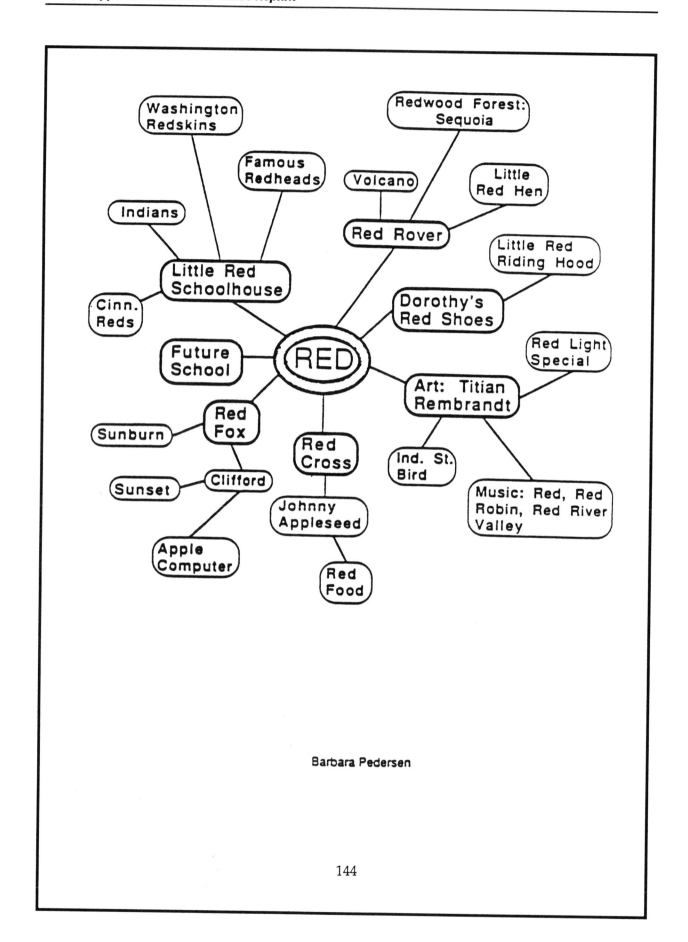

Barbara Pedersen

144

INDEX

N